DOMESTIC TERRORISM
AND
INCIDENT MANAGEMENT

DOMESTIC TERRORISM AND INCIDENT MANAGEMENT

Issues and Tactics

By

MIKI VOHRYZEK-BOLDEN, PH.D.

Professor, Criminal Justice Division
California State University, Sacramento

GAYLE OLSON-RAYMER, PH.D.

Adjunct Professor, Departments of History and Education
Humboldt State University

JEFFREY O. WHAMOND, M.S.

Investigator, California Highway Patrol
Hazardous Materials Specialist

Charles C Thomas
PUBLISHER • LTD.
SPRINGFIELD • ILLINOIS • U.S.A.

Published and Distributed Throughout the World by

CHARLES C THOMAS • PUBLISHER, LTD.
2600 South First Street
Springfield, Illinois 62704

©2001 by CHARLES C THOMAS • PUBLISHER, LTD.

ISBN 0-398-07225-6 (hard)
ISBN 0-398-07226-4 (paper)

Library of Congress Catalog Card Number: 2001027976

Printed in the United States of America
SR-R-3

Library of Congress Cataloging-in-Publication Data

Vohryzek-Bolden, Miki.
   Domestic terrorism and incident management : issues and tactics / Miki Vohryzek-
Bolden, Gayle Olson-Raymer, Jeffrey O. Whamond.
      p. cm.
   Includes bibliographical references and index.
   ISBN 0-398-07225-6 – ISBN 0-398-07226-4 (pbk.)
      1. Terrorism–United States. 2. Terrorism. 3. Terrorism–Prevention. 4. Emergency
management. I. Olson-Raymer, Gayle. II. Whamond, Jeffrey O. III. Title.

HV6432.V64 2001
303.6′25–dc21

                                                                                 2001027976

Most especially to my husband, Boldini and our sons, Erin and Ben,
whose love and support is always there
To my parents, Frank and Mary Vohryzek, who inspired the quest for knowledge and
a life of learning
To my community of friends who have shown their support
in innumerable ways

MIKI VOHRYZEK-BOLDEN

This book is dedicated to the students who have taken my various courses on terrorism
over the eight years at Humboldt State
University, as well as the many law enforcement officers who have endured an histor-
ical approach to terrorism at the Law Enforcement Management Institute at Texas
Woman's University. I would
never have been able to teach international and domestic terrorism, much less write
two books, without their constant questions,
intellectual challenges, astute observations, and regular input
about content and sources. They have been—and will continue
to be—a source of inspiration to me.

GAYLE OLSON-RAYMER

To EVB for being my guiding light

JEFFREY O. WHAMOND

PREFACE

The subject of terrorism consumes our public interest and fascination. For Americans, it has taken on a particularly strong personal interest because of the bombing of the World Trade Center in New York City in February 1993 and the bombing of the Alfred P. Murrah Federal Building in Oklahoma City in April 1995. What many viewed as impossible has now become a reality–Americans are becoming victims of terrorism on American soil, and in greater numbers than we have seen in the past. The unpredictability of terrorism and apparent randomness make it virtually impossible for our government to protect all potential sites and all potential victims.

To fully understand the nature of domestic terrorism, we need a clear understanding of the basics. These basics include reviewing the complex history that spans thousands of years, grappling with definitions of a controversial and emotionally-explosive topic, acquiring a clear understanding of contemporary domestic terrorism, and examining intelligence gathering, threat analysis, and emergency responses to terrorism incident management. Such knowledge should enhance the public's understanding of domestic terrorism and law enforcement's ability to prevent and respond to its acts.

Because our book seeks to achieve a greater understanding of contemporary terrorism, it focuses almost exclusively on right-wing domestic terrorism for three primary reasons:

1. strong presence in the last twenty years;
2. projections of experts that right-wing terrorism will prevail well into the 21st century; and
3. reports of local law enforcers across the nation who are dealing with an increasing number of right-wing extremists and terrorists in their jurisdiction, as well as the prevalence of special-interest extremist and terrorist groups–ecological resistance movements, anti-environmental movements, animal rights and anti-abortion activists.

Our examination of intelligence gathering and incident management build on both the historical and descriptive portions of the text by adding a practical dimension.

MIKI VOHRYZEK-BOLDEN
GAYLE OLSON-RAYMER
JEFFREY O. WHAMOND

INTRODUCTION

Those interested in the study of terrorism and terrorists recognize the need to view these subjects in an historical and contemporary context. Our book is designed to take the reader on a journey through the historical antecedents of contemporary terrorism, to introduce ideologies and activities of right-wing and special-interest extremists and terrorists, and to describe criminal intelligence gathering policies and practices and discuss terrorism incident management strategies.

As such, we believe this book is unique in several ways because it:

- Blends a strong academic component dealing with definitional and historical issues with a strong practical element dealing with contemporary issues relevant to both postsecondary students and law enforcement practitioners.
- Draws on the expertise of three professionals who come from differing, but complementary, academic and criminal justice backgrounds.
- Includes an in-depth discussion of special-interest extremists and terrorists, intelligence gathering, and emergency responses to terrorism incident management.
- Weaves case studies into the textual discussion of domestic terrorism.
- Encourages use as both a text in an undergraduate course and as a training manual for police and fire personnel.
- Contains discussion questions to which students can respond, as well as study questions that students can research outside the classroom setting.

The book is divided into three parts. Part One, The Definitional and Historical Dimensions of Terrorism, written by Gayle Olson-Raymer, deals with the issue of terrorism in a broad definitional context. The authors feel that for the student of terrorism to understand both the evolution and current status of domestic terrorism, it is first necessary to discuss it within a wider, global context. Thus, the first three chapters deal with definitional problems associated with policymaker's and law enforcement's handling of terrorism, an historical overview of terrorism and terrorist incidents in the global community, and an historical examination of terrorism from below in the United States.

Part Two, Contemporary Domestic Terrorism, written by Miki Vohryzek-Bolden, addresses the American Hate Movement and patriot–militia activities. It also discusses the emergence of special-interest extremist and terrorist groups that advocate violence based on an ideology or belief, which may include the desire for political and social change. They include ecological resistance groups, anti-environmental movements, animal rights and anti-abortion activists. Chapter 6 presents selected case studies designed to illustrate the range of political-extremist and terrorist events in the United States during contemporary times. Chapter 7 describes the changing character of domestic terrorism in terms of the groups involved and the terrorists' use of specific tools and tactics.

Part Three, Intelligence Gathering and Emergency Response Incident Management to Terrorism, written by Jeffrey Whamond, focuses on effective criminal intelligence gathering techniques and the implementation of terrorism incident management strategies. Chapter 8 develops an understanding of the complex and interrelated system of collecting criminal intelligence information on terrorist enterprises while reinforcing the concepts of due process and privacy rights. Chapter 9 focuses on terrorism incident management strategies for prevention, threat assessment, domestic preparedness, and tactics for a unified national response to a conventional or a weapon of mass destruction incident.

ACKNOWLEDGMENTS

MIKI VOHRYZEK-BOLDEN

As the lead author, and perhaps instigator of this venture, I know that this book would not have been completed without the commitment and dedication of my two coauthors, Gayle Olson-Raymer and Jeff Whamond. While at times I assumed the role of taskmaster and nudge, my colleagues maintained a good perspective on this behavior and showed me understanding when I became frustrated with the inevitable delays that surround a collaborative project of this magnitude.

I was introduced to the subject of violence and terrorism when Dr. Tom Johnson, then Chair of the Criminal Justice Division at California State University, Sacramento (CSUS) asked me to teach our upper-division course on violence and terrorism. I was fortunate to meet Gayle who was also teaching this course at CSUS. We developed a strong friendship and professional relationship as we worked cooperatively to develop the curriculum for the course. Gayle has been my "academic inspiration" as she maintains a strong scholarly focus on all that she does in the classroom, in her scholarship, and in her training seminars for law enforcement personnel.

Jeff Whamond, our other coauthor, was perhaps more directly involved in my decision to write a textbook on this subject (in other words, he planted the seed!). Jeff and I conduct training seminars for law enforcement–investigation personnel. In his quest to expand our "business," he casually mentioned one day that there was potentially a huge market for training specialists in the area of domestic terrorism, with a focus on right-wing terrorists. This occurred at the same time I was applying for a sabbatical leave from CSUS. Thus, timing and circumstances were perfect! And as they say, "the rest is history."

The writing of a textbook is an incredibly difficult task. It takes a considerable amount of commitment, focus, and, especially, understanding from those around you who must endure your idiosyncrasies during the writing process. My husband Steve Bolden, also known as the famous Boldini, gives me the greatest gift of all, his unconditional love, for which I will forever be appreciative. Our sons, Erin and Ben, are probably too young to understand what this book writing is all about. Yet, they are the "heart of my soul" and are ever present in my thoughts, and for their very presence in my life I feel very blessed and am most thankful.

Several students of mine were helpful at different points in the process and I want to extend my thanks to them: Tim Croisdale, Amber Ferry, Jody Burgess, and Judy Ruskus. Very heartfelt thanks are extended to Ann Boynton, who gave freely and fully of her time and expertise in the preparation of this book for publication. There are scores of other friends and colleagues who supported me throughout the writing of this book. The words escape even this writer! You all know who you are and you have my profound thanks for your love and support.

On a final note, I want to acknowledge my aunt, Eileen Pearson. On July 25, 1977, a week before my doctoral defense, she sent me a card with the saying: *Follow your dreams, for as you dream so shall you become.* In the card she said, "thoughts are things—and things happen! See yourself with your Ph.D. tucked into your foxy pocket as you set off north to set the world on fire." I kept the card with me all these years because I was empowered by those words. Thank you Eileen, from the bottom of my heart.

GAYLE OLSON-RAYMER

I continue to owe my greatest debt as an educator to my doctoral mentor at University of California at Santa Barbara, Dr. Alexander B. Callow. Not a day goes by when I do not repeat his parting advice to me: "When you think you know all the answers, it's time to get out of the teaching profession."

I owe my enthusiasm for teaching about the history of terrorism from my mentor at Texas Woman's University, Dr. Jim Alexander, who is the Chairperson of the Political Science Department and one of the most nurturing educators I have ever met.

I owe my interest in and commitment to the themes emphasized in this book to my friend and colleague, Dr. Miki Vohryzek-Bolden. No matter how behind we were, how frustrated we became, how overworked we felt—Miki was always there with a smile and positive word of encouragement. I can think of no one with whom I would rather coauthor a book!

I owe my diversions and sanity to my husband, Terry Raymer, my children, Miles and Michaela, and our beautiful home and spiritual retreat within the redwoods.

JEFFREY O. WHAMOND

I would like to take this opportunity to thank my coauthors Professors Miki Vohryzek-Bolden and Gayle Olson-Raymer for their willingness to blend an academic and "street cop" approach to the topic of domestic terrorism. I would also like to thank Dr. Vohryzek-Bolden for taking the responsibility of acting as the project manager for this book. Her professional approach to setting time lines kept me on track. I would like to particularly thank Paul Knox for his thoughtful editorial work on Chapters 8 and 9. His dedication and insight are an invaluable addition to this portion of the text.

My intentions for Chapter 8 were to present the material on criminal intelligence gathering from within the framework of nationally accepted standards and practices. I would like to thank David E. Struve in consultation with Ted Prime, Matthew Anderson and Michael Roland who created the manual on "Criminal Intelligence File Guidelines." From the Simi Valley Police Department, in conjunction with Jack Morris (retired), California Attorney General's Office, Department of Justice, I would like to thank Capt. Dick Wright for his expertise in developing the "Guidelines for the Criminal Intelligence Function." From the California Peace Officers Association, Criminal Intelligence Committee, I would like to thank Robert J. Luca. Mr. Luca and the members of his committee researched and presented the materials contained in the manual "Criminal Intelligence Program for the Smaller Agency." Their manual was an invaluable reference for this project. I would also like to thank Joseph F. Barbara, Attorney, State of California Department of Corrections, for his scholarly approach in assisting me with constitutional and case-law issues. These law enforcement professionals have set the national training standards for law enforcement officers in this topical area.

In addressing Chapter 9, I wanted to present the material in a manner that included the viewpoint of our nation's counterterrorism leaders from the federal, state, and local levels. To this end, I would like to thank Professor Yonah Alexander and Mr. Donald J. Musch for the selection and presentation of public records and documents contained in Volumes 14 through 19 of *Terrorism: Documents of International and Local Control.* From Hazardous Management Associates in conjunction with the National Fire Academy, I would like to thank David M. Lesak for the GEDAPER process.

To Estela Whamond, Ruth R. Whamond, and Kathy Marsh, I would like to say a special thank you for your support and editorial review.

Finally, to my wife, Estela and sons, Joshua, Matthew, Michael and Daniel, I would like to especially thank you for your support over all these years.

CONTENTS

Page

Preface vii
Introduction ix

PART ONE: THE DEFINITIONAL AND HISTORICAL
DIMENSIONS OF TERRORISM 3
    References 4

CHAPTER 1. TERRORISM AND TERRORISTS:
    A DEFINITIONAL PERSPECTIVE 5
    Terrorism Defined 8
        The Broad Construction 9
        Victim's Status 10
        Emotional Ingredients 10
    Terrorism Typologies 11
        Terrorism from Above 12
        Terrorism from Below 13
    Terrorists Defined 14
    The Tools of Terror 18
        Assassination and Kidnapping: Tools of Terrorists Operating
            from Above and Below 19
        Enslavement and Subjugation, Imprisonment, Banishment,
            and Genocide: Tools of Terrorists Operating from Above 21
        Arson, Guns, Bombs, Hijacking, and Weapons of Mass
            Destruction: Tools of Terrorists Operating from Below 24
    Summary 29
    Discussion Questions 30
    Study Questions 31
    References 31

CHAPTER 2. TERRORISM IN THE GLOBAL ARENA:
AN HISTORICAL PERSPECTIVE 35
Ancient Times to 1800 36
   Terrorism from Above: Institutionalized Terrorism and
   American Slavery 36
   Terrorism from Below: The Assassins 38
1800 to 1900 39
   Terrorism from Above: Genocidal Policies Against the
   North American Indians 40
   Treaties and Supreme Court Decisions 40
   Federal Policies and Laws 41
   Terrorism from Below: Socialist and Anarchist Influences
   and the Haymarket Square Riot 43
1900 to 1950 45
   Terrorism from Above: Turkey and the Armenian Genocide 46
   Terrorism from Below: The Ku Klux Klan 48
1950 to 1979 50
   Covert Terrorism from Above: Argentina's "Dirty War,"
   1976–1983 51
   Covert Terrorism from Above: American Involvement in
   Guatemala's Reign of Terror 54
   Terrorism from Below: Revolutionary Philosophers 55
      Mao Tse-Tung 55
      Che Guevara 56
      Carlos Marighella 57
      Franz Fanon 57
   Terrorism from Below: Algeria and the Front de
   Liberation Nationale (FLN) 58
1980 to 2000 60
   Terrorism from Above and Below: The Taleban of Afghanistan ...61
   Terrorism from Above and Below: The Hutu Genocide of
   Tutsis in Rwanda 65
   Terrorism from Below: The *Sendero Luminoso* of Peru 68
Summary 68
Discussion Questions 70
Study Questions 71
References 72

CHAPTER 3. TERRORISM IN THE UNITED STATES: A
          RELATIONSHIP AS "AMERICAN AS APPLE PIE" 74
  Scapegoating Vigilantes 76
    Witches and Vigilantes 76
    Catholics and Vigilantes 77
    Asians and Vigilantes 79
    African Americans and Vigilantes 81
  Patriot Militias 85
    Militias in Colonial America 86
      Bacon's Rebellion 86
      The Paxton Boys 87
      The New Jersey Land Rioters 87
      The South Carolina Regulators 88
      The Green Mountain Boys 88
    Militias in Postrevolutionary and Nineteenth-Century America ...89
      Shays' Rebellion 89
      The Whiskey Rebellion 90
      The Molly Maguires 90
    Patriot Militias: 1930s through the 1950s 91
      The Farmer's Holiday Association 91
      Fascist Groups 91
  Left-Wing Extremism and Terrorism 92
    The Students for a Democratic Society and the
      Weather Underground 92
    The Black Panthers: Terrorism from Above and Below 95
  Extremists, Terrorists, and Law Enforcement Responses:
      Yesterday and Today 97
  Summary 99
  Discussion Questions 100
  Study Questions 100
  References 101

PART TWO: CONTEMPORARY DOMESTIC TERRORISM 105

CHAPTER 4: THE AMERICAN HATE AND
          PATRIOT–MILITIA MOVEMENTS 107
  Hate-Motivated Groups 108
    White Supremacists 108
    Ku Klux Klans 108

Current KKK Splinter Groups 109
Neo-Nazis 112
Neo-Nazi Skinheads 113
Christian Identity 116
Other Racist-Religious-Oriented Groups 121
World Church of the Creator 121
White Aryan Resistance (WAR) 122
Odinism 124
Black Separatist 125
Nation of Islam 125
New Black Panther Party (NBPP) 126
Patriot and Militia Groups 127
Patriot Groups 129
Militias 130
Militia of Montana 133
Arizona Patriots 134
Common Law Courts 134
Summary 135
Discussion Questions 137
Study Questions 137
References 138

CHAPTER 5. SPECIAL-INTEREST EXTREMISTS AND
TERRORISTS 140
Extremist and Terrorist Groups 140
Ecological Resistance Movements 140
Earth First! 141
Earth Liberation Front 146
Anti-Environmental Movement 146
Wise Use 147
Animal Rights 152
Animal Liberation Front 154
Anti-Abortion Activists 156
Pro-Life Action Network 157
Operation Rescue 159
Anti-Abortion Terrorists 160
Special-Interest Extremist Groups to Watch 161
Greenpeace 161
People for the Ethical Treatment of Animals 164

Summary 165
Discussion Questions 166
Study Questions 168
References 170

CHAPTER 6. CASE STUDIES IN DOMESTIC TERRORISM
            AND POLITICAL EXTREMISM 173
Randy Weaver and Ruby Ridge 174
    Background 174
    The Federal Approach and Resulting Standoff 175
    The Aftermath 177
    Discussion Questions 179
    Study Questions 180
Federal Assault on the Branch Davidian Complex in Waco, Texas . .180
    Discussion Questions 185
    Study Questions 186
World Trade Center Bombing 187
    Discussion Questions 190
    Study Questions 190
Bombing of the Alfred P. Murrah Federal Building in
    Oklahoma City, Oklahoma 191
    Discussion Questions 194
    Study Questions 194
The Freemen of Montana 195
    Discussion Questions 196
    Study Questions 196
The Unabomber 197
    Discussion Questions 201
    Study Questions 201
Summary 201
References 202

CHAPTER 7. THE CHANGING CHARACTER OF
            DOMESTIC TERRORISM 204
The Ideologies and Activities of Right-Wing and Special-
    Interest Terrorist Groups 205
International Terrorist Links 206
New and Different Terrorist Tools and Tactics 208
    Cyberterrorism and the Internet 208

Weapons of Mass Destruction 208
Third Position 213
Summary 214
Discussion Questions 215
Study Questions 216
References 216

**PART THREE: INTELLIGENCE GATHERING AND
EMERGENCY RESPONSE INCIDENT
MANAGEMENT TO TERRORISM** 219

CHAPTER 8. THE GATHERING OF CRIMINAL
INTELLIGENCE: POLICY AND PRACTICE 221
Criminal Intelligence Gathering Goals 221
Relationship of Privacy Rights to the Gathering of
Criminal Intelligence 222
Public Access to Information Gathered by Law Enforcement 225
Privacy Act Implications: Cases Relating to the Maintenance
and Dissemination of Criminal Intelligence Information
in California 226
Criminal Intelligence Filing Procedures 227
The FBI Lead Agency Responsibilities 227
The Investigation Potential and Actual Terrorist Acts 228
An Investigative Support Unit 231
Attorney General Guidelines on General Crimes, Racketeering
Enterprise, and Domestic Security Terrorism Investigations ...232
Sources and Processes of Intelligence Information 233
Investigative Techniques 233
The Internet as an Intelligence Information Source 235
Sources of Criminal Intelligence Information and the
Evaluation Process 236
Summary 238
Discussion Questions 238
Study Questions 239
Terrorism Statutes 239
Other Authorities Relating to the FBI's Investigative Jurisdiction
in Terrorism Cases 240
References 241

CHAPTER 9. TERRORISM INCIDENT MANAGEMENT:
            STRATEGIES AND TACTICS 242
    Strategies to Prevent Terrorist Incidents 242
        Partnerships for Protecting the Infrastructure from
            Terrorist Attack 243
        Support and Structure of Presidential Decision Directive-63 245
    Terrorism Prevention: Proactive Criminal Investigations 247
    Strategies for Threat Assessment 251
        FBI Threat Analysis 252
            Department of Justice/Federal Bureau of Investigation 252
            Federal Emergency Management Agency (FEMA) 252
            Department of Defense (DOD) 253
            Department of Energy (DOE) 253
            Environmental Protection Agency (EPA) 253
            Department of Health and Human Services (DHHS) 254
        Threat Assessment Trends 254
    Strategies for Domestic Preparedness 255
    Tactics to Create a Unified National Response to Weapons of
            Mass Destruction 258
        Biological Weapons 259
    Summary 263
    Discussion Questions 264
    Study Questions 264
    References 264
    Additional Information 266

Name Index 273
Subject Index 277
About the Authors 293

DOMESTIC TERRORISM
AND
INCIDENT MANAGEMENT

Part One

THE DEFINITIONAL AND HISTORICAL DIMENSIONS OF TERRORISM

GAYLE OLSON-RAYMER

It seems that for the instructors of terrorism, there is always a "teachable moment." If we wait for a month or so, something will pop up in the domestic or international arena that will demand our immediate attention and revitalize the interest of students in our classes. Before we can really immerse ourselves in the tragic circumstances of each emerging incident of terrorism, however, we must have a clear understanding of the basics. In the case of terrorism, that means grappling with definitions of a very controversial and emotionally-explosive topic, as well as reviewing a complex history that spans thousands of years. These, then, are the two primary goals of Part One:

- to discuss the many controversies about how to define terrorism and develop a rationale for the broad definition used throughout the book; and
- to examine the history of international and domestic terrorism, with a particular emphasis on case studies.

Because this book is designed for use in a wide array of interdisciplinary classrooms and law enforcement training experiences, it is important to note that these first three chapters rely heavily on the history of terrorism. Indeed, it is premised on the belief that local law enforcers and those who study terrorism must be educated about extremists and terrorists, as well as become more open to proactive and preventive anti-terrorist strategies. Fortunately, this particular belief is supported by a growing number of law enforcement personnel.

In his book, *Terrorism and Local Law Enforcement,* twenty-year veteran from the Los Angeles County Sheriff's Office Philip McVey argues that officers must be educated about the political agenda of domestic and international extremists and terrorists, as well as the history of political violence in America. Specifically, he argues for creating educated police forces where officers take specialized courses, improve their intelligence gathering on potential and actual extremist groups and individuals, and learn target-hardening techniques. An educated local law enforcement agency can then, in the words of McVey (1998), "reduce the need to enter into the paramilitary mode of operations . . ." and can instead take more "proactive approaches" (p. 153). Echoing this belief is Scott McHugh, retired Special Agent with the U.S. Department of State's Bureau of Diplomatic Security, who has commented that: "The future effectiveness of U.S. counter-terrorist operations can be improved upon by discarding the current reactive approach to terrorism and replacing it with the means to prevent terrorist operations" (as quoted in Ward and Moors 1998: 57–58).

In keeping with such beliefs, Part One is designed to be an educational journey for those who wish to learn more about the historical and contemporary contexts of terrorism. Consequently, its chapters deal with the issue of terror in a far broader context than Parts Two and Three, which exclusively discuss aspects of terrorism from below within the United States. However, to understand both the evolution and current status of domestic American terrorism, it is first necessary to discuss it within a wider context. Consequently, the first two chapters in Part One will differ in both content and theme from the remaining two-thirds of this book in at least two ways:

1. The inclusion of a broad discussion of terrorism within a *global* rather than an exclusively *domestic* context. Terrorism did not begin in the United States–thus, it does not make sense to begin our discussion with the settlement of the first American colonies. Instead, Chapter 1, "Terrorism and Terrorists: A Definitional Perspective," provides a definitional dialogue about terrorism and terrorists, while Chapter 2, "Terrorism in the Global Arena: An Historical Perspective," includes an historical overview of the evolution of international terrorism.

2. The inclusion of a series of case studies about incidents of terrorism committed both from above and below. Terrorism has never been the exclusive tool of the empowered operating from above–thus, it does not make sense to exclude an historical discussion of the use of terror in the hands of the empowered.

The third and final chapter in Part One, "Terrorism in the United States: A Relationship as 'American as Apple Pie,'" sets the tone for the remainder of the book by focusing exclusively on the history of terrorism from below in the United States.

REFERENCES

McVey, Phillip. *Terrorism and Local Law Enforcement.* Springfield, IL, Charles C Thomas, 1998.

Ward, Richard H., and Moors, Cindy S. Intelligence, terrorism, and the new world order. In Ward, Richard H., and Moors, Cindy S. (Eds.), *Terrorism and the New World Order.* Washington, D.C., Office of International Criminal Justice, 1998, pp. 45–65.

Chapter 1

TERRORISM AND TERRORISTS: A DEFINITIONAL PERSPECTIVE[1]

The death of 168 men, women, and children in the 1995 bombing of the Alfred P. Murrah building in Oklahoma City marked the end of public naïveté about the possibility of experiencing a horrific terrorist incident on American soil. Indeed, prior to 1995, most Americans believed terroristic violence was something that happened in the *international* community–not within the *domestic* borders of America. In the wake of Oklahoma City, communities, local law enforcement agencies, educational institutions, and the media began a sincere dialogue about how to respond to the terrorist threat. However, it soon became clear that no one was really clear about what terrorism was and was not.

One of the most difficult issues related to any discussion of terrorism is related to this definitional dilemma. For decades, academic experts, criminal justice practitioners, governmental officials, and even the terrorists themselves have disagreed on a definition of terrorism. Scores of definitions began appearing in the 1980s. Schmid's (1984) comparative analysis of more than 100 definitions of terrorism used between 1936 and 1981 concluded that it was not possible to provide one correct definition of terrorism because it is different things to different people. Such a conclusion gained further credence throughout the 1980s as experts continued to debate definitional components. White's (1991) survey of these various definitions found that they generally fell into one of five categories:

1. Simple definitions broadly defining terrorism as the use of force to bring about political change that do not limit terrorism to specific actions (Jenkins 1985; Laqueur 1987).
2. Legal definitions suggesting that terrorism is a form of criminal violence that violates legal codes and is therefore punishable by the state (Grosscup 1987).
3. Analytical definitions seeking to identify the problem through specific factors, such as the use of unacceptable violence aimed at innocent targets (Crenshaw 1983).
4. State-sponsored definitions maintaining that small states, especially those states

[1] An earlier version of this chapter was published in Gayle Olson-Raymer: *Terrorism: A Historical and Contemporary Perspective.* New York, American Heritage Custom Publishing, 1996. This chapter has, however, been substantially revised from the earlier version.

backed by members of the former Communist bloc, use terrorism to attack Western political viewpoints and interests (Livingstone and Arnold 1986; Netanyahu 1986).

5. State definitions holding that various Western states, especially the United States, have supported terrorist regimes that use repression and terror to maintain their power (Chomsky 1986; George 1991; Herman 1982; Perdue 1989; Stohl 1983).

White (1991) concluded that all five definitions were "viable," that there is "no standard definition of terror," and that each definition was based upon "political biases" (p. 7). In the second edition of his book, White (1998) explained several reasons why defining terrorism is so confusing and difficult:

• Terrorism's pejorative connotation ensures that a person is politically and socially degraded if they are labeled a terrorist.
• Governments, which can increase their power when they call their opponents terrorists, encourage citizens to accept abuses of governmental power in the name of a counterterrorist campaign.
• The intertwined usage of the terms *terror* and *terrorism* suggests that anything that creates terror, including military conflicts and force, is terrorism.
• Many scholars and experts insist that repressive governments that rule through terror be included in any definition of terrorism.
• The use of the term has changed from its historical use as applied to official governmental actions of terrorism, to its more contemporary usage as applied to the ac-

tivities of domestic enemies of the government (pp. 5–6).

Laqueur (1999) adds his own opinion to the definitional dilemma by concluding that "There has been no 'terrorism' per se, only different terrorisms" (p. 46).

Given such definitional latitude, policymakers, educators, and experts have had to grapple with their own personal and professional perspectives and biases about terrorism. Thus, my personal definitional struggle began in 1983 when trying to find the appropriate descriptive words for students taking a course in "International Terrorism" within the Criminal Justice Department at Sacramento State University. Most of my students were undergraduates preparing to enter the criminal justice system, military police from the neighboring bases, and local law enforcement officers working on their master's degrees. Each semester I introduced students to the way in which the emerging literature defined terrorism, most of which relied heavily upon the FBI's legalistic definition of terrorism: *Terrorism* is the unlawful use of force or violence against persons or property to intimidate or coerce a government, the civilian population, or any segment thereof, in furtherance of political or social objectives (U.S. Department of Justice 1997: i).

While the FBI's definition was fairly broad, throughout the 1970s and until 1995, the agency narrowly interpreted terrorists to be primarily people of left-wing orientation.[2] *Left-wing terrorists* are those who profess views to reform or overthrow the established governmental order in the name of the greater freedom or well-being of the common man. Theirs is considered to be a *radical* political

---

[2] After the Oklahoma City bombing, the FBI no longer relied exclusively on its left-wing interpretation of terrorism. Instead, it began to encompass a broader interpretation of its definition, one that included terrorists of many political, social, religious, and ideological persuasions.

position that advocates for extreme political change.

According to this leftist interpretation, terrorism rarely occurred in the United States. Indeed, in the five years before Oklahoma City, the FBI officially recorded a total of 19 incidents of domestic terrorism—16 of which were committed by left-wing terrorist groups (U.S. Department of Justice 1997).

Each semester, however, the law enforcement professionals whom I taught increasingly disagreed with these interpretations and many clamored for a broader context in which to examine the issue. Many identified actual and potential terrorists within their jurisdictions not as left-wing revolutionaries, but rather as right-wing extremists involved in hate crimes and special-interest terrorists tied to the animal rights, anti-abortion, and environmental movements.

Right-wing terrorists are those who profess views in opposition to change in the established governmental order; or who wish to ensure that traditional attitudes and practices are restored to the established governmental order; or who advocate the forced establishment of an authoritarian political order. Theirs is considered to be a *conservative, traditional* position that advocates for keeping or returning to the political status quo.

Special-interest terrorists are committed to a specific cause and use violent tactics to try to resolve specific issues. Such terrorists operate from either a left-wing, radical position, a right-wing conservative and traditional position, or in some cases, from a combination of both left- and right-wing positions.

The attitudes of the local officers in my courses were reinforced with the findings of the Riley and Hoffman (1995) survey of state and local law enforcement agencies about professional perceptions of the terrorist threats in their jurisdictions. In their final report, *Domestic Terrorism: A National Assessment of State and Local Preparedness,* they found that during the period under study—January 1991 through December 1992—state and local law enforcement officers around the nation defined terrorism quite differently than did the FBI. In brief, Riley and Hoffman's (1995) study concluded that:

- From 1990 to 1997, the FBI recorded a total of 33 terrorist incidents, 6 suspected incidents, and 18 preventions. In contrast, 49 percent (73 of 148) of local law enforcement respondents[3] reported some involvement with terrorism between 1988 and 1992.
- A majority of state and local law enforcement agencies broadened the FBI's perception of terrorism to include perpetration of ring-wing extremism and terrorism. States and localities most often identified right-wing hate groups (neo-Nazi, white supremacist, anti-federalist) and issue-specific organizations (anti-abortion, animal rights, environmentalist) as their greatest terrorist threats.
- Most local law enforcement agencies reported more involvement with terrorism than did the FBI.
- Most state and local law enforcement agencies noted the presence of an identified terrorist threat(s) or potential terrorist threat(s). Almost 80 percent (31 of 39) of state agencies reported an identified terrorist threat(s) in their states; 32 percent (48 of 148) of all local agencies identified terrorist groups in their jurisdictions; and 83 percent (123 of 148) of local respondents noted a potential for terrorist threats in their states and localities.

---

[3] Respondents included 75 percent (39 of 52) state law enforcement agencies; and 49.5 percent (148 of 299) of the population-based, targeted local law enforcement agencies.

After examining Riley and Hoffman's study, I began to make some definitional decisions of my own. First, it appeared necessary that to define terrorism, several other terms also needed to be defined, especially political extremism and vigilantism. Second, for teaching purposes, it made sense to develop a broad working definition of terrorism. Finally, it was essential to make distinctions between all of these definitions. Thus, it is the primary purpose of this chapter to explore the results of such definitional decisionmaking by

- introducing a broad working definition of terrorism and various terms related to the study of terrorism;
- describing two broad based typologies–terrorism from above and below–through several contemporary case studies;
- shedding some light on the backgrounds and psychological characteristics of the terrorists themselves; and
- discussing the historical and contemporary usage of the tools of terror.

TERRORISM DEFINED

Terrorism, in its most simplistic definition, can be described as a type of political extremism. But just what is political extremism?

Political extremism occurs when a political belief(s) is taken to its extreme limits with the intention of achieving a political goal(s) that aims to confront, diminish, and/or eliminate the opposition, and when such goals are pursued in an uncompromising, authoritative, belligerent, and/or bullying manner.

If we look at American history, political extremism has most often been manifested in vigilantism–another term that is rarely understood.

Vigilantism occurs when persons take the law into their own hands by intimidating, threatening, injuring, or killing targeted members of a racial, cultural, religious, ideological, behavioral, or political group for one of two political reasons: to defend and preserve the existing political, social, economic, ideological, or religious system; or to reform or destroy such a system(s).

Are these acts of terrorism? Let's examine the definition used for our purposes and then answer that question.

Terrorism occurs when persons use, or threaten to use, political violence, which is intended to instill terror within a targeted population and to achieve a political goal. Such a goal is motivated by political, social, economic, religious, or ideological beliefs that may be emotionally influenced by fear, hate, and intolerance. Terrorists rely upon actions that intentionally cause terror, as well as actions that unintentionally cause terror, but are not discontinued if the consequences become known.

If we compare these three definitions, we can make some definite distinctions:

- *Vigilantes are both extremists and terrorists.* Because the actions of vigilantes are politically extreme, all vigilantes are political extremists. Furthermore, because vigilantes move across the ideological threshold and commit politically-violent actions, they are also terrorists.
- *While some extremists are also terrorists, the vast majority of extremists are not.* Most political extremists are law-abiding citizens who are ideologically extreme, but do not resort to violence to achieve their extremist agenda.
- *All terrorists are political extremists.* Every person who commits an act of terror does so because that person chooses to take a belief to its extreme limits. When political extremists step over the politically-extreme threshold and commit violence to achieve their political goal(s), they become terrorists.

Given the diversity of law enforcement, academic, and governmental debate about a definition of terrorism, the broad interpretation used herein is bound to stir up controversy for at least three reasons:

1. A broad construction of terrorism fails to limit the topic and incorporates the use of legitimate governmental power.
2. The victim's status as either a civilian or noncivilian is not included in the definition.
3. Several emotional ingredients are included in the definition: fear, hate, and intolerance.

The Broad Construction

Some critics will argue that a broad construction of terrorism fails to limit the topic and that any politically-violent act committed on behalf of a political goal becomes an act of terrorism. Others believe that a broad definition incorrectly incorporates the legitimate use of governmental terror from above. However, we argue herein that the following advantages of a broad definition far outweigh the obvious disadvantages.

Broadening the definition recognizes the fact that terrorism and terrorists are most often defined by an individual's or a government's own moral and political perspective. A significant number of experts have noted that terrorism means different things to different people: to the people who are actually being terrorized or perceive they are being terrorized, to the perpetrators of perceived or actual terrorism, and to those who study terrorism. Governments, including the United States, selectively designate who are and who are not terrorists through a legalistic definition of terrorism.

White (1998) offers an interesting analysis of this legalistic approach. First adopted by Congress via the Omnibus Diplomatic Se-

curity and Antiterrorism Act of 1986, this definition was almost identical to that of the FBI: "terrorism is the unlawful use of force or violence designed to intimidate or coerce a government or a civilian population in the furtherance of political or social objectives" (White 1998: 7). As White (1998) explains:

> The beauty of legal definitions is that they give governments specific crimes that can be used to counter terrorist activities. Beyond that they are quite useless because they account for neither the social nor the political nature of terrorism. More important, they can be misused. . . . Under the legal guidelines of the United States, some groups can be labeled as terrorists while other groups engaged in the same activities may be described as legitimate revolutionaries. Governments friendly to the United States in Latin America, for example, have committed some of the worst atrocities in the history of the world in the name of counterterrorism. Ironically, some of the revolutionaries espouse the rights expressed in the U.S. Declaration of Independence and Constitution. Legal definitions are frequently short-sighted. (p. 7)

To illustrate just how short-sighted this approach has been, the United States continues to designate nations whose political philosophies conflict with America's as perpetrators of international terrorism—especially Cuba, Iran, Iraq, Libya, and North Korea. However, American allies are omitted from any inclusion as terrorist agents—especially Great Britain, Israel, and South Africa. We, therefore, must recognize the hypocrisy of the now-worn phrase, "What is one man's terrorist is another man's freedom fighter."

To further support our argument, it is important to note that a broad interpretation of terrorism does not allow a perpetrator to dehumanize and stereotype an adversary, to avoid addressing the grievances of those targeted for political violence, or to claim that violent actions are not those of a criminal but of a heroic figure engaged in a "just war" for freedom (Dugard 1989; Long 1990). Governments can use such justifications to claim a "state of emergency," during which constitutional and civil rights are suspended and the police are allowed to use unfettered legal authority to control dissenters, "the enemies of the people." Likewise, those without access to legitimate means of power also justify their use of terrorism in the name of freedom, self-determination, and independence.

In short, because most groups operating from above and below feel their cause is legitimate and moral, it is unrealistic to expect that anyone can make an objective distinction about what is and is not an act of terror. While we can understand the use of terrorism from both the governors and the governed, in so doing, we need not justify its usage. To truly understand terrorism, we must honestly identify and examine all who terrorize and disregard the justifications of all who terrorize; must be able to recognize terror for what it is, and avoid the pitfalls of the "just war" rationale. However, we cannot achieve such recognition if the actions of some terrorists are excused while others are condemned. Thus, it is important to broadly define all forms of politically-violent actions that are intended to terrorize.

Victim's Status

The second controversial element of this book's definition of terrorism lies in the victim's status. Some experts claim that terrorism must be defined by its target–a victim who is a civilian and is not responsible for the grievances that motivate a terrorist act (Crenshaw 1983; Laqueur 1987; Netanyahu 1986). Such a definition, we herein argue, implies that a government may legitimately and even legally target a victim who is, or who is perceived to be, responsible for such

grievances. Thus, as the history of many societies indicates and as Chapter 2 will illustrate, slaves who violently resisted the terroristic practice of enslavement were terrorized into submission. The tools for such submission, however, were and continue to be justified as legal acts of governmental necessity rather than acts of terror. This analysis contends that including the type of victim in a definition of terrorism exonerates blame and sometimes elevates some terrorists to heroic stature. It is necessary, then, to recognize that if an act of political violence, or the threat thereof, is based upon a political goal, which results in terrorizing any victim, the action is one of terror.

Emotional Ingredients

The final controversial definitional component is the inclusion of three complex emotional ingredients: fear, hate, and intolerance. Only recently have some scholars begun to make the connection between these emotions and terrorism. Hamm (1993) contends that recent Skinhead hatred of and violence toward non-Whites and Jews is terroristic in nature. Caputi and Russell (1992) argue that male fear and hatred of women, which manifests itself in the killing of women, is a type of gender-related terrorism that maintains the gender status quo.

The definition of terrorism offered herein takes these assertions several steps further by arguing that fear, hatred, and intolerance are almost always integral factors motivating a terroristic action. Indeed, these emotions historically have played significant roles in the evolution of humankind and are easily translated from generation to generation: as young people witness racial, ethnic, national, ideological, and sexual prejudices based on fear and hate, they carry that legacy into adulthood and parenthood; their children know no better than to perpetuate the cycle through intolerance. This cycle has sometimes resulted in terrorism.[4]

Throughout history, those who govern have burned witches to death, enslaved conquered enemies and persons of color, directed the Crusades, and carried out genocidal missions—all in the intolerant quest to satiate fear and hate. Those without legitimate access to power were equally imbued with fear and hatred as they formed vigilante groups to terrorize and eliminate those who were different. Because such actions historically have sought and continue to seek the curtailment of political, social, and economic lives of the victims, these actions were, and are, actually acts of terrorism motivated by hate, fear, and intolerance. And the victims of such terrorism—those who have been enslaved, oppressed, subjugated, and terrorized because of their racial, ethnic, national, ideological, and behavioral differences—have sometimes reacted to their fears by using terrorism to fight for their individual and collective survival.

To sum up our definitional discussion, terrorism is terrorism, regardless of the actual or perceived righteousness, morality, or justifications of the perpetrators. If an action uses violence from either above or below to terrorize a targeted population to achieve a political goal; if such violence is motivated by political, social, economic, or ideological grievances that may be emotionally driven by fear, hate, and intolerance; and if the action has the anticipated or unanticipated consequence of causing terror and is not discontinued once such terror is discovered, the action has been committed by a terrorist.

TERRORISM TYPOLOGIES

To understand the types of terrorism to be discussed next, it is important to first examine the historical context in which the word has been used. The word itself is derived from the Greek verbs *trein* (to be afraid) and *tremain* (to tremble). For over 3,000 years, the word was used to describe the human action of instilling fear or terror in a social context. It was not until the French Revolution that the term *terrorism* was used to describe the political action of instilling fear and perpetrating violence within a political context. In 1795, the English politician Edmund Burke was the first to say that political terrorism could be directed from above by the state.

In its earliest political context, then, terrorism was committed by state-empowered governors who repressed popular dissent. In 1866, the *Oxford English Dictionary* broadened this view with its first inclusion of the word "terrorist" by defining it as "any one who attempts to further his views by a system of coercive intimidation." By the end of the nineteenth century, then, those who perpetrated political violence either from within or outside the circles of political power were considered terrorists. Such a distinction suggests the evolution of two specific types of terrorism: terrorism from above and terrorism from below.

Terrorism from above occurs when persons who are legally empowered either covertly or overtly use, or threaten to use, political violence to maintain or defend political power within their domestic borders, or to maintain, defend, overthrow, or undermine the politi-

---

[4] Clearly, not all who experience fear, hatred, and intolerance become involved in terrorism. However, at least three factors can increase the probability that a person who hates may become involved in terror: the opportunity to commit terror becomes available; the external constraints that discourage the commission of terror are absent; and the societal norms indicating the unacceptable nature of violence are missing.

cal power of other nations within the international community.

Terrorism from below occurs when persons use, or threaten to use, political violence either to undermine or overthrow existing governmental policies or structures, or to intimidate individuals and groups they perceive as threatening to the social, political, economic, or ideological status quo.

While we posit the existence of these two types of terrorism, it is also important to note that in general, Americans tend to believe that most terrorism committed within the United States takes place from below and is committed by radical, dissatisfied citizens. In reality, much of the terrorism in most nations is introduced from above. In addition, as discussed previously, terrorism historically and contemporarily tends to be cyclical and very difficult to break:

- The cycle begins when policymakers, acting from positions of empowerment and authority, promote and sanction terrorism against those who are believed to be dangerous to the existing political system, or who are perceived to stand in the way of social, economic, and political progress.
- The cycle continues when those who are targeted by the government react to actual or perceived governmental terrorism by resorting to violence against government officials and infrastructure.
- The cycle comes full circle when policymakers use counterterrorism to react to citizens who resist governmental policies and often involves the overt and covert use of legalized terror to deny human and constitutional rights and privileges to such citizens.

Thus, usage of terrorism from above and below should be considered loose, rather than strict, typological descriptors of terrorism.

Terrorism from Above

A great deal of controversy surrounds the use of terrorism from above as a type of terrorism. Some experts have argued that terrorism occurs only when the powerless use political violence against those in power (Kirkpatrick 1979; Perlstein 1991). Others have argued that if the state holds a legitimate monopoly on violence, its actions are not terroristic but rather reflect a legitimate representation of power (Arendt 1970; Gerth and Mills 1958; Honderich 1982). Still others do not deny the existence of state terrorism, but argue instead that such repression is a long-term political problem that is separate from the problems of modern terrorism (Laqueur 1987; White 1998).

The broad construction of terrorism offered herein is firmly rooted in the belief that governmental repression is an essential component in the history of modern terrorism. In short, our interpretation contends that almost all states have used terrorism to curb dissent, quell revolutions, and silence "enemies of the state." In so doing, they have acted as terrorists by legally using or threatening to use violence against an individual or group to maintain political control. Indeed, several experts have argued that terrorism from above may be terrorism at its most frightening level of application (Chomsky 1986; Duvall and Stohl 1983; Herman 1982; Walter 1969; Wardlaw 1989).

In the vast majority of cases throughout history, terrorism from above preceded and then nurtured the grievances that stimulated terrorism from below, thus suggesting a symbiotic relationship between the two. Thus, when governments used terrorism to quell dissent, such actions put the cycle of terrorism into motion by encouraging a violent response from some dissenters who resorted to terrorism to survive annihilation or because legitimate channels for changing a repressive regime or oppressive policy were closed. This circuitous motion continued when governments responded with yet another wave of institutionalized terror to put down terror emanating from below. Ironically, the terror both from above and below was advanced for real and perceived reasons of terror perpetrated by the "other side." Both groups viewed themselves as victims rather than perpetrators of terrorism.

Terrorism from above can be both covert and overt in nature.

- Terrorism is *covertly* used from above when government personnel use acts of terror that may or may not be prohibited by their official position, but which are secretly carried out or sanctioned by the government. Such terror can be covertly planned and implemented within a government's domestic power structure, as in the case of Argentina's "Dirty War" summarized in Chapter 2. Governments can covertly sponsor terrorism within the international arena by intervening in the political power structure of another nation, as in the case of American intervention in the political affairs of Guatemala from 1954 to 1996, also summarized in Chapter 2.

- Terrorism is *overtly* used from above when governments and/or leaders openly use political violence, claiming such actions are not terroristic, but rather, are necessary to enforce their rule and defend the nation, as in the case of the Hutu's genocidal policy against the Tutsis of Rwanda summarized in Chapter 2.[5]

Terrorism from Below

Throughout history terrorism from below most often has been used as a political tool for the following reasons:

- *To achieve national self-determination* by appealing to a particular national, religious, ethnic, or racial segment of the population to join in a campaign of political violence against the government to achieve political independence, as in the case of the *Front de Liberation Nationale* (FLN) fight against French colonization in Algeria summarized in Chapter 2.
- *To foster a particular ideology or political issue* by seeking a political change that is linked to a specific ideological factor or political issue, as in the case of several American groups and lone individuals who have terrorized abortion clinics and been active in various animal liberation and environmental groups that are summarized in Chapter 5.
- *To defend or preserve communal values* by destroying any actual or perceived opposition to the political, social, religious, or economic status quo, as in the case of the Ku Klux Klan summarized in Chapter 2 and various case studies of scapegoating vigilantism discussed in Chapter 3.
- *To reform or destroy the existing political, social, religious, or economic system* through the creation of private patriot-militia groups that take the law into their own hands, as illustrated in the various case studies presented in Chapter 4.

---

[5] For an in-depth study of another overt use of terrorism from above beginning in 1652 and ending in 1993, see Chapter 4 on South Africa, "Apartheid or Freedom?" in Gayle Olson-Raymer: *Terrorism: A Historical and Contemporary Perspective*. New York: American Heritage Custom Publishing, 1996:107–160.

TERRORISTS DEFINED

Terrorists have been wielding political violence for many years. But how did these perpetrators come to be called terrorists? We have already seen that the English politician Edmund Burke made the first reference to terrorists within a political context. In this historical usage, then, terrorists operated *from above*–they were the "hell hounds . . . turned loose by the state against the people." The contemporary political usage of the word began in the late 1970s when "terrorist" became a convenient label many governments applied to those conducting left-wing political violence from below. This modern application of the term assumed that dissenters were not just harmless malcontents or violent criminals, but dangerous terrorists, enemies of the state who posed a threat to political and societal order. To rid the nation of these terrorist enemies, some governments resorted to terrorism from above, justifying the use of a "national emergency" that sometimes required the suspension of constitutional and civil rights to protect the people.

In the United States, the use of the terrorist label to identify those acting from below became increasingly popularized by both the electronic media and the Reagan administration. From the early 1980s forward, the word terrorist was deliberately applied to citizens whom the U.S. government believed to embody a direct threat to American values and beliefs; however, if a person or group used political violence for a cause acceptable to the U.S. government, then the "terrorist" label did not apply. Moreover, the same qualifications were applied to those who conducted terrorism from above. If a government leader was an "enemy" of the American people–such as Muammar al-Qaddafi of Libya–that leader was a terrorist who was trying to destroy the power and credibility of the U.S. government. If the

leader was a Western ally–such as Benjamin Netanyahu, former prime minister of Israel–that leader was a freedom fighter who was merely struggling to maintain a power base that was acceptable to the U.S. government.

Such manipulation of the term terrorist, it is herein argued, allows governments to make value-laden choices about who is and who is not a terrorist. We are then forced to make definitional decisions based upon such individual questions as the following:

- Who is right, just, and moral? Who decides: Americans? Iranians? Iraqis? Italians? Russians? Chinese?
- What is right, just, and moral? Who decides: Palestinians or Israelis? The Catholics or Protestants of Northern Ireland? The Serbians or the Croatians? The Hutus or the Tutsis?
- When is an action considered to be a legitimate act of the government, and when is it considered to be an act of terrorism? Who decides: the government that terrorizes or the people being terrorized?

To avoid making such value judgments, we must understand that "at the heart of every terrorist cause or motive is an underlying 'core of legitimacy'" (Adams 1986: 6). All groups feel their cause is right, just, and moral and, therefore, almost all terrorists consider themselves freedom fighters rather than terrorizers. Thus, to even make a distinction between freedom fighters and terrorists is useless. If their modus operandi fits the description of terrorism used herein, then we can only conclude they are terrorists, regardless of whether their cause is just or unjust, right or wrong, moral or immoral by anyone's standards.

Terrorists, then, cannot easily be typified. Over the past several decades, experts have been unable to create a composite picture of a "typical" terrorist's background, psychological makeup, political beliefs, and motivations. Instead, by the 1970s, they identified various background patterns that fit many, but not all, terrorists. Primarily, they were the following:

- single males between the ages of twenty-two and twenty-four who had some university education;
- university or college students who came from an affluent, urban, middle-class family;
- activists in left-wing, nonviolent activity on the fringes of mainstream political parties; and
- persons attracted to terrorism because it afforded a way to promote left-wing political ideologies while rejecting their middle-class values.

Several other analyses supported this general pattern while adding a few other characteristics: a high level of verbal skills, superior training, and a fervent dedication to fight for "justice" (Clutterbuck 1980; Gurr 1983; Hacker 1976; Russell and Miller 1977; Strentz 1981).

By the mid-1980s, however, researchers noted some changes in this general pattern. Increasingly, terrorists–who were still predominately male–were

- young people, often attending secondary and even elementary schools, who were less politically and technically sophisticated and educated than their predecessors;
- members of the lower and middle classes who often lived in refugee camps, impoverished peasant villages, and urban and suburban communities facing an economic downsizing, where myriad grievances had been carefully nurtured;
- youth raised by families that instilled fear and hate of their perceived and actual oppressors; and

- persons who were attracted to terrorism because they believed violence offered the only viable option to poverty, provided an avenue for personal and familial survival, offered hope for economic and social upward mobility, and/or gave them an opportunity to redress their grievances.

Such broad, descriptive backgrounds, however, tell us little about the psychological characteristics of a terrorist. Terrorist experts are divided in their findings about the terrorist psyche. Some stress the psychological flaws of terrorists, flaws that attract them to a life of violence. Others argue that terrorists are relatively free of psychiatric problems and become involved in terrorism because they perceive they have no other option for personal, spiritual, nationalistic, or cultural survival.

The psychologically flawed advocates were enthused by the autobiographical materials Kellen (1979) collected from five left-wing terrorists: Michael Baumann of the German 2nd of June Movement, Hans Joachim Klein of the German Red Army Faction, Kozo Okamoto of the Japanese Red Army, Zvonko Busic involved in pro-Croation terrorism, and Horst Mahler of the Baader-Meinhof Gang. A comparative analysis indicates that they shared several psychological flaws:

- disillusionment with society and their middle-class lifestyles;
- willingness to reject their society;
- desire to fight that society for a variety of reasons, ranging from "simple revenge to millennialist and utopian fantasies";
- preference for "the life" of terrorism that gave them a chance to be important, free, and always involved in action; and
- feelings that they, as individuals and as group members, were repressed people (Kellen 1979).

Box 1.1
Women in Terrorism

Several scholars have examined various theories about how and why women became involved in left-wing terrorism during the 1960s and 1970s. See the summary in Olson-Raymer (1996: 22–23), or refer to Georges-Abeyies (1983); Hee (1993); Huey (1992); MacDonald (1991)Morgan (1989); and Weinberg and Eubank (1987). Although women were not initially involved in any substantial capacities in early right-wing terrorist movements of the 1980s and 1990s, by the end of the century, that had changed. As Lisa Turner, founder of the right-wing organization "Women's Frontier" of the World Church of the Creator stated in 1998, "In the last year or so, we have seen a lot of changes in this area. Everyone is starting to realize that if we are going to overcome in this [racial] struggle we are going to have to do it together—Man and Woman—side by side!" (as quoted in *Intelligence Report*, Summer 1999: 13).

Increasingly, women involved in right-wing movements are seeking new, expanded roles for themselves. While most reject the "feminist" perspective of sexual equality—which is believed to be a Jewish plot to destroy the white race—they are working hard to build up the culture that they hope will replace the current society their men are trying to destroy. The basis of that culture is working to find racist White female mates for their men; using the Internet and newsletters to advise racist women to raise more children; designing "racialist" educational curriculum for women who home school; and recruiting more women into their various organizations.

Following Kellen's psychopathic analysis, McKnight (1974) found that terrorism was committed by "people lost to love and affection, twisted by hates and frustrations: perhaps no better than dangerous psychopaths" (p. 13). One study of children who grew up in the violence of Northern Ireland suggested that the origins of terrorist behavior stem directly from a disruption in moral judgment caused by early exposure to violence (Fields 1979). Psychiatrist Jerrold M. Post (1987) posited that terrorists were typically action-oriented and aggressive individuals who had suffered psychological damage in childhood

that resulted in shattered self-regard. Thus, as the terrorist searched for identity, the terrorist gradually concluded that the "establishment" must be destroyed, and in so doing, also attempted to destroy the enemy within.

Perlstein's (1991) analysis of nine political terrorists found that they generally appeared to be psychologically molded by certain narcissistic personality disturbances.[6] Perlstein (1991) defined narcissism as an "internal, intrapsychic, regulatory 'tool' that enables the individual to defend the self from damage and harm" (p. 15). In his opinion, the nine terrorists studied received "distinct and

---

[6] Perlstein's nine terrorists were Susan Stern and Diana Oughton of the Weather Underground; Donald DeFreeze and Patricia Soltysik of the Symbionese Liberation Army; Thomas Martinez from the National Alliance; Victor Gerena from Los Macheteros; Ilich Ramírez Sanchez, better known as "Carlos the Jackal"; Ulrike Meinhof from the German Baader-Meinhof Gang; and Renato Curcio of the Italian Red Brigades.

powerfully alluring psychic benefits or rewards" from their involvement in terrorism; and had suffered narcissistic injury, "massive, profound, and permanent damage or harm to an individual's self-image or self esteem," as well as ". . . profound disappointment in the self prompted by an individual's pronounced inability to measure up to what he perceives as positive and desirable standards of conduct" (Perlstein 1991: 6–8).

Crenshaw (1986), who identified risk taking as one such reward, explained that two types of reward seekers were attracted to terrorism: individualistic risk takers, the leaders who sought danger as a form of self-affirmation; and collectivistic risk takers, the followers who identified more with the need to belong to a group than with its activities. Post (1987) further posited that such group psychology may dominate the individual's psychology, producing pressure to conform and to commit acts of violence.

The school that posits the absence of psychological illness has been championed by Rubenstein (1987) who asserted that terrorists "are generally no crazier than you or I might be if some implacable authority robbed us of our land or turned our dream of a better life into ashes" (p. 5). While Merkl's (1986) studies found a general absence of psychiatric symptoms and illnesses in terrorists, they also noted the prevalence of extremist thoughts and actions–dogmatic and dramatic thought, exaggerated emotions, and thinking in black-and-white terms.

Taylor and Quayle's (1994) interviews with terrorists over a fifteen-year period echoed similar beliefs about the terrorist psyche, finding that many saw violence as a "forced response to circumstances, expressed either as a regrettable but entirely reasonable response to past violence against the community, a legitimate response to conspiracies to disadvantage the community, or in a reactive way as a response to current aggression" (pp. 29–30).[7] They were also critical of "attempts to denigrate terrorists by describing them as madmen or psychopaths," an avenue that ". . . simply serves to deflect attention from the unpalatable truth that in their own eyes and those of their supporters, terrorists are often moral, even responsible people" (Taylor and Quayle 1994: 9). Indeed,

> Personal benefit rarely figures in the terrorist's own objectives as they might articulate them, and the benefits of terrorism are almost always expressed in altruistic terms of communal rather than personal benefits. What greater altruistic motive could there be than seeking justice for your community and traditions or beliefs through exposing yourself to danger and possible death? (Taylor and Quayle 1994: 9)

This diversity of opinion about terrorist psychologies is also evident in terms of terrorist motivations. As Freedman (1979) has stated, "The context and circumstances within which terrorism . . . has been carried out are diverse in chronology, geography, and motive" (p. 390). Jeffrey Simon (1994)[8] provided several motivational "payoffs" for terrorists: humbling powerful enemies; achieving results that otherwise may be unobtainable; ensuring a powerful position in future governmental

---

[7] Interviews were conducted with members of terrorist groups in Northern Ireland, Arab and Islamic Jihad organizations, and with former members of the Italian Red Brigades, the German Baader-Meinhof gang, and other European terrorist organizations.

[8] Simon explores the "terrorist trap: the psychological, political, and social elements that make terrorism unlike any other type of conflict." These elements include the "endless nature of terrorism and its likely growth in the coming years;" the central role the U.S. government and its presidents have played "in determining terrorism's impact on this country;" and terrorism's link "to the irreversible march of technology" (Simon 1994: 9–10).

leadership; sabotaging peace initiatives or to keep tension high for various reasons; settling scores; and making money.

Others cite the need for social interaction as a major motivational factor for joining and remaining in a terrorist group.

- Della Porta's (1995) study of the Red Brigades and other Italian terrorist groups found that "cliques of people connected to each other" by a well-developed political identity tended to join together and to stay committed to the group. Thus, friendship and kinship ties were very important motivators for joining and remaining in terrorist groups.
- Crenshaw (1986) described two types of risk takers who were drawn to terrorism out of personal and social needs: the leaders drawn to danger as a form of self-affirmation; and the followers drawn to the need to belong to a group rather than identify with its activities.
- Taylor and Quayle (1994) found a socialization process involving three phases: *becoming,* motivated by socialization processes, family, ideological commitment, and real or perceived grievances; *remaining,* includes peer pressure, group solidarity, commitment to the organization, isolation from normal social interaction; and *leaving,* about which we only know from conventional wisdom and includes an increased risk of apprehension, increasing family commitment, growing older, and amnesties.

Walter Laqueur (1999) posits another motivation for "the new terrorists"—a motivation that differs from the past in that its religious and ideologically radical adherents aim to destroy society. Their brand of terrorism is aimed, "not at clearly defined political demands but at the destruction of society and the elimination of large sections of the population" (p. 81). Indeed,

In its most extreme form, this new terrorism intends to liquidate all satanic forces, which may include the majority of a country or of mankind, as a precondition for the growth of another, better, and in any case different breed of human. In its maddest, most extreme form it may aim at the destruction of all life on earth, as the ultimate punishment for mankind's crimes (Laqueur 1999: 81).

Robert Jay Lifton's (1999) frightening analysis of Japan's terrorist cult, Aum Shinrikyo, reaches a similar conclusion. Aum's religion—a global stew of apocalyptic science fiction, New Age thinking, and ancient religious practices—was the justification for its charismatic leader's world-ending vision. Given such motivations and the increasingly easy access to weapons of mass destruction, Lifton concludes that the twenty-first century may be one in which terrorists may be able to create their own holocausts.

Rather than providing a "typical" profile of the contemporary terrorist, this brief discussion of background, psychological make-up, and motivations indicates that no single terrorist background exists, no uniform series of psychological traits can be consensually identified, and no simple list of terrorist motivations can be compiled. Instead, we find many generalizations and a great deal of diversity among the terrorists themselves.

THE TOOLS OF TERROR

To commit acts of terror, terrorists throughout history have resorted to a wide array of tools, tools that remained remarkably consistent until the late twentieth century. Regardless of the types of tools used by terrorists, they are all intended to have the same effect: to commit, or threaten to commit, an act of political violence that subsequently terrorizes a targeted victim on behalf of a particular political goal.

As the following brief discussion of the most popular terrorist tools indicates, each has been used for centuries, and some have been used exclusively by terrorists from above, others by terrorists from below, and some by both. Further, these terrorist tools have remained remarkably consistent throughout history. Indeed, it was not until the late twentieth century that the tools of the trade began to change. Such changes, however, were not *revolutionary* in nature, but involved *evolutionary* modifications that were directly attributable to the growth of modern communications, transportation, and weaponry technology. For example, consider the following:

- While kidnapping has consistently been used by historical and contemporary terrorists, it has become more sophisticated with modern transportation technology. Yesterday's kidnappers seized their victims on horseback, while today's kidnappers seize their victims in cars, "hijack" trains and buses, and "skyjack" airplanes.
- While bombs have been popular tools for both historical and contemporary terrorists, they have become more deadly with advances in explosive technology. In earlier years, bombers were content with the results of crude dynamite, while today's bombers use sophisticated, high-powered plastic explosives deployed by remote-controlled devices located miles away from the bombing scene.
- While chemical weapons have been used for hundreds of years by historical and contemporary terrorists, newer contemporary weapons of mass destruction pose a frightening new technological leap. Historical proponents of chemical warfare aimed to destroy a particular target for a very particular reason, while today's proponents of

deadly chemical weapons are often rooted in apocalyptic visions for the future.

Such new technology has wrongly convinced a large proportion of the world citizenry that terrorism is a new phenomenon, that terrorists are a new breed of politically violent criminals, and that they wield dramatically new tools. Terrorism, however, is as old as humankind, and terrorists and their tools are an unfortunate but real component of our history. To illustrate this viewpoint, we need to further examine a few of the tools of terrorism that have been used over the years:

- Assassination and kidnapping: tools of terrorists operating both from above and below.
- Enslavement, imprisonment, banishment, and genocide: tools of terrorists operating from above.
- Arson, guns, bombs, hijacking, and weapons of mass destruction: tools of terrorists operating from below.

Assassination and Kidnapping: Tools of Terrorists Operating from Above and Below

Assassination is used to kill a prominent figure whose death potentially will have a political effect. Prior to the use of this term, the killing of a political leader by a disgruntled citizen was often known as tyrannicide. Early Greek and Roman history is replete with examples of citizens using tyrannicide to overthrow perceived and actual tyrants. Early Roman and Greek philosophers, playwrights, and poets often praised tyrannicide. Cicero, in *De Officiis* stated that, "There can be no such thing as fellowship with tyrants, nothing but bitter feud is possible; and it is not repugnant in nature to kill; nay, this pestilent and godless breed should be utterly banished from human society" (as quoted in Laqueur 1987: 16).

Aristotle and Seneca also viewed tyrannicide favorably, with the latter arguing that the blood of a tyrant was the most pleasing sacrifice to God. In 1159, John of Salisbury completed the "first explicit philosophic rationalization" of tyrannicide, arguing that anyone who killed a tyrant was merely carrying out God's will (as quoted in Crotty 1971: 5).

Assassination has not merely been the tool of the dissenting public. Indeed, terroristic assassination from above was recorded in early history. Perhaps the most celebrated of all early historical political assassinations from above was that of Julius Caesar, who was killed by a group of friends and Roman senators who feared the consequences of his absolute power.

Indeed, throughout history, governors most often used political assassination to suppress a political, social, economic, or ideological challenge from below. To that end, Machiavelli (1469–1527) was one of several Renaissance philosophers who believed that any illegal or criminal method of assassination was justifiable if committed in the interest of the state. In *The Prince*, published in 1532, Machiavelli praised the actions of Cesare Borgia, who paid assassins to eliminate his political opponents, touting him as "an example to be imitated by all who by fortune and with the arms of others have risen to power" (as quoted in Jaszi and Lewis 1957: 36). In 1595, the successor to the Ottoman Empire followed the example from Italy by ordering the death of his 19 brothers who would have become competitors (Stavrionos 1958).

Assassinations used by contemporary terrorists from below are generally aimed at highly visible targets who have some symbolic value for the terrorist cause. Examples include the 1991 assassination in Lima, Peru, of the Canadian director of the humanitarian organization World Mission by the Sendero Luminosa (see Chapter 2); the 1993 killing of a police officer and wounding of six others by the Egyptian terrorist group al-Gama'at al-Islamiyya[9] that was retaliating for the screening of immoral films; and the 1995 assassination of Prime Minister Yitzhak Rabin of Israel by a Jewish student who claimed Rabin had given away too much of Israel during the peace process.

Kidnapping involves abducting an individual through the use of unlawful force or fraud, with the abductors usually demanding economic and/or political ransom. Long before the word was in use, people were seized and held for ransom. Greek myths abound with stories of abductions stimulated by love: Jupiter, disguised as a white bull, carried off Europa; Paris seized Helen of Troy from her husband, Menelaus. By the tenth century, the use of kidnapping to obtain a political goal on behalf of ideological and spiritual grievances was not uncommon.

- The Muslim world apparently suffered from enough Christian kidnappings to create a formal mechanism for ransom negotiation. Thus arose a new profession, the *fakkak,* or professional ransomer, who served as an intermediary to Muslim families whose members had fallen into Christian hands.
- In 1198, the Christian Order of the Most Holy Trinity for the Ransom of Captives, the Trinitarians, received a papal sanction to begin ransom missions to the Barbary Coast. Twenty-five years later, St. Peter No-

---

[9] al-Gama'at al-Islamiyya is an indigenous Egyptian Islamic group that has been active since the late 1970s and seeks to overthrow the government of President Hosni Mubarak and replace it with an Islamic state.

lasco founded the Order of Our Lady of Mercy, the Mercedarians, whose vows included surrendering themselves as hostages to the Moors. By the thirteenth century, the Mercedarians claimed they had ransomed 59,000 captives; the Trinitarians claimed 900,000.

Kidnapping assumed a peculiar course in fifteenth- and sixteenth-century England. As incomes from landed estates declined, unmarried rich girls were sought for marriage. Often, a scorned suitor simply abducted the girl, forcing her father into marriage and financial acceptance. It was not until the seventeenth century that the word "kidnap" first appeared in the English language. In 1678, the word "kidnappers" was included in the fourth appendix of the *New World English Words Dictionary*. Its usage was broadened in 1707, when abductions of "maydens that be inheritors" was made punishable by hanging in England (Moorehead 1980).

Throughout history, kidnappers also have operated from positions of power. During the Crusades, victorious kings made fortunes by ransoming prisoners. While returning to England from the Crusades in 1192, King Richard was captured by Duke Leopold of Austria. The ransom was 100,000 marks of silver; about one-half that sum was finally paid by the English crown. Soon traveling kings and emperors began to capture and force hostages to travel with them as guarantors of their host's honorable behavior. In those cases, an important hostage from a ruling family was seized and, upon safe arrival, was then returned. The Incas of Peru employed another type of kidnapping. After conquering a warring people, the idols of the conquered were seized and held hostage. It was believed that as long as the idols were in captivity, the defeated people would not rebel against enforced authority (Moorehead 1980).

Kidnapping assumed a more modern form in the 1970s in the form of hostage taking. During the 1980s and early 1990s, hostage taking reached a peak as terrorists from all parts of the world kidnapped important figures to gain a worldwide audience for their cause. One of the most recent and well-publicized hostage-taking incidents occurred in December 1996 in Peru when the Tupac Amaru[10] took more than 500 people hostage at the Japanese Embassy in Lima. During the early negotiation process, most hostages were released, but 81 remained in captivity for 126 days before being rescued by Peruvian troops.

Enslavement and Subjugation, Imprisonment, Banishment, and Genocide: Tools of Terrorists Operating from Above

Enslavement and subjugation involve the legal and absolute control of a specific group of people. The practice of enslaving certain peoples, the "legal institutionalization of persons as property," has been a constant characteristic of human society (Tuden and Plotnicov 1970: 11). Roman civilization had such an advanced system of slavery that it has been called a "slave society," one in which slave labor in the countryside sustained the nation as a whole. In most early slave societies, the motives for enslavement were primarily political and economic. Slaves, who were necessary to keep the economy running, were readily available through political conquest, and, as such, were clearly the ob-

---

[10] The Tupac Amaru, a revolutionary movement formed in 1983, seeks to rid Peru of imperialism and establish a Marxist regime.

ject of political, social, physical, and economic deprivation. They were not subjected to the terrors of enslavement because of who they were, what they believed, or the color of their skin; rather, slaves were the victims of economic and political realities.

Economics and politics were also responsible for the decline and fall of the first "slave society." With the collapse of the Roman Empire and its cities, country estates gradually lost their ability to support slave labor. Thus, between the fifth and eleventh centuries, rural slavery throughout western Europe slowly transformed into a "dependent peasantry of serfs" (Phillips 1985: 43). While they were never completely absent from European society during this period, serfs largely replaced slaves. Although serfs were not ruled absolutely nor owned by their masters, their will was totally subordinated to the lord for whom they worked. In essence, they were politically, economically, and socially dependent on their masters. The enslaved, then, were largely replaced by the subjugated.

Slavery did not regain strength in Europe until the late-fifteenth and early-sixteenth centuries, when the demand for labor increased in European colonies. This demand opened the door to what soon became a very lucrative new type of slavery, based not merely upon economic motivation, but also upon racial inequality, fear, and hate. The black African slave trade was pioneered by the Portuguese who, in 1444, transported the first group of black African slaves to Portugal.

Shortly thereafter, the Portuguese and Spanish established sugar cane plantations in the Caribbean, thus originating the Atlantic slave trade that promoted slavery on an unprecedented scale. Between this time and 1650, it is estimated that over 350,000 slaves arrived in Spanish-American ports and 250,000 arrived in Brazil, primarily to work on the sugar cane plantations (Curtin 1969;

Lovejoy 1982). When the colonists and later the citizens of the United States engaged in the slave trade, the number of black Africans who were involuntarily enslaved skyrocketed.

It was not until 1807 that slave trading was first outlawed, with the British taking the lead. The following year, the Americans abolished the slave trade, although the institutionalized system of slavery remained legal. Thus, slavery continued to flourish in most British colonies and in the United States. Widespread abolition efforts did not begin for at least thirty more years, and slavery would not be abolished in the United States until after the Civil War. Slavery, however, has not disappeared from either the American or global landscape. In the late 1990s, journalist Kevin Bales (1999) traveled around the world in his search for contemporary enslavement. He found that about 27 million people were still enslaved on every continent and in almost every nation in the world–although the numbers were highest in Southeast Asia and North Africa.

Imprisonment and punishment of political enemies involves imprisoning and/or punishing a person(s) perceived to be an enemy of the state. One of the most dramatic examples of imprisoning and punishing began in the early fourteenth century, "the golden age of the political trial for sorcery, heresy, and witchcraft" (Russell 1972: 193). Between 1300 and 1360, ten major politically motivated trials occurred in England, France, and Italy, trials that convicted the defendants not because they worshiped the devil, but because the courtroom provided a forum for expressing "religious hatreds and fears" and punishing those who were different, prosperous, and often powerful (Russell 1972: 198). Between 1427 and 1486, over 100 "significant witch trials" occurred in secular and religious European courts, during which ". . . the rulers of society felt their status was threatened and proceeded ruthlessly against those whom they feared. Heretics, witches, and Jews were the most visible nonconformists. . . . The persecutors justified their bloody elimination of witches . . . by dehumanizing them" (Russell 1972: 286–287).

Cohn's (1975) examination of the Inquisition's four centuries concludes that the "dangers" of witchcraft were a tragic, paranoid fantasy conjured up by the Inquisitors who, frustrated in their failure to convert Europeans to Christianity, came to believe such people represented a real threat to their religion. Of those accused in England's "witch craze" of the sixteenth and seventeenth centuries, most were again religious and/or societal nonconformists (Trevor-Roper 1969). More than 90 percent were women; the few male witches were often married to an accused witch (MacFarlane 1970).

The vast majority of these so-called witches were accused during an especially difficult economic time in England, when women were actively competing with men for scarce livelihoods and were thereby seen as a threat to the male supremacist status quo. In retrospect, "the crimes . . . do not appear to have been real crimes at all but seem to have been explanations for unpleasant events in the village" (Hester 1992: 32). In short, fear of or an actual accusation of witchcraft was a type of terrorism from above that served as a method for controlling women's lives through the threat of violence (Hanmer and Saunders 1984; Hester 1992).

Unfortunately, imprisonment and punishment of political enemies continued throughout the modern era of global history. The "disappeared" of Argentina and Chile, as well as other Latin American nations during the 1970s and 1980s, are another tragic example. (See the brief case study on Argentina in Chapter 2.)

Banishment of political enemies involves compulsory, involuntary removal or exile of a person or persons from a country, or compulsory, involuntary confinement of persons in the home who are subsequently banished from public movement and communication. Banishment is a punishment as old as civilization. In ancient Greece, the ruling faction of Athens legalized the practice: those who were feared to become tyrants and those perceived as a threat to the will of the majority were expelled and sent into "honorable exile" for ten years (Shain 1989: 2). Citizens of ancient Rome who had been sentenced to death could choose between execution or exile.

One of the most elaborate experiments with banishment was the transportation policy adopted by Britain as a way to rid the kingdom of its criminal population. The first British efforts in this direction occurred in 1597 when local magistrates received Parliamentary power to exile criminals "beyond the seas." In 1615, James I granted pardons to condemned felons who agreed to be banished to the New World. But it was the Transportation Act of 1718 that institutionalized the policy of banishment as a punishment for serious crime. By 1775, when transportation to the American colonies was officially ended, over 50,000 convicts had been transported over the Atlantic (Ekirch 1987: 26–27). But transportation of criminals was not entirely abandoned; instead, between 1786 and 1856, over 150,000 felons were banished to Australia, England's first large-scale penal colony.

Genocide involves actions committed with the intent to destroy, in whole or in part, a national, ethnic, racial, religious, political, or economic group. Such actions against a group include killing its members; causing serious bodily or mental harm to members; deliberately inflicting conditions of life calculated to bring about the groups' physical destruction in whole or in part; imposing measures intended to prevent births within the group; and forcibly transferring its children to another group. Cultural genocide occurs when governments officially sanction the removal and/or repression of a particular group that subsequently eliminates and/or weakens parts of that group.

While it is unknown when the first genocide occurred, it has been postulated that it was well past the hunting and gathering stage of the human evolutionary process (Chalk and Jonassohn 1990). Once humans were able to build city states and empires, conflicts arose over access to trade, wealth, and trade routes. Wars resulted, the defeated people withdrew long enough to ready themselves to avenge their previous defeat, and the conflict assuredly occurred again. "This pattern became so common that it soon appeared that the only way to assure a stable future was to eliminate the defeated peoples once and for all" (Chalk and Jonassohn 1990: 32). At least four reasons for genocide were used to terrorize prior to 1848:

1. After the discovery of agriculture, when conflicts arose over access to wealth and trade routes, the victors sometimes used genocide *to eliminate a potential future threat* to their power. People who were not killed during or after the battle were sold into slavery and dispersed.
2. As early civilizations continued their quest to obtain more land and other resources, they sometimes used genocide *to acquire economic wealth*. In such circumstances, people found that wealth could only be acquired by forcibly occupying the land and then enslaving or exterminating the indigenous population.
3. Genghis Khan, acknowledged as "Universal Ruler" of the Mongolian people in 1206, used genocide *to create terror*. After his armies conquered and subjugated peoples, Khan offered the vanquished a choice of submission or extermination; those who selected the latter were ruthlessly killed.
4. During the Middle Ages, some nation states and churches used genocide *to implement*

and defend a belief, a theory, or an ideology. In such cases, perceived and actual nonbelievers were persecuted and sometimes executed (Jonassohn and Chalk 1987: 12–15).

From the nineteenth century forward, genocide has been used largely as a tool to eliminate a certain group of people from a nation or region because of their ethnicity, religious beliefs, race, or their perceived hindrance to the economic, political, and social progress of another people. Chapter 2 provides several brief case studies: the nineteenth-century genocide of the North American Indian at the hands of the U.S. government; the early twentieth-century Armenian genocide; and the 1994 Hutu genocide of the Tutsis in Rwanda.

Arson, Guns, Bombs, Hijacking, and Weapons of Mass Destruction: Tools of Terrorists Operating from Below

Arson has served the purposes of many terrorists throughout history. A Syrian architect named Kallinokos, the first person known to use what later became known as arson, gave Emperor Constantine Pogonatus a secret fire formula when Constantinople was under siege by the Saracens in A.D. 673. The mixture of sulfur, pitch, niter, petroleum, and quicklime was put into projectile tubes, which Constantine placed in his galleys. When confronted by hostile vessels, the projecting tubes squirted what became known as the "Greek fire" into the ships, causing them to burn fiercely. This tool's reputation of being inextinguishable "greatly enhanced its efficiency as a terror weapon. . . ." (Brodie and Brodie 1973: 15). Thereafter, fire explosives became common weapons of both warriors and terrorists.

By the late 1990s, arson still was a popular terrorist tool, accounting for about 14 percent of all incidents around the world and remaining as the primary instrument for property destruction. One of the most recent and dramatic uses of terroristic arson occurred in November 1993 and Spring 1995 when the PKK (Kurdistan Workers' Party)[11] committed a series of firebombings against Turkish diplomatic and commercial facilities in various Western European nations. One person was killed and several dozen were injured.

Guns became popular shortly after the introduction of gunpowder. It is believed that in eleventh-century China, the first type of black-powder explosive was developed of sulfur, saltpeter, and charcoal. In Western society, the Englishman Roger Bacon is generally credited with discovering gunpowder made from the same ingredients in the 1240s (Wilkinson 1966). Between the thirteenth and seventeenth centuries, most countries of Western Europe became familiar with the production and use of black powder. Gradually, Europeans learned to shoot it from cannons, muskets, shotguns, rifles, and handheld pistols.

Until the 1970s, many terrorists were content with handheld pistols and the new armor-piercing ammunition of the 1960s. However, terrorists of the 1970s preferred to use new technologically-advanced weaponry. Thereafter, the newly developed automatic assault rifles became the most sought-after "weapons of choice" for terrorists: the Soviet-designed Kalashnikov, the Czech-made Skorpion VZ 61, and the Israeli Uzi. In the 1980s, several types of shoulder-fired, precision-guided, "standoff" weapons began to be used by terrorists to attack both military and commercial aircraft:

• Soviet-made RPG-2 and RPG-7 shoulder-fired antitank rockets. These weapons have a range of at least several hundred meters, and on impact will penetrate ten inches or more of steel armor. The Irish Republican Army, as well as other terrorist groups, has used the RPG-7 grenade launcher during several attacks on Great Britain (Biddle 1986).

• Surface-to-air missiles (SAMs) and their American cousin, the Stinger. In 1978 and 1979, guerrillas used the SAM-7 to down two Rhodesian passenger jets resulting in the death of 107 people; in 1986, Sudanese rebels shot down a Sudan Airways commercial jet with a SAM, killing all 60 persons on board; and in 1988, Polisario Front guerrillas in Morocco used a SAM to down an American DC7 weather plane, killing the five-member crew. During the Soviet occupation in Afghanistan, guerrilla *muja-hadin* forces fighting the occupiers had access to approximately 5,000 Stinger and British Blowpipe shoulder-mounted missiles, most of which were supplied by the United States (Ispahani 1989/1990).

• Suitcase-size, wire-guided missiles. While similar in effect to the shoulder-fired anti-tank rockets, these weapons have a range of 1,000 yards or more and can penetrate 20 inches of steel armor and 60 inches of concrete.

Bombs, which have been used by terrorists for centuries, remain their most popular tool—accounting for about 50 percent of all terrorist incidents around the world. Guy Fawkes's infamous "Gunpowder Plot" of 1604 is often cited as the first intended modern use of the politically inspired bomb. On November 4, officials found 36 barrels of gunpowder in the cellar underneath the English House of Parliament. Fawkes and at least 12 other Catholic co-conspirators had planned to blow up Parliament, kill the Eng-

---

[11] The PKK, established in 1974, seeks to create an independent Kurdish state in southeastern Turkey where there is a predominately Kurdish population. Its primary targets are Turkish government security forces and Turkish targets in Western Europe.

lish peers assembled for the opening of the new parliamentary session, and murder King James I of England. Afterwards, they planned to kidnap the King's daughter, nine-year-old Princess Elizabeth, and pronounce her the titular Queen of England with the Earl of Northumberland, a Catholic sympathizer, as Protector. The close-knit group of young Catholic men who conceived this plot with Fawkes had resorted to such a violent plan because they felt there was no other avenue to end the laws that discriminated against the Catholic minority in England.[12]

The nineteenth century witnessed two important discoveries that helped create a new group of explosives. In 1846, Ascanio Sobrero, professor of chemistry at the University of Turin in Italy, discovered nitroglycerin; and in 1866, Alfred B. Nobel of Sweden found that mixing a particular kind of earth with the right amount of nitroglycerin made a superior explosive that he called dynamite.

The first terrorist bombs were crude devices that had to be carefully concealed and delivered by hand; such bombs placed the terrorist equally at risk as the intended victim. When reliable timing devices were invented, terrorists were able to avoid risk by placing nondescript packages in or around the intended target. Then, with the automobile's introduction, terrorists could leave a time bomb in a parked car; by the early 1960s, such timing devices had been used by terrorists in many places, including Ireland, the Middle East, South Vietnam, and the United States for a wide array of motives (Grabosky 1983; Gurr 1983; Harrigan 1966; Joesten 1962; Sobel, 1975).

One of the most deadly examples of modern bomb usage occurred in 1983, when over 12,000 pounds of plastic explosives en-

hanced by canisters of flammable gases killed 241 U.S. Marines in Beirut. The blast, which the FBI described as the "largest non-nuclear blast ever detonated on the face of the earth," created a crater forty feet wide and nine feet deep (Hammel 1985: 303).

Since the Beirut bombing, at least seven other major anti-American bombing incidents have occurred overseas during which hundreds of people died, many of whom were Americans, and thousands were injured. Foremost among these attacks were the 1995 car bombing of U.S. military headquarters in Riyadh, Saudi Arabia, in which five Americans died; the 1996 truck bombing of the U.S. Air Force base at Dhahran, Saudi Arabia, in which nineteen Americans died and more than 500 Americans and Saudis were injured; and the 1998 bombing of the U.S. embassies in Kenya and Tanzania in which 224 people died, including twelve Americans.

Terrorists have also taken advantage of such dual technologies as automatically detonated explosives and the airplane. Although bombs had first been placed in aircrafts during World War II, it was not until the 1960s that aircraft sabotage became a popular tool for terrorists. Today, the "bomb saboteur" who places a bomb on a commercial aircraft, in a car, or in a public place is among the most dangerous of terrorists because all of this saboteur's "actions are calculated to kill in quantity" (Jenkins 1992: 18). Between 1960 to 1988, 87 incidents of aircraft sabotage occurred; between 1949 and 1988, 2,939 people had died and 356 persons were wounded by sabotage or explosions; and between 1969 and 1988, there were 80 "clear-cut attempts to destroy planes," which most likely represented only half of the number actually attempted" (St.

---

[12] For a detailed and engaging history of Fawkes's experience with terrorism, see Antonia Fraser: *Faith and Treason: The Story of the Gunpowder Plot*. New York, Doubleday, 1997.

John 1991: 63, 219–220).[13] The actual bombs used by the aircraft saboteur have changed as new explosive technologies have developed.

In a more recent event, suicide bombers in a small boat slipped through Navy security and set off a blast that tore a gaping hole in the *U.S.S. Cole*. In October 2000, this terrorist incident killed seventeen crewmembers, injured 35 others, and crippled the ship that was at a refueling stop in the Yemeni port of Aden. This was the worst attack against the U.S. military since the 1996 bombing in Saudi Arabia.

Sabotage, unfortunately, has not been linked only to aircrafts and ships; increasingly, bombings target the public infrastructure

- Between 1970 and 1990, some 155 bombings occurred at the sites of civil nuclear installations in Sweden, Spain, the United Kingdom, France, Italy, Belgium, and the United States (Kupperman 1991).
- In 1984, the Shining Path of Peru blew up a strategic railroad bridge east of Lima, effectively cutting off food and mineral shipments.
- In 1991, the Irish Republican Army bombed the Victoria and Paddington railroad stations in London during rush hour, killing one man and wounding 40 others.
- In 1995, a truck filled with fertilizer and gasoline was detonated and blew up the federal building in Oklahoma City, killing 168 men, women, and children, as well as destroying the entire building.

Hijacking involves the unlawful seizure of and/or unlawful interference with a public or private transportation mode, during which the abductors usually demand economic and/or political ransom. Sixty years ago, it would have been impossible to conceive that the technological advances in air transportation would encourage a new vehicle for the modern-day terrorist. Even after the first aircraft was hijacked in May 1930, no one would have believed they were witnessing an evolutionary trend in terrorist kidnapping. Indeed, the Peruvian revolutionaries who seized that Pan American mail plane and demanded the pilot drop propaganda leaflets over Lima would have been surprised by the historical precedent they had set.

It was not until the late 1940s and early 1950s that illegal diversion of aircraft for political reasons began to occur on an occasional basis, thereby modernizing the ancient practice of kidnapping. Thereafter, the airplane made mass kidnapping possible through the practice that variously became known as air piracy, hijacking, and skyjacking. While the word "hijack" first appeared in American slang during Prohibition, it referred specifically to robbing a bootlegger of his liquor and literally meant "to steal in transit" (Phillips 1973: 259). It was not until February 19, 1958, that the term hijacking was first applied to the seizure of an airplane by the London *Times,* which, on August 10, 1961, was also the first to use the term *skyjack* (St. John 1991).

Hijacking was soon used to achieve political asylum, escape from Communist nations, or enter a Communist nation where the hijacker would be safe from political prosecution in a Western nation. Even before the official term was used, between 1947 and 1952, St. John (1991) identified 23 hijacking incidents: 20 cases involved Eastern Europeans who sought political asylum in Western Europe, and three cases occurred in Asia. Because the only actual crime that had been committed was the theft of the airplane, and

---

[13] Perhaps the most well-known and tragic of these was the December 21, 1988 bomb explosion of Pan American Flight 103 over Lockerbie, Scotland in which 270 people died.

because the planes were usually returned, Western nations often regarded the hijackers as heroes, escaping the tyranny of Communism–never terrorists–who were not deserving of punishment.

By the late 1950s, when anyone could fly on a commercial aircraft, this new transportation technology was ready to be tapped by terrorists operating from below. Raoul Castro, Fidel's brother who was also involved in the guerrilla-based revolution against President Batista, pioneered the first modern political hijacking and provided the model for future terrorists. In October and November 1958, several of Raoul's guerrilla warriors hijacked two private Cuban planes and brought them to a jungle-based temporary airport. Over the next one-and-a-half years, at least 18 politically motivated hijackings occurred. By the autumn of 1961, "the full range of human, technological, and national problems involved in hijacking had emerged" (St. John 1991: 8–9).

For the next several years, however, only about four hijackings occurred each year, none of which were politically significant. In 1967, the hiatus ended with the occurrence of two important hijackings: the diversion of a Russian-built Egyptian plane to Jordan with 41 passengers on board; and the hijacking of a private plane flying from Spain and diverted to Algiers with the former president of the Congo on board. Thereafter, "a tiny little seed was sown; an ominous little seed that grew slowly, unobtrusively into an enormous, ugly, parasitic growth" (Arey 1972: 67). Between August 1967 and February 1968, a "worldwide phenomenon" ensued that led to "a virtual epidemic of hijacking" (St. John 1991: 10). Indeed, between 1972 and 1988, the U.S. Federal Aviation Administration registered a total of 364 hijackings (U.S. Department of Transportation 1986: 13).

While hijacking continued throughout the 1990s, only a few were real "spectaculars"

that dominated news coverage. One of the most recent occurred in late December 1999, when an Indian Airlines jet was hijacked after it took off on a scheduled flight from Katmandu, the capital of Nepal, to New Delhi. During the first few days of the ordeal, the hijackers fatally stabbed one hostage, unloaded the slain man's body, and released 27 captives, most of them women and children, during a stopover in Dubai, United Arab Emirates. However, more than 150 hostages remained in captivity on board the jet for over a week while the hijackers increased their pressure on the Indian government by demanding that it pay them $200 million and release 35 jailed militants. At the time of this writing, the identities of the hijackers remained uncertain, but they appeared to be either Kashmiri or Pakistani terrorists who were violently opposed to rule of the predominantly Muslim territory of Kashmir by secular, but predominantly Hindu, India. Their goal was to create either a separate Kashmiri state or a United Nations-sponsored plebiscite that would allow Kashmir to join Islamic Pakistan.

Weapons of mass destruction–such as chemical weapons and nuclear explosives–are designed to bring about absolute devastation. The use of chemical weapons wielded from above dates back at least as far as the Peloponnesian War "when tar pitch and sulfur were mixed to produce a suffocating gas" (Vetter and Perlstein 1991: 168). By 1899, chemical weapons had become common enough to be outlawed by the Hague Convention. Only 16 years later during World War I, German soldiers released lethal gas near the Belgian town of Ypres, killing 5,000 French troops and injuring another 10,000. By the war's end, about 124,000 tons of chemicals had been released by both sides, killing 91,000 soldiers and injuring another 1.3 million (Vetter and Perlstein 1991).

Despite the passage of the Washington Treaty after World War I outlawing the use of poison gas in war and the Geneva Protocol in 1925, the Italians used mustard gas in their conquest of Ethiopia; the Spanish dropped chemical bombs on Morocco; the Japanese launched over 800 gas attacks in Manchuria; and the Egyptians used chemical agents during the Yemeni Civil War (Kupperman 1991).

More recently, during the horrific civil war between Iraq and Iran, the former used chemical weapons against the latter. Within the context of this war, the use of chemical weapons took a dramatic turn. In March 1988, the Iraqi government used chemical weapons not as an instrument of war, but as a terroristic instrument of hatred against its own citizens. Claiming that the targets were Iranian troops who held the Iraqi border town of Halabja, the real targets were the dissident Kurds, an ethnic group long held in disdain by much of the Iraqi population and by their president, Saddam Hussein. The combination of mustard gas, cyanide, and nerve gas was indiscriminately administered against innocent civilians, killing some 2,000 Kurdish civilians (Joyner 1993). In September, after a number of Kurdish villages in northern Iraq were struck by chemical weapons, over 60,000 Kurds fled into refugee camps in southern Turkey.

From the 1970s forward, various governments have reported that terrorist groups operating from below had possession of chemical weapons. Israel security agents and police found canisters of a potent poison that were presumed to have been brought in by terrorists. In 1975, German entrepreneurs were apprehended in Vienna attempting to sell nerve agents to Palestinian terrorists. Approximately 400 kilograms of intermediate compounds for the manufacture of nerve agents were discovered in a terrorist safe house in West Germany in the late 1970s (Kupperman 1991: 95–96). Chapter 7 discusses recent right-wing threats from weapons of mass destruction in more detail.

SUMMARY

The primary goal of this chapter has been to provide a definitional framework for a more in-depth study of terrorism and terrorists. In so doing, this chapter has introduced several themes that will be reiterated throughout the book.

1. Terrorism is best defined within a broad context that both recognizes the subjectivity of human interpretation and rejects definitions based on the perpetrators' justifications of legitimacy and morality for some terroristic actions and condemnation of others. In the broadest sense, terrorism occurs when an action uses violence from either above or below to terrorize a targeted population on behalf of a political goal; when such violence is motivated by political, social, economic, religious, or ideological grievances that may be emotionally driven by fear, hate, and intolerance; and when the action has the anticipated or unanticipated consequence of causing terror and is not discontinued once such terror is discovered. Further, regardless of who commits an act of terror–those acting from above under legal guise or those acting from below with no legal ability to change the power base–the perpetrators are terrorists.

2. In general, terrorism can be explained within the framework of two broad typologies: terrorism from above and below. Terrorism from above involves the overt and covert use of political violence conducted from a position of established authority to maintain and defend positions of power against actual or perceived "enemies of the state." Terrorism from below involves the use of political violence by dissenters who wish to challenge or overthrow official state power.

3. There is no "typical" profile of the contemporary terrorist. Indeed, no single terrorist background exists, no uniform series of psychological traits can be consensually identified, and no simple list of terrorist motivations can be compiled. Instead, we find many generalizations and a great deal of diversity among the terrorists themselves.

4. Despite the inability to create a solid terrorist profile, since the mid-1980s, researchers have identified a series of general characteristics that describe many contemporary terrorists. Terrorists tend to be predominately male and are younger, as well as less politically and technically sophisticated and educated, than their predecessors of the 1960s and 1970s; are recruited into terrorism primarily from the lower to middle classes, often from refugee camps, impoverished peasant villages, and economically depressed urban and suburban communities where a myriad of political, economic, social, religious, and ideological grievances have been carefully nurtured; come from families where they had been raised to fear and hate their oppressors; have firsthand experience both with their grievances and violence through actual and perceived victimization; and are attracted to terrorism because they believe violence offers the only viable option to poverty, provides an avenue for personal and familial survival, and/or gives them an opportunity to redress their grievances.

5. In general, the tools of terrorists from both above and below have remained remarkably consistent throughout history. It was not until the late twentieth century that the tools of the trade began to change. Such changes were really modifications of the old tools and, as such, were not *revolutionary* in nature. Rather, they involved *evolutionary* improvements that were directly attributable to the growth of modern communications, transportation, and weaponry technology.

DISCUSSION QUESTIONS

1. How do the terms *vigilante, extremist,* and *terrorist* compare and contrast?

2. What is the difference between terrorism from above and below? After rereading White's (1998) opinions about why terrorism is so difficult to define, as well as the definitional section at the beginning of the chapter, do you believe terrorism from above should be included in a definition of terrorism? Why or why not?

3. Why is terrorism often considered to be cyclical in nature? Do you agree or disagree with the thesis of this chapter that throughout history, the cycle has most often begun with terrorism from above? Why or why not?

4. Compare and contrast the descriptive backgrounds and psychological mindset of terrorists prior to the 1980s with those of contemporary terrorists. How have terrorists from both generations been influenced by left-wing and right-wing political philosophies?

5. How would you explain the phrase, "What is one man's terrorist is another man's freedom fighter?" How is this phrase related to the quote by Adams (1986) that "at the heart of every terrorist cause or motive is an underlying 'core of legitimacy'?" (p. 6).

6. Do you agree with the assertion that the tools of terror have not radically changed but rather have been modified over the years? How has modern communications, transportation, and weaponry technology changed such tools?

7. Identify and explain at least three of the major themes in this chapter. With which do you most agree? Least agree? Why?

8. Based on the information presented in this chapter, what do you believe is the likelihood of terrorists using weapons of mass destruction in the twenty-first century?

STUDY QUESTIONS

1. List the pros and cons of a broad definition of terrorism. Then, create a series of arguments that either support or refute such a broad definition. Research the arguments of at least two authors who were cited in this chapter and use their views to support your position.

2. Think about the position advocated in this chapter that terrorism in most nations–the United States included–often is introduced from above. Research an example of such institutionalized terrorism in the United States and show how the cycle was then perpetuated.

3. Investigate an example of how terrorism was initially begun from below within the United States. Then, select another nation and illustrate how the cycle of terrorism began with an incident from below.

4. Research an actual incident that illustrates, in your opinion, the use of the phrase, "What is one man's terrorist is another man's freedom fighter."

5. Many experts have argued that the media has done a great deal to confuse the public about how terrorism should be defined and how Americans think the U.S. government should respond to terrorists. Using at least three sources, learn more about the role of the media in terrorism. Then support or refute the assertion that the media should be allowed to fully exercise its freedom of the press privileges when handling terrorist incidents.

6. Robert Jay Lifton's book on Aum Shinrikyo concludes that "Aum stepped over a line that few had even known was there. Its members can claim the distinction of being the first group in history to combine ultimate fanaticism with ultimate weapons in a project to destroy the world. . . . We can no longer pretend that such a line does not exist, that another group, even a small one, might not be capable of similar world-ending zealotry" (Lifton 1999: 343–344). Conduct more research on weapons of mass destruction, concentrating on the possibility of their usage by terrorist groups. Then, learn as much as possible about how well law enforcers are or are not prepared for terrorist usage of weapons of mass destruction at the federal, state, and local levels.

8. Watch at least two movies that have been released in the last thirty years that deal with terrorist issues (*Missing, American History X, Arlington Road, Z, Air Force One, In the Name of the Father, Silkwood, Patriot Games* are just a few examples). What do they tell you about terrorism? Are they based on real situations–and if so, how accurate is the portrayal and how might it have been improved to include greater accuracy? Are the plots made up–and if so, how realistic is the portrayal and how might it have been improved to create greater realism? Do you think most Americans, as well as people around the world who see such movies, base their opinions about terrorism on what they see at the theater? How and why?

REFERENCES

Adams, James: *The Financing of Terror.* New York: Simon & Schuster, 1986.

Arendt, Hannah: *On Violence.* New York: Harcourt Brace, 1970.

Arey, James: *The Sky Pirates.* New York: Scribners, 1972.

Bales, Kevin: *Disposable People: New Slavery in the Global Economy.* Berkeley, CA: University of California Press, 1999.

Bell, J. Bowyer: *Transnational Terror.* Washington, DC: American Enterprise Institute, 1975.

Biddle, Wayne: It must be simple and reliable. *Discover:* 22–31, June 1986.

Brodie, Bernard, and Brodie, Fawn M.: *From Crossbow to H-Bomb.* Bloomington, IN: Indiana University Press, 1973.

Caputi, Jane, and Russell, Diana E. H.: Femicide: Sexist terrorism against women. In Radford, Jill, and Russell, Diana E.H. (Eds.): *Femicide: The Politics of Woman Killing.* New York: Twayne Publishers, 1992, pp. 13–24.

Chalk, Frank, and Jonassohn, Kurt: *The History and Sociology of Genocide: Analysis and Case Studies.* New Haven: Yale University Press, 1990.

Chomsky, Noam: *Pirates and Emperors: International Terrorism in the Real World.* New York: Claremont Research and Publications, 1986.

Clark, Rulard C.: *Technological Terrorism.* Old Greenwich, CT: Devin-Adair, 1980.

Clutterbuck, Richard: *Terrorism and Guerilla Warfare: Forecasts and Remedies.* New York: Routledge, 1990.

Cohn, Norman: *Europe's Inner Demons.* New York: Basic Books, 1975.

Crenshaw, Martha (Ed.): *Terrorism, Legitimacy, and Power.* Middletown, CT: Wesleyan University Press, 1983.

——: The psychology of political terrorism. In Hermann, Margaret G. (Ed.): *Political Psychology: Contemporary Problems and Issues.* San Francisco: Jossey-Bass, 1986, pp. 379–413.

Crotty, William J. (Ed.): *Assassinations and the Political Order.* New York: Harper and Row, 1971.

Curtin, Philip D.: *The Atlantic Slave Trade: A Census.* Madison: University of Wisconsin, 1969.

David, B.: The capability and motivation of terrorist organizations to use mass-destruction weapons. In Merari, Ariel (Ed.): *On Terrorism and Combatting Terrorism.* Landham, MD: University of America Press, 1985.

Della Porta, Donatella: *Social Movements, Political Violence, and the State: A Comparative Analysis of Italy and Germany.* Cambridge: Cambridge University Press, 1995.

Dugard, John: International terrorism and the just war. In Rapoport, David C., and Alexander, Yonah (Eds.): *The Morality of Terrorism: Religious and Secular Justifications,* Second Edition. New York: Columbia University Press, 1989, pp. 77–98.

Duvall, Raymond, and Stohl, Michael: Governance by terror. In Dekker, Marcel (Ed.): *The Politics of Terrorism,* Second Edition. New York: Marcel Dekker, 1983, pp. 179–219.

Ekirch, A. Roger: *Bound for America: The Transportation of British Convicts to the Colonies, 1718–1775.* New York: Oxford University Press, 1987.

Fields, Rona M.: Child terror victims and adult terrorists. *Journal of Psychohistory, 7,* 497–512, 1979.

Fraser, Antonia: *Faith and Treason: The Story of the Gunpowder Plot.* New York: Doubleday, 1997.

Freedman, Lawrence Zelic: Why does terrorism terrorize: a psychiatric perspective. Paper presented at the Conference on Psychopathology and Political Violence, University of Chicago, November, 1979.

George, Alexander: *Western State Terrorism.* New York: Routledge, 1991.

Georges-Abeyie, Daniel E.: Women as terrorists. In Freedman, Lawrence, and Alexander, Yonah (Eds.): *Perspectives on Terrorism.* Wilmington: Scholarly Resources, 1983, pp. 71–84.

Gerth, Hans, and Mills, C. Wright: *From Max Weber.* Glencoe: Free Press, 1958.

Gonzalez, Raul: Coca and subversion in the Huallaga. *Lima Quehacer, 48,* 58–72, September–October 1987.

Grabosky, P. N.: The urban context of political terrorism. In Stohl, Michael (Ed.): *The Politics of Terrorism,* Second Edition. New York: Marcel Dekker, 1983, pp. 51–76.

Grosscup, Beau: *The Explosion of Terrorism.* Far Hills: New Horizon Press, 1987.

Gurr, Ted Robert: Some characteristics of political terrorism in the 1960s. In Stohl, Michael (Ed.): *The Politics of Terrorism.* New York: Marcel Dekker, 1983.

——: Political terrorism: Historical antecedents and contemporary trends. In Gurr, Ted Robert (Ed.): *Violence in America: Protest, Rebel-*

lion, Reform, Volume 2. Newbury Park: Sage, 1989, pp. 201–230.

Hacker, Frederick: *Crusaders, Criminals, Crazies: Terror and Terrorism in Our Time.* New York: W.W. Norton, 1976.

Hamm, Mark S.: *American Skinheads: The Criminology and Control of Hate Crime.* Westport: Praeger, 1993.

Hammel, Eric: *The Root: The Marines in Beirut, August 1982–February 1984.* San Diego: Harcourt Brace Jovanovich, 1985.

Hanmer, Jalna, and Saunders, Sheila: *Well-Founded Fear.* London: Hutchinson, 1984.

Harrigan, Anthony: Combat in cities. *Military Review, 46:* 26–30, May 1966.

Hee, Kim Hyun: *Tears of My Soul.* New York: William Morrow, 1993.

Herman, Edward S.: *The Real Terror Network: Terrorism in Fact and Propaganda.* Boston: South End Press, 1982.

Hester, Marianne: The witch-craze in sixteenth- and seventeenth-century England as social control of women. In Radford, Jill, and Russell, Diana E.H. (Eds.): *Femicide: The Politics of Women Killing.* New York: Twayne Publishers, 1992, pp. 27–39.

Honderich, Ted: Political violence, the alternative and probability. In Honderich, Ted (Ed.): *Collected Seminar Papers, No. 30.* London: Institute of Commonwealth Studies, University of London, 1982.

Huey, Jacqueline: Political ideology and female terrorism. Paper presented at the annual meeting of the American Society of Criminology, New Orleans, Louisiana, November 1992.

Intelligence Report: All in the Family. Alabama, Southern Poverty Law Center. Summer, 12–19, 1999.

Ispahani, Mahnaz: *Pakistan: Dimensions of Insecurity, Aldelphi Papers 246.* London: Brassey, 1989/90.

Jaszi, Oscar, and Lewis, John D.: *Against the Tyrant: The Tradition and Theory of Tyrannicide.* Glencoe: Free Press, 1957.

Jenkins, Brian: *Will Terrorists Go Nuclear?* Santa Monica: RAND, 1976.

——: Reentry. In Jenkins, Brian (Ed.): *Terrorism and Personal Protection.* Boston: Butterworth, 1985, pp. 426–433.

——: Terrorism: A contemporary problem with age-old dilemmas. In Howard, Lawrence (Ed.): *Terrorism: Roots, Impact, Responses.* Westport: Praeger, 1992, pp. 13–23.

Joesten, Joachim: *The Red Hand.* London: Abelard-Schumann, 1962.

Joyner, Christopher C.: Chemoterrorism: Rethinking the reality of the threat. In Oan, Henry H. (Ed.): *Terrorism and Political Violence: Limits and Possibilities of Legal Control.* New York: Oceana, 1993, pp. 115–125.

Kellen, Konrad: *Terrorists: What Are They Like? How Some Terrorists Describe Their World and Actions.* Santa Monica: RAND, 1979.

Kirkpatrick, Jeanne: Dictatorships and double standards. *Commentary, 68:* 34–45, November 1979.

Kupperman, Robert: Emerging techno-terrorism. In Marks, John, and Beliaev, Igor (Eds.): *Common Ground on Terrorism: Soviet-American Cooperation Against the Politics of Terror.* New York: W.W. Norton, 1991, pp. 88–103.

Laqueur, Walter: *The Age of Terrorism.* Boston: Little, Brown, 1987.

——: *The New Terrorism: Fanaticism and the Arms of Mass Destruction.* New York: Oxford University Press, 1999.

Leventhal, Paul, and Alexander, Yonah (Eds.): *Preventing Nuclear Terrorism.* Lexington: Lexington, 1987.

Lifton, Robert J.: *Destroying the World to Save It: Aum Shinrikyo, Apocalyptic Violence, and the New Global Terrorism.* New York: Metropolitan Books, 1999.

Livingstone, Neil C., and Arnold, Terrell E. (Eds.): *Fighting Back.* Lexington: Heath, 1986.

Long, David E.: *The Anatomy of Terrorism.* New York: Free Press, 1990.

Lovejoy, Paul E.: The volume of the atlantic slave trade: a synthesis. *Journal of African History 23:* 473–501, 1982.

MacDonald, Eileen: *Shoot the Women First.* New York: Random House, 1991.

MacFarlane, Alan: *Witchcraft in Tudor and Stuart England: A Regional and Comparative Study.* London: Routledge, 1970.

McKnight, Gerald. *The Terrorist Mind.* Indianapolis: Bobbs-Merrill, 1974.

Merkle, Peter H. (Ed.): *Political Violence and Terror: Motifs and Motivations.* Berkeley, CA: University of California Press, 1986.

Moorehead, Caroline: *Hostages to Fortune: A Study of Kidnapping in the World Today.* New York: Athenum Press, 1980.

Morgan, Robin: *The Demon Lover: On the Sexuality of Terrorism.* New York: W.W. Norton, 1989.

Netanyahu, Benjamin: *Terrorism: How the West Can Win.* New York: Farrar, Straus, Giroux, 1986.

Olson-Raymer, Gayle: *Terrorism: A Historical and Contemporary Perspective.* New York: American Heritage Custom Publishing, 1996.

Perdue, William D.: *Terrorism and the State: A Critique of Domination Through Fear.* Westport: Praeger, 1989.

Perlstein, Richard M.: *The Mind of the Political Terrorist.* Wilmington: Scholarly Resources, 1991.

Phillips, William D.: *Slavery from Roman Times to the Early Transatlantic Trade.* Minneapolis: University of Minnesota Press, 1985.

Post, Jerrold M.: Terrorist psycho-logic: Terrorist behavior as a product of psychological forces. Paper presented at the Interdisciplinary Research Conference on the Psychology of Terrorism. Woodrow Wilson Center for Scholars, Washington, DC: March 1987.

Riley, Kevin Jack, and Hoffman, Bruce: *Domestic Terrorism: A National Assessment of State and Local Preparedness.* Santa Monica: RAND, 1995.

Rubenstein, Richard E.: *Alchemists of Revolution: Terrorism in the Modern World.* New York: Basic Books, 1987.

Russell, Charles, and Miller, Bowman H.: Profile of a terrorist. *Terrorism: An International Journal, 1:* 41–70, 1977.

Russell, Jeffrey Burton: *Witchcraft in the Middle Ages.* Ithaca: Cornell University Press, 1972.

Schmid, Alex: *Political Terrorism: A Research Guide.* New Brunswick: Transaction Books, 1984.

Shain, Yossi: *The Frontier of Loyalty: Political Exiles in the Age of the National State.* Middleton, CT: Wesleyan University Press, 1989.

Simon, Jeffrey: *The Terrorist Trap: America's Experience with Terrorism.* Bloomington, IN: Indiana University Press, 1994.

Sobel, Lester A. (Ed.): *Political Terrorism.* New York: Facts on File, 1975.

St. John, Peter: *Air Piracy, Airport Security, and International Terrorism: Winning the War Against Hijackers.* Westport: Quorum Books, 1991.

Stavrionos, L. S.: *The Balkans Since 1453.* New York: Rinehart, 1958.

Stohl, Michael: Myths and realities of political terrorism. In Stohl, Michael (Ed.): *The Politics of Terrorism.* New York: Marcel Dekker, 1983, pp. 1–22.

Strentz, Thomas: A terrorist organizational profile: a psychological role model. In Alexander, Yonah, and Gleason, J.M. (Eds.): *Behavioral and Quantitative Perspectives on Terrorism.* New York: Pergamon Press, 1981, pp. 86–104.

Taylor, Maxwell, and Quayle, Ethel: *Terrorist Lives.* New York: Macmillian, 1994.

Trevor-Roper, Hugh: *The European Witch-craze of the Sixteenth and Seventeenth Centuries.* Harmondsworth: Penguin, 1969.

Tuden, Arthur and Plotnicov, Leonard (Eds.): *Social Stratification in Africa.* New York: Free Press, 1970.

U.S. Department of Justice, Federal Bureau of Investigation: *Terrorism in the United States, 1994.* Washington, DC: U.S. Government Printing Office, 1997.

U.S. Department of Transportation, Federal Aviation Administration, Office of Civil Aviation Security: *U.S. and Foreign Registered Aircraft Hijackings, 1931–1986.* Washington, DC: U.S. Federal Aviation Administration, 1986.

Vetter, Harold J., and Perlstein, Gary R.: *Perspectives on Terrorism.* Pacific Grove: Brooks/Cole, 1991.

Walter, Eugene Victor: *Terror and Resistance: A Study of Political Violence with Case Studies of Some Primitive African Communities.* New York: Oxford University Press, 1969.

Wardlaw, Grant: *Political Terrorism.* New York: Cambridge University Press, 1989.

Weinberg, L., and Eubank, W. L.: Italian women terrorists. *Terrorism: An International Journal, 9:* 241–262, 1987.

White, Jonathon R.: *Terrorism: An Introduction.* Pacific Grove: Brooks/Cole, 1991.

——: *Terrorism: An Introduction,* Second Edition. Belmont: Wadsworth, 1998.

Wilkinson, Norman B.: *Explosives in History.* Chicago, IL: Rand McNally, 1966.

Chapter 2

TERRORISM IN THE GLOBAL ARENA: AN HISTORICAL PERSPECTIVE

Since early civilization, people throughout the world have used terror both from above and below in order to achieve political goals motivated by political, social, economic, religious, and ideological grievances. In general,

- Terrorists from above have included empowered government and religious leaders who used terror to maintain power, suppress those desiring change or reform, and institutionalize racist and nativist policies that discriminated against, enslaved, or subjugated people because of who they were and what they believed.
- Terrorists from below have included unempowered and dissatisfied citizens who used terror to overthrow governments and acquire political power, to seek freedom and equality, or to maintain the social, political, economic, religious, or ideological status quo.

From ancient times to the present, terrorism has been a constant ingredient of humankind's political, social, economic, and religious history. Indeed, today's terrorists are not *revolutionary* new actors in the domestic or international arenas, but rather, as we pos-

tulate herein, their goals, grievances, and actions are *evolutionary* advances along the historical continuum of terror. In fact, the actions of terrorism and terrorists have not substantially changed over the years; instead, they have new names, newer and more technologically sophisticated tools, and span a greater geographical arena. Indeed, when contemporary terrorists are compared with their historical counterparts, they share remarkable similarities.

- Historically, the rulers of nations (kings, dictators, czars, popes, and priests) justified the use of terror within their own boundaries as a legal right of the state or an ordained gift from God. Those without legitimate means of power (revolutionaries, zealots, vigilantes, and "traitors") rationalized the use of terror within their own boundaries as a necessary tool for overthrowing corrupt leaders, obtaining political and spiritual freedom, gaining support for an ideological cause, and for intimidating persons who were "different" into accepting the communal status quo.
- Contemporarily, the same actors act with different appellations. The empowered presidents, military dictators, and funda-

mentalist spiritual leaders view themselves as justifiable defenders of the political, social, and economic status quo. The unempowered freedom fighters, nationalists, patriots, and terrorists see themselves as bulwarks against imperialism, oppression, state terrorism, and moral and spiritual decay.

To illustrate such historical continuity, this chapter will briefly examine the evolution of terrorist thought and activity from ancient times to the present. Additionally, it will provide a series of illustrative case studies for each of five loosely designated time frames: ancient times to 1800; 1800 to 1900; 1900 to 1950; 1950 to 1979; and 1980 to the present.

ANCIENT TIMES TO 1800

During the first several millennia of world history, terrorists operating from above used terror primarily to control actual and perceived threats to their power, as well as to enslave certain people within their domestic borders. Terrorists operating from below used terror primarily to reform or overthrow existing political and religious orders. To achieve such goals, both justified the use of terror as illustrated in the two brief case studies that follow:

1. terrorism from above committed by the American colonies and the federal government in its institutional enslavement of

a distinct race of people—black Africans; and
2. terrorism from below committed by the Order of the Assassins, a twelfth-century band of Shi'ite Muslim terrorists against Sunni Muslims and other apostates.

Terrorism from Above: Institutionalized Terrorism and American Slavery

In 1619, a small number of black Africans arrived in colonial America bound to several different types of servitude.[14] Within 40 years, Blacks would be legally restricted to only one type of servitude: enslavement, the buying of human beings for the condition of permanent bondage. For almost 250 years, from 1619 to 1865, Blacks who were bought were physically and emotionally terrorized under the legal system of slavery. The very nature of their involuntary servitude and enslavement marked slaves as victims of terrorism. That is, slavery was designed to instill terror in a targeted population; to achieve the political goal of denying basic human rights and liberties to an entire race of people for the purpose of maintaining white political, social, and economic power. Further, the goal of such terror was motivated by political, social, economic, religious, and ideological beliefs emotionally fueled by fear, hate, and intolerance.

Enslavement in the colonies involved at least two distinct forms of terrorism: the forcible kidnapping and resettling of some-

---

[14] Other types of servitude existed in the American colonies. Almost 50 percent of those who wished to come to North America but had no money or transportation came as indentured servants, apprentices, tenants, or bond servants whereby they promised four to seven years of servitude to an unknown master. After their contractual term of servitude was over, these individuals received the full rights of freed men and women. During the period of servitude, however, their political, social, and economic status was similar to that of slaves. They were not only owned by their masters, "They could be hired out, sold, or auctioned, even if that meant separating them from their families. They could be beaten, whipped, or branded. If they ran away, they could be punished by an extension, often a multiplication, of their term of servitude" (van der Zee 1985: 31–32).

where between 12 and 15 million black Africans in the Caribbean and English colonies;[15] and the legalization of slavery that subsequently institutionalized a system of terror throughout the South. This case study focuses on the latter form of terrorism–legal enslavement of black Africans beginning in colonial times and ending after the Civil War.

From the earliest British colonial settlement in North America, labor was a problem for the colonists. When Virginians discovered the profitability of growing tobacco in 1617, they confronted a labor crisis: there simply were not enough white servants for the tasks at hand. Black slavery, already a thriving business in the Caribbean, was believed to be the answer. Not only did the system of racial bondage appear to solve the South's economic needs, but also seemed to ameliorate its social needs. Slavery became the white man's "method of regulating race relations, an instrument of social control" over a black race they feared and hated (Stampp 1965: 387). Thus, well-developed moral and legal justifications provided a defense for terroristic racism.

Moral justification fell to the colonial clergy who rationalized that to be a Christian living in colonial America meant being civilized, not barbaric; English, not African; White, not Black (Jordan 1974). Christian masters taught slaves that God made them slaves, an act of insolence against whites was an act against God, and God wanted them to respect their master's power and superiority (Stampp 1965).

Legal justifications for slavery, initially from colonial rulers, were passed on to the new nation's founding fathers, and were, in turn, bequeathed to their heirs. Beginning in 1661 and progressing through the end of the

century, every English colony passed a series of laws that restricted slaves to the black race and legally defined all slaves as property, thus confining slaves to an inferior legal, social, and moral status. By the end of the nineteenth century, further legal refinements hardened the institutional structure of slavery: slaves were legally bound to obey their masters and respect all Whites; their movement and communication with both Blacks and Whites was strictly controlled and limited, they could not learn to read and write, they were prohibited from purchasing or possessing liquor, and they could not be armed.

Such moral and legal rationales not only justified the economic and social motives for slavery, but also emphasized the "humaneness" of the system. Many Whites claimed that their paternalistic actions were positive, humane endeavors justly rewarded by the loyalty of their slaves who were grateful and happy under white tutelage. However, such rationales could not disguise the fact that slaves were not free and lived under a system of institutionalized terror. Slaves who disobeyed any rules were terrorized into submission. Slave conspirators who participated in aborted rebellions or who were suspected of planning a rebellion received harsh penalties. After Gabriel Prosser's planned revolt in Richmond in 1800 was uncovered, about 40 slaves were arrested, and 20, including Prosser, were executed. Upon discovery of Denmark Vessey's planned revolution for Charleston in 1822, scores of slaves were arrested; 35 were executed (Brown 1975). After Nat Turner's rebellion, he and many of his supporters were captured and hung.

Slave patrollers, white men who were deputized volunteers or paid professionals,

---

[15] Estimates vary for the number of slaves that came to the colonies between the 1660s and 1808 (the year slave trading was outlawed by the United States). Most sources suggest that as many as 50 million Africans were actually kidnapped for enslavement in the Americas. Less than one-third, however, survived capture, transport to the colonies, and resettlement on a plantation in North or South America.

also terrorized slaves. As such, they were legally empowered by state legislatures to protect plantation society by "prowling Southern roads enforcing the curfew for slaves, looking for runaways, and guarding rural areas against the threat of black uprisings" (Bullard 1991: 7). All patrollers were allowed to forcibly enter slave dwellings on any plantation at any time, and to administer up to 39 lashes to any slave who was caught without a pass, was insolent, or had broken some rule defined by the patrollers themselves.

In addition to myriad slave codes, violent punishment of resisters, and the terror of slave patrollers, the U.S. Supreme Court upheld slavery as a legal institution of human bondage. The Dred Scott (1857) decision determined that "a Negro has no rights a white man was bound to respect."[16] Thereafter, in the eyes of federal law, slaves were property not people, and thus, they could not be U.S. citizens nor did they have any right to petition the court. Clearly, such governmental actions and decisions contributed to a terroristic environment unique to the United States, where slavery was absolutely defined by race and culture and Black people were relegated to a life in which human rights and dignity played no role.

Terrorism from Below: The Assassins

The Order of the Assassins, a twelfth-century band of Muslim terrorists, evolved from a division that arose within Islam after Muhammed's death in A.D. 632. Because he had not named a successor, internal dissension arose among Muhammed's followers about a legitimate heir. Muslims who believed the first caliph (successor to the Apostle of God) should be elected from Muhammed's *tribe* became known as Sunni Muslims. Those who believed the caliph should be a direct descendant of Muhammed's *family* became known as *Shia* or *Shi'ites,* the "partisans of Ali" (the son-in-law of Muhammed's favorite daughter, Fatima.)

The Sunnis prevailed and elected Abu Bakr, the father of Muhammed's young wife, Aisha. Thus began a series of assassinations related to the succession argument. In 661, Ali was assassinated, and in 680, Ali's son and Muhammed's grandson, Husayn and many of his followers were also assassinated. Some 20 years later, the Shi'ites declared they would no longer follow the caliphs and would instead elect an *iman* from the descendants of Ali to lead the true believers of the Muslim faith. This division between Sunni and Shi'ite was further complicated in 873, when the twelfth iman died without an heir and the fledgling party of Ismail broke away from the Shi'ites.

Shortly thereafter, the *Assassins* (hashish-eaters) were founded by Hasan-i-Sabbah, a Shi'ite who had become an Ismaili. The Assassins, who were believed to use *assass* (hashish) to increase their courage while committing various acts of terror, organized an "underground force of missionaries and murderers . . . to carry the Ismaili word to the many and strike down the powerful few among the Sunni majority . . ." and was "determined to unleash organized terrorism, destroying selected enemies and thereby intimidating others among the unconverted" (Ford 1985: 101–102).

For almost 200 years, the Assassins remained a powerful force in the Arab world

---

[16] Dred Scott was a slave owned by John Emerson who resided in Missouri, a slave state. Emerson, an army physician, had lived two years in Illinois and another two years in Wisconsin Territory, areas where slavery was illegal. Scott's attorney unsuccessfully argued that by living four years on free soil, Scott was a free man.

by using terror to convince the populace to accept their interpretation of Islam and to overthrow the enemies of Islam, the members of the Sunni political, military, and religious establishment. The innumerable victims of the Assassins forced the Arab community to regard these early terrorists as a "profound threat to the existing order, political, social, and religious" (Lewis 1968: 139). What is equally as important, however, is the fact they were "no isolated phenomenon, but one of a long series of messianic movements, at once popular and obscure, impelled by deep-rooted anxieties, and from time to time exploding in outbreaks of revolutionary violence" (Lewis 1968: 139).

1800 TO 1900

The nineteenth century witnessed a spirit of domestic unrest that blanketed much of the world.

- In Russia and Europe, the growing urban bourgeoisie and proletariat classes were increasingly unhappy with their lives under aristocratic and often tyrannical monarchs. In addition, a more diverse, and eventually dissatisfied, student intelligentsia was growing as students from different social and economic classes entered Russian and European universities.
- Throughout Europe and the United States, the Industrial Revolution resulted in uneven economic development, thus emphasizing the differences between the haves and have-nots and stimulating discontent among the impoverished, underprivileged working classes.
- The U.S. government, imbued with the spirit of manifest destiny, began its march westward across the northern continent; in its quest for territorial expansion, the gov-

ernment made it clear that nothing would stand in the way of the progress of the white, Christian American.
- Many governments, feeling threatened by growing reform and revolutionary movements, began to use terror to silence "enemies of the state"; such actions gave rise to terrorism from below, which increasingly became more philosophically and programmatically organized.
- Growing imperialist impulses of the most powerful governments in the world led to increased colonial empires and conflict between nations.

Under such circumstances, terrorism from both above and below thrived. The terrorists who operated from above in the nineteenth century did so with terrifying success, a success that was inevitable because they held absolute power and a virtual "monopoly of the right to kill enemies of society and to ask its citizens to kill enemies of the state, or be killed doing it" (Libaridian 1987: 203).

This legalistic and absolute right to inflict terror was accompanied by what Gay (1993) has called the "cultivation of hatred" whereby the rulers of the world suspected "the people" and any democratic impulses, and terroristically punished persons who resisted their rule. One of the most tragic examples of such absolute power was the battle waged by the U.S. government against the American Indian—a battle that was genocidal in consequence and is further explained in the next case study.

Terrorists operating from below were deeply affected both by the terroristic actions wrought by the empowered of Russia and Europe, as well as by the thoughts and writings of two emerging streams of political philosophy that fueled what has been called "the modern era of terrorism" (Vetter and Perlstein 1991: 31). Socialist and anarchist thought clearly modernized terrorism, yet it did not create a distinctly new type of political violence. Instead, the beliefs outlined next simply added philosophical form and substance to what had been expressed previously through spontaneous terror perpetrated by the unempowered.

Terrorism from Above: Genocidal Policies Against the North American Indians

Before the Constitution was signed, the Northwest Ordinance of 1787 mapped out the manner in which the U.S. government would deal with the Indian nations. The Ordinance proclaimed that the government would observe "the utmost good faith" in dealing with Indians and promised that their lands would not be invaded or taken except "in just and lawful wars authorized by Congress." At the same time, however, the Ordinance provided a blueprint for national expansion into Indian Territory. Thus, from the very beginning of the U.S. government, Indian policies have been contradictory—in writing, most aimed to act in good faith toward the Indians; but in practice, these policies endorsed actions most beneficial to the non-Indian population.

When the Constitution was written, it included a provision that established federal authority over the conduct of Indian relations. In Art. 1, Sec. 8 (the Commerce Clause) the Constitution declares that "The Congress shall have the power to regulate Commerce with foreign nations and among the several states, and with the Indian tribes." Thus, the Constitution specified that there were three governmental entities within the United States with forms of sovereignty—Indian tribes, state governments, and the federal government. The Constitution, then, recognized the inherent sovereignty of Indian governments—sovereignty that was not derived

from any other government, but rather from the Indian people themselves.

Because Indian nations were sovereign, the federal government immediately faced what non-Indians soon called the "Indian problem." While European Americans wanted to move westward and conquer all the land to the Pacific Ocean, it was clear that the hundreds of sovereign Indian nations were not going to willingly or voluntarily give up their land. Consequently, the U.S. government took two steps:

1. signing hundreds of treaties with Indian nations—treaties which, in turn, were bolstered by a series of U.S. Supreme Court decisions; and
2. passing dozens of laws designed to define relations between the federal government and Indian nations.

Treaties and Supreme Court Decisions

Treaties were legal, government-to-government agreements between two legitimate governments—the United States and an Indian nation. When an Indian nation signed a treaty, it agreed to give the federal government some or all of its land as well as some or all of its sovereign power. In return, the Indian people entered into a trust relationship with the federal government in which the government promised to provide benefits and services in perpetuity. The trust responsibility bound the United States to represent the best interests of the tribe, protect the safety and well-being of tribal members, and fulfill its treaty obligations.

This basis for the federal relationship with Indian nations and for tribal sovereignty gradually was redefined by the U.S. Supreme Court as early as 1823. Beginning with *Johnson v. McIntosh*, the Supreme Court has produced two competing theories of tribal sovereignty:

1. Indian nations have inherent powers of sovereignty that predate the "discovery" of America by Columbus; and
2. Indian nations have only those attributes of sovereignty that Congress gives them.

Over the years, the Court has relied on one or the other of these theories in deciding tribal sovereignty cases. Whichever theory the Court favored in a given case largely determined the powers the tribe had and what protections they received against federal and state government encroachment.[17] Thereafter, Indians had a kind of limited sovereignty that was to be governed by paternalistic trust and subject to the interpretation of the U.S. government. In other words, Indian nations would have to trust the U.S. government to do what was best for them.

Between 1778 and 1868, 371 treaties were signed. These treaties, each of which eventually was abrogated, focused primarily on the way the U.S. government would handle Indian land and the resources on those lands. In 1871, Congress formally ended the government-to-government treaty-making power. No longer would Indians have any negotiating power or say about their treatment at the hands of the U.S. government. Thereafter, such determinations would be made as Congress and the Executive Branch passed various federal policies and laws.

Federal Policies and Laws

From 1830 throughout the remainder of the nineteenth century, at least four specific policies were adopted by the federal government, each of which led to the genocide of the Indian tribes and each of which was supported by a series of laws: removal, reservations, allotment and assimilation, and elimination.

Removal policies were adopted in the early 1830s and dramatically altered the lives of the Cherokee, Creek, Chickasaw, Choctaw, and Seminole peoples who lived on land that many Americans felt could be more profitably farmed and settled by non-Indians. However, all five nations had signed treaties with the federal government guaranteeing the right to live in their ancestral lands and maintain their sovereign systems of tribal government. Not surprisingly, these nations were unwilling to give up their land and to negotiate new treaties with the federal government that would give away part of their land.

President Andrew Jackson decided that a new federal policy would be necessary in order to remove the Indians from their lands. Thus, he supported the Removal Act of 1830 which gave him the right to make land "exchanges" by forcibly removing the five nations from their ancestral lands against their will. Between 1830 and 1840, somewhere between 70,000 and 100,000 Native Americans living in the East were forcibly resettled by the U.S. Army. Many others were massacred before they could be persuaded to leave; an

---

[17] At least three U.S. Supreme Court decisions—known collectively as the Marshall Trilogy—set this precedent: In *Johnson v. McIntosh* 21 U.S. (8 wheat.) 543 (1823), the Court held that while the Indians were the rightful occupants of the land, tribes had no power to grant lands to anyone other than the federal government. The federal government, in turn, held title to all Indian lands based on the "doctrine of discovery—the belief that initial discovery" of lands gave title to the government responsible for the discovery. As a result, the right of Indians to complete sovereignty was limited as European Americans had exclusive title to the land that they had "discovered." In *Cherokee Nation v. Georgia* 30 U.S. (5 Pet.) 1, 8 L. Ed. 25 (1831), the court found that Indians were neither U.S. citizens, nor independent nations, but rather were "domestic dependent nations" whose relationship to the United States "resembles that of a ward to his guardian." Consequently, Indian nations did not possess all the attributes of sovereignty that the word "nation" usually implies. In *Worcester v. Georgia* 31 U.S. (6 Pet.) 515, 8 L. Ed. 583 (1832), the Court held that state laws did not extend to Indian country. This ruling clarified that Indian tribes were under protection of the federal government and that Congress had plenary, or overriding power, over all Indian tribes.

unknown number died from disease, exposure, and starvation suffered during the Trail of Tears as well as on other enforced, long-distance marches westward to Indian Territory. Eventually, more than 40 tribes were forcibly removed to the area that came to be known as Indian Territory—the area that is now Oklahoma.

While the removal policy helped to alleviate the immediate "Indian problem," as more and more Americans continued to move westward they found many other Indian tribes living in freedom throughout the continent. Because these Indians prevented non-Indians from settling in many desirable areas, and because many white settlers did not feel safe living amidst the Indian "danger," another new policy was created to deal with the Indians. This time, Indians would be confined to a land reserved exclusively for their own use—areas that came to be called reservations.

Reservations were created by men who believed that if Indians could be confined to one particular geographical place reserved for them, they would become "civilized" and assimilated into American life—that they could shed their Indian ways and take on the qualities of white men. Thus, the reservations were to make sure the remaining tribes were converted to Christianity, taught English, and learned to become profit-motivated, small-scale farmers.

Some Indians adjusted to the Americanizing influences of the reservation. However, the vast majority did not become more like the white man. Indeed, most fought to maintain their Indian culture and traditions. The reservation system survived for almost twenty years before it was clear that all Indians were not going to be confined and that the vast majority were not going to become Americanized. Thus, a new policy was created—allotment.

Allotment was designed to detribalize the Indian by destroying the idea of communal land ownership on the reservations. Many Americans had come to believe that Indians would never become Americanized as long as they lived in large reservations where they owned their land communally and were allowed to celebrate their cultural and spiritual traditions. Further, American policymakers believed that the reservation did not give the Indians an incentive to improve their situation. The federal government's new policy was signed into law as the Dawes Severalty Act of 1887.

The Act allowed the president to give, or allot, portions of certain reservation land to individual Indians—160 acres to each head of family and 80 acres to others—to establish private farms, and authorized the secretary of interior to negotiate with the tribes for purchasing "excess" lands for non-Indian settlement. Each head of family would receive final title to the land and American citizenship after a 25-year period during which they had willingly assumed responsibility for the land. Any land remaining after allotment would be sold to Whites; all proceeds were to be used to "civilize" Indians on the reservation.

At the same time that the Dawes Act was being conceptualized, American policymakers were also experimenting with another new *assimilation* policy. Some reasoned that for Indians to really become assimilated, Indian children would have to be taken from their tribal environment and reeducated. Within a few years, federal authorities forced Indian parents to either send their children to an off-reservation boarding school, or to boarding schools established in remote areas of Indian reservations. There, Indian children were forced to shed their "Indianness" and were forbidden to wear traditional clothing, speak their native tongue, practice their religious and cultural rituals, or use their family name.

The results of the boarding schools' policy and the Dawes Act were catastrophic: American Indians lost even more of their land; between 1887 and 1934 when the Dawes Act was repealed, tribal lands dwindled by 60 percent—from 138 million acres to 48 million, 20 million of which were arid or semi-arid. Additionally, all Indian people suffered enormous loss of their cultures, languages, and family traditions.

Ultimately, allotment and assimilation policies failed to assimilate Indians and force them to accept a more settled, Americanized way of life. Toward the end of the nineteenth century, a large number of Indians and several Indian nations still lived in communal groups that refused to live on reservations or to be involved in allotment. Thus, the federal government moved ahead with another policy to deal with these recalcitrants—elimination.

Elimination grew out of a belief that Indian resistance was equivalent to a declaration of war against the United States. Using such a rationale, in the late 1800s, the U.S. Army declared war on several tribes, began eliminating resisters, and sought to absolutely subjugate any survivors. However, war was hardly a last resort nor was it something used only at the end of the nineteenth century. A review of official military records, some of which are incomplete, shows that from 1776 to 1907, the U.S. Army was involved in 1,470 official actions against Indians (Utter 1993). These figures do not include actions against the Indians undertaken by either the U.S. Navy—of which there were probably dozens—or the hundreds of hostile actions undertaken by private armies and citizens against American Indians.

The vast majority of military Indian fighting under the auspices of the U.S. government occurred between 1866 and 1891. According to official records for this 25-year period, the Army was involved in 1,065 combat engagements with Indians. In total, 948 soldiers were killed and another 1,058 wounded, as well as 4,371 Indians who were killed and another 1,279 who were wounded (Utter 1993).

By the turn of the century, the consequences of intentional American federal policy toward American Indians had not only been disastrous, but were the results of genocidal governmental policies.

- The Indian population had dramatically decreased. Between 6 and 10 million native peoples lived in the United States at the time of its birth; by 1900, less than 250,000 people remained and the majority of tribes had dwindled to the brink of extinction.
- Most surviving Indians had been forced onto reservations or lived on allotted lands where they were expected to shed their "Indianness" and become civilized, Christianized, and Anglicized.
- The self-sufficiency, cultural integrity, and ecological balance that characterized the Indian tribes at the time of European settlement had been destroyed. From the early 1800s forward, Native Americans were forced into a position of economic dependency upon the U.S. government.
- The majority of Indian tribal land holdings had passed into white ownership.

Terrorism from Below: Socialist and Anarchist Influences and the Haymarket Square Riot

The circumstances under which socialism and anarchism grew were directly related to the political climate in nineteenth-century Europe. As the Industrial Revolution spread across the continent, some Europeans began to criticize the emerging power of the capitalists and the subsequent absence of power within the growing urban working class. These were the democrats of the 1800s, who primarily "believed in middle-class democracy and were reluctant to take to the streets, if the legislative process was available. They would fight to seize power . . . but they usually worked for the rational development and transfer of organized political power" (White 1991: 57).

By the middle of the century, the democrats had begun to split into two political camps. On one side were those who favored a constitutional vehicle for obtaining liberty–the democrats. On the other side was a small group that supported the reorganization of class structure and the redistribution of wealth as an equally important ingredient for obtaining liberty–the radical democrats who came to be known as socialists. To the socialists, capitalism was ultimately undemocratic; true democracy could only be achieved through the communal ownership and control of all means of production.

The German philosophers and writers Karl Marx (1818–1883) and Friedrich Engels (1820–1895) became the first to clearly articulate the socialist philosophy. In 1847, Marx and Engels were commissioned to write a statement of principles by a network of revolutionary groups operating in a number of European cities. Their program, known as *The Communist Manifesto,* was the first systematic statement of modern socialist philosophy and goals. The Manifesto argued that during every period of history, the prevailing economic system that produces the necessities of life determines the political organization of that society.

Thus, the history of society was marked by the ongoing struggles between the governors and the governed, the exploiters and the exploited. Capitalism exemplified this struggle and, as such, was a corrupt and outdated political system destined to be overthrown by a worldwide working-class revolution in the form of a massive seizure of power by the proletariat–the working class. In the course of the proletarian revolution, socialists Marx and Engels argued that terrorism was justifiable only in the process of seizing power, but not for individual acts of murder to satisfy political or personal grievances.

Unlike the socialists, anarchists believed that all government was evil and would always conflict with the rights of the people. As such, anarchism sought to abolish private property and to destroy all existing governments. Four men especially articulated anarchist philosophy and its achievement through the use of political violence: the Russian revolutionaries Mikhail Bakunin, Peter Kropotkin, and Sergey Nechaev; and the German author, Karl Heinzen.

1. Mikhail Bakunin (1814–1876) sought the creation of an ideal society consisting of a loose federation of local communities, each with a maximum of autonomy and each holding the means of production in common. The use of terror against oppression was seen as a natural reaction of the oppressed against their oppressors.
2. Peter Kropotkin (1842–1921) contended that because the capitalist economic system backed by various governments was immoral, the only moral response was violent action that would awaken the masses into supporting a revolution. His method for such awakening was "propaganda by the deed," the use of violence as a form of political communication by propagandizing the action through the media.
3. Sergey Nechaev (1847–1882) extolled the virtues of political violence used to counteract the oppressive, nondemocratic forces operating from above. He called upon young revolutionaries to "grasp the fact that it is considerably more humane to stab and strangle dozens, nay hundreds, of hated beings than to join with them to share in systematic legal acts of murder" (as quoted in Laqueur 1987: 67–68).
4. Karl Heinzen (1809–1880) advocated using the bomb as a perfect revolutionary

tool. When it was indiscriminately planted, its detonation would create constant disorder, which, in turn, would maximize the conditions for revolution.

It has been argued that the violence of these anarchists was generally limited to rhetoric (Laqueur 1987; White 1991). The "propaganda of the deed," however, did become reality on several occasions. One of the first major incidents occurred in the United States with the anarchist bombings of May 1886 during the Haymarket Square riot in Chicago. The roots of the incident went back to widespread labor unrest that had erupted in the late 1800s across the United States. With each strike from labor radicals—a few of whom were fueled by socialist and/or anarchist political philosophy—the corporations were backed by security police and often soldiers who were empowered to use violence to keep workers from disrupting production.

This was the general pattern that described the events that began in April 1885, when the president of the McCormick Reaper Works was forced by a workers' strike to restore a 15 percent wage cut. For over one year, Cyrus H. McCormick, Jr. explored every possible way to break the workers' union. By February 1886, McCormick had introduced new machinery that abolished the jobs of the skilled iron molders who had led the April walkout. At that point, he declared a general lockout, replaced his remaining employees with nonunion labor, and hired 300 armed Pinkerton detectives to protect the strikebreakers.

Tensions heightened on May 1, 1886, when 300,000 workers in 13,000 establishments throughout the nation laid down their tools in support of the eight-hour day and 40,000 strikers peacefully demonstrated in Chicago. Three days later, serious trouble erupted. At the end of the workday, about 200 strikers gathered outside McCormick's. Some rocks were tossed into a group of strikebreakers, forcing them back into the factory. The police immediately appeared and were greeted with a shower of stones. In response, the policemen drew their revolvers and fired into the crowd. While exact casualties were never established, at least two strikers were killed, many other strikers were wounded, and the assistant superintendent of the factory was badly hurt; no policeman was seriously injured.

On May 4, a crowd generally assumed to be organized by prominent anarchists held a protest meeting near Haymarket Square. The meeting proceeded without incident, and the crowd began to disperse at the appearance of rain clouds. As the last speaker was concluding, a contingent of policemen marched in and ordered the meeting to be closed. The speaker objected, stating that the gathering was peaceful. Concurrent with the police captain's insistence on closure, a bomb was thrown into the police ranks. The officers opened fire on the crowd, killing and wounding a number of civilians, as well as some of their own men. Sixty-seven policemen were hurt, and eight eventually died (Avrich 1984).

Despite the fact that the bomb thrower was never apprehended, eight well-known Chicago anarchists were brought to trial and convicted of murder: four were hanged, a fifth committed suicide in his cell the day before the executions, and the others received long prison terms. In 1893, the three survivors were pardoned by Governor John Peter Altgeld, who criticized the judge for conducting the trial with "malicious ferocity" and stated that trial evidence failed to prove that the anarchists had been involved in the bombing.

1900 TO 1950

In the early twentieth century, terrorism gained more recognition on the international arena than on the domestic stage. Indeed, in just over thirty years, one world war ended, only to sow the seeds for another that would occur within twenty short years. Right-wing fascism grew to unprecedented proportions, bringing dictators to power in Germany and Italy who would institutionalize terror in a manner previously unrecorded by humankind. Successful, but bloody, revolutions in Russia and China led to socialist governments whose very philosophies threatened those of Western democratic nations. Finally, many peoples of African, Asian, and Indian nations began to openly chafe under the oppressive colonial yoke of their European rulers. Clearly, the violence of these decades provided fertile ground for the growth of terror from above and below.

During no other time in modern history did terrorism that was legally authorized through executive, legislative, and/or constitutional means achieve such horrific proportions. The "Bolshoi Terror" wrought by Joseph Stalin, leader of the Soviet Union from 1928 to 1953, began on August 5, 1937 when he signed Order No. 00447 mandating that all prison camps across the Soviet Union be emptied. Over a two-year period, at least 14 million people perished—prisoners used as slave labor, as well as Russian intellectuals, anti-revolutionaries, ethnic minorities, and university students. In July 1997, the remains of 9,111 of these victims—all of whom had been stripped down to their underwear, bound hand and foot, and lined up along the edge of trenches where they were each shot in the back of the head—were found in a mass grave covering two and one-half acres in a Karelian forest, 245 miles north of St. Petersburg.

One of the least publicized, but still hotly debated examples of terrorism from above that occurred was the Armenian genocide, subject of the following brief case study. But terrorism from below also flourished during this period. Vigilante-type terrorism in the United States especially gained immense popularity during this period with the post-Civil War birth of the Ku Klux Klan and its early-twentieth-century resurgence, the subject of the case study discussed shortly.

Terrorism from Above: Turkey and the Armenian Genocide

Prior to World War I, the Armenian people lived primarily in Russia, Persia, and Turkey, where they had been subjected to ethnic abuse and terror for several decades. As early as 1878, the Armenians unsuccessfully appealed to the Congress of Berlin to help gain administrative reforms from the Ottoman Empire. Their plight became desperate in 1894 when 25 villages and hundreds of Armenians were killed in Bitlis, Turkey by nomadic Kurds and Turkish troops. After an Armenian protest in Constantinople, mass killings were organized by Turkish officials in which about 30,000 Armenians perished (Gross 1970: 555). Similar massacres occurred the following year, resulting in at least 6,000 Armenian fatalities. Afterward, a British diplomat reported that "the intention of Turkish authorities is to exterminate the Armenians" (Miller 1936: 426).

The terroristic policies of the Turkish government intensified for the approximately 1.7 million Armenians who lived in Turkey on the eve of World War I. On November 2, 1914, Turkey entered the war on the side of Germany and the Austro-Hungarian empire. Immediately thereafter, the Russians invaded Turkish Armenia, and, subsequently, many Armenian political groups refused to actively cooperate with the Turkish government against Russia. By the winter of 1915, three of the seven Armenian provinces were the center of the combat area.

On May 30, 1915, the Ottoman minister of the interior signed an order for the mass transfer of the Armenian population from these areas to Iraq and the Syrian desert. Inhabitants were given two days to prepare themselves for resettlement. Simultaneous with the order, 650 Armenian leaders were arrested in Istanbul and most officers and soldiers of Armenian origin were removed from the army. The official reason for resettlement was to prevent any possibility that the Armenian presence would harm the state's internal security; in reality, however, the policy effectively squelched all organized resistance.

The exact number of those who perished in the "resettlement" effort is unknown; various sources claim that somewhere between 600,000 and 1.5 million Armenians died or were massacred (Kuper 1982; Kurz and Merari 1985; Wilkinson 1983). Many witnesses, including Red Cross officials and Western diplomats, have called the action systematic genocide. An eyewitness account by Arnold Toynbee stated that "deportations were deliberately conducted with a brutality that was calculated to take maximum toll of lives en route. . . . My study of the genocide that had been committed in Turkey in 1915 brought home to me the reality of Original Sin" (Toynbee 1967: 242).

The memoirs of the American ambassador to Turkey, Henry Morgenthau, stated that it was

> absurd for the Turkish Government to assert that it ever seriously intended to 'deport the Armenians to new homes'; the treatment which was given the convoys clearly shows that extermination was the real purpose. . . . Out of the combined convoy of 18,000 souls just 150 women and children reached their destination. (Morgenthau 1919: 318)

In their moving book weaving together the oral interviews of 103 survivors of the Armenian genocide, Miller and Miller (1993) provide a convincing portrayal of a people who were terrorized by the Turkish govern-

ment. One of the most poignant is that of Aghavni, who was about 20 years old at the time of the genocide and the oldest of all survivors who were interviewed. As Aghavni recalled, one month before neighbors in her town of Sivas were deported, many local Armenian political leaders were imprisoned, 60 men were hanged in one day, and many others were killed outside the city limits—including her husband.

When Sivas got its deportation orders, Aghavni fled with her entire family. Three days into the journey, her mother and the donkey that carried their few possessions were shot. For seven months, she and her mother-in-law took turns carrying and holding the children as they walked. At the end of the journey, her grandmother had drowned, both her children and mother-in-law had died, and two aunts, an uncle, and a brother were killed.

After World War I, approximately 80,000 Armenian survivors who had been resettled in Syria returned to Turkey, which had become a French protectorate. When the French left Turkey in September 1920, between 50,000 and 60,000 Armenians returned to Syria and Lebanon, thus beginning the present-day diaspora of the Armenian peoples. Mid-1980 estimates indicated that about 5 million Armenians, many of whom longed to return to their homeland, lived in various parts of the world: between 50,000 and 60,000 remained in Turkey; approximately 4 million lived in various districts of the former Soviet Union; approximately 500,000 and 100,000 resided in the United States and Canada respectively; and some 300,000 settled in Europe (Kurz and Merari 1985).

The first 50 years of living in diaspora produced little protest from the Armenian community about the alleged genocide. It took an important event to trigger the emergence of protest and, eventually, of two major Armenian terrorist movements. In a 1974

U.N. Human Rights Commission report, an expert reported on the prevention and repression of the crime of genocide. Paragraph 30 of the draft report stated that, "Passing to the modern era, one may note the existence of relatively full documentation dealing with the massacre of the Armenians, which has been described as the 'first genocide of the twentieth century" (Chaliand and Ternon 1983: 3). However, when the final report was presented to the Human Rights Commission, paragraph 30 had been deleted.

Shortly thereafter, debate about the Armenian genocide began within the international community. The Armenians argued that the Ottoman government carefully and systematically planned and then implemented genocide of its Armenian citizens via outright massacres and forced marches into Iraq and Syria. This was alleged to occur because the Turks felt Armenian claims to land in the east would block their dreams of a greater union of all Turkish peoples. The Turkish government, however, persistently referred to this event as a collective population transfer in which great care was taken to prevent the Armenians from being harmed. Further, they claimed Armenian accusations comprised a vindictive propaganda campaign against modern Turkey; indeed, the government has consistently claimed no genocide was ever committed against the Armenians in the Ottoman Empire before or during World War I.

The refusal of both the United Nations and the Turkish state to recognize the facts of the Armenian genocide encouraged the organization of two terrorist groups: the Justice Commandos for the Armenian Genocide (JCAG), and Armenian Secret Army for the Liberation of Armenia (ASALA). Both groups are committed to liberating occupied Armenian lands and reintegrating them into

a new nation. To that end, between 1975 and 1985, they launched 188 terrorist incidents in 22 countries on four continents (Gunter 1986).

While the intensity and dimensions of their efforts have since decreased, both JCAG and ASALA continue to use terrorism to achieve their long-term liberation goals. In the meantime, terrorism has helped both groups achieve at least two short-term successes: propelling the tragedy of the Armenian genocide and the resulting diaspora into the international arena; and the growth of a new generation of young Armenians living in diaspora who have been raised with inner pride about and identity with their Armenian heritage.

Terrorism from Below: The Ku Klux Klan

Ironically, the originators of what became the most popular of all American vigilante movements did not have terror in mind when they created the Ku Klux Klan (KKK). Rather, in early 1866 when six young ex-Confederate soldiers from Pulaski, Tennessee, organized the KKK to have fun, and play pranks on the public.[18] It would have been hard for them to imagine that within a few months, the Klan would become America's first "secret vigilante terrorist network," consisting of hate-filled Klansmen who "threatened, flogged, and murdered countless black and white women and men" in order "to bolster the crumbling foundations of Southern supremacy against political inroads by blacks, Republicans, and Northern whites" (Blee 1991: 12–13).

The Klan's initial terroristic wave was short lived. For reasons that remain unclear, in January 1869, the Grand Wizard ordered

---

[18] The Ku Klux Klan was named for the *kuklos* (Greek for "circle"), thus signifying a circle of club members.

the national organization to disband; by the mid-1870s, his mission was accomplished; all that remained were sporadically-operating local and unorganized KKK bands in a few regions of the South.

Almost 50 years later, a second Klan was reborn with frightening vigor. By 1921, nearly 100,000 members comprised the "invisible empire." In the early 1920s, in Indiana alone an estimated 32 percent of all women were members of the WKKK, Women of the Ku Klux Klan (Blee 1991). By 1925, an estimated five million Americans across the nation had joined a local Klan (Bullard 1991). Just what catapulted the Klan into such an exalted status is still unclear. Some credit D. W. Griffith's heroic portrayal of the KKK vigilantes in *The Birth of a Nation*. Others cite the creative efforts and economic greed of its second-generation founder, William J. Simmons. Still others point to the slick marketing campaign and economic opportunism of Klan promoters (Blee 1991; Chalmers 1981; Wade 1987). Why the revitalized Klan became such a success is no mystery. When Simmons marched 15 supporters up Atlanta's Stone Mountain to light a match to a huge pine cross, he was reigniting an old flame of racial hatred. Indeed

> The Klan's underlying ideas of racial separation and white Protestant supremacy echoed throughout white society in the 1920s, as racial and religious hatreds determined the political dialogue in many communities. Few white-controlled institutions or organizations in the United States either practiced or espoused racial integration or equality, allowing the Klan to proudly proclaim its continuity with established sentiment among whites. (Blee 1991: 17–18)

What made this second Klan remarkable was not the racist and nativist rhetoric that historically and contemporarily appealed to a large number of Americans, but two other factors: the expansion of its victims to include anyone considered a traitor to the white race; and its "explicit call to violence in defense of white supremacy" (Blee 1991: 17). However, it was not Simmons national organization that specifically promoted violence. In fact, when Georgia granted a charter for the Knights of the Ku Klux Klan on December 4, 1915, Simmons described it as a "purely benevolent" fraternal order dedicated to social vigilance. Violence and terror instead, primarily became the tool of local Klan members, who, when they wished to punish a perceived enemy of the white race, acted without fear of reprisal.

The Klan's success in the state of Texas provides an excellent example of its terroristic influence during this period. In 1922, over 200,000 Klansmen had been organized under the first Grand Dragon in Texas, Dr. A. D. Ellis, an Episcopal minister. The vows of Klan members, "to protect God, Country, Home, Womanhood, the South, and White Supremacy," were not only sacred, they were also respected by officials in high office who allowed Klansmen to resolve their doubts of propriety and to act without fear of retribution (Chalmers 1981: 40–41). Thus, Klansmen confidently spread fear and terror into the hearts of the local black citizens.

In Denton, Texas, the Klan took two Negroes from jail and flogged them. A Negro bellhop in Dallas was flogged, KKK was branded on his forehead with acid, and he was dumped in front of the hotel. A warning, signed KKK, sent striking Negroes back to the cotton fields of Corsicana at the old rate of 50 cents per 100 pounds of cotton. When a Negro dentist was kidnapped and whipped, the resulting rumors of retaliation and racial warfare brought the Klan out, armed and deputized, to patrol the streets of Houston (Chalmers 1981).

Blacks, however, were not the only targets of the Klan's terroristic drive to instill
morality.

A white man in Timson, who had recently
separated from his wife, was taken out and
beaten. So were a Brenham man who spoke
German, a divorced man in Dallas, a bank
cashier in Bay City, a lawyer from Houston
who annoyed girls, and another attorney who
participated in Negro lawsuits and sometimes
won. A woman was taken from a hotel where
she worked in Tenha, stripped, beaten with a
wet rope, and tarred and feathered, over the
disputed question as to whether her second
marriage had been preceded with a di-
vorce. . . . Jewish-run businesses were boycotted. . . . One unfriendly tabulation of
affairs in Texas credited the Klan with over
five hundred tar-and-feather parties and
whipping bees, plus other threats, assaults,
and homicides. (Chalmers 1981: 41–42)

Local Klan members also infiltrated the
political machines of several states as well as
local law enforcement agencies and the
courts: Texas voters sent Klansman Earl
Mayfield to the U.S. Senate in 1922; in Georgia, Alabama, California, and Oregon, Klan
members helped elect governors; and in Colorado, Oklahoma, Arkansas, Indiana, and
Ohio, the Klan achieved a great deal of local
and statewide power.

The Klan's power, however, was short
lived. In Colorado, Grand Dragon Dr. John
Locke was asked to step down after a short
jail term for federal tax fraud and continued
bad publicity about his personal and political
life. When the corruption of Locke and Klan
leaders in other states was finally uncovered,
membership plummeted.

By 1927, national membership had dwindled to 350,000, and from the mid-1930s
until the end of World War II, the few remaining local Klans had become little more
than fraternal societies. Notable exceptions

occurred in Florida, where throughout the
1930s, approximately 30,000 members continued their night-riding terroristic activities
aimed primarily against Blacks; in the Carolinas during late 1939, where KKK groups terrorized textile workers who were trying to
unionize; and in Georgia where Klansmen
flogged over 50 people between 1939 and
1940 (Bullard 1991).

After World War II, with the arrival of a
new wave of European Jewish immigrants
and the return of young Black soldiers who
hoped for better social and economic opportunities at home, a handful of Klan members
seized an opportune moment to advocate terror. Two months after VJ Day, the Association
of Georgia Klans marched up Stone Mountain and lit barrels of fuel oil to form a cross
300 feet long. Their message was "to let the
niggers know the war is over and that the
Klan is back on the market" (Wade 1987: 276).

For the next ten years, Klan activity was
primarily confined to statewide and local efforts, such as that in Georgia whereby members spewed racist and nativist rhetoric and
leveled violence against Blacks, union members, Jews, Catholics, and a new target, Communists. Such efforts were continued locally;
they remained small in scope and never
achieved national prominence. However, the
very fact of their existence, as well as the fear
of a new and revitalized Klan rebirth, kept the
local non-White, non-Protestant, and immigrant population in a perpetual state of fear. It
would not be until the mid-1950s that the
Klan would experience renewed energy and
increased physical violence when the Civil
Rights movement began. (See Chapter 4.)

1950 TO 1979

For these thirty years, terrorists continued to be influenced by historical continu-

ities. At the same time, however, terrorists from both above and below were increasingly influenced by at least three contemporary realities:

1. The "conventions of violence" that historically governed acceptable and legitimate levels of violence, broke down after 200 years of warfare.
2. Justifications that terrorism should be used to bolster a political cause rather than affect political change became more commonplace.
3. Attention to left-wing, Marxist philosophies enhanced by the growing revolutionary fervor of a new generation of revolutionaries.

Consequently, both terrorists from above and below became emboldened during this period.

As discussed in Chapter 1, terrorism can be covertly used from above when government personnel use acts of terror that are prohibited by their official position, but which are secretly carried out within its domestic borders, such as in the case of Argentina's "Dirty War" discussed next. Governments also covertly sponsor terrorism within the international arena by intervening in the political power structure of another nation, such as the case of American intervention in the political affairs of Guatemala from 1954 to 1996 discussed shortly.

Terrorism from the unempowered also thrived during this period and was largely fueled by the left-wing thoughts of Mao Tse-Tung, Che Guevara, Carlos Marighella, and Franz Fanon–each which are summarized later in this chapter. While this era was filled with left-wing political revolutions, one of the most interesting, violent, and long-lasting was that of the *Front de Liberation Nationale* in Algeria–the subject of the last case study for this period.

Covert Terrorism from Above: Argentina's "Dirty War," 1976–1983

Between 1966 and 1976, rural and urban guerrilla warfare was a fact of life in Argentina. Revolutionary terrorist groups advocating political change carried out bombings, kidnappings, and attacks on military camps and police stations; government-supported groups responded with counterterrorist efforts by conducting retaliatory murders of revolutionaries and anyone suspected of sympathizing with them. Thus, when a coup bringing a three-party military junta to power quietly occurred on March 23, 1976, few Argentineans were surprised, and some were even encouraged.

The new leaders promised that "this government will be imbued with a profound national spirit, and will respond only to the most sacred interests of the nation and its inhabitants" (as quoted in Simpson and Bennett 1985: 47). Yet within two days, the legal machinery was in motion that terrorized Argentineans for the next seven years. The "process of national reorganization" began by suspending the national constitution and passing a series of official "orders" that "cleansed" the educational system by dismissing "dangerous" left-wing, revolutionary members of all secondary schools and universities, and arresting student activists and alleged subversives; enforced strict censorship codes for the media; allowed terrorists to be shot on sight; and mandated a ten-year jail sentence for anyone propagating subversive material or material offensive to the military.

This and other legal methods, supported what came to be called the "dirty war"–a terroristic battle covertly facilitated within the higher echelons of all three parties comprising the military junta and overtly carried out by military force. As people began to disappear in great numbers, repression tightened, the dirty war escalated, and the junta denied any official involvement. It was not until Argentina's new leader, Dr. Raul Alfonsin came to power in December 1983, that Argentineans began to learn the truth. Dr. Alfonsin made two commitments to the nation: to establish a national commission inquiring into the fate of "the disappeared"; and to prosecute those who were allegedly involved in the disappearances.

In 1984, the report of the Argentine National Commission on the Disappeared (CODEP) established positive identities of 8,960 of the estimated 11,000 persons who had disappeared; found that about 20,000 people had been arrested, many of whom had been tortured and raped in one of 340 clandestine jails; and estimated that 2 million Argentineans fled the country to escape the possibility of death or imprisonment. Of those known to have disappeared, the vast majority were young adults aged twenty to thirty-five who were generally educated, politically aware, and suspected of sympathizing with left-wing terrorists or perpetrating left-wing terrorism. At least 172 of the disappeared were children who were taken from their parents. Some were sold, some were given to childless couples, and some were murdered; 160 were adolescents aged 13 to 18, and 52 were over age 55 (Argentine National Commission on the Disappeared 1986).

In CODEP's moving "Prologue" to their report, "Nunca Mas," commission members left no doubt about the use of covert official terrorism by the military junta:

> The armed forces responded to the terrorists' crimes with a terrorism far worse than the one they were combating, and after 24 March 1976 they could count on the power and impunity of an absolute state, which they misused to abduct, torture and kill thousands of human beings. . . . From the huge amount of documentation we have gathered, it can be seen that human rights were violated at all levels by the Argentine state during the repression carried out by its armed forces. Nor were they violated in a haphazard fashion, but systematically, according to a similar pattern, with identical kidnappings and tortures taking place throughout the country. How can this be viewed as anything but a planned campaign of terror conceived by the military high command? How could all this have been committed by a few depraved individuals acting on their own initiative when there was an authoritarian military regime, with all the powers and control of information that this implies? How can one speak of individual excesses? The information we collected confirms that this diabolical technology was employed by people who may well have been sadists, but who were carrying out orders. (Argentine National Commission on the Disappeared 1986: 1–2)

The first and only trial conducted in Latin America against high-ranking military officials began on April 22, 1985, and lasted five months. State prosecutors charged each of nine Argentinean military commanders with the abduction, torture, or murder of a specified number of victims. Two defendants received life sentences; one was sentenced to 52 months in jail; two others were sentenced to eight and 17 years of imprisonment, respectively; and the final four were acquitted. The court's defense of its opinion consisted of several arguments:

- While the commanders did not, as individuals, abduct or torture anyone, the instructions they issued to the armed forces for dealing with subversives and terrorists made them responsible for the acts of others.
- Each of the three parties that comprised the junta were autonomously involved, and there was no evidence of a coordinated plan of terror between them.

- In each branch of the armed services, a sustained pattern of abduction, torture, and murder existed that could not possibly be explained as the individual excesses of a few aberrant officers.

In short, the Argentine government clearly had been involved in covert violence designed to cleanse the nation of subversive, revolutionary individuals perceived to be a threat to the power structure. Not only had constitutional rights been suspended due to a so-called national emergency, but people were systematically tortured and killed by persons with the legal authority to commit such terrorist actions. However, the trial did not bring an end to the legacy of terrorism from above in Argentina.

The next chapter occurred in October 1989 during the rule of the new Argentinean president, Carlos Monem. One of his first actions was to grant amnesty to all leaders on both sides of the dirty war—the left-wing civilians and the right-wing military members, including all five junta members who were tried and convicted under President Alfonsin's rule. Then, in December, he issued a formal pardon to all those tried and involved in the 1985 trial in the hope that it would help all Argentineans to heal and forgive.

However, many people persisted in their efforts to get the government to admit its involvement.[19] In March 1995, ten years after nine commanding officers had been tried, the extent to which the Argentine government had been involved became public knowledge when a military officer admitted that the dirty war had actually occurred. He then described the deaths of thousands of political opponents suspected of left-wing activism. Weak from incessant torture, thousands were forcibly placed in airplanes, injected with sedatives by a navy doctor, undressed by officers, and then their unconscious bodies were thrown into the Atlantic Ocean. He also accused the Roman Catholic Church of complicity by claiming that many military chaplains acted as counselors for officers who were distressed by what they were forced to do. They rationalized such deaths as "a Christian form of death" ("Grisly revelations on 'dirty war'" 1995: A13).

A month later, the army chief of staff, Gen. Martin Balza, formally admitted that the army had been wrong to kidnap and kill thousands of political dissidents during the dirty war. He stated that "The army did not know how to take on terrorists by legal means . . . It employed illegitimate methods, including the suppression of life, to obtain information" ("Argentine army finally admits to killings" 1995: 10).

Subsequent to such admissions, efforts were intensified to deal with the victims and perpetrators of the dirty war. In August 1997, the Argentine government announced that it would issue $3 billion in bonds sometime in 1998 to compensate relatives of the "disappeared." Each of the families of the government's estimated 9,000 victims was to receive $220,000.[20] Then, in November 1999, Argentina's former president Leopoldo Galtieri,

---

[19] Most active in this fight to force the government to admit its involvement in the "dirty war" have been the Mothers of the Plaza de Mayo. Their ongoing and heroic battle is described by Marguerite Guzman Bouvard in *Revolutionizing Motherhood: The Mothers of the Plaza de Mayo* (1994). Additionally, two excellent movies chronicle their efforts: the academic-award winning *The Official Story* and the documentary, *Madres de Plaza de Mayo*. Further, an excellent article chronicles the experiences of one victim of the dirty war—a child who was taken from her parents at birth, renamed, and adopted—only to be found by the Mothers of the Plaza de Mayo. See Sebastian Rotella, "Terrible Secret: In Argentina, an 'Open Wound'" *Los Angeles Times* (Sunday, October 25, 1998).

[20] Human rights agencies, however, have estimated that the number of the "disappeared" was really about 30,000.

Gen. Jorge Videla, former navy chief Emilio Massera, and 95 other military officers who presided over the years of terror in Argentina were indicted on charges of torture, terrorism, and genocide.[21]

Covert Terrorism from Above: American Involvement in Guatemala's Reign of Terror

From 1954 to 1996, Guatemala was under nearly continuous military control;[22] during the last 36 of those years, it was also involved in a bloody civil war in which right-wing military regimes attempted to destroy their left-wing guerrilla opponents. During the civil war, more than 100,000 people were killed, another 40,000 "disappeared," 100,000 fled the country, over 200,000 children were orphaned, and one million people were displaced from their homes. Additionally, the Guatemalan army destroyed over 440 villages–primarily those populated by the indigenous Mayans who make up about 60 percent of Guatemalans.

The human tragedy of the Guatemalan civil war has been further exacerbated by the gradually-emerging public acknowledgment

of U.S. complicity in these years of terror. American involvement began in 1954 when President Eisenhower approved a plan to overthrow the election of the popularly elected, left-wing president of Guatemala, Jacob Arbenz Guzman.[23] Complicity continued under the Reagan administration that turned a blind eye to the growth of Guatemalan death squads that committed human rights abuses against the indigenous population, burning their villages and slaughtering inhabitants.

While U.S. military advisers and CIA operatives were not necessarily involved in the planning and execution of these atrocities, official documents from the National Security archives clearly show that U.S. policymakers not only knew what was going on in Guatemala and did nothing to end the terror, but also supported such terror in a variety of ways:[24]

- On December 3, 1966, the Department of State received a secret cable from General Porter describing a request made to him by the Guatemalan Vice Defense Minister for U.S. assistance in the covert training of special kidnapping squads that would target leftists. Although Porter declined, he went on to recommend that the United States "fully support current police improvement programs and initiate military psychologi-

---

[21] The indictment was brought by Spanish Judge Baltasar Garzon who earlier had won the arrest of former Chilean dictator Augusto Pinochet Ugarte. The move has heated up the historical controversy between Spain, Latin America's former colonial master, and the domestic affairs of some Latin American countries. At the time this book went to press, little was known about the outcome of the indictment.

[22] Guatemala was under military rule from 1954 to 1985. However, even after elections restored civilian leadership in 1985, the military was still in charge behind the scenes and Congress and the president largely served at the will of the generals (Anderson 1996).

[23] For an account of U.S. involvement in the CIA coup, see Stephen Schlesinger and Stephen Kinzer: *Bitter Fruit: The Untold Story of the American Coup in Guatemala.* Garden City: Anchor, 1983. For a political history of U.S. involvement with United Fruit in Guatemala see Paul J. Dosal: *Doing Business with the Dictators.* Wilmington, Scholarly Resources, 1993.

[24] For a summary of and access to 32 documents submitted to the State Department, see the National Security Archives at http://www.gwu.edu/~nsarchiv/NSAEBB/NSAEBB11/docs/

cal warfare training and additional counter-insurgency operations training."[25]

- On March 29, 1968, the Department of State received a secret memorandum from Viron Vaky of the State Department's Policy Planning Council who, upon return from Guatemala, wrote an indictment of U.S. policy therein. Vaky argued that the Guatemalan government's use of counter-terror was indiscriminate and brutal and had impeded modernization and institution building within the country. Furthermore, he stated the United States had condoned such tactics. "This is not only because we have concluded we cannot do anything about it, for we never really tried. Rather we suspected that maybe it is a good tactic, and that as long as Communists are being killed it is all right. Murder, torture and mutilation are all right if our side is doing it and the victims are Communists." Vaky urged a new policy in Guatemala that rejected "counterterror" as an accepted tactic and represented a "clear ethical stand" on the part of the United States.[26]

In short, during most of the civil war years, the United States allocated security assistance to the Guatemalan government, knowing full well that some of these monies were supporting terrorist activities in Guatemala. In December 1990, President Bush froze the delivery of security assistance in the wake of the murder of American citizen Michael DeVine. In 1995, it was reported that although overt military aid was indeed halted in 1990, millions of dollars of secret CIA funds continued to flow to the Guatemalan armed forces during the ensuing years. Those funds were finally cut off after knowledge of the funds became public.

In early 1999, an independent truth commission's report on the Guatemalan's terroristic campaign also pointed to the extent of American involvement in the civil war. Consequently, in March 1999, President Bill Clinton not only acknowledged American involvement in the Guatemalan civil war, he also told a gathering in Guatemala City that U.S. support for security forces that engaged in massacres, executions, torture, and "disappearing" was wrong. In short, for the first time in the twentieth century, a president of the United States admitted the immorality of American involvement in Latin American terrorism, apologized to its people, and expressed regret for the nation's role in Guatemala.

Terrorism from Below: Revolutionary Philosophers

Terrorists from below were greatly effected by the left-wing thoughts and actions of four revolutionary thinkers who published and violently practiced their philosophies during this period: Mao Tse-Tung, Che Guevara, Carlos Marighella, and Franz Fanon.

Mao Tse-Tung

Even though he never applied the words to the concept, Mao Tse-Tung was the first to systematize guerrilla warfare, a type of terrorist activity that had been evolving since the beginning of humankind. In 1935, when he became the chairman of the Chinese Communist Party's Politburo, Mao gave coherent organization to what had previously been a crude set of military tactics employed by revolutionary groups that lacked armies.

---

[25] See the primary document at http://www.gwu.edu/~nsarchiv/NSAEBB/NSAEBB11/docs/03-01.htm.
[26] See the primary document at http://www.gwu.edu/~nsarchiv/NSAEBB/NSAEBB11/docs/05-01.htm.

Realizing at the outset that his forces were numerically and technologically inferior to those of his opponents, Mao substituted political power for the lack of conventional military power. He thus declared a "people's war" into which he planned to enlist the rural peasantry, his guerrillas.

To recruit his "people's army," Mao said it was essential to:

- Politically mobilize the rural populace by convincing them that the ultimate success of the peoples' war depended on the support and beliefs of all the people, and that their superior political motivation and beliefs could wear down the enemy by waging a protracted military campaign–a war of attrition.
- Invoke a new, radical strategy that only the Chinese peasantry, not the urban elite, offered any hope for real change and for recovering Chinese dignity.
- Espouse a revolutionary ideology that utilized both violence and terror, arguing that "Political power grows out of the barrel of a gun," and that change comes only through violence, extreme, shocking violence in which the masses must be coerced into participating if the corrupt state is to be annihilated.

Mao's "Red Terror" was used from below against two targets: the corrupt government; and any unwilling, nonsupportive peasants. Between 1949 and 1950, civil liberties and individual rights took a backseat to revolutionary necessity as Mao's terrorists confiscated the property of private landholders and killed the landed gentry. In the mid-1950s, terror was focused on peasants who were forced to organize into state collectives. Thus, Mao successfully employed terrorism from below to win the revolution; once in power, Mao used terrorism from above to maintain control and to protect the state.

Che Guevara

In the late 1950s, Che Guevara began to build upon Mao Tse-Tung's premise that the rural populace could be politically mobilized for a people's war against the power structure. Che developed the theory of "rural guerrilla warfare" that grew out of his experiences in Cuba and his subsequent belief that peasant-based revolutions could be used around the world to acquire political power. Such ideas formed the basis for his first book, *Guerrilla Warfare*, which was published in 1960. Two other publications explain the methods for such warfare, *Guerrilla Warfare: A Method* (1963), and *To Create Two, Three . . . Many Vietnams* (1967). All of his writings reiterated the following themes:

- It is unnecessary to wait until all conditions for revolution exist; revolutionary activity itself can create favorable conditions. The existing socioeconomic conditions for the rural peasants in Latin America invited revolution.
- The principal enemies of the Latin American people and their revolution were American imperialists, landowners, and the wealthy bourgeois.
- Basic social and economic changes in Latin America could only be accomplished through an armed revolution of popular forces. In turn, popular forces led by the people could successfully wage an unconventional war against a conventional army with superior manpower and resources.
- Armed fighting can be most successful in underdeveloped rural countries, especially in Latin America.
- Terror is justified if it promotes revolutionary conditions necessary to overthrow the enemy. Political terrorism was valuable only if it promoted revolution and eliminated oppressive opposition. Terror was never to be used against the rural masses

who were already repressed by the enemy, or against any civilian forces.

Carlos Marighella

Marighella adapted Che's themes to his concept of "urban guerrilla warfare." Marighella felt rural guerrillas could not generate the support of urbanites. Instead, guerrillas needed to be trained to deal specifically with urban war. As such, the principle task of the urban guerrilla is to wear down the military dictatorship and its forces, and attack and destroy the wealth of the Brazilian upper-class.

Marighella's urban guerrilla was required to have a wide range of qualities, from courage and initiative and good marksmanship, to being a good walker and knowing the art of disguise. Additionally, the urban guerrilla had to know how to live among the urban population, dress appropriately, and work at an ordinary urban job. Most importantly, the urban guerrilla required specialized training that included the art of fighting, self-defense, electronics, map reading, flying, first aid, and other functional and survival skills; instruction on how to use weapons and explosives; and an understanding that one's skills gave one several advantages over the enemy.

As explained in Marighella's *Minimanual of the Urban Guerrilla* (1969), urban guerrillas must discredit and harass their oppressors (North Americans, executives of foreign firms, the Brazilian upper class); destroy goods and belongings of their oppressors; become committed revolutionaries whose first duty was to do whatever was necessary to further the revolution; engage in guerrilla and psychological warfare designed to transform the country's political situation into a military one so that the military could be overthrown by the guerrillas; be willing to read and understand the list of revolutionary reading supplied by Marighella; and become familiar with a list of possible actions to take against authorities and be able to select those actions with a great deal of care.

Franz Fanon

Franz Fanon was the first to adopt a more radical approach to terrorism during this period. Fanon's political ideology was shaped by his direct personal experiences as a psychiatrist practicing during Algeria's struggle for liberation. Gradually, Fanon came to believe that his patients' psychiatric disorders were the direct result of their unjust social situation at the hands of French colonial rulers. It was futile, he felt, to treat a patient and send that patient back into the same environment that was responsible for the illness. What had to change were not the people, but the social and political conditions that dictated and terrorized their lives. Thus, his involvement with the Algerian Liberation Front (Front de Liberation Nationale-FLN) began: he hid FLN members in the underground struggle; offered rooms for secret meetings; and relayed information, arms and other materials. While in exile, Fanon began writing *The Wretched of the Earth* in which he introduced the philosophy of terror for terror's sake.

- The social and economic systems of African nations, as well as other underdeveloped nations that had been exploited by western imperialists, needed total change for man to be free.
- The quest for freedom did not end by creating free states through revolution; man must be free and must work to ensure his freedom. The goal, therefore, was to create social and political institutions that will allow man to express his freedom.
- Using violence for violence's sake, or expressing oneself and one's desire for free-

dom through violence against oppressors, was always acceptable. Violence for violence's sake was useful and productive, even if it fails to enhance the revolutionary cause of guerrilla warriors. The end need not always justify the means; violence as a means was justifiable in and of itself as an expression of freedom.

• Violence is both therapeutic and helpful. As a "cleansing force," it can "free the native from his inferiority complex and from his despair and inaction; it makes him fearless and restores his self-respect" (Fanon 1982: 73).

While the tactics and philosophies of all four men were widely read by would-be and actual left-wing revolutionaries from around the world, they have been particularly well applied in Algeria where guerrilla warfare has been and continues to be an ordinary occurrence from 1954 to the present.

Terrorism from Below: Algeria and the Front de Liberation Nationale (FLN)

Between November 1954 and July 1962, Algeria was involved in a protracted guerrilla war with its French colonial governors. During those eight years, one-ninth of the total population perished by death, mutilation, and other war-related crimes; approximately one-third of the country's infrastructure was partially or completely demolished; and over one million professionals, skilled workers, and civil servants fled the country in search of a new homeland.

This struggle for Algeria's independence from France was waged and won, in part, by the *Front de Liberation Nationale* (FLN), which sought to free Algeria from a nonrepresentative French colonial regime and to establish a new national entity. Their battle began on

November 1, 1954, with a wave of low-level violence that swept across the rural areas of Algeria. For the first two years, the FLN's guerrilla efforts were aimed primarily at three targets: French citizens in rural French villages, pro-French Algerians living in Algeria, and rural Muslim Algerians who were forced to learn "a certain Islamic puritanism" (Hutchinson 1978: 44).

In 1956, the FLN opened a terrorist bombing campaign against Europeans living in urban Algerian locations. A year later, it expanded operations into metropolitan France. Because the French government viewed FLN actions as seditious acts of a few extremists, it justified the use of military force, torture, and brutality–terror from above–against the enemies of French nationalism. Thus, the French army terrorized the native Algerians by destroying their crops and orchards, forcing millions into concentration camps, and torturing FLN leaders. Such terror drove a further wedge between the Muslim population of Algeria and the French-born populace, allowing the FLN to recruit more volunteers and gain valuable support for their political cause.

The battle progressed, military victory for the FLN seemed unlikely. Consequently, a new FLN goal emerged: gaining popular, worldwide support for its cause. As explained by one FLN member:

> Our brothers know that we are outnumbered and outgunned by the colonialist army and hence, cannot achieve great, decisive military victories. Which is better for our cause? To kill ten enemies in some gulch in Telergma, which will go unnoticed, or one in Algiers, which will be written up in the American press the next day? If we are going to risk our lives, we must make our struggle known. . . . Let us reflect on the consequences of our acts and be sure that they will be profitable, that they will unfailingly draw attention to the noble struggle of our people and its army. (as quoted in Gaucher 1968: 230)

While the FLN's guerrillas failed to gain military victory against the French army, it eventually won the political victory; indeed, the FLN's persistence and high visibility turned the tide of international opinion. In time, FLN members were viewed as freedom fighters who justifiably fought the repressive measures of the French. In so doing, FLN guerrilla tactics, coupled with the world opinion that the terrorists had so carefully cultivated, helped Algeria gain its independence on July 5, 1962.

After the FLN leader Ahmed Ben Bella became the nation's first president, Algeria became a socialist state. In 1976, the first constitution was adopted in which the FLN was proclaimed the country's only legal political party. As such, the FLN became responsible for nominating all candidates for political office.

For over ten years, the FLN ruled in relative peace. However, when oil prices crashed in 1986, domestic unrest ensued. Thereafter, the one-party government sharply cut back its socialist welfare net. Unemployment and popular frustration increased. In 1988, rioting in Algiers resulted in the death of several hundreds of citizens. In the aftermath, the president promised elections. Consequently, more than 50 new political parties emerged. The fundamentalist Islamic Salvation Front (FIS)–the first legal Islamist political party in the Arab world–had the largest following.

The FIS won the first round of national elections in December 1991–gaining 188 seats of 231. The military was both shocked and worried by these results and forced the president to resign in January 1992. On January 11, 1992, just five days before the next elections in which the FIS was expected to win control over the Algerian Assembly, the FLN-controlled army seized power. Thus, the FLN–a group that won political power through a terroristic battle fought from below–became the terrorizer fighting from above against an emerging threat. Thereby, the army canceled elections, arrested thousands of FIS members, and installed a five-man High State Committee to govern during a two-to-three-year transition period.

In July 1992, convicted FIS leaders were sentenced to up to 12 years in jail for sedition and advocating holy war against the Algerian government. Shortly thereafter, military and secret antiterrorist courts sentenced about 400 convicted Islamic terrorists to death and banned the FIS. In response, the FIS began a terroristic struggle from below in which members sought to destroy the secular state and replace it with a fundamentalist Islamic State. Thereafter, Algeria was embroiled in a terrorist war waged by the FIS and its military arm–The Islamic Salvation Army–and other Islamic extremist groups.[27]

By the end of the 1990s, the estimated death toll after almost ten years of violence in Algeria was over 70,000. The nation was over $30 billion in debt and had an unemployment rate of about 28 percent. Poverty and hunger was widespread. Two-thirds of the jobless were under 30 years old. Further, the terroristic struggle had become more complex. Another fundamentalist Islamic group arose in 1997–the Armed Islamic Group (GIA)–and became the avowed enemy of the FIS. Consequently, civil war in Algeria was no longer just between the various fundamentalist Islamic groups and the Algerian government, but also between the terrorist groups themselves. In essence, the GIA believes the army of the FIS is involved in secret peace talks with Algeria's military regime. Thus, the GIA launched a series of

---

[27] Armed Islamic Movement Group (an offshoot of FIS), Armed Islamic Group, Hezbollah, Repentance and Emmigration (al-Takfir wa'l Hija), and Afghan veterans of the Afghanistan war.

terroristic attacks against the FIS to halt any peace accord because of its belief that a radically new Islamic society is the only answer to the current terror gripping Algeria.

In response, the Algerian military has undertaken a counterterrorist campaign. Military courts execute civilians; strict curfews have been in effect; security forces arrest suspects who are later found dead in public places; pro-government death squads patrol urban and rural areas; FIS leaders are hunted and slaughtered. The cycle had come full circle—it began with the regime of perceived terrorism from above by the French colonial power; furthered with terrorism from below by the FLN that ultimately ended with the FLN in control; continued with the FLN refusal to allow opposition parties with fundamentalist goals play a role in the government; broadened with terrorism from below by the Islamic-based FIS and GIA; and came full-circle with counterterrorism from the FLN.

1980 TO 2000

In the previous period, terrorism became more grievance-based, violent, and morally justified. While these characteristics continue to greatly influence this most recent phase of terroristic activities from both above and below, terrorism has also become more technologically advanced and more dramatically influenced by political goals grounded in right-wing racial and ethnic hatred, as well as in fundamentalist religious and ideological extremism. None of these changes, as we have previously argued and will continue to argue, have created a revolutionary new type of terrorism, but rather, each has moved terrorism ahead along an evolutionary time line. While the technological advances that have dramatically affected the tools of terrorism were discussed in Chapter 1, our discussion

herein will focus on the ethnic hatreds and ideological shifts that have increasingly influenced modern terrorist actions.

Fundamentalist religious ideologies have prompted recent terrorist exploits in the United States as well as in the Middle East where the world has witnessed the emergence of Islam as a potent global force. Beginning in the 1960s, many Muslims began to question the political, economic, and social authority of their increasingly modernizing and Westernizing nations. Some believed that modernization had promoted dependence on Western nations and encouraged political and social imitations of Western society that threatened the unique religious nature of their Muslim identity. Rather than expressing loyalty to their nation—through nationalist ideology—they expressed loyalty to the fundamentals of their religion.

For a few of the most politically extreme—like the Armed Islamic Group of Algeria discussed earlier—Islam provides a self-sufficient ideology for a nationalistic model believed to be a valid alternative to secular state systems. That is, some fundamentalists have become religious nationalists, believing that their nation is a divine creation with specific God-given purposes and features.

Islamic fundamentalists believe that the Muslim world is in a state of decline because it has departed from the straight path of Islam. Thus, Muslim governments and societies must be revitalized by implementing and enforcing Islamic law that will, in turn, create an Islamically guided and socially-just state and society. The pace, direction, and extent of change must be subordinated to Islamic beliefs and values to protect them against the penetration of Western values. While the vast majority of Islamic fundamentalists are ideologically extreme in their political viewpoints, only a few have resorted to the use of violence against two targets:

Box 2.1
Nationalism vs. Religious Nationalism

Nationalism is an ideology that gives priority to the nation over other communities, postulates the unique character of the nation, and attaches sentiments of belonging, loyalty, solidarity, and legitimate political authority to the nation.

Religious nationalism is the belief that nations are divine creations with specific God-given purposes and features; have a unique relationship with the Creator from which specific obligations and exclusive rights are derived; and certain roles in the great divine plan, the outcome of which frequently is revealed and included as central to the national identity.

---

1. Western governments: especially Britain, France, and the United States; and
2. Un-Islamic or unjust Arab regimes: especially Egypt, Iran, Lebanon, Algeria, and Afghanistan.

The case study presented next describes the cyclical use of terrorism first from below and then from above as wielded by the Taleban of Afghanistan.

In addition, over the past several decades, an increasing number of cruel regimes have marketed racial and ethnic hate that, in turn, has resulted in almost unbelievable terrorism that the Western press has since labeled "ethnic cleansing." While ethnic cleansing has been the "terror of choice" for many Croats and Serbs, it has also been used extensively in Africa. As the case study on Rwanda will indicate, ethnic cleansing has become a modern-day form of genocide–and a cyclical example of how terrorism from above begat terrorism from below.

Finally, beginning in the 1980s, terrorism from below in Latin America increasingly involved left-wing political violence that "defied the traditional models applied to Latin American guerrilla and terrorist movements" (White 1998: 62). As the case study on *Sendero Luminoso* will indicate, its terroristic

exploits involve indiscriminate terrorism against anyone who does not support its cause.

Terrorism from Above and Below: The Taleban of Afghanistan

Throughout their history, most Afghanis have not viewed themselves as residents of an Afghani nation, but rather of their traditional Muslim community that, in turn, is defined by ethnicity and tribal affiliation. Indeed, according to many scholars, "the only thing all Afghans have in common is Islam" (Oliver 1990: 30). This split in perceptions–the Afghani state versus the Muslim community–encouraged the growth of two worlds in Afghanistan: one that was increasingly modern, urban and tied to the civil bureaucracy, and one that was traditional, rural, and tied to the tenants of Islam. As the centralized state continued its modernization process, it began to usurp political, social, and economic decisionmaking power from the rural areas, further widening the gap between the two worlds.

Resistance movements to modernization and non-Islam influences in the government began in 1958 among students at the Univer-

Box 2.2
Historic Relations Between Ethnic, Tribal, and Clan Groups in Afghanistan

For centuries, the area that has come to be called Afghanistan has been populated by several prominent ethnic groups: the Pashtun/Pathan of the east and west; the Tajik of the north; the Hazara of central Afghanistan; the Uzbek of the north, and several others living primarily in the south and northeast. In addition to their ethnic identity, every Afghani also has a tribal identity that is traced through one's father. One's tribe or clan has its own autonomous values that define traditional rights and customs, honor, and vengeance, and one's interpretation of Islam, and rely on specific institutions. For instance, most ethnic Pashtuns claim tribal identity with the Durrani—the tribe controlling most centralized power in Afghanistan since 1747. The Durrani, in turn, are divided into several familial clans. Thus, throughout its history, allegiance within Afghanistan has been determined by ethnicity and tribe—and the tribe's interpretation of Islam. Allegiance, then, has not been given to the state, or to the state's interpretation of Islam.

During the twentieth century, another identity factor claimed importance—that of Shi'ite versus Sunni Muslim. The vast majority of Afghanis are Sunni Muslims. However, beginning in the 1970s, with the rise of Islamic fundamentalism throughout the Middle East, both groups formed foreign alliances that pitted them against each other. The Shi'ite fundamentalists, most of whom came from the Hazara ethnic group in central Afghanistan, allied themselves with Iran. The Sunni fundamentalists, most of whom were Pashtans not tribally affiliated with the Durrani, allied themselves with Saudi Arabia, Egypt, and Pakistan.

This religious and cultural structure has deeply influenced the evolution of Islamic fundamentalist thought and activity in Afghanistan, beginning with the creation of a tribal confederation organized in 1747 by Ahamd Shah of the Poplozay clan. Shah's tribe, now known as the Durrani, maintained power until 1978, during which time the confederacy conquered and controlled the nation primarily for pillaging and exacting tribute. Despite the Durrani's lack of loyalty to a centralized state, an autonomous locus of power was established with the rise of the tribe. Indeed, the Durrani aristocracy and the great families of other tribes that became linked with it built the semblance of a state that maintained its influence through the use of patronage and genealogy.

Throughout the last 200 years, the Durrani have struggled to gain centralized power and autonomy from the tribal lives and communities where real power was exercised under the ulama—Islam scholars of the community who did not care who was in charge of the state as long as it supported the *Sharia* (The Islamic Path of God) and protected Islam. The Durrani, then, were the driving force behind modernization. By the turn of the twentieth century, modernization was used to increase state power through two avenues: creating an army that, in turn, required an increased supply of weapons and money by establishing a manufacturing industry; and imposing the *Sharia* instead of tribal common law.

Yet, the state remained in existence, not because the Durrani were proficient at holding on to their elusive power, but because of the financial subsidies and weapons freely provided by various foreign governments that were interested in maintaining Afghanistan

Box 2.2 *Continued*

as a buffer state, especially England and Russia. Consequently, the boundaries of the modern state were determined by the strategic requirements of the English and Russians, rather than to any ethnic or historic boundaries. Thus, the nation's eastern boundary cut right through the Pashtan ethnic group, which led to problems of the 1990s.

sity of Kabul who were taught by professors steeped in anti-Soviet and anti-Western thought. The professors were also opposed to traditional views of the community Muslim scholars, the ulamas, and concerned about the growing infiltration of communists within the Afghan state machinery. Gradually, many students began to believe that a true return to Islam was essential, that this must be accomplished by establishing an Islamic state ruled by strict Islamic law, and that such a state could only be created via a successful Islamic revolution.

In July 1973, Prince Muhammad Daoud, a Pashtan nationalist who favored an independent Pashtan-ruled Afghan state and was backed by the communists, carried out a successful coup. Daoud, a passionate anti-fundamentalist, immediately arrested most student leaders. In response, the radicals, led by Gulbuddin Hekmatyar with support from Pakistani President Bhutto, began receiving training from the Pakistan army. In 1975, the Afghan fundamentalists began a rebellion that was brutally crushed by the end of the year. The rebellion failed not because it couldn't oust Daoud, but rather because it received virtually no support from the Afghani people in the Islamic-oriented, traditional rural areas. The people simply "did not see the Islamic political movement as being a bulwark of Islam" so they failed to support them or come to their defense (Oliver 1990: 76). The lessons for the survivors were simple: there could be no victory without close

links with the ulama who influenced traditional society or without close contact with the peasants.

With this in mind, the fundamentalists took refuge in Pakistan. There, the fundamentalist movement split into two factions by 1977:

• The moderate element led by Borhanuddin Rabbani who attracted the Persian-speaking populace and a wider coalition of Afghanis, including the ulama.
• The radical element led by Hekmatyar who attracted the Pashtun and created a largely homogeneous and disciplined group of political activists.

In April 1978, while the fundamentalists were busy infighting, a communist coup occurred. Consequently, for the first time since 1747, power shifted from the Durrani Pashtun to the Ghilzay Pashtun—members of the lower ethnic classes with professed allegiance to socialism. Additionally, many reforms advocated by the Ghilzay involved state encroachment upon the traditional social, economic, and cultural patterns of tribal Islamic Afghans. Within months, widespread resistance spread to two-thirds of the country. This was the beginning of the Afghan civil war that was to last from 1978 to 1992.

It began as a guerrilla war in mid-1978 after Afghan resistance forces, led primarily by Islamic fundamentalists, challenged the communist-backed government. The war intensified in December 1979 when the Soviet

Union invaded Afghanistan with the intent of incorporating the country into its sphere of influence. After ten years of controversial involvement, the last Soviet soldiers left Afghanistan on February 15, 1989. However, the Soviets had placed President Najibullah in power in 1986–and he remained seated after they left. The war lingered on as the rebels attempted to oust Najibullah, a task that was not accomplished until April 1992 when rebel forces seized Kabul and announced the formation of an Islamic government.

Both the nature and outcome of this war is significant because of what it tells us about Islamic fundamentalism.[28]

- It was the first war of liberation won by an Islamic movement, which sought to create an Islamic state rather than a nationalist or socialist state.[29]
- It marked the first and only time that radical Islamic fundamentalists in a Sunni Muslim nation were able to involve traditional peasants and the ulama in a united battle against a common enemy.

Thus, the war was won primarily because the disparate forces of Islam, the two worlds of Afghanistan, were able to unify. However, such unity worked only to slay a common enemy, not to establish a new government based upon a common Islamic ideology or vision. After the rebels toppled the Soviet-backed president, their fragile coalition fell apart around the question of how their *jihad–* or holy war–should be interpreted.

- The fundamentalists felt the jihad had been an *offensive* action designed to topple an illegitimate secular state. Once the war was won, they interpreted it as a full-scale offensive revolution that would naturally lead to the formation of an Islamic government and implementation of the *Sharia* from the centralized Islamic government.
- The traditionalists felt the jihad had been a *defensive* action designed to protect Islam from foreign encroachment and from increasing state secularization. Once the war was won, they interpreted it as a defensive struggle that would bring about a return to life as it was prior to the communist takeover and the implementation of the Sharia from the ulama.

In short, the war marked the decline of Soviet influence, the rise of Islamic fundamentalist influence, and the beginning of a civil war in Afghanistan. The seeds of this war were formally sown on April 25, 1992, when political leaders of ten major rebel factions agreed on the composition of an interim Afghan government that would take over government ministries and installations. Within a few months, Burhanuddin Rabbani, a leader of the rebel group, Islamic Society, became president.

Fighting began, especially between five major rebel groups that have been supported by Iran, India, Pakistan, and Saudi Arabia. In the first four years of the war, 35,000 Afghans died. In 1994, Hekmatyar and his allies tried to oust Rabbani from control, and in the ensuing battle Kabul was reduced to rubble. Rabbani

---

[28] An often-discussed factor in winning the war was U.S. backing of the fundamentalist forces in their fight against the Soviet-backed government. During the 1980s, the CIA gave the *mujahedeen* rebels an average of $500 million annually in military aid, including Stinger anti-aircraft missiles. Two million Afghans died in the fighting and over 6 million became refugees (Cooper 1996).

[29] It was not the first time that a guerrilla movement had assumed power in a Muslim country; this had been done both in Algeria and South Yemen. However, the liberators in both nations adopted their ideology and political organization from Western models like Marxism and nationalism–not Islam. The last purely Muslim revolts were the anticolonial revolutions in the Sudan by the Mahdist movement and in Central Asia by the Basmachis–both of which were doomed because they could not adapt to the modern world.

remained in power and Hekmatyar was thrown out of the city. That autumn, an alliance of rebels from radical fundamentalist groups formed under the leadership of Mullah Mohammad Omar. Known as the Taleban, the group had captured the southern province of Kandahar by September 1994. In the next six years, Taleban rebels seized huge tracts of land in southern, western, and eastern Afghanistan—until by the beginning of 2000, they controlled 90 percent of the entire nation.

The Taleban, in the southeastern city of Kandahar, historically has been a bastion of Islamic fundamentalist conservatism. Because its founders were scholars in Islamic religious schools, the movement took the name *Taleban* meaning "religious student." Within months, the Taleban had attracted a 10,000-member army consisting of mujahedeen who were dedicated to ending the communist-controlled government, former refugees from camps in neighboring Pakistan, and former communist government soldiers. Pakistan and Saudi Arabia have continuously provided military and financial help.

Where it was in control, the Taleban imposed strict Islamic rule upon all Afghanis. Its goal is to merge the secular and sectarian realms of Afghan society into the purist Islamic state in the world. The new government is to be based on the teachings of the *Koran* and a strict interpretation of the *Sharia* by

- Prohibiting women from working outside the home except in health-related professions; girls from attending school; all Afghans from attending music recitals, concerts, and dances, watching movies and television, and participating in certain games, especially kite flying and chess; women from lingering in public or speaking to strangers; and surgeons from operating on members of the opposite sex.
- Requiring men to grow full beards and women who appear in public to cover their entire bodies by wearing the *burqa*.
- Supporting and enforcing new laws demanding that adulterers be stoned to death, murderers be executed by firing squad or slow strangulation, thieves be subjected to the amputation of the offending hand(s) and/or feet, and those guilty of engaging in illicit sex receiving 100 lashes.

In short, the Taleban, which began as a group of political extremists, mounted a successful terroristic campaign from below against the government and traditional Afghani rulers. By late-2000, it maintained power over 95 percent of the nation and was continuing its battle for the remainder of Afghanistan. In so doing, the Taleban has instituted a coercive and terroristic rule from above by enacting strict Islamic rules over society.

Indeed, as these words are being written, the world's most radical contemporary Islamic fundamentalist group is in control of most of Afghanistan and is seeking recognition by United Nations as the only legitimate ruler in the nation.[30] Thus, regardless of how long the civil war continues and who wins the conflict, it is clear that an Islamic state—whether liberal, moderate, or extreme—will be the outcome.

Terrorism from Above and Below: The Hutu Genocide of Tutsis in Rwanda

From the seventeenth century until the monarchy was overthrown in 1961, the king-

---

[30] As of this writing, the United Nations still recognized Rabbani's government as legitimate rulers of Afghanistan. Rabbani continues to fight against Taleban encroachment on his small corner of Afghanistan.

dom of Rwanda was a highly stratified state based on class and ethnicity. Society consisted of three peoples:

1. The Hutu (85 percent): noblemen, military commanders, local officials, and cattle farmers.
2. The Tutsi (14 percent): largely subsistence farmers, but also comprised the ruling class consisting of the king and his court.
3. The Twa (1 percent): hunters and potters.

For over 300 years, the privileged Tutsis believed themselves racially and intellectually superior to the other two classes, while the vast majority of Rwandans—the Hutus—felt oppressed and enslaved by the Tutsis. Such class and racial antagonisms were exacerbated by at least two policies under the colonial rule of Belgium from 1919 to 1962: the Tutsis were allowed to remain in control of the puppet monarchy; and a formal identity-card system was created to force all people to classify themselves as either Hutu or Tutsi.

In 1959, the Hutus staged a successful revolt against the Tutsi monarchy and created a one-party dictatorship, which they maintained until 1990. Once in power, the Hutus began to harass and threaten the Tutsis. Such actions led to a cycle of terroristic violence between the two groups.

- The Hutus—operating from above—ousted Tutsis from power and began harassing and threatening those with traditional privileges.
- In response, the Tutsis—operating from below—created a guerrilla-terrorist group, the *Inyenzi*, composed of refugees living in Uganda, Burundi, and the former Zaire (now the Republic of the Congo).

The Hutus' responded with counterterrorism by executing prominent Tutsi leaders. The subsequent violence led to the deaths of 20,000—mostly Tutsis—as well as the exile of between another 400,000 to 500,000 Tutsis. Although Hutu attacks against the Tutsi significantly decreased after 1966, discrimination was still widespread. A relative peace set in for 25 years until a new wave of terror struck in October 1990 when Tutsi exiles invaded Rwanda. Over the next two years, armed terrorist groups, working together with Rwandan civilian officials and some government soldiers, killed at least 2,000 civilians solely because they were Tutsi. At least another 8,000 were imprisoned without being charged; hundreds of those were beaten, tortured, and raped. Authorities at all governmental levels, including the president of Rwanda, consented to these actions. These hostilities ended August 1993 when both sides agreed to create a power-sharing government in Rwanda.

The worst round of genocidal actions began in April 1994 when the presidents of Rwanda and Burundi died in a mysterious airplane crash. Rwanda's Hutu-led army, terrorists, and even civilians went house-to-house hunting down and killing Tutsis and Hutus favoring reconciliation. Civilians were often forced into killing. "Their options . . . were either to kill or to be killed or to see their families be killed," reported the former Canadian commander of the U.N. peacekeeping mission in Rwanda (Davies 1998:A8). Between April and July of 1994, a massive genocide occurred that resulted in tragic and astonishing human costs:

- Somewhere between one-half and three-fourths of the entire Rwandan Tutsi population was systematically exterminated by the Hutu. Some experts put the number between 800,000 and 850,000 Tutsis—out of a total of less than a million Tutsis in Rwanda (Prunier 1996). Those who survived have not only been traumatized, but live in continual fear of Hutu reprisals.

Box 2.3
Rwandan Hutu Extremists in Surrounding Countries

According to Human Rights Watch, the perpetrators of the Rwandan genocide re-built their military infrastructure in Zaire. Once settled in Zaire, the Rwandan Hutu extremists began to apply its ethnic-cleansing strategies to Zaire's local Tutsi residents. By mid-1996, it was apparent that the Rwandan Hutu exiles living in Zaire were coordinating their efforts with other Hutus in the eastern Congo and Burundi, as well as with tribes with anti-Tutsi animosities. The result was what many people called a regional ethnic-cleansing effort.

In Zaire, Laurent Kabila used the Tutsi-led Rwanda army to help him in his successful 1997 coup against the Zairian dictator Mobutu Sese Seko. Subsequently, Congolese tribal militias—terrorists known as the Mai-Mai—and members of Mobutu's defeated army joined with Rwandan Hutus living in the Congo in attacks on the Tutsis, both in the Congo and Rwanda. This conflict widened into a full-fledged war in August 1998. Rwandan and Ugandan rebel Tutsis attacked the Congo and captured the western river port town of Matadi. They announced that they would continue to march toward Kinshasa with the intent of overthrowing Kabila's government.

Burundi has also been under attack from 1997 to early 2000. There, Tutsis have held economic and political power almost continuously since their independence. Fighting between Burundian Hutu rebels, often with assistance from Rwandan rebels, and the Tutsi-dominated military has led to over 150,000 deaths since 1995.

- The Hutu population was branded *genocidaires*—perpetrators of genocide. This label will probably remain for generations.
- The lives of the surviving children were shattered. A survey conducted by UNICEF in 1996 found that more than 2,500 children—most of whom were accused of murder—lived in decrepit, filthy, and crowded jail cells throughout the country; tens of thousands of children were in orphanages; 50,000 children were homeless and were searching for their parents; and most children were psychologically traumatized by the violence they witnessed, and that some actually committed suicide.

In late 1994, a Tutsi-dominated army drove the extremist Hutus from Rwanda and regained governmental power. About one million Hutus fled to Zaire (now the Republic of the Congo) along with its leaders and a 30,000-person-strong army and the civilian terrorist groups. There, the Hutu exiles have formed alliances with other Hutus in neighboring nations—alliances that plan to regain control not only over Rwanda, but over other regional nations with Hutu populations. What began over 40 years ago as a terroristic war of genocide within the internal borders of Rwanda has now become a regional problem for the central African nations of Rwanda, Burundi, and the Congo—all of which have substantial Tutsi populations. By mid-2000, the terroristic perpetrators of genocide—the Hutus—were believed to have two distinct goals for the region: to kill as many Tutsis as possible, and in so doing, to gain political and economic power in Rwanda, Burundi, and the Congo.

Terrorism from Below: The Sendero Luminoso of Peru

In 1981, Abimael Guzman, professor of philosophy at the San Cristobal de Huamanga University in Ayacucho, Peru, founded the *Sendero Luminoso* (SL), or Shining Path. Guzman's goal was to take Peru back to the cooperative agricultural system perfected by the Incas. His choice of Ayacucho was strategic; the village was not only steeped in Incan tradition, but its Indian *campesinos* (peasants) were dissatisfied with their impoverished lives and frustrated by the failure of promised land reforms. Based upon Maoist principles, Guzman's strategy was twofold:

1. to begin the revolution in remote areas where, after he built regional military support, it would spread to more prosperous districts and finally take over the cities; and
2. to ruthlessly eliminate all enemies–anyone who refused to support the Shining Path.

Guzman's five-phase process–which he felt might take as many as 50 years to complete–included mobilization, agitation, and propaganda; sabotage and rural guerrilla activity; generalization of violence into guerrilla war; establishment and expansion of bases and liberated zones; and blockading of towns and cities by peasant armies, leading to the collapse of the government (Clutterbuck 1990: 117).

During its first years of operation, the Sendero Luminoso concentrated on the first phase. By 1982, it had launched the second, more violent phase and had committed over 2,900 attacks of sabotage and guerrilla activity (Clutterbuck 1990: 118). In 1983, 500 murders were attributed to SL activities (Vetter and Perlstein 1991). Additionally, in 1983, ac-

tivities spread to the Upper Huallaga River Valley and extended to the drug trade (Gonzalez 1987). While the SL is not directly involved in the drug trade, it extorts money for cultivating and exporting coca; accepts money and arms from drug traffickers in return for preventing or deterring interference from the police, army, and the U.S. Drug Enforcement Administration; charges traffickers "departure fees" for each plane filled with coca paste; and fights with rival gangs of drug traffickers for its fair share of the profits. The Shining Path, then, is one of the first terrorist groups in modern times that has successfully combined a guerrilla campaign and Maoist goals and philosophy with wide-scale involvement in the drug trade. The terrorists provide protection for the drug traffickers, and, in turn, the drug traffickers provide the SL with necessary financial and arms assistance.

In November 1984, the Sendero Luminoso attacked the main base of an American-sponsored crop substitution program near Tingo Maria and killed 19 local employees (Clutterbuck 1990). From that time onward, the SL moved into its third phase, designed to hurt the economy through the violent disruption of communications, mines, factories and the destruction of the tourist trade. It has been variously estimated that, from the time it moved into this phase through the 1980s, between 12,000 and 15,000 people had died at the hands of the SL (Clutterbuck 1990). From the mid-1990s forward, the SL has lacked the resources to renew a widespread guerrilla campaign. It has, however, resorted to individual acts of terrorism.

SUMMARY

The primary goal of this chapter has been to provide an historical framework for an in-depth study of terrorism both in the international and domestic political arenas. In so doing, this chapter has also introduced several new themes, which will be used throughout the book.

1. Terrorism is as old as humankind. Thus, contemporary terrorists are not radical new actors in the drama of political violence; rather, their actions, goals, and grievances have simply evolved from those of their historical mentors. What has changed throughout history is not the horrendous violence wrought by terrorism or the perpetrators themselves, but the grievances of the terrorists, the political philosophies of their mentors, the technological sophistication of their tools, and the acceptance of violence as a legitimate and moral way to achieve political goals. None of these, however, are revolutionary changes; instead, they represent evolutionary changes along a lengthy historical time line.

2. Terrorism is cyclical in nature–originating from above or below, intensifying when the targets of terror respond in kind with terror, and recycling with the use of counterterrorism. Additionally, it is not unusual for a group to use terrorism from below in order to overthrow a terrorist regime, and then once in power, the former critics of governmental terror often resort to the use of terrorism from above in order to squelch opposition to their new regime.

3. Throughout history, terrorism most often originated from above, by persons in power who, both intentionally and unintentionally, institutionalized and used political terror against those who threatened their power base. Historically, the dispensers of terror from above (monarchs, dictators, czars, popes, and priests) justified their use of terror as a legal right of the state or an ordained gift from God. Contemporarily, those operating from above have new titles: presidents, military dictators, fundamentalist spiritual leaders, each of whom view themselves as legitimate defenders of the political, social, religious, and/or economic status quo. Such leaders usually disguise terrorism as a "legitimate use of power," necessary and justifiable to maintain "public safety" and act "in the best interest of the people."

4. Historically, terrorists operating from below (revolutionaries, zealots, and "traitors"), rationalized the use of terror as a defensive struggle necessary to overthrow corrupt leadership, obtain political and spiritual freedom, and fight for individual and collective survival. Contemporarily, those operating from below (freedom fighters, nationalists, guerrilla warriors, racial revolutionaries, fundamentalists) believe they are fighting defensive battles against imperialism, one-world conspirators, governmental oppression, state terrorism, and moral and spiritual decay. Such terrorists believe their cause to be just.

5. Throughout the last 200 years, terrorists from above and below have been deeply influenced by the revolutionary ideologies of many socialists and anarchist philosophers. Nineteenth-century terrorists received inspiration and adopted socialist strategies from Marx and Engels, as well as Bakhunin and his fellow Russian anarchist philosophers. Twentieth-century terrorists readily combined Marxian rhetoric with those of a new generation of revolutionaries who advocated guerrilla warfare. Mao Tse Tung, Che Guevara, and Carlos Marighella adapted guerrilla warfare to distinctly rural and urban locales; proposed that terror was to be used as a way to change existing political structures and transform them into Marxist governmental systems; and determined that terror was a tool to be used only to overthrow the abusers of power, never against inno-

cent civilians. Franz Fanon revised this latter tactic by claiming that terror was a useful, justifiable means for achieving freedom and, in some cases, for acting as a cleansing force necessary to survival. Thereafter, for some terrorists, terror was not merely to be used as a means to gain an end, but rather as an end unto itself.

6. Terrorism has been inextricably interwoven into our past, it is a subjective rather than objective phenomenon, and its cyclical nature ensures its longevity. If we accept these arguments, then we must also accept that it is impractical to expect that terrorism can be eradicated any more than we can expect to eliminate crime. This does not mean, however, that we should throw up our hands in defeat. While we cannot expect to end international terrorism on a so-called macrolevel, we can learn how to mitigate its consequences by examining the historical and contemporary reasons for its occurrence. In addition, on a microlevel, we can make strides against domestic hate-related terrorism by educating ourselves about fear and intolerance, resisting the forces of terrorism, and forcing terrorists to be accountable for their actions.

DISCUSSION QUESTIONS

1. Some experts would disagree with one of the themes in this chapter—that today's terrorists are not revolutionary new actors in the domestic or international arenas, but rather their goals, grievances, and actions are evolutionary advances along the historical continuum of terror. Do you agree or disagree with this thesis? Why or why not?

2. Do you agree or disagree with the section in which the American system of slavery is called a terrorist action from above? Why or why not? Why do you think other books about and scholars of terrorism rarely, if ever, use American slavery as an example of terrorism?

3. Many scholars have argued that the U.S. government's policy of allotment under the Dawes Severalty Act of 1887 was one of the most terroristic pieces of federal Indian legislation. Would you agree or disagree with this analysis? Why or why not?

4. In the case study of the Armenian genocide, it is mentioned that in 1920, "the present-day diaspora of the Armenian peoples" began. What is a diaspora? Provide examples of one other historical diaspora, as well as two examples of contemporary diasporas. Were any of these the consequence of terrorism from above or below? Explain.

5. Do you think that the CIA involvement in Guatemala from 1954 to 1996 was an act of covert terrorism from above, or a legitimate act of governmental power? Defend your opinion with supportive facts and documentation.

6. How do the left-wing political theories of Mao Tse-Tung, Che Guevara, Carlos Marighella, and Franz Fanon compare and contrast? How do they compare and contrast with the philosophies of Marx and Engels?

7. Terrorism in Algeria continues as the government uses terror to combat the efforts of the Islamic fundamentalists who seek its demise, and as the various Islamic terrorist groups fight each other for control over the terroristic battle from below. What are the most recent facts and figures about terrorism in Algeria? Based upon what you know about the situation, do you think peace will come to Algeria in the near future? Under what circumstances might that be possible?

STUDY QUESTIONS

1. In many of the case studies involving terrorism from above, right-wing governments sought to terrorize left-wing opponents. Using this model, begin an investigation into another nation—excluding the United States—that has followed this path. Describe how the cycle of terrorism began from above, how it continued from below, and the manner in which governmental counterterrorism was used.

2. Covert terrorism from above has been alleged to have been used many times in the 1970s and 1980s by the U.S. government—especially within Latin America. Some examples include the CIA's involvement in the coup against Chili's Salvador Allende, U.S. complicity in the Iran–Contra scandal, and American support of right-wing guerrillas in El Salvador. Pick one of these examples—or any other in which you are interested—and describe how and why the U.S. government got involved and the extent of American involvement. Then, explain why you agree or disagree with allegations that such involvement was an act of governmental terrorism from above.

3. As described previously, in March 1999, President Bill Clinton in a precedent-setting admission told a gathering in Guatemala City that U.S. support for security forces that engaged in massacres, executions, torture, and "disappearing" was wrong. Do you believe Clinton's statement was a wise one? Why or why not? Do you think it was a correct assessment of the CIA's involvement?

4. Using newspaper and Internet sources, examine the most recent terroristic chapter that surrounds the lives of the Hutus and Tutsis—not only in Rwanda, but in the Republic of the Congo and Burundi as well. Is there any hope that this cycle of terror can be broken?

5. In his recent book *The Debt: What America Owes to Blacks,* Randall Robinson argues that slaves should receive reparations for the labor that made America great prior to the Civil War. And the great-great-granddaughter of a slave in South Carolina is also demanding reparations from Aetna—which sold policies in the 1850s that reimbursed slave owners for financial losses when their slaves died. Both advocates for reparations support the creation of some sort of foundations that would benefit minority education and businesses. After researching more about the reparation issue, answer the following questions: Should governments compensate those who have been victims of terrorism? Why or why not? What other groups in the United States have asked for reparations? What have been the results? Do any of the discussions about reparations equate the atrocities to acts of terrorism? Should they?

6. What is the United Nation's official definition of genocide? Upon examination of that definition, do you agree or disagree with the assertion that nineteenth-century governmental policies resulted in genocidal consequences for the American Indians? Why or why not? Do you think genocide is an act of terrorism? Why or why not?

7. Some experts on the Ku Klux Klan attribute the release of D. W. Griffith's movie, *The Birth of a Nation* to the KKK's resurgence of power in the early 1900s. After watching this movie, do you think the Klan is portrayed in a favorable light? Explain. Can you discuss any other movies that have positively portrayed vigilante violence in a manner that might have swayed audience opinion? Movies that negatively portrayed vigilante violence in an influential manner?

8. Review one of the four sources in Footnote 19 about the fight of the Mothers of the Plaza de Mayo to force the Argentinean

government to admit its involvement in the "dirty war." The Mothers' endeavors are one of several around the world that have selected to fight terrorism with nonviolent protest and pressure rather than resort to terrorism from below and perpetuate the cycle of terror. Summarize the most recent efforts of the Mothers and then learn more about similar endeavors in Northern Ireland, Israel, and the lands currently governed by the Palestinians. How do they compare and contrast?

REFERENCES

Anderson, John Ward: Generals in Retreat. *Washington Post Weekly Edition:* 18, December 16–22, 1996.

Argentine National Commission on the Disappeared: *Nunca Mas: The Report of the Argentine National Commission on the Disappeared.* New York: Farrar, Straus & Giroux, 1986.

Avrich, Paul: *The Haymarket Tragedy.* Princeton: Princeton University Press, 1984.

Blee, Kathleen M.: *Women of the Klan: Racism and Gender in the 1920s.* Berkeley, CA: University of California Press, 1991.

Bouvard, Marguerite Guzman: *Revolutionizing Motherhood: The Mothers of the Plaza de Mayo.* Wilmington: Scholarly Resources, 1994.

Brown, Richard Maxwell: *Strains of Violence: Historical Studies of American Violence and Vigilantism.* New York: Oxford University Press, 1975.

——: Historical patterns of American violence. In Gurr, Ted Robert (Ed.): *Violence in America. Volume 2: Protest, Rebellion, Reform.* Newbury Park: Sage, 1989, pp. 23–61.

Bullard, Sara (Ed.): *The Ku Klux Klan: A History of Racism and Violence,* 4th ed. Montgomery: Southern Poverty Law Center, 1991.

Chaliand, Gerard, and Ternon, Yves: *The Armenians: From Genocide to Resistance.* London: Zed Press, 1983.

Chalmers, David M.: *Hooded Americanism, The History of the Ku Klux Klan,* 3rd ed. Durham: Duke University Press, 1981.

Clutterbuck, Richard L.: *Terrorism and Guerilla Warfare: Forecasts and Remedies.* New York: Routledge, 1990.

Cooper, Kenneth J.: War engulfs Afghanistan again. *San Francisco Chronicle:* A1, September 23, 1996.

Davies, Karen: Rwanda killings called avoidable. *San Francisco Chronicle:* A8, February 26, 1998.

Dosal, Paul J.: *Doing Business with the Dictators.* Wilmington: Scholarly Resources, Inc., 1993.

Fanon, Franz: *The Wretched of the Earth.* New York: Grove, 1982.

Ford, Franklin L.: *Political Murder: From Tyrannicide to Terrorism.* Cambridge: Harvard University Press, 1985.

Gaucher, R. *The Terrorists.* London: Secker & Warburg, 1968.

Gay, Peter: *The Cultivation of Hatred.* New York: W.W. Norton, 1993.

Gonzalez, Raul: Coca and Subversions in the Huallage. *Lima Quehacer, 48,* 58–73, September–October 1987.

Gross, Feliks: Political violence and terror in 19th and 20th century Russia and Eastern Europe. In Kirkham, James F., Levy, Sheldon G., and Crotty, William J. (Eds.): *Assassination and Political Violence: A Staff Report to the National Commission on the Causes of Prevention and Violence.* New York: Bantam, 1970, pp. 519–598.

Guevara, Che: *Guerrilla Warfare.* New York: Vintage, 1960.

Gunter, Michael M.: 'Pursuing the Just Cause of Their People,' A Study of Contemporary Armenian Terrorism. Westport: Greenwood Press, 1986.

Gurr, Ted Robert: Political terrorism: Historical antecedents and contemporary trends. In Gurr, Ted Robert (Ed.): *Violence in America: Protest, Rebellion, Reform,* Vol. 2. Newbury Park: Sage, 1989, pp. 201–230.

Hutchinson, Martha Crenshaw: *Revolutionary Terrorism: The FLN in Algeria 1954–1962.* Stanford, CA: Hoover Institution Press, 1978.

Jordan, Winthrop D.: *The White Man's Burden: Historical Origin of Racism in the United* States. New York: Oxford University Press, 1974.

Kuper, Leo: *Genocide: Its Political Use in the Twentieth Century.* New Haven: Yale University Press, 1982.

Kurz, Anat, and Merari, Ariel: *ASALA: Irrational Terror or Political Tool.* Boulder, CO: Westview, 1985.

Laqueur, Walter: *The Age of Terrorism.* Boston: Little, Brown, 1987.

——: *The New Terrorism: Fanaticism and the Arms of Mass Destruction.* New York: Oxford University Press, 1999.

Lewis, Bernard: *The Assassins: A Radical Sect of Islam.* New York: Basic Books, 1968.

Libaridian, Gerald L.: The ultimate repression: the genocide of the Armenians, 1915–1917. In Wallimann, Isidor, and Dobkowski, Michael N. (Eds.): *Genocide and the Modern Age: Etiology and Case Studies of Mass Death.* Westport: Greenwood, 1987, pp. 203–235.

Marighella, Carlos: *Minimanual of the Urban Guerrilla.* Berkeley, CA: Long Time Comin', 1969.

Marx, Karl, and Engels, Frederick: *The Communist Manifesto.* New York: Monthly Review Press, 1964.

Miller, Donald E., and Miller, Lorna Touryan: *Survivors: An Oral History of the Armenian Genocide.* Berkeley, CA: University of California Press, 1993.

Miller, William: *The Ottoman Empire and Its Successors.* Cambridge: Cambridge University Press, 1936.

Morgenthau, Henry: *Ambassador Morgenthau's Story.* Garden City: Doubleday, 1919.

Oliver, Roy: Afghanistan: an Islamic war of resistance. In Marty, Martin E. and Appleby, R. Scott (Eds.): *Fundamentalism and the State: Remaking Polities, Economies, and Militance,* Vol. 3. Chicago: University of Chicago Press, 1991, pp. 491–510.

——: *Islam and Resistance in Afghanistan.* New York: Cambridge University Press, 1990.

Olson-Raymer, Gayle: *Terrorism: A Historical and Contemporary Perspective.* New York, American Heritage Custom Publishing, 1996.

Prunier, Gerald: *The Rwanda Crisis: History of a Genocide.* New York: Columbia University Press, 1996.

Rotella, Sebastian: Terrible secret: in Argentina an 'open wound.' *Los Angeles Times,* October 25, 1998, p1, 10–11.

San Francisco Chronicle, "Argentine army finally admits to killings," April 22, 1995: p. A10.

San Francisco Chronicle, "Grisly revelations on 'dirty war,'" March 8, 1995, p. A13.

Schlesinger, Stephen, and Kinzer, Stephen: *Bitter Fruit: The Untold Story of the American Coup in Guatemala.* Garden City: Anchor, 1983.

Simpson, John, and Bennett, Jana: *The Disappeared and the Mothers of the Plaza: The Story of 11,000 Argentineans Who Vanished.* New York: St. Martin's Press, 1985.

Stampp, Kenneth M.: *The Peculiar Institution: Slavery in the Ante-Bellum South.* New York: Random House, 1965.

Toynbee, Arnold: *Acquaintances.* London: Oxford University Press, 1967.

Utter, Jack: *American Indians.* Lake Ann: National Woodlands Publishing, 1993.

van der Zee, John: *Bound Over: Indentured Servitude and American Conscience.* New York: Simon & Schuster, 1985.

Vetter, Harold J., and Perlstein, Gary R.: *Perspectives on Terrorism.* Pacific Grove: Brooks/Cole, 1991.

Wade, Wyn Craig: *The Fiery Cross: The Ku Klux Klan in America.* New York: Simon & Schuster, 1987.

White, Jonathon R.: *Terrorism: An Introduction.* Pacific Grove: Brooks/Cole, 1991.

Wilkinson, Paul: Armenian terrorism. *The World Today,* September 1983, pp. 340–350.

Chapter 3

TERRORISM IN THE UNITED STATES: A RELATIONSHIP AS "AMERICAN AS APPLE PIE"

To many Americans, colonial history is a bore. Students always want to know what they could possibly learn from the European settlers who arrived in America with their austere clothing and puritanical values. Students in a domestic terrorism course are even more skeptical of beginning their analysis with a lesson in American history. Nonetheless, it is in the seventeenth century that our story begins.

If we carefully reexamine the character and background of the Anglo-Europeans who settled the North American continent, we can make two observations that will form the foundations of this chapter:

1. Many of the first European colonists were already politically extreme when they arrived in North America. Such colonists took their religious ideas to an extreme limit by intentionally confronting the opposition, and when that did not work, they set out to eliminate the opposition in an uncompromising, authoritative, and sometimes, bullying manner.

2. While many colonists remained committed extremists, others took their extreme ideas one step further by acting on them in a politically-violent manner; in so doing, they became terrorists acting from below. Such colonists took the law in their own hands by using intimidation, threats, injuries, and sometimes death either to defend and preserve their communal status quo, or to make political, social, and economic changes in American society.

Terrorism from below, then, is as "American as apple pie." It has been an integral part of the colonial and American political, social, and economic landscape. Indeed, in keeping with one of the primary themes of Part One, it has been an evolutionary rather than a revolutionary part of American history. This ongoing thesis is not surprising in light of the fact that sixteenth- and seventeenth-century Europeans often resorted to political violence as a justifiable mode for expressing their political, social, and economic grievances[31]–

---

[31] Urban political violence was common in sixteenth- and seventeenth-century Europe, especially between peasants and their landlords and between the urban poor against privileged aristocratic rulers. At some times, such violence was especially extreme. For instance, in sixteenth-century Lyon, Huguenots (French Protestants) were killed and butchered, their various body parts were then sold openly in the streets (Stannard 1992: 61). Political violence also played a role in rural Europe. Anti-landlord violence became more frequent as peasants throughout Europe organ-

and some of those protestors were among the first colonists to arrive in North America.

If we combine this colonial predisposition to use political violence to settle grievances with the life-threatening situations faced by frontier families, it is no wonder that many Euro-Americans became what Stock (1996) has called "rural radicals" who developed a series of extremist beliefs that became the central core of their lives:

- Independent land ownership comprised the basis for strong, self-defensive communities that were necessary to conquer the physical hardships of frontier life.
- Bigness threatened the fabric of rural life—especially big business and big landowners. Capitalism in and of itself was sound, but it must be fueled and controlled by small, local producers and businessmen.
- Government must be controlled at the local level, not at the state or federal level.
- White control over the land was not only essential to political, social, and economic progress, but was preordained by God.
- Families were to be governed by traditional patriarchal relationships.
- Christianity—especially Protestantism—was the one true faith.
- Government rule should act in the best interests of all white people, not just a select few who were empowered, and should reflect the views of ordinary white people about personal liberty and material prosperity.
- If the people legally expressed their political, social, and economic grievances to those in power, and such legal grievances failed to bring about change, then political violence was justified in order to restore liberty.

When these fundamental beliefs were challenged or threatened, some frontiersmen responded with political violence to defend or preserve communal values by destroying the actual or perceived threat to their communities. In so doing, these men became what we have called *scapegoating vigilantes*. In addition, when some men used political violence to reform or destroy the existing political, social, religious, or economic system so that their beliefs could be restored, they organized what we have called *patriot militias*. In both capacities–defending or destroying the communal status quo–these men were the first American terrorists.

Again, a study of the historical facts indicates that resorting to vigilantism or forming patriot militias were not merely occasional aberrations. As Stock (1966) indicates, between 1650 and 1750, rural and urban colonists were involved in somewhere between 75 and 100 political riots and rebellions against those who were empowered. Gurr (1989) found that more than 70 political, ethnic, and labor riots occurred in New York City between 1788 and 1834, and that as many as 500 vigilante movements occurred between the 1760s and 1909.

This chapter presents a series of case studies that illustrate two trends within American society:

1. particular actions of both scapegoating vigilantes and patriot militias from the early seventeenth century through the 1950s; and
2. left-wing philosophies and actions of student protest groups and Black militants from the late 1950s to the early 1970s.

It is hoped that after this discussion, a clear connection will be drawn between the histor-

---

ized to defend themselves against their impoverished status. For example, the Peasants Revolt in Germany (1524–1525) involved tens of thousands of peasants–100,000 of whom died when revolting against changes landlords made in agrarian policies.

ical actions of America's early terrorists and the contemporary actions of today's terrorists who are the subjects of Parts Two and Three.

SCAPEGOATING VIGILANTES

Scapegoating vigilantes were fueled largely by fear, intolerance, and hatred of those who were racially, ethnically, spiritually, and/or behaviorally different from white, Protestant Americans. In all cases of such vigilantism, we see the actions of Americans who felt the safety and social, economic, and political integrity of their communities were under attack by some group or individuals who were different—or who were perceived to be different—from the majority of people within their communities. They used violence and terror to rid the community of the actual or perceived threat and to restore it to the status quo.

The following case studies provide just a few historical examples of scapegoating vigilantism against the following targets: witches and vigilantes, Catholics, the Chinese, and African Americans.

Witches and Vigilantes

Forty years after the first European colonists settled in North America, the first accusation of witchcraft was made. Between 1647 and 1691, 83 witchcraft trials were held. Additionally, community members threatened hundreds of women—if their behavior did not change to fit the communal status quo, then they would be subjected to accusations of witchcraft. Accused witches had two choices:

1. Admit involvement in witchcraft and stand trial for the crime. If found guilty, they were imprisoned and upon release,

subjected to public humiliation, political banishment, and destruction of their economic well-being for the remainder of their lives.
2. Deny involvement in witchcraft and stand trial for the crime. Such persons were found guilty and their punishment was almost always death.

The threat of banishment or death in seventeenth-century New England actually intimidated and terrorized some colonial women into changing their behavior to conform to the status quo. Dozens who refused were incarcerated and ostracized. At least 22 people who would not admit their guilt were executed.

Such hysteria reached its peak in 1692 in Salem, Massachusetts, where hundreds of accused witches were arrested, tried, and found guilty; 19 people were hung, one man was pressed to death, and at least 150 persons were imprisoned. However, when we take a closer look at the accused witches of Salem by examining surviving primary documents, we find some interesting characteristics. These women were

- generally older, between the ages of 41–60, and more outspoken than younger women in the community;
- often widows, or "women alone" who were the only women in colonial New England who had the right to sue, make contracts, and buy or sell property; and/or
- usually known in the community for some type of personal eccentricity and behavior believed to threaten the communal status quo (Demos 1970).

Now, if we take a closer look at Salem, we also find some interesting facts. By the late seventeenth century, Salem was essentially split into two political, social, and economic spheres:

1. The traditional agrarian farming area of West Salem Village. Community members who were farmers held the reins of political and economic power that they felt were increasingly threatened by the growing mercantile population from East Salem Town.
2. The rising commercial area of East Salem Town. Community members who were largely small merchants began to challenge the traditional social, political, and economic power of the agrarian residents in West Salem Village.

Those who accused the witches were almost exclusively drawn from the farmers of West Salem, while 82 percent of the accused witches lived in East Salem. Given such demographic information, Boyer and Nissenbaum (1974) concluded that women who were different posed a real or perceived threat to the spiritual and communal status quo. It is herein argued that these accused witches were terrorized either into conformity or an admission of consorting with the devil. In so doing, the accusers of Salem were among the first scapegoating vigilantes–or terrorists–in colonial America.

Catholics and Vigilantes

Anti-Catholic feelings came to North America with English settlers whose intolerance stemmed from both their hatred of Catholicism and of the Irish. Consequently, anti-Catholicism quickly became institutionalized into colonial law. In every colony but Pennsylvania, celebrating mass was a public offense and the colonial governments of Rhode Island, Pennsylvania, and New Hampshire denied Catholics the right to vote.

With the legalization of anti-Catholic feelings, colonial communities increasingly hosted anti-Catholic activity:

• In Maryland, the only colony founded by a Catholic, anti-Catholicism was waged by Protestant colonists who comprised the majority of the population. When Parliament took Maryland away from the Catholic proprietors of the colony in 1654, a Protestant assembly was established and thereafter, Catholics were regularly persecuted. Maryland was returned to the Calverts in 1658. At least four formal rebellions were led by the Protestants against their Catholic proprietors in 1659, 1676, 1681, and 1691.[32]
• New York in the early 1700s was the scene of repeated anti-Catholic demonstrations.
• In Massachusetts Bay Colony, Catholics were banished; those who dared return did so on pain of execution by community members.

Anti-Catholicism continued to flourish in the newly created United States. New Jersey became the first state to stipulate in its constitution that Catholics could not hold state offices. North Carolina and Georgia followed suit in 1776 and the next year Vermont's constitution required all state office holders to swear they were Protestants (Coates 1987).

By the early 1800s, newspapers, books, and pamphlets appeared in which Catholics were ridiculed and portrayed as irresponsible alcoholics. *The Awful Disclosures of Maria Monk* (1836), which sold more than 300,000 copies before the Civil War, were the alleged con-

---

[32] Such Catholic–Protestant conflict began when the English Civil War broke out in 1642 between the Puritan-dominated Parliament and the Catholic King Charles I. Parliament, with the help of Protestant Oliver Cromwell, won and the King was beheaded in 1649. Parliament took Maryland away from the Calvert family (the original proprietors) and established a Protestant assembly in the colony.

fessions of a former nun who described "depraved priests, licentious nuns, and monastic orgies" (Olson 1994: 169).

In the 1840s, anti-Catholicism increased with the arrival of thousands of Irish immigrants fleeing the Potato Famine. Thus, anti-Catholic, anti-immigrant vigilantism arose, especially in American cities.[33]

- On Christmas Day, 1806, mobs in New York City disrupted Catholic religious services.
- In 1833, after a drunken Irishman killed a man in Charleston, Massachusetts, enraged citizens smashed and burned the Irish section of town while the troops stood by and did nothing.
- In 1834, in the same town, an angry mob of Protestant workmen attacked the Ursuline Convent. According to one onlooker, "The crowd of truckers and bricklayers, aided by volunteer firemen, ransacked it from top to bottom, smashing furniture and piling combustible materials in the center of the rooms. Amid cheers and jeers, the ornaments of the altar and cross were hurled on the pyre just after midnight, and the building . . . went up in a roar of flames" (as quoted in Bennett 1988: 27).
- In 1844, Protestant rioters destroyed a weaver's neighborhood where most residents were Irish Catholics and then attacked a Catholic Church.
- In 1854, a mob destroyed the Irish ghetto in Lawrence, Massachusetts.

Nineteenth-century anti-Catholicism peaked in 1850 when an obscure fraternity was founded in New York City. The Order of the Star Spangled Banner (OSSB) quickly became known as the American Party or the Know Nothings.[34] All members pledged never to vote for a Catholic or foreign-born political candidate. In addition, members who held any political office promised to help remove all Catholics and aliens from any positions of authority and to deny them jobs and profits in private business or public offices (Bennett 1988). Finally, its political platform stated that no Catholics or foreign-born Protestants could hold an office. During the 1854 election, the Know Nothings emerged as the nation's second largest party; members elected five senators and 43 representatives to Congress. During the 1856 election, the Party's presidential candidate, Millard Fillmore, won 21 percent of the vote.

While anti-Catholicism was not absent for the remainder of the century, it was not until the rebirth of the Ku Klux Klan in the 1920s that it regained prominence. Indeed, during this decade, anti-Catholicism was more deeply embedded in American society than it ever had been before or after the Klan's resurgence. As one historian has explained, "To a highly fragmented, disorganized Protestant America, the Catholic constituted a tightly organized, disciplined, well-financed fighting force. The diverse legions of Protestantism saw themselves as being under attack, and this meant America in danger" (Chalmers 1981: 113). In essence:

> The Klan's main concern . . . was the looming danger of Roman Catholicism. . . . For the most part the rank and file listened approvingly to revelations that Lincoln, McKinley, and Harding had been done in by the

---

[33] In the 1830s, Irish Catholics accounted for one-third of all immigrants. Between 1840 and 1844, over a quarter of a million Catholics arrived in the United States. By 1840, membership in American Catholic churches reached 660,000; in the next decade, that number tripled (Bennett 1988).

[34] Because OSSB members pledged to say nothing when asked about the club, writer Horace Greeley called them the "Know Nothings" in a November 1853 article in the *New York Tribune*.

Knights of Columbus and that 90 percent of the deserters in World War I had been Roman Catholics. The Klan's standard piece of campaign literature . . . was the famous forged "Knights of Columbus Oath." Copies of the alleged pledge, by which Catholic laymen promised to "hang, burn, boil, flay, and bury alive" all non-Catholics, were distributed by the tens of thousands all over the country. . . . One popular story was that every time a boy was born to a Roman Catholic family, the father added a rifle and ammunition to his local church's arsenal. (Chalmers 1981: 111)

Examples of KKK terrorism against Catholics abound in the following:

- In 1921 in Oregon, the Klan developed a widespread recruitment campaign based upon anti-Catholicism. In several communities, an "escaped nun" invited to a Protestant church would tell of her ordeals as a Catholic and Klan lecturers spoke out against "the Roman Octopus which has taken control in the nation's capital" while announcing that "this is white, Protestant and Gentile man's country, and they are going to run it" (Chalmers 1981: 86). A local editor in Marshfield who tried to refute anti-Catholic stories was boycotted as a Papist. The Klan elected city officials in Astoria, Tillamook, and Eugene.
- In 1922 in Greenville, Mississippi, the primary role of the Klan was to defend their community and their state against the menace of Roman Catholicism. During a local Klan meeting that year, the speaker claimed that the Pope had recently bought huge tracts of land opposite West Point Academy and overlooking the nation's capitol; that convents were actually brothels and the confessional a place of seduction; and that local churches were storing arms in their basements in preparation for the Pope's plan to seize the U.S. government.

- In 1922 in Sacramento, California, the Klan began to make regular appearances at the Westminster Presbyterian Church at 13th and K Streets. In June, Reverend Harrison announced that the Klan was doing more for the moral and spiritual life of the community than any other organization outside of the church. Reverend Redburn then pointed to the real peril in Sacramento: "Nearly all the bawdy houses, bootleg joints, and other dives are owned or controlled by Romanists. A member of the Catholic faith may go to Mass in the morning and lie drunk in the gutter all day. . . ." (as quoted in Chalmers 1981: 123).

Asians and Vigilantes

Anti-Asian actions in the United States are directly tied to various waves of Asian immigration over the past 150 years. The first large wave of Asian immigration began in 1848 when many Chinese fled the poverty and famine of Southern China, which had been hit by a series of floods and crop failures.

The Chinese initially were drawn to the West Coast–and especially to California– where they mined gold and worked in the railroads as cheap labor. By 1870, the Chinese represented 20 percent of California's labor force, even though they constituted only 0.002 percent of the entire U.S. population. They comprised a large percentage of labor in mines, railroad, factories, and the fishing industry, and many also worked on large wheat and fruit farms where they became the nation's first seasonal workers. As the Chinese presence increased in California, a large wave of anti-Chinese sentiment arose–sentiment that eventually promoted extremist legislation and labor policies:

- In 1850, the California legislature passed a Miner's Tax forcing the Chinese to pay taxes on any mining claim.[35] Thereafter, white miners in most California counties violently began to expel the Chinese from mining camps.

- In 1854, California's Supreme Court overturned the murder conviction of a white man who was found guilty on the eyewitness testimony of Chinese workers. The Court's finding that "Chinese and other people not white" could not testify in court against whites invited anti-Chinese vigilantism.
- In the 1870s, San Francisco's office of the Cigarmakers' International Union distributed a circular across the western United States stating that manufacturers who employed Chinese imposed a great injury to our white working men and women. The union asked readers to boycott these firms and began to attach special labels to their products proclaiming "Made by white labor," or "Made by white men."
- In 1880, the California legislature prohibited marriage between a white person and a negro, mulatto, or Mongolian.

As a consequence of such legislation, many Chinese in California and other parts of the West became the victims of vigilantism.

- In October 1871, as Los Angeles police tried to end an argument about the status of a woman contractually bound as a worker to a Chinese community, two policemen were killed. More than 500 Whites entered Chinatown, burned dozens of buildings, and lynched 15 people.
- In 1877, five members of the Order of Caucasians in Chico, California, shot five Chi-

nese workers and then set them on fire (Stock 1996).

- In 1873, a journalist in Montana wrote, "We don't mind hearing of a Chinaman being killed now and then, but it has been coming too thick of late . . . soon there will be a scarcity of Chinese cheap labor in the country. . . . Don't kill them unless they deserve it, but when they do–why kill 'em lot" (as quoted in Lyman 1970: 76).
- In September 1885, after a fight between a white miner and two Chinese miners near the Chinese community at Rock Springs, Wyoming, white residents voted for the immediate expulsion of the Chinese. Seventy-five armed men marched on the Chinese section of town and forced the entire population to flee. They then burnt the town to the ground, looted the houses, and shot every "Chinaman" in sight (Stock 1996: 105).

In the late 1870s, Californians began to lobby Congress heavily to pass a law dealing with Chinese immigration. Consequently, the Chinese Exclusion Act of 1882 prohibited entry into the United States of all Chinese people except teachers, students, merchants, tourists, and officials. The act was so successful that Chinese immigration to the United States declined from 39,500 in 1882 to only 10 in 1887.[36]

After the Exclusion Act, large numbers of young Japanese laborers, as well as smaller numbers of Koreans, began arriving on the West Coast where they replaced the Chinese as cheap labor in building railroads, farming, and fishing. As a result, anti-Japanese actions soon grew on the West Coast. California

---

[35] The Foreign Miners' Tax was enforced almost exclusively against the Chinese. They had to pay 50 percent of all revenues gained from mining operations during the first four years the law was in effect. During the next sixteen years (the law was repealed in 1870), Chinese were forced to pay 98 percent of their revenues (Lyman 1970).

[36] The Act was not repealed until 1943–and then, only because the United States was soliciting assistance from China during World War II.

again took the lead when in 1913, it passed the Alien Land Law prohibiting land ownership for "aliens ineligible for citizenship" (Asians) and limited their lease of agricultural land to three years.[37] In 1920, the Land Law was amended to prohibit leasing land to "aliens ineligible to citizenship." By 1925, similar laws were passed in Washington, Arizona, Oregon, Idaho, Nebraska, Texas, Kansas, Louisiana, Montana, New Mexico, Minnesota, and Missouri.

In 1922, the U.S. Supreme Court ruled in *Takao Ozawa v. the United States,* 260 U.S. 178; 67L.Ed. 199: 43 F. Supp. Ct. 65 that Asians were neither White nor Black and, therefore, were ineligible to become citizens. Ozawa had unsuccessfully argued that he should be considered as a person under the Constitution, an individual with the moral character necessary to become an American citizen. Later that year, the Cable Act passed by Congress stipulated that "Any woman who marries an alien ineligible for citizenship shall cease to be a citizen of the United States." Then, the 1924 Immigration Act forbade immigration of Asians (except Filipinos), denied all Asians naturalization rights, and prohibited Asians from marrying a Caucasian and owning land.

Such legislation not only greatly curtailed the rights of Asians living in the United States, but it also encouraged vigilante violence against the Japanese. Such violence escalated tremendously in 1942 after Pearl Harbor when former President Franklin Roosevelt authorized Executive Order No. 9066, which permitted the War Department to prescribe Military Areas for Japanese relocation, to evacuate any persons from these areas, and to relocate them in internment camps. The order forcibly placed 110,000 Japanese, many of whom were second- and third-generation American citizens, in ten internment camps across the United States where most remained throughout the war.

African Americans and Vigilantes

In addition to slaves being terrorized from above by the nature of enslavement as a legal institution as discussed in Chapter 2, free black persons were also subject to the whims of white vigilantes. Mob violence in the form of urban race riots was especially terroristic. Between 1824 and 1849, Werner (1972: 4) traced 39 riots in northern cities instigated by Whites "as a result of real or imagined assaults by blacks on the established structure." By the outbreak of the Civil War, racial tensions in urban America had worsened. Black soldiers were threatened and thrown off horse-drawn streetcars in Washington, Philadelphia, and New York. Throughout 1862 and 1863, several violent urban riots were led by racist or pro-Southern Whites who protested issues related to the Civil War.

Between July 13 and 17, 1863, the most violent of these riots occurred in New York City. In just four days, more people participated and died and more property was destroyed than in any other riot in modern history (Gilje 1987). Estimates of the total number killed range from 119 (Cook 1974) to over 1,000 (Gilje 1987). Additionally, 35 soldiers and 32 policemen were seriously wounded, 38 soldiers and 73 policemen were lightly wounded, and 128 rioters and victims were seriously wounded (Cook 1974; Kohn 1986). Over 12,000 Blacks were victimized in

---

[37] The Naturalization Act of 1790 required that applicants for naturalized citizenship reside in the United States for two years, provide "proof" of good character in court, and that they be White. Thus, Asians could not become naturalized citizens and became known as "aliens ineligible for citizenship"; thereafter, only Asians born in the United States could be American citizens. This law was not nullified until 1952.

some way, including 5,000 people whose homes were deliberately destroyed. As one eyewitness reported, racism was largely behind the rioters' actions and their subsequent use of terrorism.

> If [a Negro was] overtaken, he was pounded to death at once; if he escaped into a negro house for safety, it was set on fire, and the inmates made to share a common fate. . . . A negro lodging house . . . was soon in ruins. Old men, seventy years of age, and young children, too young to comprehend what it all meant, were cruelly beaten and killed. . . . At one time there lay at the corner of Twenty-seventh Street and Seventh Avenue the dead body of a negro, stripped nearly naked, and around it a collection of Irishmen, absolutely dancing or shouting. (as quoted in Headley 1882: 207–208)

Born of the shame and anger over the Confederacy's defeat in the Civil War, vigilante violence again erupted soon after Robert E. Lee's surrender. Without the legal institution of slavery that legitimized terrorism against Southern Blacks, many Whites searched for another effective and socially acceptable method to keep the newly freed Blacks "in their place." Vigilantism appeared to be the perfect solution; it was not long before hate-filled white vigilantes began to engage in "well-documented terrorism" against Blacks (Wade 1987: 25).

> In Hinds County, Mississippi, alone, whites killed an average of one African American a day, many of them servicemen, during Confederate Reconstruction. . . . In Louisiana in the summer and fall of 1868, white Democrats killed 1,081 persons, mostly African Americans and White Republicans. In one judicial district in North Carolina, a Republican judge counted 700 beatings and 12 murders. (Loewen 1995: 151)

In addition, much was done to ensure that the freed Blacks were denied access to educational facilities. From 1865 to 1867, various mobs in the South "occasionally burned school buildings and churches used as schools, flogged teachers or drove them away, and in a number of instances murdered them" (Loewen 1995: 153).

Citizen vigilantism ushered in a new wave of terrorism when the Ku Klux Klan (KKK) was created in 1866 (see Chapter 2). During the brief three years of its life as a formal organization, the KKK successfully spread its hate-filled message: vigilante-style terrorism was not only an effective means of gaining political and social goals, but also an acceptable means. Indeed, terrorism became an accepted and regular practice of some white Southerners who intimidated, threatened, and killed African Americans. Between 1882 and 1951, at least 4,730 persons, 70 percent of whom were Black, were executed by lynch mobs in the South (Brown 1975).

At the same time that KKK tactics were gaining popularity in the South, racist vigilante violence was taking another shape in southern cities: the urban riot during which the White, majority community provoked a one-sided attack against members of the black community. The intended result of such riots was "racial massacres of blacks by whites" (Brown 1975: 211). The earliest cases, recorded in 1866, resulted in the deaths of 34 Blacks in New Orleans and 40 Blacks in Memphis.

It was over 30 years later that another wave of riots erupted, this time beginning in Wilmington, South Carolina. By 1898, Wilmington's black population had achieved notable economic and social success. Not only did many Blacks hold political office, others were successful businessmen, lawyers, doctors, and editors. Many members of Wilmington's white population were increasingly uncomfortable with such success. Their discomfort was transformed into violence shortly after the editor of a local black newspaper asserted that sexual assaults by black men on white women were not attacks, but rather were merely white accusations about instances that had been provoked by white women.

On December 9, a "Declaration of White Independence" announced the intention of the white community to remove Blacks from office and from jobs and to close down the black paper. Within 24 hours, Whites began to attack Blacks; when the riot was over, at least 30 Blacks were dead, all of Wilmington's leading black officeholders were forced out of office, and many prominent businessmen fled to find jobs in the North.

Atlanta experienced the next large riot. In September 1906, a prominent southern editor commented that because black men were raping white women in unprecedented numbers, such criminals should be castrated. White mobs, responding to the call to end black rape, began attacking black communities. After six days of rioting, hundreds of Whites and Blacks were injured, 25 Blacks and one White died, hundreds of black businesses were destroyed, and thousands of Blacks were forced to leave the city.

Shortly after World War I, white racial hostility toward black Americans heightened. The labor boom during the war had lured over 750,000 Blacks northward seeking jobs. With the war's end and the subsequent return of thousands of black soldiers to American soil, both groups were perceived as a threat. Northern black laborers, it was feared, would be competing for a dwindling number of jobs. In addition, the returning soldiers, Whites feared, would use "black aggressiveness" in their desire to alter the status quo of white dominance in race relations (Brown 1975: 212).

Consequently, the "communal riot" evolved whereby "large, relatively evenly-matched sections of each community attacked members of the other communities" in massive, uncoordinated battles (Janowitz 1976: 261–286). Within a few years after the war, at least 26 such racially motivated riots occurred in cities throughout America (Wade 1987).

One of the worst took place in Chicago during the summer of 1919. For several years prior to 1919, Chicago had become a hotbed of racial unrest. During the war, southern Blacks migrated in massive numbers, stimulating competition between Whites and Blacks for housing and jobs. Entire urban areas became designated "white" or "black," with sporadic skirmishes breaking out in so-called contested areas.

On July 27, 1919, a young black man wandered onto Lake Michigan beach, a beach claimed as "white." For one week, independent white and black mobs attacked communities and individual victims of the opposite race. By August 2, over 500 people had been injured in the riots; 15 Whites and 23 Blacks had died. Chicago, however, was merely one example of the racist violence that swept through American cities after the war.

> Mass attacks by whites wiped out or terrorized black communities in the Florida Keys, in Springfield, Illinois, and in the Arkansas Delta, and were an implicit, ever-present threat to every black neighborhood in the nation. Some small communities in the Midwest and West became "sundown" towns, informally threatening African Americans with death if they remained overnight. African Americans were excluded from juries throughout the South and in many places in the North, which usually meant they could forget about legal redress even for obvious wrongs like assault, theft, or arson by whites. . . . Every time African Americans interacted with European Americans, no matter how insignificant the contact, they had to be aware of how they presented themselves, lest they give offense by looking someone in the eye, forgetting to say "sir," or otherwise stepping "out of their place." Always, the threat of overwhelming force lay just beneath the surface. (Loewen 1995: 159)

Concurrent with this new wave of racial riots was the rebirth of the second KKK (see Chapter 2). The Great Depression and World War II brought a temporary reprieve from Klan activity and rioting, but not from racial prejudice. Segregation was the rule in the South as well as common practice in the North. Blacks could not buy houses in many Minneapolis communities, could not work in construction trades in Philadelphia, and could not be hired as department store clerks in Chicago. Racial rioting, however, found its way back into urban life in 1942, when over a dozen military and civilian riots and industrial sit-downs occurred during which Whites and Blacks fought. In 1943, another 19 such riots were recorded, the worst of which took place in Detroit where, after two days of rioting, 25 Blacks and 9 Whites had died (Dahlke 1952).

It was almost ten years before widespread vigilantism again became a popular tool of racists. In response to the *Brown v. Board of Education* 347 U.S. 483 ruling in 1954, many white vigilante groups openly organized in protest. Economic pressure, intimidation, and propaganda were used to bolster the violence and terror that "became an enduring part of the arsenal to keep black children out of white schools" (Morris 1984: 28).

Among such groups were various, revitalized KKKs that were suspected of "more than 150 bombings and hundreds of arsons and shooting across the South, in which dozens of people died and untold others were injured" (Bullard 1991: 84). The primary targets were black Civil Rights activists and white "traitors" to the race who joined their black colleagues in a quest for peace and equality.

Even more influential than the Klan were the White Citizen Councils (WCCs) of the southern states. Organized in the 1950s, WCC members from white business communities used their considerable power to completely control the lives of Blacks who were believed to pose a danger to the political and economic status quo.

> Blacks who tried to register to vote, who signed a petition for school desegregation, who belonged to the NAACP, who spoke out for equality received the treatment. Bankers would deny loans; black merchants couldn't get credit from wholesale houses or sometimes could not get supplies even with cash; insurance policies were canceled; employees were dismissed; renters were evicted from their homes; mortgages were recalled. Blacks dependent on whites for employment or credit were often forced to boycott black ministers or doctors or craftsmen who were violating the racial etiquette. (Bloom 1987: 99)

Perhaps even more frightening than the organized activities of the Klan and the Councils were the unorganized and often spontaneous actions of racist individuals, groups, and mobs who terrorized southern Blacks in general, and civil rights activists in particular.

- Southern NAACP leaders were "bludgeoned, pistol-whipped and shot at" and local black leaders were "threatened, arrested, intimidated and harassed" (Marable 1984: 47).
- Between 1955 and 1958, 530 cases of terroristic violence and intimidation were perpetrated against individuals "who questioned the South's tradition of segregation" (Bloom 1987: 101).
- In 1955, a 14-year-old black teenager visiting Mississippi from Chicago who whistled at a white woman was kidnapped, pistol-whipped, stripped naked, shot through the head with a .45 caliber Colt automatic, barb-wired to a 74-pound cotton gin fan, and dumped into 20 feet of water in the Tallahatchie River (Bloom 1987).
- During 1961, Freedom Riders were harassed and assaulted throughout the South:

white mobs in Anniston, Alabama, attacked and burned one bus; white racists in Montgomery, Alabama, pulled Freedom Riders off the bus and administered a brutal beating; a group of 26 other Freedom Riders in Jackson, Mississippi, received 67-day jail sentences for sitting in the whites-only section of the city's bus depot (Marable 1984).

- In 1963, routine violence in the South related to integration included dozens of cases in eight states of police brutality before, during, and after arrests; bombings of houses, schools, churches, businesses, and persons known to be involved in integration; fires deliberately set to burn black businesses, homes of activists, and a youth camp in North Carolina; shootings conducted by police and citizens against voter registration workers, black attorneys, and ordinary citizens during integration rallies; and the assassination of two civil rights leaders, William L. Moore and Medgar Evers. During the summer, the U.S. Justice Department noted that 758 demonstrations had occurred and that almost 14,000 people had been arrested in the South.
- In 1964, the Mississippi Freedom Summer Project brought white college students from the North to register black voters in the South. Early in the summer, three male volunteers, one Black and two Whites, were murdered. Within a short period of time, 1,000 people were arrested, 35 shooting incidents were recorded, 30 homes and other buildings were bombed, 35 churches were burned, 80 people were beaten, and at least 6 persons were murdered. As one Freedom Summer participant recalled,

> We tried to pull ourselves together and "Keep on Keepin' on," but it was impossible. The weeks of tension and strain, coupled with Wayne's [a co-worker] brutal death, could not be ignored. Hate and viciousness seemed to be everywhere. We realized that the only

thing keeping us from sharing Wayne's fate was dumb luck. Death could come at any time in any form: a bullet between the shoulder blades, a fire bomb in the night, a pistol whipping, a lynching. I had never experienced such tension and near-paralyzing fear. (as quoted in Sellars 1973: 106)

PATRIOT MILITIAS

From colonial society forward, patriot militias were largely fueled by their anger toward unresponsive governors, landowners, and capitalists. Their targets most often were federal and state legislators who levied unfair taxes, officials who enforced debtor laws, landlords who perpetuated tenancy and factory owners who exploited urban and rural workers. Stock (1996) explains that many colonists belonging to such militias—the people she calls "rural producer radicals"—were primarily small independent and tenant farmers living on the frontier who had at least two common desires:

1. Independent land ownership and production that was free from the oppression of large landlords and absentee proprietors.
2. Control over local affairs that would free them from unfair political and economic decisions made by unresponsive and disinterested eastern colonial governors.

When it became clear that legal avenues were closed for frontier farmers who sought such goals, many elected to fight the system with political violence. Such patriot-militia violence began in colonial America, continued in postrevolutionary America and throughout the nineteenth century, staged a limited comeback between the 1930s and 1950s, and burst into the 1970s with a renewed commitment to terror. The remainder of this section discusses a few case studies during three loosely defined periods: colonial America, postrevolutionary and nineteenth-century America, and the 1930s through the 1950s. Part Two illustrates many more contemporary endeavors from the 1960s to the present.

Militias in Colonial America

Within the first several decades after European colonization, a political, social, and economic split occurred between the rural frontier and the urbanized eastern communities. Accompanying this division were several well-known rebellions by patriot militias who tried to force the unresponsive eastern policymakers into meeting their demands for protection, lower taxes, and adequate criminal justice resources desperately needed on the frontier. Some dissatisfied men created private, armed militias that often attacked Indians in what they considered to be self-defense; released those jailed for debt or nonpayment of taxes; attacked tax collectors or prevented them from entering their homes and communities; refused to recognize the authority of existing criminal justice and taxing agencies; and sometimes created their own judicial systems and methods of tax collection. Among the most well-known of these patriot militia efforts were Bacon's Rebellion, the New Jersey Land Rioters, the Paxton Boys, the South Carolina Regulators, and the Green Mountain Boys.

Bacon's Rebellion

In 1676, frontier farmers in Virginia's back country had become quite disillusioned with the colonial legislature that continued to levy high taxes and had failed to provide farmers and their families with adequate defense against the Indians. To these farmers, the colonial elite seemed more concerned with providing for the eastern elite than with

protecting frontier families. Consequently, a small back-country landholder named Nathaniel Bacon raised a frontier militia of about 500 men—mostly freed white indentured servants, small farmers, and a few free black men—to protect themselves against the Indians.

Their initial goal—to destroy all American Indians in their region—was an early example of "racial radicalism among rural people" (Stock 1996: 114). Bacon's army marched against both friendly and enemy Indian peoples, massacring all with whom they came into contact. Governor Berkeley's decision to charge Bacon with treason was based upon two fears:

1. the colony's trading alliances with friendly Indian nations might be disrupted or destroyed; and
2. an armed militia of economically discontented and diverse colonists was a huge threat to the colonial government.

Bacon responded to the charge by marching his army to the colonial capitol at Jamestown and burning it to the ground. Berkeley escaped, Bacon died soon thereafter of dysentery, and then the governor returned to the capitol. Bacon's supporters who were unable to flee were captured and imprisoned. Although Bacon's patriot militia was destroyed, it emphasized two important lessons—one for the frontier farmers and another for the empowered governmental leaders.

1. To the frontier farmers, the rebellion reinforced their belief that political violence was a legitimate manner in which to seek relief for political grievances.
2. To the governors, the rebellion solidified their fear of an armed militia that was organized out of hatred of an alien race and was composed of diverse, disenfranchised, and disillusioned white and black men

who knew they were more alike than different.

As Stock (1996) laments,

> Such experiences would ultimately lead to the quintessential American paradox: the coexistence of a society devoted to personal liberty and a society that legalized slavery. In the dirty work of Bacon and his men we can see the vague outlines of a culture that could glorify the use of violence in the name of freedom and equality and not see any contradiction at all. (p. 115)

The Paxton Boys

In December 1763, frontiersmen from the Paxton District in Pennsylvania responded to the growing outbreak of Indian violence and the colonial government's refusal to come to their aid. Fifty-seven men created a militia that attacked a nearby village of Christian Susquehannock Indians. Six Indians were killed and all huts and possessions were destroyed by fire. When the Paxton Boys learned that the colonial legislature planned to move the surviving Indians to a secure facility in Lancaster, they were furious. After all, no government aid had been forthcoming after Indians had terrorized their families and farms!

After the Indians were moved to Lancaster, militia members broke into a workhouse and killed every man, woman, and child they found. By February, an even larger militia marched to Philadelphia to demand the execution of all Indians and that more money be spent on western defense. They were met by Benjamin Franklin who promised that the provincial assembly would consider their requests. The Paxton Boys went home, only to be disappointed that no governmental relief was forthcoming. Thus, they continued to fight the Indians and began to

harbor an abiding mistrust of the government—a mistrust that erupted over twenty years later when the new federal government began to tax their whiskey.

The New Jersey Land Rioters

By the 1740s, tensions ran high between colonial proprietors and squatters and between landlords and tenants in New Jersey. In essence, for almost 100 years the proprietors and landlords had lived on fortunes acquired from landownership and those who squatted on and rented their land. The latter were frustrated not only with their inability to purchase and produce on their own land, but with the economic and political barriers built by the empowered proprietors and landlords who did not wish to relinquish their land or control. When both the landowners and the colonial legislature ignored their grievances, rebel groups organized themselves to attack proprietors and landowners, as well as their property and the basis of their power. As Stock (1996) relates:

> In New Jersey . . . rebels pulled down the houses of tenants who cooperated with the proprietors and set barns and fields ablaze in midnight raids of terror. . . . When New Jersey proprietors began arresting squatters . . . the rebels took the law into their own hands. Samuel Baldwin was rescued by a crowd of 150 men reportedly armed "with clubbs, Axes, and Crow barrs." Each time a leader was jailed, larger and larger mobs gathered to free the man. . . . In one incident, the rioter was freed and the sheriff put in jail. . . . Between 1745 and 1748, the rioters' supporters in the assembly filibustered, allowing no laws to be passed to end the violence, while prominent rebel leaders began organizing as if they were the government of New Jersey. One leader, Amos Roberts, established his own judicial system, army, and system of tax collection. (pp. 27–29)

The South Carolina Regulators

In the 1760s, a similar rift developed between South Carolina's wealthy planters from the east coast and the small subsistence farmers of the backcountry who paid their taxes, but had no sheriffs, or courts, had to travel long distances to register land sales or deeds and to bring lawsuits for debts, and were not allowed to serve in the colonial legislature. Life on the frontier had not been easy and by 1767 many settlers were exhausted from fighting Indians as well as the crime associated with widespread drinking, gambling, and shooting matches. In November, a citizen militia arose to "regulate" affairs by burning cabins of known outlaws and those believed to harbor them, whipping and sometimes killing gang members and their families, and attacking and driving out of town "lewd" women, unfaithful husbands, neglectful fathers, and unproductive community members.

The movement was immediately popular in three South Carolina counties where the Regulator movement had the support of between 6,000 and 7,000 men out of the area's total white taxable population of 8,000 (Zinn 1995). The governor ordered the Regulators to disperse, but to no avail. Three factors brought an end to the Regulators by the end of the decade:

1. The Circuit Court Act of 1769 that provided for courts and magistrates in the South Carolina backcountry.
2. The opening of new lands in the trans-Appalachian frontier that gave poor men a chance to own their own farms.
3. The rise of a counterterrorist vigilante movement—the Moderators—who challenged regular violence with their own brand of flogging, kidnapping, and imprisonment.

The Green Mountain Boys

Just 15 years after the first Anglo-European settlement appeared in Vermont, three provincial governments and dozens of farmers were battling over its destiny. Although it had originally been part of the Massachusetts Bay Colony, King George II ruled in 1741 that all claims by Massachusetts in Vermont were invalid. Since New York and New Hampshire still claimed land in Vermont, an all-out struggle began between landlords, speculators, squatters, and small farmers. After the King upheld New York's claim to the land, many rural folks vowed they would never live under the system of landlords and proprietary titles, nor would they purchase land from New York speculators—land upon which they had been living for years.

In 1770, Ethan Allan, an army officer who had been building a farm near New Perth, created a citizen militia and government of his own. The Green Mountain Boys resisted the King's orders, ignored the power of the New York speculators and landowners, and created its own court and penal system. In addition,

> It attacked small farmers who honored the New York titles, replaced them with its own men, and in at least one case sacked an entire village. Likewise, the Green Mountain Boys emptied jails, closed courts backed by crowds as large as five hundred, and punished local officials who accepted the authority of the New York government. One man received two hundred lashes on his bare back as punishment for the crime of serving as a justice of the peace. (Stock 1996: 32)

When the Revolutionary War broke out, the Green Mountain Boys threw their lot with the patriots, as they would not back a king who had given their land to New York. After the war, the fear of an alliance with New York kept them from joining the new American government. Instead, they created an independent Republic of New Connecticut that the Continental Congress refused to recognize. It was not until 1791 that the people of Vermont felt confident that they could join the United States without being tied to New York.

Militias in Postrevolutionary and Nineteenth-Century America

After the Constitution was signed, patriot-militia activities were not eliminated. Indeed, while many militia supporters had backed the American Revolution, the Constitution's creation of a strong federal government was the antithesis of what they hoped would be the result of the revolution. Rather than keeping political, social, and economic power at the local level, the Constitution instead created a centralized federal system of government, strong federal courts proclaimed to be the supreme law of the land, and an armed federal militia that could be used to put down domestic unrest.

Patriot militias were created to protest what was believed to be overzealous federal legislation that threatened the local governance of frontier communities, and to challenge the elitist system of corporate management that exploited laboring men and women. Typical of such patriot-militia activities was Shay's Rebellion, the Whiskey Rebellion, and the Molly Maguires.

Shays' Rebellion

In the aftermath of the Revolutionary War, many Americans struggled with the political and economic consequences of independence. Beginning in 1786, many Massachusetts farmers faced bad harvests, a shortage of hard currency, deep debts, and heavy taxes. Many knew they could not pay their taxes and might face the loss of their farms or imprisonment. Furthermore, many were disenfranchised by the state's constitution that, in 1870, raised property qualifications for voting and holding state office.

Consequently, illegal conventions arose in some western counties to organize opposition to an unresponsive legislature. Simultaneously, a group of armed farmers and veterans of the Revolutionary War were organized by Luke Day–a veteran and former inhabitant of debtor's prison–to formally petition the county General Court. Day stood with 1,500 armed farmers in front of the General Court, forcing adjournment of the session. Similar militias in other counties set debtors free and forced more courts to adjourn.

Daniel Shays entered this politically charged atmosphere in 1786. Shays was a poor farm boy who joined the Continental Army, was wounded in action, and resigned in 1780 after he was not paid. Upon returning home, he found himself in court because he could not pay his debts. When Shays heard talk that Luke Day was going to be indicted for his militia activity, he organized 700 armed farmers, most of whom were war veterans, and marched with them to Springfield. Upon arrival, so many men joined his ranks that the judges were forced to postpone hearings for the day.

In Boston, the legislature passed a riot act and a resolution that suspended habeas corpus so that people could be kept in jail without trial. In protest, Shays began marching 1,000 men to Boston. Turned back by a blizzard, the militia was met by a private army funded by Boston merchants. Several battles ensued, Shays fled to Vermont, and many of the captured rebels were tried for treason. In one county, six were sentenced to death. In another case, 33 rebels stood trial and six were condemned to death. A few were pardoned–including Shays–while some were hung.

The Whiskey Rebellion

America's first secretary of the treasury, Alexander Hamilton, immediately set about to devise an innovative financial program to overcome the fiscal problems that had plagued the U.S. government under the Articles of Confederation. Beginning in 1789, he convinced Congress of the wisdom of passing a variety of domestic excise taxes, including a duty on spirits that were distilled in the United States. The tax–which required a 25 percent charge on all production and sale of liquor–subsequently raised the price and cut the demand for corn whiskey that farmers in western Pennsylvania had sold locally and bartered for eastern goods. For grain farmers, distilling was an essential home industry as their crops could rot prior to reaching market unless they were converted to whiskey.

Resistance to the tax grew as farmers challenged the authority of a distant government in the east. In 1794, a group known as the Whiskey Rebels began attacking tax collectors and refusing to pay their taxes. As President Washington's Cabinet members began hearing the news of the protest, some sympathized with the farmers and saw the rebellion as justified civil disobedience against harsh legislation. Others, led by Hamilton, saw the rebellion as a direct challenge to the federal authority of the new constitutional government. To him, the government's only choice was swift and effective military action against a dangerous faction of malcontents. His argument proved persuasive to the president who personally rode with an army of 13,000 men–a force larger than the one he commanded during the Revolutionary War–against the small, poorly armed rebels. As soon as the rebels saw the huge army march-

ing against them, they quickly dispersed and the rebellion was effectively terminated.[38]

The Molly Maguires

In the early to mid-1860s, large numbers of Irish, Welsh, and English immigrants began to work in Pennsylvania's Schuylkill County anthracite coal fields. In keeping with the social and economic traditions of England, the Irish received the lowest status and paying positions. Resentment soon festered among the Schuylkill Irish. In the 1840s, rumors began about a secret Irish society of coal miners who violently settled disputes with management and were vehemently opposed to being drafted into the Civil War. Between 1860 and 1862, over a dozen murders were attributed to this obscure organization that targeted capitalist mine owners whom the miners perceived were greatly exploiting their workers.

In late 1863, violence escalated in the mine region, violence attributed to what became known as the Molly Maguires–a group of armed men who blackened their faces during their attacks. The attacks included the deaths of four management-level men during a five-week period; the deaths of two mine superintendents along with 16 other mine-related murders that occurred between 1865 and 1866; and the deaths of five more managers, as well as six assaults and 27 robberies in 1867.

Between 1870 and 1874, violence again escalated as the debate between management and the miners' union about wages ended in two strikes–one in 1871 and another in 1875. Management, with the help of the state legislature, broke the strikes and the union, arguing that the real issue was a union that engaged in vigilantism. Three highly publi-

---

[38] After the Rebellion was crushed, about 2,000 distillers fled to Kentucky which was not yet a state and thus, not subject to the tax. There, they set up their stills and began their whiskey-making enterprises.

cized trials began in January 1876. Twenty men were tried, found guilty, and executed–thus putting an end to the Molly Maguires.

Patriot Militias: 1930s through the 1950s

During the Depression and the beginning of the New Deal, a few Americans continued to harbor grievances against the government. In addition, with the outbreak of World War II, several anti-Jewish organizations arose that emulated Hitler's political, social, and economic philosophies. While extremism was still alive and well in both urban and rural America, as well as scapegoating vigilantism as discussed earlier, only a few people formed organized patriot militias. Two of these examples are discussed next: the Farmer's Holiday Association and Fascist groups.

The Farmer's Holiday Association

Created in 1932 to take a "vacation" from marketing their goods, the Farmer's Holiday Association was a national organization of farmers who vehemently disagreed with two governmental policies: increasing national, versus local, control over their products; and increased evictions of farmers due to Depression foreclosures. Consequently, members took extreme measures by pledging not to sell any of their products below the cost of production and to take whatever action was necessary–violence included–to stop evictions and foreclosures. In so doing, they created small militia-like units of members who were involved in the following activities:

- In August 1932, farmers in Minnesota, Iowa, and the Dakotas set up roadblocks to keep farm products from markets. In at least five locations, violence erupted. In

Racine, Wisconsin, a farmer's son was shot with a .38-caliber bullet.
- February 1933, 1,000 farmers used force to stop a sheriff's sale at a North Dakota farm in Finley. Two weeks later in Minot, a similar forceful demonstration occurred (Corcoran 1990).
- In Le Mars, Iowa, an armed group of farmers kidnapped a local judge, beat him, and threatened to kill him if he didn't sign a pledge not to foreclose on any more property. "They led him out of town, tied him, blindfolded him, and beat him, threatening to kill him" (Stock 1996: 83).

Fascist Groups

According to Stock (1996), more than 120 fascist organizations existed in the United States during the 1930s and 1940s. Based in both urban and rural America, these groups believed that the New Deal was part of a Jewish conspiracy to overthrow the American government. Some also believed that a paramilitary counteroffensive against the government could prevent the United States from entering World War II.

Two of the best-known fascist leaders during this time were William Dudley Pelley and Gerald B. Winrod. Their shared beliefs shaped the growing fascist movement:

- America was plagued by a moral decay that was the product of urbanization and immigration.
- The New Deal constricted the independence of American farmers and small businessmen, championed labor organizations, funded lewd art projects, recognized the Soviet Union, and repealed Prohibition.
- The Roosevelt administration had given too much power to the Jews.
- Rural America was the only real America and the men and women who lived on farms were the only real Americans.

While neither man was ever accused of an act of political violence, their anti-Semite and anti-communist rhetoric encouraged vigilante tactics. Furthermore, both men organized small fascist-fueled patriot militias.

- Pelley organized the Silver Legion, which later became known as the Silver Shirts. Members dressed in special military hats, shirts, and pants that resembled those of Hitler's elite SS forces; followed elaborate rituals; and regularly marched in military-style musters. In several midwestern cities, Silver Shirts threatened, harassed, and attacked Jews.
- Winrod founded the Defenders of the Christian Faith, which at one time had 150,000 members. One of its primary beliefs was that the Nazis were entirely justified in their attacks on the Jews.

In 1958, the first organized neo-Nazi group appeared in the United States—the American Nazi Party founded by George Lincoln Rockwell. Rockwell took three specific paths to widen the appeal of Nazism for an American audience:

1. He coined and popularized the term "white power." He then broadened the idea of a master race from the narrow German concept of the Aryan master race to include people from white, working class, immigrant homes. Rockwell understood the power involved in telling young people who were emotionally insecure as well as those who had normal teenage problems that they could be members of a master race.
2. He distanced his brand of Nazism from the murder of millions of Jews by building the Holocaust denial myth that has since become the central belief of modern neo-Nazis.
3. He divorced Nazism from atheism because he believed that nothing motivated Amer-

icans more than a religious experience. He eventually linked his neo-Nazi movement directly to the slowly evolving Christian Identity theology. (See Chapter 4.)

LEFT-WING EXTREMISM AND TERRORISM

In the late 1950s, a great spirit of unrest arose among many American youth who were increasingly dissatisfied with the U.S. government. Some were college educated, and most were well-versed in left-wing socialist and anarchist thought. As the trauma of the Cold War, the McCarthy era, and American involvement in Vietnam unfolded within the domestic landscape, a few of these young people began to advocate for a revolutionary overthrow of the American system of government. In so doing, they became left-wing extremists and sometimes they stepped over the ideological threshold into terrorism.

As we learned in Chapter 1, left-wing extremists are those who profess views to reform or overthrow the established governmental order in the name of the greater freedom or well-being of the common man. Most prominent among these advocates were the Students for a Democratic Society, their splinter group the Weather Underground, and the Black Panthers.

The Students for a Democratic Society and the Weather Underground

Like many movements of the 1950s and 1960s, the Weather Underground was not born overnight. Instead, it evolved slowly, beginning in the late 1950s when a small but vocal group of students peacefully began protesting several political issues, thereby forming the nucleus of the Students for a Democratic Society (SDS). Founded in 1959 as a revival of an older Socialist educational organization called the Student League of Industrial Democracy, the original SDS sought to promote greater active participation of American students through the resolution of current problems: poverty, unemployment, racism, campus injustice, and free speech. Their target for criticism was "the Establishment"–especially the federal, state, and local government power structure–and the university's paternalism.

Early SDS activists held intellectual discussions and meetings, wrote and distributed position papers to college campuses around the nation, and worked to recruit new members. As a contemporary participant observed, SDS activists were not terrorists; rather, they committed

> acts whose primary motive is to demonstrate and express where the student stands. . . . What unites these demonstrations is not a coherent ideology of protest or reform, much less an organized political group, but a personal sense of ethical obligation to take a visible stand against injustice or oppression. (Keniston 1971: 118)

The SDS took its first well-publicized political stance in 1962 when forty-five supporters issued the "Port Huron Statement" calling for an alliance of Blacks, students, peace groups, and liberal organizations to bring about a "progressive realignment" of the Democratic Party. After President Kennedy's assassination and with America's growing commitment to Vietnam, SDS interest in the antiwar movement heightened. In January 1965, 25,000 U.S. troops were stationed in Vietnam and were actively fighting in the War. In protest, on April 17, 1965, the SDS sponsored the first national demonstration against the war in which "massive civil disobedience" was used (Kohn 1986: 76).

By 1966, U.S. forces had increased to 184,000. In protest, SDS members and thousands of sympathizers peacefully picketed, marched, and burned draft cards in communities across the nation. Until late 1967, most anti-draft and anti-government SDS efforts were peaceful. This approach changed between October 16–22, 1967, during "Stop the Draft Week" when student leadership passed from nonviolent proponents into the hands of militant activists who claimed the right to self-defense and take the offensive against the enemy.

The factors that contributed to such a radical change were simple: many white militants were fed up with "too little, too late"; and some student leaders had become radicalized by the failure of the American government to listen to their peaceful pleas for change and peace. Thus, as the war escalated, so did the discontent and the violence:

- In 1968, violence broke out at Columbia University and at the Democratic National Convention in Chicago.
- In 1969, violent confrontations occurred between students and police over campus military and corporate recruiting activities, the Vietnam War, and university policies.
- In May 1970, the violence turned deadly when a large wave of protests occurred in reaction to the U.S. and South Vietnamese invasion of Cambodia: activists at Kent State University in Ohio set the ROTC building on fire and two days later, National Guardsmen fired into a crowd of jeering students, killing four and wounding nine. By May 10th, at least 448 campuses reported they had either been affected by strikes or had been forced to close down (Gurr 1989).

Subsequently, student protesters gained more media coverage, and the most visible symbol of violent protest–the SDS–became

America's best-known radical group, feared by both the police and the Establishment. Its membership grew and with such growth came new factions and philosophical splits. At the 1969 SDS Convention in Chicago, a dispute arose between those SDS members advocating more militancy and those advocating less. Eleven of the most militant members formed a new group–the Weathermen–who were dedicated to the concept of a revolution that could only be accomplished through terror. In their 16,000-word programmatic thesis, "You Don't Need a Weatherman to Know Which Way the Wind Blows," the Weathermen required that its members:

- Prepare for a major international struggle that opposed U.S. imperialism, chauvinism, and racism. Working-class whites must work in a supportive capacity to aid "America's black colony with guerrilla warfare."
- Plan for a militant, armed struggle that would inflict material damage to imperialist and racist institutions by whatever means possible.
- Create a mass base of working-class, non-student support–"the first revolutionary street gang in history"–comprising alienated, disenfranchised, and oppressed youth to operate a worldwide war against the American empire.

The Weathermen were very clear about using terror: because members were unable to accept the state as it was, they must resist with violence and terrorism. Destruction, to Weathermen, was an act of *positive* resistance. Their first nationally organized instrument of destruction, the "Days of Rage" held during October 8–11, 1969, in Chicago, was designed to put the Establishment "up against the wall" through a widely supported, well-attended antiwar demonstration in which armed conflict with the police was inevitable. During the four days, only about 200 sup-

porters gathered to fight the Establishment, which resulted in millions of dollars in property damage, scores of injured policemen, and the arrest of 68 Weathermen.

At their National War Council Meeting in December 1969, leaders decided they would neither raise bail money, nor appear at trials. Instead, they went underground and changed their name to the Weather Underground. On May 25, 1970, the Underground released its first communiqué to the *New York Times,* stating its revolutionary intentions:

> Ever since SDS became revolutionary, we've been trying to show how it is possible to overcome the frustration and impotence that comes from trying to reform this system. Kids know the lines are drawn; revolution is touching all of our lives. Tens of thousands have learned that protest and marches don't do it. Revolutionary violence is the only way.

Revolution against the Establishment and "the pigs" was declared and the Underground promised that "within the next 14 days we will attack a symbol or institution of American justice." On June 9th, the New York Police building was bombed. Between 1970 and 1972, the Underground carried out several dozen bombings and other violent actions, all of which were claimed and identified in the Underground's 1974 publication, *Prairie Fire.*

From 1974 through 1981, the Underground was not active above ground. Many of its members were wanted in connection with bombings during the 1970s, but they eluded capture. However, on October 20, 1981, the Underground again emerged as members robbed a Brink's armored truck, seized $1.6 million, and killed two policemen at the Nanuet National Bank near Nyack, New York. A massive police investigation soon indicated the involvement of well-known Underground members Kathy Boudin, Judy Clark, Donald Weems, and

David Gilbert, as well as several others. In 1982, ten indictments were handed down: five suspects were involved in a two-year trial; the remaining five are still fugitives— Herald Wayne Williams, Marilyn Buck, Susan Rosenburg, Dr. Alan Berkman, and Cheri Laverne Dalton. Of those who were on trial, Weems, Clark, and Gilbert claimed they were "prisoners of war" and the court had no right to try them; they received 75 years to life for the robbery and three murders. Sam Brown got the same sentence. Kathy Boudin, one of the groups' most vocal and active members, was allowed to plead guilty in return for a 20-year-to-life sentence, even though she refused to give information about other co-conspirators who had escaped.

Little was heard from the Underground for two years after the trial. Then, in August 1986, the FBI announced that 50 pounds of explosives, blasting caps, and a detonating cord had been found in a Santa Fe Springs rental storage space that was linked to six suspected terrorists, all members of the Underground. As of this writing, the six members were being sought in purported plots to disrupt the 1984 Summer Olympics and to break a Puerto Rican nationalist out of federal prison.

The Black Panthers: Terrorism from Above and Below

In 1963, a handful of black-power advocates were tired of waiting for freedom, fed-up with nonviolent tactics that did not bring justice and equality, and turned off by a political system that institutionalized racism and perpetuated exploitation of Blacks. The Black Panther Party (BPP) differed from previous black activists primarily because they actively enlisted poor black people in a revolutionary battle of self-defense.[39] Cofounders Huey Newton and Bobby Seale quickly began to educate their followers in revolutionary theories.

> We read the work of Franz Fanon, particularly *The Wretched of the Earth,* the four volumes of Chairman Mao Tse-Tung, and Che Gueverra's *Guerrilla Warfare. . . .* We read these men's works because we saw them as kinsmen; the oppressor who had controlled them was controlling us, both directly and indirectly. We believed it was necessary to know how they gained their freedom in order to go about getting ours. However, we did not want merely to import ideas and strategies; we had to transform what we learned into principles and methods acceptable to the brothers on the block. (Newton 1973: 123)

The Panthers sought to overthrow the existing American social order, a social order that was reinforced by an almost all-white police force that the BPP felt was a terroristic symbol of an oppressive and repressive government. Initially, BPP methods for achieving their goals were not terroristic; in fact, many members wanted to stay within legal boundaries until conditions were ripe for revolution. The idea was,

> As long as we kept everything legal, the police could do nothing, and the people would see that armed defense was a legitimate, constitutional right. In this way, they would lose their doubts and fears and be able to move against their oppressor. (Newton 1973: 136)

Accordingly, one of the BPP's initial endeavors was to use armed patrols of black men to protest the presence and activities of the police and observe police conduct in black communities. If the police were en-

[39] Initially, the BPP was called The Black Panther Party for Self Defense, thus emphasizing the survivalist goals of the organization. In 1964, "for Self Defense" was removed from the title.

gaged in conduct that the BPP found objectionable, the Panthers confronted the officers and advised the person of their legal rights.[40]

The BPP soon expanded its endeavors into the educational and service arenas, guided by the philosophies of a ten-part program for freedom and empowerment.

> We want freedom. We want power to determine the destiny of our Black Community. We want full employment for our people. We want an end to the robbery by the white man of our Black Community. We want decent housing, fit for the shelter of human beings. We want education for our people that exposes the true nature of this decadent American society. We want education that teaches us our true history and our role in the present-day society. We want all black men to be exempt from military service. We want an immediate end to police brutality and murder of black people. We want freedom for all black men held in federal, state, county and city prisons and jails. We want all black people when brought to trial to be tried in court by a jury of their peer group or people from their black communities, as defined by the Constitution of the United States. We want land, bread, housing, education, clothing, justice, and peace. (www.afrom.org/history/panthers/10point.html)

Soon, however, tactics became more terroristic as Panthers became engaged in shootouts with the police, hence the famous phrase, "Off the Pig!" Within a short time, the BPP had adopted an urban guerrilla-warfare campaign consisting of rooftop snipings, midnight ambushes, and mass shoot-outs. Among their earliest actions were the following:

- May 1967, a contingent of Panthers burst into a California legislative session armed with shotguns and rifles, to prove their right to bear arms in self-defense.

- April 1968, when two armed policemen in Oakland approached Panther members in their cars, Panthers shot first; a 90-minute battle ensued in which three policemen were killed, Eldridge Cleaver was wounded, and seven others arrested. Cleaver was indicted, released on bail, and fled the country, finding political asylum in Algeria.

- In 1969 at Cornell University, armed black students, responding to a threat by armed white students, seized a university building and held it for several days. Similar actions were repeated on campuses across the nation.

- In December 1969, 14 Chicago policemen stormed Illinois's Panther Chairman's apartment at 5:00 A.M. with a search warrant for illegal weapons; they were greeted with a shotgun blast, and police fired between 83 and 99 bullets in response.

By early 1970, the *Wall Street Journal, Time Magazine,* and an independent poll conducted for ABC-TV in several large American cities found a "a surprising level of support within the black community" (Richardson 1993: 6–9). It has been variously estimated that by late 1968, the BPP had 5,000 active members and thousands of supporters from across the nation (Marable 1984). A secret FBI report to President Nixon in 1970 reported that "a recent poll indicates that approximately 25 percent of the black population has great respect for the Black Panther Party, including 45 percent of blacks under 21 years of age" (Zinn 1990: 455).

By mid-1971, the Panthers had divided into two factions, one headed by Huey Newton and another by Eldridge Cleaver. Cleaver's faction became known as the Black Liberation Army (BLA), whose more militant members were allegedly responsible for several police killings in New York and San

---

[40] Until the 1970s in California, persons could legally carry a weapon as long as it was not concealed.

Francisco, as well as several armed robberies. By late 1973, police believed that most BLA members were either imprisoned or had been killed in police shoot-outs; no BLA organizational activities have since been reported. Newton's faction took over the largest number of BPP members and created a new image for the Panthers, one of gradualism rather than extremism. By the late 1970s, the Panthers were known as peaceful agitators. Ten years later, the few known and active Panthers operated a shoe distribution program, an extermination service, and several health care clinics in Oakland.[41]

EXTREMISTS, TERRORISTS, AND LAW ENFORCEMENT RESPONSES: YESTERDAY AND TODAY

These case studies reinforce one of the primary themes of this chapter–that contemporary terrorists have a great deal in common with their historical counterparts. Indeed, the grievances that fueled historical vigilantism are still alive and lurking in the minds of more than a few American "patriots." For instance, the scapegoating vigilante terrorists of yesterday and today:

- targeted and still target people who are different, or who are perceived as being different, from the community status quo; and
- perpetrated and still perpetrate violent actions that have been and still are fueled by fear, intolerance, and hatred of those who are racially, ethnically, and spiritually different from white, Anglo-Protestant Americans.

In addition, the patriot-militia terrorists of yesterday and today:

- targeted and still target the empowered who are perceived to be withholding rights and services, irresponsibly enforcing laws, levying unjust taxes, and exploiting poor, white people; and
- perpetrated and still perpetrate violent actions that have been and still are fueled by the anger of politically, economically, and socially unempowered people who seek to change, balance, or overthrow those in power and replace the system with a more responsive and representative government.

But there are also some definite differences–differences that are evolutionary rather than revolutionary in nature. For instance, until the 1970s, most of the scapegoating and patriot-militia groups remained dedicated to their singular goal–they wished to either retain the political, social, spiritual, and/or economic status quo as defined primarily by white, Protestant Americans; or they wished to change or overthrow the policies and procedures of unrepresentative government, landowning, and capitalist officials.

However, as Part Two will illustrate, over the past twenty years, some of these groups have come together to form a common agenda with a common enemy. Many have combined their extreme racist beliefs typical of historical scapegoating, with the beliefs typical of historical patriot militias–that the government is dominated by persons who do not listen to the needs of the "real" American people. Thus, the common enemy for many of today's political extremists and terrorists has become the U.S. government and its various representatives.

---

[41] For more information from a first-hand, retrospective view of former Black Panther Party members, see Elaine Brown, *A Taste of Power: A Black Woman's Story* (New York: Pantheon, 1993); and Earl Anthony and David Hilliard, *This Side of Glory* (Boston: Little, Brown, 1993).

However, even this is not a radical departure from the past. Indeed, as the left-wing case studies on the Weather Underground and the Black Panthers illustrated, the U.S. government always was the primary target of their extremist ideologies and terroristic activity.

In the cases of both left-wing and right-wing terrorism, all too often, the specific governmental representative targeted by contemporary terrorist groups has been the local law enforcer. If we again dig deep into the roots of American history, we can better understand why. Indeed, as policing became more professionalized through the years, law enforcers played different roles with the two types of vigilante and left-wing terrorists.

Throughout the eighteenth and nineteenth centuries, when law enforcement agencies were gradually evolving, one of the most important goals of the police was to enforce the community status quo. In most cases, this meant either ignoring, and in some instances, actually supporting, scapegoating vigilantism. Indeed, without either the toleration or support of law enforcement, vigilantism would not have been as all-pervasive. For example, in the late 1700s many southern cities developed uniformed, armed, and paid municipal police forces to deal specifically with slave control and the suppression of slave rebellion. The primary responsibility of these urban police officers was to enforce the racist status quo. Charleston, Virginia, was the first to establish such a force in 1783; Savannah followed in 1796; Richmond in 1801; and New Orleans in 1805.

In his study of the New Orleans Police Force, historian Dennis C. Rousey (1996) illustrates how such racism prompted the creation of a modern police force. He contends that the majority of nineteenth-century police reforms were motivated by racism, ethnic prejudice, and a disruptive party spirit—especially during the 1850s when the Know Nothings were in power. The Know Nothings systematically stripped the police force of the majority of its immigrant officers and replaced them with officers sympathetic to their anti-immigrant, anti-Catholic cause. Thereafter, police were often used to intimidate ethnic voters and to perpetrate violence against those who challenged such intimidation.

The elected mayor of New Orleans in 1858, Gerad Stith, a Know Nothing, candidly announced his views about the political role of the police: "The force is to be constituted of men favorable to the principles which are professed by the American Party" (as quoted in Rousey 1996: 79). Rousey also claims that this struggle between the Know Nothings and the local democrats in most American cities of the 1850s led not only to an incredible amount of vigilante-type violence, but also to the loss of many immigrant police jobs (Rousey 1996).

However, while law enforcers were instrumental in either tolerating or supporting some racial extremism of scapegoating vigilantes, their role with patriot militias and left-wing radicals was quite the opposite. During colonial times as well as the first several decades of the New Republic, special militias were put together by colonial legislatures to suppress patriot militias with governmental violence. With the growth of urban police departments in the early to mid-1800s, it then became the job of law enforcement agencies to actively enforce the law and suppress any militia activity.

This role persisted throughout much of the twentieth century. Thus, clear into the 1980s, we saw law enforcers who, at worst, were active in the KKK groups and at best, were sympathetic to the cause and failed to suppress their terroristic exploits. In contrast, law enforcers—often at the behest of the FBI—were expected to crack down hard on those who had organized left-wing groups like the Weather Underground and the Black Panthers, as well as right-wing patriot militias.

This mixed legacy of law enforcers supporting one group of vigilante terrorists while actively suppressing other groups of patriot militias and left-wing radicals has served as ammunition for many of today's terrorists. Some of them see law enforcement as the historical enemy; others lament the passing of bygone days when law enforcers were the Klan. Thus, current anti-law enforcement attitudes are another example of the evolutionary rather than revolutionary attitudes of contemporary terrorists.

SUMMARY

1. Terrorism from below is as "American as apple pie" and as such, has been an evolutionary rather than a revolutionary part of American history. Indeed, contemporary terrorists have a great deal in common with their historical counterparts. An analysis of the ideologies, goals, and actions of early American extremists and terrorists illustrates that they are not a new breed of political activist, but rather, are the historical outgrowth of the vigilante tradition that has been an integral part of American society from colonial times to the present.

2. European colonists who immigrated to North America in the sixteenth and seventeenth centuries often resorted to political mob violence as a justifiable mode for expressing their political, social, and economic grievances.

3. As the American frontier moved westward, many frontier families who were faced with life-threatening situations became "rural radicals" who developed a series of extremist beliefs that became the central core of their lives: strong, self-defensive communities were necessary to conquer the physical hardships of colonial life; independent landownership comprised the basis for strong, self-defensive communities; bigness—especially big business and big landowners—threatened the fabric of rural life; government must be controlled at the local level, not at the state or federal level; white control over the land was not only essential to political, social, and economic progress, but was preordained by God; families were to be governed by traditional patriarchal relationships; Christianity—especially Protestantism—was the one true faith; government rule should act in the best interests and reflect the views of all white people, not just a select few who were empowered; and if the people legally expressed their political, social, and economic grievances to those in power, and such legal grievances failed to bring about change, then mob action was justified in order to restore liberty.

4. Some colonists—and later on, Americans—stepped over the line from extremism and into the sphere of political violence. In so doing, they became terrorists. During the first 350 years of American history, such terrorist activities can be divided into three categories: scapegoating vigilantism, patriot militias, and left-wing terrorists.

5. The "revolution" today's extremist and terrorist groups claim to support is not radical. Rather, it seeks a return to a bygone era of simplicity and clear definitions of authority. Most contemporary extremists wish to restore America to the land it was at its birth—a land ruled by empowered white Christian men; a land in which there was no federal income tax, no guarantees of freedom for persons of color, and no women's suffrage; and a land ruled by the first ten amendments of the Constitution. Such dreams are hardly radical; they compose the political, economic, and ideological foundations of our nation.

6. Law enforcers have a mixed legacy of involvement with early terrorism. Historical-

ly, law enforcers have supported the activities and goals of one group of vigilante terrorists–scapegoating vigilantes–but have been expected to actively suppress the other group–patriot militias, as well as left-wing radicals. Such actions have served as ammunition for many of today's terrorists who either see law enforcement as the historical enemy, or lament the end of law enforcement support of vigilantism designed to protect the status quo.

DISCUSSION QUESTIONS

1. Explain how well you think this chapter has supported its central thesis–that terrorism from below is as "American as apple pie?" If you do not feel this thesis has been adequately supported, how do you think it could be strengthened?
2. Do you think all vigilante activity in America has been terroristic in intent and action? Explain.
3. Why are the beliefs of frontier families explained by Catherine McNichol Stock considered to be extremist? Are they extremist by historical standards or by contemporary standards? Both? Neither?
4. Do you agree or disagree with the conclusion that those who accused persons of witchcraft in colonial America were among the country's first terrorists? Why or why not?
5. It has been argued that the forcible relocation of 110,000 Japanese into camps during World War II was one of the worst examples of terrorism from above. Would you agree or disagree with the thesis that relocation was also the culmination of decades of anti-Asian, especially anti-Japanese, terrorism from below throughout the west coast? Be sure to back up your answer with facts and figures.

6. Richard Drake's (1989) study of the Italian terrorist group, the Red Brigades, ends with a chilling assessment: that "left- and right-wing radicals could exist in such threatening numbers suggests, at the very least, some serious limitations in Italy's political structures . . . recent reverses [in Italian political life] have eliminated neither the social factors that permitted terrorist groups to become a major force in Italian life nor the cultural legacy that has disposed Italian revolutionaries to embrace political violence in the way they have" (p. 65). Do you believe his assessment is applicable to the Weather Underground–that is, that the factors of American political life have not eliminated the political or cultural problems that gave rise to the Underground's terrorism? Why or why not?

STUDY QUESTIONS

1. The video *Rosewood,* which is available for rent from your local video store, deals with an infamous incident of vigilante violence during which a white mob destroyed the black settlement of Rosewood, Florida, in 1923. After watching the video, use the Internet to discover the most recent community and court actions in terms of reparation for the destruction of the town and its people. (http://www.freenet.scri.fsu.edu/eoc/rosewood.txt9/98) Write a brief summary of your findings and conclude with a statement about whether or not the actions at Rosewood, in your opinion, were acts of vigilante-style terrorism. Then, critique the movie in terms of its accuracy as well as its portrayal of an actual terrorist incident.
2. The four case studies discussed in the first part of this chapter are but a few historical examples of scapegoating vigilantism.

Conduct some research about other historical examples of American terrorism from below. Select a particular incident of scapegoating vigilantism and then write your own case study. Be sure to explain the historical background for its growth, the goals and actions of those involved in terrorism, and the consequences on the victims.

3. The case studies discussed in the second part of this chapter are a few historical examples of patriot militias. Conduct some research about other historical examples of American terrorism from below. Select a particular militia movement and then write your own case study. Be sure to explain the historical background for its growth, the goals and actions of those involved in terrorism, and the consequences on the victims.

4. Anti-Catholicism in the United States is deeply tied to anti-Irish thoughts and deeds. Explore the historical foundations of scapegoating vigilantism committed against the Irish. Write a case study about how the Irish fared in America at the hands of those who hated and feared them. How did victimization affect the Irish people in general? Are the Irish still subject to vigilante tactics today? Why or why not?

5. Locate a copy of the video, *A Family Gathering,* originally shown by the Public Broadcasting System in the early 1990s. This story follows the life of the Yasui family that originally settled in Hood River, Oregon, in 1908 and is based on the family's biography by Lauren Kessler, *Stubborn Twig.* Using the video, the book, or both as a reference, determine whether the experiences of three generations of the Yasui family in America included being victims of terrorism from below and/or terrorism from above.

6. In times of war, Americans have questioned the loyalty of immigrants from an enemy nation—and sometimes they have made such persons victims of terrorism. This was clearly the case with Japanese internment during World War II. With the onset of World War I, many Americans were concerned about the loyalty of German Americans. Using at least two sources, trace the rise of anti-German legislation and vigilante activities that occurred in the United States throughout World War I.

7. By the mid-1970s, left-wing ideologies as well as support for terrorism had lost a great deal of popularity among American youth. Using at least two outside sources, research possible reasons why young people turned away from such beliefs and actions.

8. The movie *Catherine* was a hit in the late 1970s when it featured a "poor little rich girl" who turned to terrorism. After viewing this film, answer the following: Do you think it was based on a real-life story? If so, whose life and what group? How accurate is this story in terms of the involvement of young people in terrorism during the 1960s and 1970s? What did you learn from the film that would help you to better understand left-wing terrorism during the period under study?

9. Rent the recent movie *Panthers.* After viewing this film, compare it with what you have learned in the book about the Black Panthers, as well as at least one other written source about the Black Panthers Party. How accurate is the portrayal of the Panthers? How might it have been improved to include greater accuracy?

REFERENCES

Anthony, Earl and Hilliard, David: *This Side of Glory.* Boston: Little, Brown, 1993.

Bennett, David H.: *The Party of Fear: From Nativist Movements to the New Right in American History.* Chapel Hill: University of North Carolina Press, 1988.

Bloom, Jack M.: *Class, Race, and the Civil Rights Movement.* Bloomington, IN: Indiana University Press, 1987.

Boyer, Paul, and Nissenbaum, Stephen: *Salem Possessed: The Social Origins of Witchcraft.* Cambridge: Harvard University Press, 1974.

Brown, Elaine: *A Taste of Power: A Black Woman's Story.* New York: Pantheon, 1993.

Brown, Richard Maxwell: *Strains of Violence: Historical Studies of American Violence and Vigilantism.* New York: Oxford University Press, 1975.

Bullard, Sara (Ed.): *The Ku Klux Klan: A History of Racism and Violence,* 4th ed. Montgomery: Southern Poverty Law Center, 1991.

Chalmers, David M.: *Hooded Americanism: The History of the Ku Klux Klan,* 3rd ed. Durham: Duke University Press, 1981.

Coates, James: *Armed and Dangerous: The Rise of the Survivalist Right.* New York: Hill and Wang, 1987.

Cook, Adrian: *The Armies of the Streets: The New York City Draft Riots of 1863.* Lexington: The University of Kentucky Press, 1974.

Corcoran, James: *Bitter Harvest, Gordon Kahl and the Posse Comitatus: Murder in the Heartland.* New York: Penguin, 1990.

Dahlke, H. Otto: Race and minority riots—a study in the typology of violence. *Social Forces, 30,* 1952: 419–425.

Demos, John: *Underlying Themes in the Witchcraft of 17th Century New England.* Washington, DC: American Historical Association, 1970.

Drake, Richard: *The Revolutionary Mystique and Terrorism in Contemporary Italy.* Bloomington, IN: Indiana University Press, 1989.

Feagin, Joe R., and Hahn, Harlan: *Ghetto Revolts: The Politics of Violence in American Cities.* New York: Macmillan, 1973.

Gilje, Paul A.: *The Road to Mobocracy: Popular Disorder in New York City, 1793-1834.* Chapel Hill: The University of North Carolina Press, 1987.

Gurr, Ted Robert (Ed.): *Violence in America: Protest, Rebellion, Reform,* Vol. 2. Beverly Hills: Sage, 1989.

Headley, Joel T.: *Pen and Pencil Sketches of the Great Riots.* New York: E. B. Trent, 1882.

Janowitz, Morris: *The Last Half-Century: Societal Change and Politics in America.* Chicago: University of Chicago Press, 1976.

Keniston, Kenneth: *Youth and Dissent: The Rise of a New Opposition.* New York: Harcourt Brace Jovanovich, 1971.

Kessler, Lauren: *Stubborn Twig: Three Generations in the Life of a Japanese American Family.* New York: Penguin, 1993.

Kohn, Stephen M.: *Jailed for Peace: The History of American Draft Law Violators, 1658-1985.* Westport: Greenwood, 1986.

Loewen, James W.: *Lies My Teacher Told Me: Everything Your American History Textbook Got Wrong.* New York: The New Press, 1995.

Lyman, Stanford M.: Strangers in the cities. In Wollenberg, Charles (Ed.): *Ethnic Conflict in California History.* Santa Monica: Tinnon-Brown, 1970, pp. 70–82.

Marable, Manning: *Race, Reform and Rebellion: The Second Reconstruction in Black America.* Jackson: University of Mississippi Press, 1984.

Morris, Aldon D.: *The Origins of the Civil Rights Movement: Black Communities Organizing for Change.* New York: Free Press, 1984.

National Advisory Commission on Civil Disorders: *Report of the National Advisory Commission on Civil Disorders.* Washington, DC: U.S. Government Printing Office, 1968.

Newton, Huey: *Revolutionary Suicide.* New York: Ballantine, 1973.

Olson, James S.: *Ethnic Dimensions in American History.* New York: St. Martin's Press, 1994.

Richardson, Edwina: The FBI's Role in the Destruction of the Black Panther Party. Paper presented at the Annual Meeting of the American Society of Criminology. Phoenix, AZ, October 1993.

Rousey, Dennis C.: *Policing the Southern City: New Orleans, 1805-1889.* Baton Rouge: Louisiana State University Press, 1996.

Sellars, Cleveland: *River of No Return.* New York: William Morrow, 1973.

Stannard, David E.: *American Holocaust: Columbus and the Conquest of the New World.* New York: Oxford University Press, 1992.

Stock, Catherine McNichol: *Rural Radicals: Righteous Rage in the American Grain.* Ithaca, NY: Cornell University Press, 1996.

Wade, Wyn Craig: *The Fiery Cross: The Ku Klux Klan in America.* New York: Simon & Schuster, 1987.

Weather Underground Organization: *Prairie Fire: The Politics of Revolutionary Anti-Imperialism.* San Francisco, CA: Communications Company, 1974.

Werner, John M.: Race riots in the United States during the age of Jackson, 1824–1849. Ph.D. dissertation, Indiana University, 1972.

Zinn, Howard: *A People's History of the United States, 1492–Present.* New York: Harper Collins, 1995.

Part Two

CONTEMPORARY DOMESTIC TERRORISM

Miki Vohryzek-Bolden

As Part One illustrated, not only does domestic terrorism present itself in a myriad of forms in the United States, but terrorists display different motives and justifications. In light of the World Trade Center Bombing in New York City in February 1993, the bombing of the Alfred P. Murrah Federal Building in Oklahoma City in April 1995, and the more recent series of anthrax scares in the Los Angeles region in 1998, domestic terrorism continues to be a topic of macabre fascination. No longer are Americans witnesses to acts of terrorism—we are increasingly becoming victims of terrorism on American soil. Terrorism's unpredictability and randomness make it virtually impossible for our government to protect all potential sites and all potential victims.

As a society, we are becoming more vulnerable to acts of terrorism. As Bruce Hoffman (1986) notes, "we should not be lulled into thinking that the United States is either immune to violence from political extremists within our own borders or that the terrorist acts which occur here do not warrant attention" (p. 4).

To enhance our reader's ability to analyze terrorism, Part Two presents terrorist groups in three main categories: hate-motivated, patriot-militia right-wing, and special-interest groups. Such categorization recognizes that while there are subcategories within the main groups and each organization will not have all of the same characteristics as the other groups, there can be ideological overlap between the groups in terms of their beliefs.

Chapter 4 focuses on hate-motivated and patriot and militia groups. Chapter 5 discusses the emergence of special-interest extremist and terrorist groups that advocate violence based on an ideology or belief, such as ecological resistance groups, the anti-environmental movement, and animal rights and anti-abortion activists. Chapter 6 presents selected case studies designed to illustrate the range of political extremist and terrorist events in the United States during contemporary times. Chapter 7 describes the changing character of domestic terrorism in terms of the groups involved and the terrorists' use of specific tools and tactics.

Chapter 4

THE AMERICAN HATE AND PATRIOT–MILITIA MOVEMENTS

By the 1980s, the influence of left-wing extremists and terrorists had dramatically decreased. As such, it was a relatively short-lived experience in the United States. Smith (1994) suggests that when American terrorism reached its peak in the mid-1980s, the government had improved its counterterrorist tactics and its arrest procedures enough to contribute to the decimation of a number of left-wing groups. At the same time, however, right-wing ideologies gained a great deal of popularity among many American extremists. Thus, for the last twenty years, domestic terrorism has been perpetrated for the most part by right-wing terrorist groups (Smith 1994).

As stated in Chapter 1, right-wing extremists are those who profess views in opposition to change in the established governmental order, or who wish to ensure that traditional attitudes and practices are restored to the established governmental order, and/or who advocate the forced establishment of an authoritarian political order. Theirs is considered to be a conservative, traditional position that advocates for keeping or returning to the status quo, as opposed to left-wing extremists who have a radical political position that advocates for extreme political change.

As Chapter 3 illustrates, the United States has always had far-right groups with political agendas and hateful ideologies. Stern (1996) notes that although such groups are new in many ways, they adhere to a philosophy that has its roots in other American far-right foundations over the last 100 years and beyond–that government has been taken over by unseen interests plotting to enslave ordinary Americans. Thus, it is our belief that the United States will continue to be vulnerable to acts of terrorism by right-wing groups.

The Intelligence Project of the Southern Poverty Law Center (SPLC) indicated that 457 hate groups and group chapters actively operated in the United States in 1999. At the same time, hate groups operated 305 Internet sites that sent hate-motivated messages around the world. Additionally, the SPLC reported 217 active "patriot" groups in the United States, as well as 263 Internet sites linked to such groups (SPLC 2000).

Part of the increase over the years is due to the addition of local chapters of organizations, and not necessarily the creation of new groups. We also believe that this number is not static and will vary each year. Thus, readers are encouraged to review currently available documents to examine trends in the creation, organization, and deployment of domestic terrorist groups. Finally, while we recognize the presence of all these right-wing groups, we focus our discussion on the major hate-motivated and patriot groups operating in the United States in the 1990s.

HATE-MOTIVATED GROUPS

The American hate movement comprises three distinct yet interrelated philosophical underpinnings: white supremacy, other racial-religious orientations, and black separatism. The organizations represented in each of these three groups include:

1. White supremacist movement: various KKK splinter groups; National Alliance; Neo-Nazis; Neo-Nazi Skinheads; and Christian Identity. The Christian Identity movement includes the Phineas Brotherhood; Posse Comitatus; Aryan Nations; The Order; Aryan Brotherhood; and The Covenant, the Sword and the Arm of the Lord.
2. Other racial-religious groups: World Church of the Creator; White Aryan Resistance; and Odinism.
3. Black separatist groups: Nation of Islam and the New Black Panthers.

The primary sources of information about these groups are provided mostly by two organizations, the Anti-Defamation League (ADL) and the SPLC. Specific cites will be noted when material is drawn from other than these sources.

White Supremacists

White supremacists are individuals or groups who adhere to right-wing rhetorical traditions of anti-Semitism and believe in the superiority of white people over minorities, and argue that white people have the right to subjugate people of other races.

The following case studies describe the justifications of five groupings of white supremacists: Ku Klux Klans, KKK Splinter groups, Neo-Nazi, Neo-Nazi Skinheads, and Christian Identity.

Ku Klux Klans

The KKK was and is motivated by political, social, and ideological grievances that were emotionally influenced by fear and hate. As Chapter 2 illustrates, the KKK began as a group committed to having fun and playing pranks on the public. It quickly evolved into a secret vigilante-terrorist network that employed beating, flogging, hanging, and burning at the stake in pursuit of its goal to rebuild the foundations of Southern supremacy against political inroads by Blacks, Republicans, and Northern Whites (Blee 1991).

Laqueur (1987) identifies three historical periods of Klan activity, the first two of which are discussed in Chapter 2. In essence, the three Klan's did not have much in common with each other:

1. The First Klan (1865–1872), a white supremacist by-product of the Reconstruction period, was a secret, violent association attacking recently emancipated Negroes;
2. The Second Klan (1915–1944) also stood for white supremacy, but campaigned causes such as patriotism and attacked bootleggers and wife-beaters; and
3. The Third Klan (1960–1975) more closely resembled the traditional focus of The First Klan.

There were numerous accounts of beatings, shootings, cross-burnings and bombings in southern communities during the Third Klan phase. By the mid-1960s, cross-burning and night rides were ever present in the South. These actions were designed to terrorize Blacks, and intimidate and harass civil rights workers in their attempts to enroll black voters (Poland 1988; Vetter and Perlstein 1991). Three major KKK events of the 1960s included the following:

1. September 1963 bombing of the 16th Street Baptist Church in Birmingham, Alabama, which killed four black girls;
2. June 1964 killing of three civil rights workers near Philadelphia, Missouri; and
3. 1964 incidents in McComb, Missouri, in which eighteen bombs were detonated in black churches and homes (George and Wilcox 1992).

In these and other incidents, KKK members and others affiliated with the KKK were arrested and in most cases, convicted of their crimes. The harassment of the civil rights workers in particular prompted the FBI to initiate prosecution in federal courts of the alleged perpetrators. "President Johnson even appealed to all Klan members to withdraw from the organization 'before it was too late'" (Poland 1988: 28).

The ADL estimates the combined total membership by the mid-1990s of all Klans, including splinter groups, was approximately 2,500 to 3,000. This is considerably less than ADL estimates of 9,700 to 11,500 KKK membership in 1981, and their postwar estimates of a high of 55,000 (George and Wilcox 1992). The membership decline is attributed to a number of factors:

- successful prosecution of Klan members across the country;
- stiff sentences;
- the SPLC's creative use of civil law against what was then the largest and strongest

Klan faction, the United Klans of America (see Box 4.1);
- passage of hate-crimes and antiparamilitary legislation across the country; and
- intense internal factionalism and the tendency to divide into even smaller splinter groups.

Current KKK Splinter Groups

While the KKK has splintered into several smaller groups over the past ten years, we have focused on eight of the most influential.

1. *United Klans of America Inc. (UKA):* Founded in 1960, the UKA was the largest Klan organization of the 1960s and 1970s. Headquartered in Tuscaloosa, Alabama, it was led by Imperial Wizard Robert Shelton and espoused the traditional philosophy of hate. The official publication of the UKA was *The Fiery Cross.* During the era of the civil rights revolution, the UKA was implicated in many brutal acts of violence, including a number of murders (see Box 4.1 for further description).
2. *The Christian Knights of the Ku Klux Klan (CK):* The CK was formed in 1985 by long-time Klansman Virgil Griffin and was based in Mount Holly, North Carolina. The teachings of the Christian Knights include the command to "its membership to arm itself with firearms to prepare for a race war between white persons and Black persons" (Schwartz 1996: 248). The Christian Knights are active in North Carolina, South Carolina, Kentucky, and Tennessee and are considered the largest Klan organization in the Carolinas. The group holds occasional rallies and cross-burnings, and several members have been convicted on state charges of arson and federal counts of conspiracy to violate civil rights.

Box 4.1
Southern Poverty Law Center's (SPLC) Case against United Klans of America (UKA)

In March 1981, Michael Donald, a young black man, was abducted and lynched by Henry Hays and James Knowles–both members of the national UKA and of local Alabama Klavern 900. According to the later testimony of another Klavern 900 member, Johnny Matt Jones, Hays had stood up at a Klavern meeting two days before Michael Donald was lynched and suggested killing a black person if Josephus Anderson, a black man accused of murdering a white policeman, was acquitted. The following day, an Alabama jury composed of eleven Blacks and one White, acquitted Anderson.

In 1983, Henry Hays was tried for the death of Michael Donald. The jury found him guilty and delivered a life sentence without possibility of parole. The judge, however, overruled that sentence and imposed the death penalty–which was only the second time in Alabama history that a white person was sentenced to death for murdering a black person. James Knowles, who admitted to the abduction and murder of Michael Donald in 1983 after a two-year investigation, pled guilty to the federal charge of violating Donald's civil rights in return for his testimony against Hays on murder charges. He received a life sentence with possibility of parole.

For the SPLC, the sentences of Hayes and Knowles was not enough. Instead, the organization decided to take on the UKA in a precedent-setting civil lawsuit. The resulting suit alleged that

• Donald was a victim of the Klan, not just his two executioners.
• Klan officials at the national and local level had plotted his death.
• The UKA was an organization that historically sought to fulfill its goal of the "God-given superiority of the white race" through violence.
• The UKA's Imperial Wizard Bobby Shelton had an official policy that encouraged or condoned local units to commit criminal actions in order to carry out UKA goals.

As such, the lawsuit had two primary goals: to put the UKA permanently out of business by holding it financially responsible for past violent actions; and to force other Klans and right-wing hate groups across the country to understand the legal consequences of embracing racist violence.

On June 14, 1984, the SPLC filed a complaint in federal court in Mobile, Alabama, on behalf of Buelah Mae Donald, Michael's mother. The suit sought $10 million in damages from the UKA, Inc., Bobby Shelton, Bennie Hayes, James Knowles, three other identified Klansmen, and several other unidentified Klansmen. The court found for the SPLC and ordered the UKA to pay $7 million. Buelah Mae Donald only collected UKA assets of about $50,000. However, for her as well as the SPLC, it was a victory for it was never the money they wanted, but rather the demise of the UKA. Furthermore, it was a major victory because it set a precedent for suing right-wing racist organizations for their responsibility in racist violence.

3. *The Knights of the Ku Klux Klan (KKKK, Louisiana Faction):* David Duke incorporated the KKKK in Louisiana in 1974. Duke, considered a charismatic and polished speaker, had been a Klan member since 1973 when he began recruiting on college campuses in an effort to enlist other "intellectuals" (George and Wilcox 1992). Duke also accepted women on equal terms with men. In 1975, Duke's Klan held the largest Klan rally ever in Walker, Louisiana, with 2,700 people in attendance. He has consistently captured media attention and drawn hundreds into his organization, which in the mid-1980s, reached a peak of 3,500 members (Wade 1987). One of Duke's lieutenants, Bill Wilkinson, split to form his own Klan, Invisible Empire, Knights of the Ku Klux Klan (see later). After many years of feuding with Wilkinson, Duke turned his organization over to Alabama Grand Wizard, Don Black.

4. *The Knights of the Ku Klux Klan (KKKK, Arkansas Faction):* Based in Harrison, Arkansas, and led by Thom Robb, the KKKK, by the 1990s, was the largest and most active Klan faction operation in the United States. The KKKK experienced defections in 1994, contributing to a decline in membership from its high in 1993 of more than 1,000 members. By the end of the decade, the ADL indicated that it was active in about seven states with a hard core membership of about 500. While the organization espouses racist and anti-Semitic sentiments, it has also urged followers to avoid harsh racist language, emphasizing instead their "love of the white race." Like many leaders in today's KKK, Robb is a "pastor" in the Christian Identity movement.

5. *Federation of Klans (FOK):* Ed Novak, following his defection from the Arkansas-based Knights of the Ku Klux Klan, formed the FOK in April 1994. Novak, a strong advocate of secrecy and militancy, did not engage in the other Klan's more traditional tactic of staging numerous public events. The Federation of Klans engaged in few activities and by the late 1990s, organizational infighting led to the defection of several members.

6. *Knights of the Ku Klux Klan (Michigan Faction):* This faction is a splinter group of Thom Robb's Arkansas-based Knights of the Ku Klux Klan. Three Klan members from Michigan, Indiana, and Illinois founded the Michigan faction in 1994. Holding strong to the racist and anti-Semitic beliefs of the KKK, the Michigan faction discarded the moderate public image pushed by Robb in favor of a return to the Klan's earlier days of holding rallies in full Klan regalia. It is estimated that by the mid-to-late 1990s, the organization had about 50 members.

7. *The Invisible Empire, Knights of the Ku Klux Klan (IE):* Founded in 1975, the IE was at one time the largest Klan group in the nation. Members of the organization were encouraged to engage in confrontational tactics and openly carry and display weapons. In its first several years, the IE was involved in a series of encounters with black civil rights demonstrators that resulted in violence, arrests, and wide media coverage. After a number of other civil rights violations, a Federal court, in 1993, found the IE guilty of conspiracy to deprive marchers in Forsyth County, Georgia, of their civil rights. The group was ordered to disband, turn in its membership list of nearly 3,000, and pay $37,500 to a group of marchers. Several members broke away after the court settlement to form their own organizations.

8. *The Keystone Knights of the Ku Klux Klan:* In September 1992, Pennsylvania members of the Invisible Empire formed their own Klan. The Keystone Knights maintain

---

Box 4.2
Thomas (Thom) Arthur Robb

Thom Robb is the Grand Wizard of the KKKK. A printer by profession, Robb is a pastor of the Identity-oriented Church of Jesus Christ and adheres to the anti-Semitic, racist beliefs inherent in that ideology:

"I hate Jews. I hate race-mixing Jews. We've let Antichrist Jews into our country and we've been cursed with abortion, inflation, homosexuality and the threat of war. Anglo-Saxon and kindred people are the true Israel. Identity breaks the power Jewry has over America" (Schwartz 1996: 125)

He began publishing his first hate sheet, *The Message of Old Monthly*, in Tucson, Arizona, and in the late 1990s, published it from his home in Harrison, Arkansas, under the name *The Torch*. Robb has attempted to improve the Klan's image, including exchanging his Klan robes for business suits. He has also encouraged his followers to avoid harsh racist rhetoric and emphasize a public image of love of the white race. This effort is designed to improve the sellability of the Klan. In 1994, several members broke away from Robb because they found his message "too soft" and wanted to engage in more militant action. The new group headed by Ed Novak named itself the Federated Knights of the Ku Klux Klan (Schwartz 1996).

---

their largest presence in Pennsylvania but also have active offices in other states. They hold occasional rallies and cross-burnings and, in 1995, joined with the International Knights of the Ku Klux Klan to form a new organization called the International Keystone Knights. They are attempting to recruit new members, particularly in Ohio and Connecticut, and publish an anti-Semitic and racist newsletter called *The Keystone American*.

Neo-Nazis

A neo-Nazi group is one that generally adopts or advocates traditional Nazi symbolism, including the swastika or approximate equivalent; wears uniforms and other paraphernalia; uses the term *Nazi* or some variation; and demonstrates reverence for or appreciation of Adolph Hitler and the Third

Reich (George and Wilcox 1992). The neo-Nazi's consider themselves the heirs to Hitler's racial and political program. The term *neo-Nazi* has been applied in many cases to groups that are anti-Semitic and racist.

It is important to acknowledge that not all anti-Semitic or racist groups are neo-Nazi. In 1987, the ADL estimated that the hardcore membership in the avowedly neo-Nazi groups in the United States was at a peak of 1,000 to 1,200. Ten years later in 1998, the SPLC reported that the number of active neo-Nazi groups in the United States was at an all time high of 151. By 1999, the number had decreased somewhat to 130.

There are a number of influential neo-Nazi groups in the United States:

- *National Socialist White People's Party (NSWPP)*–formed by racial activist Harold Covington, aka Winston Smith, NSWPP has become one of the most active groups on the Internet that has spawned new activity in a number of states.

- *American Nazi Party*–one of two organizations claiming to descend from the original American Nazi Party that was headed by George Lincoln Rockwell. Based in Chicago, it claims affiliates in California and Texas.
- *National Socialist Vanguard*–based in The Dalles, Oregon, it focuses its efforts on trying to recruit high school students.

The most influential of all remains the National Alliance.

National Alliance: Willis Carto established the National Alliance in 1968 as the Youth for Wallace campaign, supporting the presidential bid of Alabama Governor George Wallace. After Wallace, Carto renamed his organization the National Youth Alliance to support his radical, antidemocratic cause. In 1970, William Pierce, a former officer in the American Nazi Party, joined him. By 1970, Carto and Pierce were feuding and, since 1974, Pierce has led the National Alliance from his compound in Hillsboro, West Virginia.

Pierce promotes "reaching out to white elites" that involves holding rallies, leadership conferences, and cultural fests. Pierce's influence in the United States has been driven not only by his organizing efforts, but also by the stature of his race-war novels, *The Turner Diaries* and *Hunter,* which attack the "mongrelization" of the white race and depicts the assassination of mixed-race couples. Pierce also has chapters in at least eleven countries in South America and Europe.

Pierce is the editor of *National Vanguard* (magazine) and the *National Alliance Bulletin* (internal newsletter). The Alliance also publishes *National Vanguard Books,* a catalog of racist and anti-Semitic literature. These publications, along with a web site, are used to recruit and/or attract new supporters. The Alliance also holds frequent meetings, lectures,

and social gatherings for members and potential recruits. As of the late 1990s, the ADL estimated that the group was active from coast to coast, had reported membership of 1,000, experienced significant growth in California, and was the largest and most active neo-Nazi organization in the nation.

Neo-Nazi Skinheads

The Skinhead movement began in the early 1970s in England, where gangs of menacing-looking, tattooed teenagers in combat boots started to hang out in the streets. Their original style of dress and behavior was meant to symbolize patriotic, anti-immigrant working-class attitudes. In time, racist and neo-Nazi beliefs started to become popular among some Skinheads, while other Skinheads retained their original beliefs. The Skinhead movement then spread throughout Europe and to the United States.

The neo-Nazi Skinheads appeared in the mid-1980s in the United States. Initially, they were characterized by shaven heads, neo-Nazi insignia, their clothing, and tattoos on their skin, and use of violence against Blacks, Jews, other minorities, and homosexuals. Their warrior subculture glorifies aggression and sacrifice (Cotter 1999). They glorify Adolph Hitler and dedicate themselves to fulfilling his dream of a world run by white, Aryan people.

By the early 1990s, the Skinheads had split into three groups: the SHARPS (Skinheads Against Racial Violence), Trads (Traditional Skins), and Racist, Neo-Nazi Skins. It is the latter group that is violently tied into the neo-Nazi movement. Such skinhead groups

- almost uniformly are white youths between the ages of 13 and 25, with males outnumbering females;
- almost always have two things in common: the fear that their chance at achieving the

---

Box 4.3
The Turner Diaries–William Pierce

"What will you do when they come to take your guns?"

The Turner Diaries, a novel first published in 1978, portrays the violent overthrow of the federal government and the systematic killing of Jews and nonwhites to establish an Aryan world. Its teachings are popular among far-right extremists; as a "terrorism manual," it has inspired several major acts of violence. Reference is made to the need for an American Nazi revolution by an all-white army: "the people had their share of the Jews and their tricks. . . . If the Organization survives this contest, no Jew will–anywhere. We'll go to the utmost ends of the Earth to hunt down the last of Satan's spawn" (Shinbaum 1996: 2). Pierce goes on to write that, "If the White nations of the world had not allowed themselves to become subject to the Jew, to Jewish ideas, to Jewish spirit, this war would not be necessary. We can hardly consider ourselves blameless. We can hardly say we had no choice, no chance to avoid the Jew's snare. We can hardly say we were not warned" (Shinbaum 1996: 2).

The *Turner Diaries* is seen as the likely inspiration for the violent extremist group known as The Order, which was active in the 1980s when it committed a series of crimes including murders, robberies, counterfeiting, and the bombing of a synagogue. Timothy McVeigh, convicted of bombing the Federal Building in Oklahoma City [executed by lethal injection on June 14, 2001], actively promoted the book before the April 1995 bombing (Shinbaum 1996).

American Dream is disappearing because white people are moving down the socio-economic ladder, while all minority people are moving up; and the feeling that in addition to losing their economic status, they are also losing their gender status–their opportunity to be real men and prove their masculinity;

- often attract youth because of a simplistic black-and-white world view–you are either loyal to the white race, or you are part of the ZOG (Zionist Occupied Government); because of the excitement of buying into a politically-incorrect ideology; or because of the scapegoatism that gives them a reason for why their lives are so messed up; and
- actively recruit two types of young people: students in junior and senior high school in

communities experiencing some type of economic or racial change and where racist or homophobic graffiti has begun to appear; and youth incarcerated in jail and juvenile detention facilities who need some sort of protection from inside as well as a subculture to come home to once they are released.

There is no single national Skinhead organization in the United States. There are, however, loosely linked networks of Skinhead gangs operating in many communities. The average neo-Nazi gang ranges in size from fewer than ten to several dozen members. The majority of the members are white youths between the ages of 13 and 25. They come from widely varying economic and fa-

---

Box 4.4
William Pierce

William Pierce, a native of Atlanta, Georgia, received his doctorate in physics from the University of Colorado in 1962. Soon after, Dr. Pierce became an untenured assistant professor of physics at Oregon State University, where he taught from 1962 to June 1965 and briefly joined the far-right John Birch Society. In the summer of 1965, he quit his teaching position to take a job in Connecticut as a laboratory researcher. In 1966, he resigned from his senior research scientist position at the Connecticut aerospace firm to join George Lincoln Rockwell's American Nazi Party. Pierce became editor of *National Socialist World,* a quarterly aimed at intellectuals and the academic community that was published by Rockwell's World Union of National Socialists. After Rockwell's assassination by a follower in 1967, Pierce became a principal leader in the American Nazi Party.

In writings and broadcasts, Pierce weaves a detailed and complex story of a Jewish-run world conspiracy that must be defeated through revolutionary means. Pierce believes it is necessary to engage in the violent overthrow of the U.S. government to achieve that return to a white America. In a "Guest Commentary" in the August 1990 issue of *WAR* (a publication of the California-based White Aryan Resistance), Pierce wrote:

"It is clear that if most White males would respond to their rage in a direct, physical way, as skinheads do, then we would have no race problem, no Jewish problem, no homosexual problem, and no problem with White race traitors in America. Our cities would be clean, decent, safe, and White once again after a relatively brief period of bloodletting" (as cited in SPLC 1999: 14–15; Schwartz 1996).

---

milial backgrounds, including broken homes or single-parent families. Individual members also tend to be highly mobile, with little to tie them to a particular location.

The social marginality of the Skinheads and other youth gangs, their young age, and their socioeconomic detachment from organized society make some of them potential front-line soldiers for neo-Nazi movements, whose elderly members either cannot afford to get directly involved in extralegal activities or constantly suffer from manpower shortage (Sprinzak 1995). Evidence suggests that Skinheads hook up with these more-organized racists and anti-Semitic groups like the KKK and other hate groups, such as the Aryan Nations, the Church of the Creator, and the White Aryan Resistance (WAR).

White power (oi) music, a brand of rock and roll whose lyrics send a message of bigotry and violence, is the Skinhead's main propaganda weapon and its chief means of attracting young recruits. It has played a vital role in the spread of the Skinhead subculture over the last twenty years (Cotter 1999). There are a number of racist bands (e.g., Max Resist and the Hooligans, Bound for Glory), many of which play at Skinhead festivals around the world. Resistance Records, a major producer of Skinhead music in Detroit that is owned and directed by National Alliance leader William Pierce, publishes a magazine, *Resistance,* which focuses on Skinhead music. Another means of attracting and retaining members is through the maintenance of home pages on the World Wide Web.

Skinhead groups have developed their own leadership and appeal, distinct from adult Klan and neo-Nazi groups (Ross 1995). Some Skinheads want a race war in the United States. Ross (1995) refers to them as the "urban guerrillas" of the hate movement. Several arrests were made in the 1990s of Skinhead gang members for plotting to incite a race war by bombing churches and attempted and/or actual assassinations of Jewish or African American church leaders.

The ADL states that up to the late 1990s, Skinheads have been responsible for no fewer than 41 murders of racial minorities (African Americans, Latinos, Asian Americans), homosexuals, homeless, and other Skinheads. In addition, Skinheads have been involved in thousands of lesser crimes: stabbings, shootings, beatings, thefts, and synagogue desecrations (Sprinzak 1995).

Christian Identity

The Christian Identity movement has its roots in British or Anglo-Israelism, which is a belief that the true descendants of the Biblical Jews are the people who today inhabit the British Isles. Christian Identity is a belief system that provides both a religious base for racism and anti-Semitism and an ideological rationale for violence against minorities and their white allies.

The Christian Identity movement came on to the American scene in the late 1970s and early 1980s. Early leaders included Wesley Swift, a former Klan member and retired U.S. Army Col. William Potter Gale, both active in the far-right and hate movements for more than 20 years. They carried their anti-Jewish message with such public statements as "All Jews must be destroyed." In fact, Swift is the single most significant figure in the early history of Identity. He was responsible for popularizing Christian Identity in right-wing circles. Swift died in 1970, and Gale died in 1988.

In general, advocates of Christian Identity believe the following:

- All the Old Testament stories were about the Aryan people, not the Jews. Through a series of migrations, these Aryan–white, Christians who comprised the "Ten Lost Tribes"–settled in Northern Europe. The people now known as Jews were a small group of rabble who remained in Palestine and did not migrate.
- God deliberately segregated the races by implanting Eve with two seeds: from Adam's seed sprang Abel and the white race, and from Satan's seed came the wicked Cain and the Jewish race. In anger, God cast Adam, Eve, and Satan out of the Garden of Eden and decreed eternal racial conflict. Cain killed Abel, then fled to the jungle where he mated with animals and created the nonwhite "mud people."
- God is white and Jesus is an Aryan, not a Jew. The white race is God's chosen people who were called to America to achieve God's plan–white domination of the earth and all nonwhite people, including the Jewish spawn of Satan.
- Christians are biblically obligated to engage in an apocalyptic battle against the evil, satanic forces of nonwhites and Jews. The Whites must destroy these enemies or risk the destruction of the white race.
- The Bible demands racial and religious segregation, because God deliberately did not create people equally. White people sin if they marry, associate with, or tolerate the behavior of a Jew, a person from another race, or homosexuals.
- The United States is a "Christian Republic" governed by Christian Biblical law. Only the Bible, the first Ten Amendments of the

Constitution, and the Articles of Confederation need to be obeyed by true Christian Americans.

• A Jewish-led conspiracy of bankers, minorities, and corrupt government officials use the IRS and Federal Reserve Board to manipulate the economy for personal gain, to control the news media and the courts, and to destroy the white race.

By 1987, an estimated 50 preachers served between 7,000 and 20,000 members of Identity congregations. By the end of 1998, SPLC reported an all-time high of 62 congregations with an estimated membership of about 50,000. By 1999, however, Identity groups suffered the first major decrease of the decade—with 46 active groups. Indeed, the SPLC reports that young racists increasingly see Identity as passé because its Christian ideology requires long hours of study and is not very exciting. Additionally, Identity leaders are growing old with many dying or retiring. Interest was so low in 1999 that the annual national conference in Idaho at the Aryan Nations complex for over ten years was cancelled. Additionally, Identity preacher Richard Butler's loss of a lawsuit has bankrupted the major Identity Church in the nation (see the section on Aryan Nations later).

The Christian Identity philosophy has been adopted by a number of loosely connected groups that proclaim themselves Christian Identity Churches and attempt to claim a tax exemption. More recently, the Christian Identity movement's racist ideology and anti-Semitic philosophy has linked together an assorted collection of extremist groups. The neo-Nazi National Alliance, for example, has found the Identity's views helpful in promoting and defending their violent and hateful ideas and actions.

In the 1980s, several Christian Identity groups adopted a millenarian belief in the imminent Second Coming of a White Aryan Christ. They believed this would occur after a seven-year period of tribulation, a modern-day Armageddon, when the entire world would change dramatically. Jews and other "mud people" would be eliminated and genuine Anglo-Saxons would finally take over (Sprinzak 1995). For this reason, many Identity preachers recommend that their followers live in isolated encampments, mostly in the racially homogenous Northwest and arm themselves in preparation for the 'great moment.'

A more recent tenet gaining popularity among Christian Identity believers is support of the use of violence if it is perpetrated to punish violator's of God's law. This includes, for example, killing interracial couples, abortionists, homosexuals, and robbing banks and perpetrating frauds to undermine the "usury system."

The following groups adhere to the philosophy of Christian Identity and are discussed next: Phineas Brotherhood; Posse Comitatus; Aryan Nations; The Order; Aryan Brotherhood; and The Covenant, the Sword and the Arm of the Lord.

Phineas Brotherhood: The Phineas Brotherhood takes its name from Phineas, the great nephew of Moses, as written in Numbers 25:1–18 (Kaplan 1997). Phineas killed two people violating God's law of maintaining the racial purity of his chosen people. The Lord then spoke to Moses saying he would give Phineas a covenant of peace for his actions, "and it shall be to him and his descendants after him a covenant of an everlasting priesthood, because he was zealous for his God and made atonement for the children of Israel." Although the history of the Phineas Brotherhood is difficult to document, it is more of a philosophy than an organization.

Posse Comitatus: The Posse Comitatus (Latin for "power of the county"), founded in 1969 by Henry Beach, was a loosely organ-

---

Box 4.5
Second Coming of Christ and Christian Identity

Christian Identity beliefs view the events leading up to the Armageddon and Christ's return to earth as inevitable. It is believed that these events are part of a cleansing process that is needed before Christ's kingdom can be established on earth. During this time, Jews and their allies will attempt to destroy the white race using any means available. The result will be a violent and blood struggle—a war between God's forces, the white race and the forces of evil, the Jews and nonwhites.

This concept of the Second Coming of Christ appears to be a combination of pre-millennialism and postmillennialism, which are views held by Christians of different denominations concerning the period preceding or during the Second Coming of Christ. Premillennialists believe that God's law on earth will only be established with the Second Coming. Postmillennialists, however, contend that God's law has to be established by man before the Second Coming can occur.

The view of what Armageddon will be varies among Identity adherents. Some contend there will be a race war in which millions will die; others believe that the United Nations, backed by Jewish representatives of the anti-Christ, will take over the country and promote a New World Order. One Identity interpretation is that white Christians have been chosen to watch for signs of the impending war in order to warn others. The result will be a battle of forces between good and evil. After the final battle is ended and God's kingdom is established on earth, only then will the Aryan people be recognized as the one and true Israel (see FBI 1999; Schwartz 1996; SPLC 1997; Sprinzak 1995).

---

ized group of Christian Identity activists dedicated to survivalism, vigilantism, and anti-government agitation. They were especially active in the early to mid-1980s. They adhere to the teachings of the Identity movement. Posse Comitatus members also believe that the federal government is controlled by enemies, referring to ZOG and Jews, and that all governmental power is rooted and should return to the county, not federal, level.

The Posse attracted Klan members and other anti-Semites and operated in a decentralized fashion, with semiautonomous units appearing in several communities. In the 1970s and early 1980s, Posse members sent death threats to a U.S. senator and many local Posse officials attempted to arrest law enforcement personnel and spoke of the need to lynch uncooperative public officials if they refused to follow (Stern 1996).

The group came to our collective attention when in 1983, active Posse member Gordon Kahl murdered two federal marshals in North Dakota and became a fugitive. Kahl eventually died in a shoot-out with Arkansas law enforcement officials in which a local sheriff was also killed. In 1987, William Potter Gale (one of the founders) and four other associates were convicted of threatening the lives of Internal Revenue Service agents and a Nevada state judge. All were sentenced to federal prison, although Gale died shortly after sentencing. After several other Posse leader convictions, the group has been relatively quiet. Today's militias, however, echo the Posse's hostility to federal authority.

Aryan Nations: Based in Hayden Lake, Idaho, Aryan Nations was founded by the Reverend Richard Butler in the mid-1970s. It was formed around Butler's Church of Jesus Christ Christian, which was affiliated with the Christian Identity movement. Aryan Nations militantly advocates anti-Semitism and the establishment of a white racist state, reflecting a Nazilike philosophy. Beginning in the 1970s, the Aryan Nations held the World Congress of Aryan Nations to bring together white supremacists to participate in activities such as courses on urban terrorism and guerrilla warfare. It also hosted youth gatherings, which attracted numerous Skinheads.

Prison outreach has been an important aspect of the Aryan Nations activities. Members correspond on an ongoing basis with prison inmates through letters and their prison outreach newsletter, *The Way.* Internet is also more prominent. In 1996, Aryan Nations published a "Declaration of Independence" for the Aryan race over the Internet that argues that it is necessary for Aryans to alter their former systems of government which reflect a ZOG, and to be a free and independent nation with no political connections to the federal government. As such, Aryan people would have the full power to "levy war, conclude peace, contract alliances, establish commerce, and to perform all other acts which independent nations may of right do. . . ." Their belief in ZOG is that the Jews control the government and engage in covert actions to take away their arms, rights, and so forth. They see ZOG as a threat and therefore, as a justification to advocate a violent overthrow of the government.

Beginning in the late 1990s, Aryan Nations experienced internal difficulties, which resulted in shifts in leadership roles for Butler, and the departure of several key members to form their own group. In September 2000, the Aryan Nations was dealt a serious blow. On September 7, the SPLC won an important civil case when a Kootenai County, Idaho, jury found Butler and the Aryan Nations grossly negligent in hiring and training security guards who shot at and assaulted Victoria Keenan and her son Jason in July 1998. The Keenans won a $6.3 million jury award and to satisfy the judgment, the Kootenai County Sheriff seized Butler's assets at the Aryan Nations compound near Hayden Lake—a 20-acre property containing the neo-Nazi's church, barracks, and Butler's home. Butler also agreed to no longer use the name Aryan Nations and to transfer any interest in the name to the Keenans. In late October, Butler moved off the property and by the turn of the twenty-first century, Butler was operating a new organization, the Aryan National Alliance out of the suburban home of a fellow racist.

The Order: Robert J. Mathews, a recruiter for the National Alliance and an activist in the Aryan Nations, founded the Order (also known as *Bruders Schweigen* or Silent Brotherhood) in 1983. It started slowly with eight members and drew its membership from the National Alliance, Aryan Nations, and various Klan splinter groups. Many of the crimes for which Order members were convicted resembled terrorist acts described in *The Turner Diaries.* For example, the group had a counterfeiting operation at the Aryan Nations compound in Hayden Lake, Idaho, that was eventually exposed, and they planted a bomb in a Boise, Idaho, synagogue that caused minor damage but no injuries.

Order members also committed a number of robberies, including the hijacking of a Brink's armored truck near Ukiah, California, as a means of generating funds for salaries, mobile homes, uniforms, vehicles, and weapons. They also used the money to purchase parcels of land in Idaho and Missouri for paramilitary training camps and reportedly donated funds to fellow extremists, including the Aryan Nations and the National

Alliance. Financing their revolution was only part of The Order's agenda; the other part involved carrying out the agenda against its enemies. The Order assassinated perceived enemies, including some of its own members. Another victim was Alan Berg, a controversial Jewish talk-radio personality in Denver, who was murdered outside his home in June 1984 after he repeatedly berated right-wing and white-supremacist extremists on his call-in program. One of the Order's most celebrated events occurred when Mathews escaped from the FBI in December 1984 and held off 200 law enforcement officers for more than 36 hours, until he died after the ammunition with which he barricaded himself exploded.

On December 30, 1985, nine men and one woman, all members of The Order, were convicted and sentenced to terms of 40 to 100 years in prison, as well as stiff fines. Another member, tried separately, was sentenced to life and 12 others pleaded guilty to various crime. An Order member at the 1985 trial reflected the Order's revolutionary program in the following statement: "The end goal, bluntly, was the annihilation of the Jewish race." The group is basically defunct even though some of its incarcerated members continue to propagandize from their prison cells.

Aryan Brotherhood: The Aryan Brotherhood is a white-supremacist prison gang that was formed on the West Coast in the 1960s and is tied to the Aryan Nations. They target Blacks and Jews and reportedly engage in extortion, drug operations, and violence in prisons. Silence and secrecy are traditional within the gang, and many members have tattoos with a swastika and the Nazi SS lightning bolt.

James Ridgeway, author of *Blood in the Face,* a history of twentieth-century American radical right, states that the Brotherhood's motto is "Kill to get in. Die to get out." While California's Department of Corrections maintains data on Brotherhood gang membership in its prisons, it is more difficult to estimate the number of gang members in all prisons. We do know that its membership extends to many prisons across the United States.

The Covenant, the Sword, and the Arm of the Lord (CSA): Founded in 1971 by James Ellison, the CSA was a paramilitary survivalist group that operated an Identity-oriented communal settlement near the Arkansas–Missouri border. The CSA's anti-Semitism was based on its Identity-movement doctrine that declared: "We believe the Scandinavian-German-Teutonic-British-American people to be the Lost Sheep of the House of Israel which Jesus was sent for" (Schwartz 1996: 210). The Jews are "the seed of Satan, not the seed of God" (Schwartz 1996: 210). Another member stated, "We do believe non-whites and Jews are a threat to our Christian, white race" and that "Jews are financing the training of Blacks to take over most of our major cities" (Schwartz 1996: 210).

The inhabitants of the settlement believed American society was approaching economic collapse, famine, rioting, and a coming war. They stockpiled arms, food, and wilderness survival gear and trained in the use of weapons in a mock village called Silhouette City. This survivalism, a self-sufficient stocking of arms and supplies, is practiced in preparation for Armageddon. They also operated a training school that offered courses in urban warfare, riflery and pistolcraft, military tactics, Christian martial arts, and wilderness survival. CSA leaders engaged in a series of criminal activities in 1983, including the firebombing of an Indiana synagogue and the arson of a Missouri church.

In April 1985, 200 FBI agents raided the CSA compound and seized hundreds of weapons, bombs, an antitank rocket, and quantities of cyanide allegedly intended to poison the water supply of an unnamed city.

The CSA leaders and several other CSA activists were sentenced to lengthy federal prison terms on racketeering and illegal weapons charges. These convictions in effect led to the demise of this group.

Other Racist-Religious-Oriented Groups

Beginning in the 1980s, several new racist groups with religious overtones that were distinctly non-Christian began attracting attention. Most prominent among these have been the World Church of the Creator, White Aryan Resistance, and Odinism.

World Church of the Creator

In 1973, Benhardt "Ben" Klassen, a former Florida state legislator and state chairman of George Wallace's 1968 presidential campaign, announced the formation of the Church of the Creator (COTC) in Lighthouse Point, Florida. The tenets of Klassen's race-based religion, called Creativity, are detailed in his 511-page book *Nature's Eternal Religion.* Among its 16 commandments is the following:

> It is our sacred goal to populate the lands of this earth with White people exclusively. The group's war cry will be "Rahowa," short for RAcial HOly WAr. "RAHOWA! In this one word we sum up the total goal and program of not only the Church of the Creator, but of the total White Race, and it is this: We take up the challenge. We gird for total war against the Jews and the rest of the goddamned mud races of the world–politically, militantly, financially, morally and religiously. . . . We regard it as a holy war to the finish–a racial holy war. . . . No longer can the mud races and the White Race live on the same planet and survive" (Schwartz 1996: 199).

Over the next ten years, Klassen attracted few followers. He published his second book, *The White Man's Bible,* in 1981 which presents a program for the survival, expansion, and advancement of the white race. In May 1982, COTC headquarters moved from Florida to Otto, North Carolina, and Klassen began publishing a monthly newsletter called *Racial Loyalty.* With his strong rhetoric, Klassen's was one of the few American hate groups to gain an international audience, with active members in Sweden, Canada, and South Africa. His call-to-arms attracted followers in the United States who committed acts of harassment and even murder. In the early 1990s, in fact, COTC emerged as one of the most violent hate groups on the radical right, attracting several hundred neo-Nazi Skinheads and other white supremacists from the United States and around the world.

During the late 1980s and into the 1990s, the COTC experienced leadership shifts that resulted in COTC headquarters moving back to Florida. In 1993, following several bombings by COTC members, Klassen committed suicide, leaving a smoldering pile of shredded documents. COTC suffered a decline in membership following Klassen's death but was resurrected by Matt Hale in 1996.

Renamed the World Church of the Creator (WCOTC) and based in East Peoria, Illinois, its stated goal is "making this an all-white Nation and ultimately an all-white world" (ADL 1999: 1). Hale appointed himself "Pontifex Maximus," an ancient Roman title designated for the Church's supreme leader. Members distribute the WCOTC's thirty-page anti-Semitic and anti-black propaganda booklet titled *Facts that the Government and the Media Don't Want You to Know.* A key leader of Hale's, Benjamin Nathaniel Smith, spent July 4th weekend in 1999 murdering a black man and an Asian man and wounding nine others.

Under Hale's leadership, WCOTC adheres to the following beliefs:

- "Creativity," the theology of the Church, is a "racial religion whose prime goal is the survival, expansion and advancement of the white race" (ADL 1999: 1). For "Creators . . . every issue, whether religious, political, or racial, is viewed through the eyes of the White Man and exclusively from the point of view of the White race as a whole."
- The white race–except Jews, Christians, and homosexuals–is responsible "for all progress on this earth." Conversely, minority groups–the "mudpeople"–are destroying civilization (ADL 1999: 1).
- Christians are part of a Jewish conspiracy to take over the world.
- To prevent the destruction of the white race, white people must engage in RAHOWA (RAcial HOly WAr) by striving harder to get their message of white superiority and rule across to as many people as possible.

Thus, Hale's church poses a new and different threat to American youth primarily because his ideology varies decidedly from any others in the white-supremacist movement because he

- Actively recruits women–something very few white supremacist groups do–as activists, but not feminists for the cause.
- Shuns Christianity and provides a home for racists who don't need a religious rationale for racism.
- Seeks to create a small, elite cadre of violent, committed, young followers from any part of the political spectrum.

According to the ADL, as of July 1999, WCOTC has over 35 post office box addresses across the United States and two overseas. Members of the group have carried out aggressive leafleting and recruiting campaigns in various cities. One of its recent exploits occurred in July 2000 with the insertion of a hate-filled flier into copies of a free local publication in Pekin, Illinois. The flier brought attention to the upcoming one-year wedding anniversary of Edgar and Shannon Sandoval. In part, the flier described their marriage as "Beastiality," a "wedding of the blond white woman with the mongrel, Filopino animal savage! . . . The World Church of the Creator and Reverend Matt Hale say today that such actions must be punished by DEATH!"

WCOTC also operates 22 web sites, including a site designed specifically to teach "racialist thinking" to young children and another geared toward recruiting women. The SPLC states that although Hale boasts that WCOTC has had as many as 30,000 followers, in reality there are fewer than 150 dues-paying members and only about a dozen are at the group's core.

White Aryan Resistance (WAR)

In 1980, Tom Metzger left the Knights of the Ku Klux Klan, where he rose to the position of Grand Dragon in California, to form the White Aryan Political Resistance (WAPA) to support "pro-white" candidates for political office. In 1983, Metzger changed the name to White American Resistance then White Aryan Resistance to reflect a more revolutionary philosophy. WAR advocates violence against non-Aryans:

> The Jews hate the White Race and are working to crush our people. . . . Jewish Marxism killed more than 200 million people. If the Holocaust were true, the world would have to kill over 194 million Kikes just to break even with the crimes of Jewish Marxism. . . . Charles Manson said that Hitler was a cool dude who leveled the Jews' karma. How true. There is no such thing as anti-Semitism, only karmic justice (ADL 1996: 26).

Box 4.6
Matt Hale

Matt Hale was born on July 27, 1971, and attended Bradley University in Peoria, Illinois, where he graduated with a baccalaureate in political science in May 1993. A biography authored by Hale indicates that his natural instincts, his knowledge of the historical inequality of the races, and his fascination with Adolf Hitler had all come together to provide him a purpose to life–doing his part to keep the white race intact (see http://www.ra-howa.com/hale.htm). While at Bradley, he made national news after putting up fliers on school bulletin boards advertising an upcoming meeting of the American White Supremacist Party (AWSP). After dissolving the AWSP, Hale tried to open a chapter of the National Association for the Advancement of White People (NAAWP), a group founded by David Duke. The NAAWP leadership never recognized this group and Hale abandoned this project but soon after discovered Klassen's Church of the Creator. In June 1998, Hale graduated from the Southern Illinois University School of Law and then passed the Illinois State Bar. The Fitness and Character Committee of the Illinois State Bar denied his application for a law license and that decision was appealed. On July 2, 1999, the Hearing Board ruled against Hale. Later that year, the U.S. Supreme Court refused to hear Hale's case, thus upholding the lower court's decision.

During law school, he actively sought recruits for the Church of the Creator. For the past five years, he has put out a monthly Creativity newsletter, placed many Creativity shows on cable access, and continues to run the WCOTC (Anti-Defamation League [ADL] 1999a).

Metzger publishes a tabloid entitled *WAR,* in which writers engage in some of the most outspoken and vehement racist anti-Jewish rhetoric in the neo-Nazi movement (Stern 1996). Metzger promoted the growth of the Skinhead movement. It published a youth magazine preaching hate, devoted a section to neo-Nazi Skinhead music, developed computer links between Skinheads and other hate groups in the United States, and established a small California organization called Aryan Youth Movement (Hamm 1993).

WAR has a site on the World Wide Web and operates telephone hotlines that provide the viewer–listener with recordings of white supremacist news and philosophy. In 1991, it began selling T-shirts featuring the cartoon character Bart Simpson in full Nazi uniform saluting in Nazi fashion and saying "Pure Nazi Dude!" A lawsuit claiming illegal infringement of copyright resulted in Metzger agreeing to a judgment barring him from further sale or use of Simpson material.

Odinism

Because both the FBI and the SPLC has recently stated that some neo-Nazis are adopting Odinism, it is important to look at the beliefs and activities of Odinists–not because Odinism in and of itself is a problem, but because some extremists and terrorists are using the religion to fit their own purposes.

Odinism, also known as Asatru, is an ancient, pre-Christian religion that originated in northern, eastern, and western parts of Europe thousands of years ago. It was officially eliminated about 800 years ago by the Catholic Church when the King of Sweden converted to Christianity. While many continued to practice the faith, most practitioners were forced underground. In the late 1940s and early 1950s, most Western nations repealed laws that made the practice of pagan religions illegal. Since that time, there has been an increasing number of converts to many of the pagan religions, including Odinism.

Today's Odinists are not practitioners of a blended religion, but rather, seek through study, investigation, and meditation, to reestablish a faithful version of one of the world's oldest religions. In short, Odinists believe that

- Religion is natural, organic, and ancestral. All genuine religion comes out of the ancient, natural, and indigenous past of its people. Genuine religion has no founder, as do cults that are designed to enslave their followers usually under the guise of freedom.
- Odinism is the ancient, ancestral, pre-Christian religion of the white race that grew out of northern, eastern, and western Europe. It has a wide pantheon of gods and goddesses, including *Odin,* the father of all gods; *Frigga,* the mother of all gods; *Freya,* the goddess of sensuality; *Frey,* the god of the feast and fertility; *Tyr,* god of battle and justice; *Thor,* son of Odin and god of defense and revenge; and *Njord,* god of the sea.
- Main rules of Odinist conduct are listed in the Nine Charges:

  1. To maintain candor and fidelity in love and devotions to the tried friend: though he strike me I will do him no scathe.

  2. Never to make a wrongsome oath: for great and grim is the reward for the breaking of plighted troth.
  3. To deal not hardly with the humble and lowly.
  4. To remember the respect that is due great age.
  5. To suffer no evil to go unremedied and to fight against the enemies of family, nation, race and faith: my foes will I fight in the field nor be burnt in my house.
  6. To succor the friendliness but to put no faith in the pledged word of a stranger people.
  7. If I hear the fool's word of a drunken man I will strive not for many a grief and the very death groweth out of such things.
  8. To give kind heed to dead men: straw-dead, sea-dead or sword-dead.
  9. To abide by the enactments of lawful authority and to bear with courage and fortitude decrees of the Norns. (www.paganlibrary.com/reference/odinism.php)

Several neo-Nazi groups, especially Skinheads, recently have become involved with Odinism. While this religion does not advocate violence and is neither extreme nor racist in origin or beliefs, racist Skinheads are attracted to it largely because of its Anglo-Saxon, white roots. Involvement from the right-wing first came to the attention of law enforcers with the FBIs publication of *Project Megiddo* in October 1999. In this report, the FBI warned law enforcers about possible millennium-related violence and specifically mentioned various patriot and hate-related groups, certain Christian sects, and Odinists as possible domestic terrorists (FBI 1999). To date, however, there has been no connection between Odinists and extremist activism or terrorist violence.

Black Separatist

By the 1990s, organizations that monitor hate crimes throughout the nation targeted several black hate groups. The most well-known and organized is the Nation of Islam, which has a long history of activism in the United States. One of the most recent, well-known, and barely organized is the New Black Panther Party.

Nation of Islam

Elijah Muhammad founded this American Black Muslim group during the 1930s, teaching that Allah (God) had appeared to him in human form and appointed him as a special prophet. Muhammad preached that the black man was created by the Supreme Being, the white man by an evil wizard–scientist named Yacub who, although he lived to age 152, never saw the "bleached out devil race" he created.

Muhammad forwarded a message of black pride and advised his followers to discard their slave names, often in favor of a simple "X." Strongly stressed were competitive private enterprise, self-reliance, and strict separation of the races. Their "separatist" belief is best seen in the Nation of Islam's request that the U.S. government give them at least one state where only Blacks would be allowed to live. Islam's appeal to black Americans hinged on the belief that up to one-fifth of all the Africans brought as slaves to this country were Muslims before they were forced to convert to Christianity.

In the early 1950s, Malcolm Little, who later became Malcolm X, joined the Nation of Islam. Malcolm X, a former felon, intensified an already vigorous recruitment in urban ghettoes and prisons. Yet, upon Malcolm X's return from a pilgrimage to Mecca, he relinquished some of his racist beliefs, defected from the Nation of Islam, and became an orthodox Muslim. He was assassinated shortly thereafter and his influence on the Nation of Islam subsequently decreased.

In 1975, Muhammad died at the age of 77 at which time he had built a following of 500,000. His son, Wallace Deen Muhammad, who inherited the leadership, changed the organization's name to the World Community of Islam in the West and turned it toward orthodox Islam and cooperation with the Whites. In contrast to both Malcolm X and Wallace Muhammad, another member, Louis Farrakhan, strictly adhered to the message of Elijah Muhammad. In 1978, Farrakhan formed his own group, taking with him the original name, Nation of Islam, and the beliefs of Elijah.

Minister Louis Farrakhan has led the Nation of Islam for the last twenty years. He and his followers have expressed prejudice against Whites, Catholics, the United States, and homosexuals, but their most extreme statements are directed at Jews. According to the ADL, Farrakhan has said that whites are "blue eyed devils" (ADL 1999b: 1), that Jews are "bloodsuckers" (ADL 1999b: 1), that Jews controlled the slave trade, and currently control the government, the media, and various black individuals and organizations. According to George and Wilcox (1992), among Farrakhan's more extreme statements have been charges that

- The American government has "poured drugs into" cities with large black populations.
- AIDS in Africa has been part and parcel of a white plot to gain control of that continent's minerals.
- Jews are wicked and practice a "dirty religion."
- "Hitler was a great man" (p. 349).

In addition, the Nation of Islam's weekly paper, *The Final Call,* often advertises anti-Semitic publications for purchase. In essence,

---

Box 4.7

Muhammad's Beliefs	*Orthodox / Traditional Islam*
He was a prophet	Seventh-century Muhammad was the final prophet
Blacks are superior to Whites in all ways	Eschews racism
Only Blacks allowed	Accepts all people
God is human	God is not human
No life after death	Life after death

Box 4.8
Understanding the Fundamentals of Islam

Muslims believe in one God, called Allah–the same God worshiped by Christians and Jews. Islam, which essentially means submission to the will of God, repeats the message of Abraham, Moses and Jesus: Obey God's commandments. Muslims believe that the Jewish and Christian religions wavered from that basic commitment, prompting God to reveal His truth once again to Mohammed from 610 to 632 A.D. They believe the Koran, Islam's sacred scripture, contains the word of God as received by Mohammed. Islam calls on its followers to satisfy five basic rites, the five pillars of Islam–declaration of faith, prayer, fasting during Ramadan, annual money offering to help the poor, and one pilgrimage to Mecca during their lifetime. Religious Muslims adhere to a strict code of personal behavior: no sexual relations outside of marriage; homosexuality is considered a sin; alcohol and mind-altering drugs are strictly forbidden; and no gambling since it violates the principle that all income should be gained form productive work.

In light of our discussion regarding domestic terrorism and Islamic fundamentalism, it is also important to note that Islam, like Christianity and Judaism, forbids suicide. To be killed in a holy war (jihad) guarantees paradise after death (Stencel 1993: 363–383).

---

the Nation of Islam, as a social movement of the right, is highly religious, stresses ethnocentricity, and advocates racial separatism and nationalism. These comments, however, must be reviewed in light of Farrakhan's agreement in spring 2000 to reunite with Orthodox Muslims.

New Black Panther Party (NBPP)

The roots of the NBPP go back to Milwaukee around 1990 when city alderman Michael McGee organized a Black Panther Militia that threatened to launch "urban guerrilla warfare" if black urban poverty was not alleviated with a large infusion of government funds. Sometime during the next few years, the group changed its name to the NBPP and organized chapters in Dallas–where it was led by Aaron Michaels–and Indianapolis–where it was led by Mmoja Ajabu.

The New Black Panthers, unlike their predecessors of the 1960s and 1970s, focused almost exclusively on hate rhetoric about Whites, Jews, and the U.S. government. McGee and Michaels outlined the new party's direction during a demonstration in May 1993 when they called for separating the races and overthrowing the U.S. government.

In 2000, very little is known about the NBPP's organization and ideology. It appears that the party is currently a federation of about 35 chapters in at least 13 cities with informal but important links to some black Muslim and other small black groups. Khalid Muhammad, the Panther's leader since 1998 and a former spokesman for the Nation of Islam, says the chapter leaders meet annually and maintain informal communications. In terms of their specific beliefs, that, too, is uncertain. However, during a fall 2000 speech in Detroit to an all-black crowd at the First Holy Temple of God in Christ, Muhammad remarked:

> I'm here to tell you that God has a people, that God has chosen a people. And it's not some hooked-nose, bagel-eatin', lox-eatin', perpetrating-a-fraud, just-crawled-out-of-the-caves-and-hills-of-Europe, so-called, wannabe, imposter Jew! . . . There's only two kinds of white folks: bad white folks and worse white folks . . . Malcolm X said if you find one good, kill him first, before he turns bad. Because he's only faking. . . . Whatever organization you are with or whatever religion, finally we have got a black united front that is being formed. . . . But we don't accept any white people at all. So your white girlfriend can't come with you, white boyfriend, white wife, they can't come. . . . Black power! Black

power! Black power! (as quoted in SPLC Fall 2000: 23).

Since the mid-1990s, the NBPP have used confrontational, armed demonstrations designed to gain attention from the media. They have been especially active in Texas, beginning with the May 1996 disruption of a Dallas school board meeting where Panthers threatened to enter with loaded weapons; the June 1996 black solidarity march in Greenville in response to the racist arsons in two black churches; in 1997 again in Dallas where they requested the creation of a separate school district for black students; and in 1998, clad in fatigues and brandishing shotguns and assault weapons, appeared at a KKK rally in Jasper to protect the black community in the wake of the brutal murder of James Byrd, Jr. In addition, in 1998, Muhammad organized his most public activity to date–the first of the Million Youth Marches that grew out of Louis Farrakhan's Million Man March of 1995. In 1998, about 10,000 black youth came to the march in Harlem. By 1999, attendance was about 2,000 and in 2000, only about 200 came to hear Muhammad's message.

Despite the increasing attention of the NBPP over the past year, it has not sparked the support from many black people. Instead, it has been labeled as a racist organization by many Whites, Jews, and Blacks across the nation.

PATRIOT AND MILITIA GROUPS

In October 1992, Identity Pastor Pete Peters convened an invitation-only gathering of 160 Christian men at a lodge in Estes Park, Colorado, to form a new coalition of anti-government patriots (Levin 1998). During that weekend, a network of militant anti-government zealots was created including Identity,

Posse Comitatus, Aryan Nations, neo-Nazis, tax resisters and Second Amendment advocates (Dees 1996). An important coalition was formed between Identity and other racist extremists on the one hand and nonracist, ultraconservative, and fundamentalist activists on the other—bound together by their antipathy for the federal government.

As we learned in Part One, belonging to extremist anti-government groups that conspire to overthrow the U.S. government is not new. Indeed, contemporary patriot groups like their historical counterparts, generally adhere to or advocate extreme anti-government doctrines. The patriot movement embraces a series of antagonisms toward American government, including opposition to gun control, taxation (including the belief that the Internal Revenue Service is in fundamental conflict with the individual's right to the fruits of his property and his labor), and the existing legal system (Durham 1996).

Patriot groups range from what are basically civil organizations that meet periodically on weekends to paramilitary groups that believe that a master plan exists to impose a United Nations-directed dictatorship. Many patriot organizations have adopted a strategy of "leaderless resistance," a term coined by Louis Beam, a former Grand Dragon of the KKK. This strategy is one where a movement is broken down into small cells of operatives, so they can act with greater stealth and avoid infiltration by the authorities. They are organized around ideology, not leaders.

In 1999, the SPLC estimated that 217 patriot groups were actively involved in anti-government activities. This was one-half the 1998 total of 435 patriot groups, and a 75 percent decrease over the 1996 all-time high number of 858. Of those active in 1999, 145 were "patriot" groups that include publishers, ministries, and citizens' groups opposed to the Zionist-oriented "New World Order" or

adhere to extreme anti-government doctrines; another 68 were citizen militias; and 4 were common-law courts.

In general, all three components of the patriot movement share the following beliefs:

- The federal government is involved in a conspiracy to disarm citizens and control the population. Once citizens are disarmed, they will not be able to resist the "one world dictatorship" advocated by the conspirators—the U.S. government, the United Nations, and foreign troops.
- Congress, the courts, the Federal Reserve System, the IRS, and the Supreme Court have established an "absolute tyranny" over Americans by subverting the original intent of the Constitution and Bill of Rights as written by the founding fathers.
- The Constitution permits the organization of private armies and gives citizens the right to carry weapons.
- The "real" Constitution has been suspended since 1933 when the Emergency Banking Act gave the president regulatory powers in times of war or emergency. Thus, a state of emergency remains in force and Americans are actually living under martial law, or an "unconstitutional dictatorship" of hidden exploiters in Washington, D.C.
- Unjust and immoral taxes have been imposed on the people without their consent.
- The time for traditional political reform has passed and their freedom can only be secured by resisting the nation's laws and attacking its institutions.
- The government has increasingly become anti-Christian, by supporting tax-funded abortions, a homosexual agenda, and public education that is anti-Bible, antifamily, anti-American, and anti-Constitutional.

Their activities, however, are somewhat different as the following discussion indicates.

Box 4.9
Leaderless Resistance

Former Klansman and Aryan Nations Ambassador at-large Louis Beam promoted the concept of leaderless resistance. This concept of leaderless resistance is often promoted by right-wing extremists as the most effective method of conducting terrorist operations and criminal activity. According to this concept, individuals who want to engage in criminal behavior are encouraged not to join active above-ground groups such as militias. Instead, extremists are encouraged to band together to form small autonomous cells of five to seven people that operate independently of one another. Cells do not operate hierarchically and do not have a single repeating structure.

The rationale behind this strategy is that it is harder for law enforcement to detect, monitor, infiltrate, and neutralize the criminal activities of small independent cells, compared with large above-ground groups. Individuals are encouraged to form very small, or even one-person cells. In theory, cells with more than one person are to consist of only close associates who can be trusted and will not discuss group activities and operational methods outside their cell.

It is the responsibility of each cell to acquire the necessary skills and intelligence to carry out their criminal acts. Proponents of this concept believe that since the United States is a target-rich environment, cells will instinctively know where, when, and how to act. Moreover, right-wing information mediums, such as periodicals, chat rooms, bulletin boards, Internet sites, and so forth, will keep each person informed of events (Abanes 1996; Beam 1992).

Patriot Groups

This category of publishers, ministries, and citizens' groups comprises the largest proportion of the entire patriot movement. The vast majority of these are tied to what has been called the sovereign citizens' movement, which, in turn, is based on members' interpretation of common law. As it arose in England, common law consisted of custom and tradition as interpreted by local judges, who in turn, respected the customs and common law of society. The common law for many sovereign patriot groups is that

- All government above the county level is illegitimate; the sheriff is the highest legitimate authority in the land.

- Sovereign citizens have the right to lawfully assemble to exercise their sovereignty and make their own laws.
- Sovereign citizens do not recognize federal law, thus, they do not have to pay state or federal taxes.
- Persons who interfere with sovereign citizens are guilty of obstructing the common law; such interference may constitute an act of war. (SPLC 1997)

This movement gradually gained momentum in the early 1990s. Foremost among such groups was the so-called freeman movement, which was popularized by the Freemen of Montana. In 1996, the Freemen sequestered themselves on a ranch and held the FBI at bay for eighty-one days before surrendering to authorities (see Chapter 6). The Freemen declared that they were exempt from the laws of the country and used bogus liens and money orders as part of a pseudolegal system of common law to defy the authority of actual courts and harass government officials.

This anti-government militancy of the Montana Freemen has inspired like-minded activists in at least twenty-three states to file bogus liens, pass phony checks, and deny the legitimacy of the U.S. government. Some adherents to this philosophy are using the Internet to teach people how to avoid paying taxes, drop out of the Social Security system, and defraud federal and state governments. Arrests and some convictions have occurred as a result of actions taken by adherents to the Freemen philosophy.

Another prominent group of sovereign citizens advocates for the total political separation from the federal, state, and local governments by creating a new "nation." The Republic of Texas (RoT) in Fort Davis was the first to burst on the patriot scene when its self-styled ambassador and consul general, Richard McLaren, proclaimed its existence in January 1996. According to members of RoT as indicated on their web site:

> The Republic of Texas never died—it was just covered up with a blanket called the State of Texas for a century and a half . . . it's time we throw off that dusty blanket and come back into the light as a nation of free men and women who won't bow down to the false God of government. A nation where the people are truly free. (www.texasrepublic.com)

RoT members do not recognize the existence of the State of Texas and instead, believe that the Republic of Texas declared in 1845 is the only legitimate government within the current Texan boundaries. RoT gained notoriety in April 1997 when McLaren kidnapped a married couple near his property, which is located on a rugged tract of land called the Davis Mountains resort in west Texas. According to McLaren, he had "arrested" the couple and held them as prisoners of war for five days only after Jeff Davis County Sheriff Steve Bailey had illegally "kidnapped" the RoT commander, Robert Schneidt, for trespassing in McLaren's subdivision.

The kidnapping sparked a week-long armed standoff with 300 police at his group's compound. McLaren was arrested, tried, convicted of ordering followers to kidnap the couple, and sentenced to 99 years in state prison. He will be eligible for parole in 15 years but will then have to serve 12 more years in federal prison for a second crime—issuing almost $2 billion in bogus warrants to help fund his movement. Since McLaren's conviction, the Republic has splintered into several different groups that in 1999, formally operated in at least six different locations within Texas. The statewide leadership continues to be involved in the following activities:

- Maintaining their web site.
- Publishing *Texas Independence Magazine.*
- Spreading the word among the 50,000 members whom RoT claims to have "signed on as sovereign citizens."

By the end of the 1990s, most members of the sovereign citizens' movement found themselves communicating more through the Internet than in active organizations of citizens who regularly met. In 1999, the SPLC found 263 Internet sites linked to the patriot movement.

Militias

Individuals who flock to the militia movement are estranged from the political process that we take for granted. They are people who see their government as the enemy and who believe its laws and legal system are used not to help and protect them, but to take away their rights, infringe on their beliefs, and destroy their way of life. They are people who respond to what they believe is a higher call. Rather than obey the laws, they resist them as a matter of principle–even to the death (Dees 1996).

The contemporary militia movement is a mass social movement. Self-styled defensive paramilitary groups coalesced in the early 1990s around far-right hatred of big government. The organizing principle of the militias is that the government has been taken over by evil forces and could not be reformed but must be combated with arms (Stern 1996). Militia members are united in their quest to protect American constitutional rights and in their view that the federal government is infringing on those rights. However, the patriot-militia movement is not easily defined. It has no single national organization or leadership. Rather, it consists of previously unrelated groups and individuals that have found a common cause in their deep distrust of the government and in their eagerness to fight back.

The militias are organized on local and state levels. They are usually structured around a core of local leaders with a fluctuating band of followers. Most militia groups participate in paramilitary training, survivalist tactics, and emergency medical treatment. Some actively pursue change through lobbying efforts with their elected representatives. Organizations finance their activities through membership fees, fundraisers, lectures and training seminars, the sale of videotapes, T-shirts, and publications.

The movement is characterized by a continuum. There are people who gather regularly to discuss the Constitution and perceived federal intrusions. Other individuals trade conspiracy theories, some of them anti-Semitic, at gun shows, on talk radio, and over the Internet. Finally, some individuals are members of heavily armed underground paramilitary units. There appear, however, to be a

core of beliefs: apocalypticism and a view that the federal government is part of the New World Order that seeks to undermine our rights. As we approached the millennium, there were efforts to unify the militias nationally but retain local control. There have been "calls" for members of the militia to meet in a specified location to show support for the movement but in many cases, the call was not heeded because militia members did not identify with the problems of that area.

In the 1990s we witnessed a new generation of armed organizations, the citizen militias. These militias, the largest of which are in Michigan and Montana, believe in a strict interpretation of the second amendment that reads: "A well-regulated militia, being necessary to the security of a free State, the right of the people to keep and bear arms, shall not be infringed." They believe that when the government does not protect the rights of its citizens, the militia shall assume that responsibility.

Two of the more notable leaders in the militia movement include Linda Thompson and Col. James "Bo" Gritz. Linda Thompson, an Indianapolis-based attorney, has proclaimed herself the Acting Adjunct General of the Unorganized Militia of the United States. Thompson frequently travels to militia gatherings and gun shows and communicates with fellow militia supporters on a computer bulletin board she operates with her husband, Al Thompson. Col. James "Bo" Gritz is a former Green Beret who formed a Constitutional Covenant Community in northern Idaho called Almost Heaven. The settlement is widely believed to be a paramilitary complex. Gritz opposes gun control and urges supporters to resist any attempts by the federal government to "take away their guns."

At least two militias have greatly influenced the entire movement and deserve mention here: the Militia of Montana and the Arizona Patriots.

Box 4.10
James "Bo" Gritz

Bo Gritz was born on January 18, 1939, as an only child. His father, an Army Air Corps pilot, was shot out of the sky in November 1944. Bo attended the Fort Union Military Academy and, at age 18, enlisted in the Army. He was court-martialed twice but was acquitted while still in basic training. He became a Green Beret and Special Forces lieutenant colonel during six years of combat duty in Vietnam. He commanded a mobile guerrilla force assigned to missions in the "dark zones" of North Vietnam, places that had never been penetrated by U.S. forces. General William Westmoreland saw Gritz as a classic American war hero.

After retiring from the military in 1979, Gritz took up the campaign for American prisoners of war (POW) whom he maintained were still being held in the jungles of Laos. While on his mission to document the presence of POW's, Gritz alleged he learned of the involvement of U.S. officials in the lucrative heroin trade and became severely disenchanted with the federal government. During the late 1980s, Gritz's anger at the government translated into his first venture into politics, and the beginning of his lengthy engagement with white supremacists. At the urging of Willis Carto, founder of the Liberty Lobby, Gritz agreed to run for vice president on the far-right Populist Party ticket. The convention nominated David Duke to head up Gritz's ticket. Duke won 0.05 percent of the national vote and in 1992, when Gritz headed the ticket, he captured 0.1 percent.

Gritz became more prominent in hate-group circles in August 1992 when he negotiated an end to the siege on Ruby Ridge in Idaho that involved Randy Weaver and federal authorities. James Aho, an Idaho State University professor who has written extensively on the white-supremacist movement in the Pacific Northwest says Gritz "compromises himself by associating with people who are racist. But he's not an out-and-out racist. I've never been able to find evidence of that" (as cited in Stuebner 1998: 15). Many view him as the "true American hero" that gives him credibility, particularly among some militia members.

He has trained thousands of anti-government zealots to prepare for Armageddon, through his survivalist, paramilitary training sessions which he calls S.P.I.K.E. (Specially Prepared Individuals for Key Events). These S.P.I.K.E. sessions began in February 1993. The training involves such topics as counterintelligence maneuvers, cryptography, and weapons combat. Gerald "Jack" McLamb, a retired Arizona police officer, assists him in this training and is involved with Gritz in the construction of a "Christian Covenant Community" in central Idaho, near the small town of Kamiah, called Almost Heaven. Critics call the isolated 280-acre settlement a heavily guarded base of operations for patriot tax protesters, anti-Semitic fanatics, and a haven for anti-government extremists and bigots (Abanes 1996; Stuebner 1998: 10–15).

Box 4.11
John Trochmann

John Trochmann moved to Noxon, Montana, in the mid-1980s and brought with him his white supremacist history and beliefs. He attended a taxpayer meeting convened because people were concerned about their property taxes and advised residents to "refuse to pay. . . . Those government people taxed you at a meeting where you didn't get to vote. That's illegal government. . . . Common law, constitutional law says taxation without representation is illegal" (Stern 1996: 68). Trochmann also believed in the presence of a "shadow government" or "banking elite" that many believed meant Jews. He also believed that sometime in the next century, America's white population would perish.

Trochmann was a Christian Patriot, believing that the Constitution and the Bill of Rights were meant to empower white men and that any government that wanted to uphold the rest of the Constitution (i.e., amendments after number ten including racial discrimination) violated the organic Constitution and the common law and was, accordingly, illegal and worthy of armed opposition (Stern 1996).

Militia of Montana

The Militia of Montana (M.O.M.) is probably one of the most visible and most extreme of militias. John Trochmann with his brother David and David's son Randy founded M.O.M. Headquartered in Noxon, Montana, M.O.M. was formed to protest the 1992 federal raid against white supremacist Randy Weaver (see Chapter 5). Trochmann maintains that the militias have a singular mandate: "Return to the Constitution of the United States" (Abanes 1996: 69).

M.O.M. believes the government is attempting to strip Americans of their second amendment rights. It sees the government at the heart of a conspiracy to take guns away from the patriots and tax them into poverty, strip them of their constitutional rights, and place them under the government of a one-world government (Dees 1996). Their message, like most patriot groups of the early 1990s, is more anti-government than racist.

Their material on how to form a militia is perhaps one of its greatest contribution to the movement. It provided the information on which other militia sprouted up across the country and is widely read in militia circles (Dees 1996). M.O.M. distributes a catalog offering numerous videotapes and publications on a variety of conspiracy themes, and a comprehensive bombmaking and warfare manual, *The Road Back*. An eight-page pamphlet titled *The Militia* discusses the history of the militias and their origins in the United States. Their monthly newsletter *Taking Aim* regularly warns readers of impending tyranny.

Some members of the organization circulate neo-Nazi publications among themselves. One such book, *Seed of the Woman,* is a novel detailing the wild exploits of several young neo-Nazis. Its favorable depiction of Nazi-inspired slaughter and its promotion of Nazi doctrines make it a prescription for violence against Jews, Blacks, homosexuals, and others. There is evidence to suggest that they have ties to Liberty Lobby, an organization Willis Carto founded in Washington, D.C., in 1955. Liberty Lobby disseminates anti-Semitic propaganda through three main vehicles:

1. *The Spotlight,* a weekly tabloid newspaper, established in 1975, with a circulation of about 100,000;
2. Radio talk shows, Radio Free America, and Editor's Roundtable; and
3. *The Barnes Review,* a monthly magazine devoted to historical revisionism and conspiracy-theory propaganda.

Arizona Patriots

Ty Hardin founded the Arizona Patriots in 1982 as an anti-Semitic group with an emphasis on stockpiling weapons and baiting public officials. The Patriots gained public notice in the 1980s by its efforts to clog the Arizona court system with nuisance lawsuits. Several heavily armed members discussed plans to murder government officials and in 1986, federal agents raided a patriot camp and confiscated a home-made blowgun, night-vision goggles, gas masks, spent shell casings, and numerous rocket-ammunition crates. They also found plans to bomb a Phoenix synagogue and the Simon Wiesenthal Center in Los Angeles. The FBI arrested eight members of the group, and several were convicted of federal crimes. While the group had disbanded by the late 1980s, ADL indicates that recent reports suggest the group may be reconstituting itself.

Common Law Courts

Common law courts have often been called the perpetrators of paper terrorism because they use bogus liens and arrest warrants to harass and terrorize their targeted victims.

• *Liens.* Members of the movement file fake liens against law enforcement officers, state attorneys, and judges who have brought cases against them, as well as anyone they perceive to be interfering with their common law rights or religious and political beliefs. Although the liens have no legal effect, they often sit in court records and credit bureau files that become a nightmare when the "target" tries to have them removed.
• *Arrest warrants and "Wanted" posters.* Members issue these for prominent public officials after these officials have been "indicted" by common law grand juries.

For example, in the mid-1990s, Hamilton, Montana, municipal court judge Martha Bethel was told if she didn't dismiss charges on a routine traffic ticket issued to one of the local "sovereign citizens" a warrant would be issued for her arrest. This was followed by months of anonymous phone threats. Later, a federal law enforcement agent alerted Bethel that a murder contract had been put out on her.

Such actions have tied up the resources of law enforcers and other criminal justice personnel with these phony lawsuits, liens, and courts. So how big of a danger do common law courts pose? In 1996, the SPLC identified 131 common law courts active in 35 states–a 35 percent increase over 1995. However, it also noted an incredible decrease of these courts by 1998–31 actual courts–and again in 1999 with a total of four operational courts. What accounts for such de-escalation? Is it a lack of interest? Failure to achieve their goals? In fact, the decrease is due to a widespread backlash by the state authorities who were tired of dealing with common law swindles and threats.'

As of mid-1998, eighteen states had passed legislation that outlaws the activities of common law courts and strengthens existing sanctions.[42] Another eight states (California

---

[42] Idaho, Montana, Washington (1995); Hawaii, Michigan, Missouri, Montana (second time), Ohio (1996); Colorado, Florida, Georgia, Idaho (second time), Nevada, Oklahoma, Oregon, South Dakota, Texas, Utah, Wisconsin, Wyoming (1997).

included) were considering similar legislation.[43] The conduct prohibited by the legislation is fairly uniform. The laws

- outlaw filing undocumented liens,
- make it easier to get undocumented liens lifted,
- criminalize participation in "sham legal processes,"
- impose harsh penalties for intimidating public officials by threatening them with liens or common law "criminal verdicts," and
- outlaw using liens to punish officials for "nonperformance" of imaginary duties.

However, the penalties greatly differ. Some states—like Montana—have harsh penalties. Under the Montana Anti-Intimidation Act of 1996, politically motivated threats against public officials are punishable by up to ten years in prison and fines of as much as $50,000. Some states, however, offer only civil remedies for the aggrieved party.

SUMMARY

Over the past several decades, Americans have witnessed the rise of an evolutionary breed of right-wing extremists and terrorists—people who are most often aligned with the politically-extreme right-wing. Such right-wing extremists and terrorists are not highly organized but more of a breeding ground from which individual terrorists and small terrorist groups have emerged and continue to develop (Laqueur 1999). They engage in mutual help and show solidarity on occasion, but there is no central command and little coordination. There are ideological differences between these groups. Some

groups strongly adhere to an anti-Semitic belief while others believe in a cataclysmic break in history and the emergence of a New World (millenarian).

Data collected by the SPLC—one of the nation's most respected private hate-monitoring organizations—indicate that in 1999, there were 457 active hate groups, as well as 217 active patriot groups operating within the United States. Members of these right-wing groups have committed bank robberies, bombings, and murder. We know that the groups vary in size and that the manner in which they spread their message varies—from holding annual conventions and cultural fests; publishing magazines, journals, books, and weekly tabloids; maintaining sites on the Internet; and holding public rallies.

The largest of the two groups—the American hate movement—comprises three distinct yet interrelated groups of white supremacists, racial-religious extremists, and black separatists.

1. White supremacists adhere to right-wing rhetorical traditions of anti-Semitism, the superiority of white people over minorities, the belief that white people have the right to subjugate people of all other races, and often, the desire to create an all-white Aryan nation.
2. Racial-religious extremists belong to groups that have radical religious ideologies that are distinctly non-Christian and often anti-Christian in nature.
3. Black hate groups, including the Nation of Islam and the New Black Panther Party, espouse racist, anti-white rhetoric and propose an extremist agenda of black nationalism.

Patriot groups cling to an elaborate conspiratorial theory that the ongoing economic and political events (e.g., legal limits on gun

---

[43] Alaska, Arizona, California, Kansas, Kentucky, New Mexico, Pennsylvania, and South Carolina.

ownership) are part of a much larger plan to "enslave Americans by disarming the population and making the currency worthless" (SPLC 1997: 4). Many believe that these gun-ownership restrictions, in particular, mirror events described by Pierce in *The Turner Diaries,* where he writes about the U.S. government banning the private possession of firearms. The eventual result will be the New World Order—a one-world government either administered by the United Nations or governed by the ZOG—Zionist Occupied Government. The patriot movement uses alternative systems of communication (e.g., gun shows, computer bulletin boards, Bible camps, pamphlets) to tie the far right together. The use of these alternative systems also suggests distrust for the mainstream media sources. National news services are viewed as official mouthpieces of the government.

By the end of the 1990s, distinctions between the hate and the patriot movements began to diminish. Increasingly, patriot movements embraced racist rhetoric and welcomed members from the racist right-wing into their organizations. However, many patriot groups continued to maintain that they were patriots, not racists. Additionally, over the last ten years, both movements have experienced intense factionalism, resulting in the division of ever-smaller groups—groups that often have adopted the phantom cell structure of leaderless resistance that is designed to minimize the risk of law enforcement penetration. These cells are encouraged to act alone, without communicating directly with the leadership of the movement (Stern 1999). Thus, individuals and groups operate independently of each other and never report to a central headquarters or single leader for direction or instructions. This strategy ensures the movement will survive.

Survival, however, has recently been questioned given the decrease of far-right activity that began in 1998. For instance, in 1999 the SPLC noted the active involvement of 457 hate groups—compared with the 537 recorded in 1998. The decrease in the number of patriot groups has been even more impressive. In 1999, the SPLC tallied a total of 217 patriot organizations, representing one-half of the 435 active groups in 1998 and a decrease of more than 75 percent from the 858 groups that operated in 1996.

Several factors have contributed to the decline in both patriot and hate activity. First, many members have become bored and tired of working for a cause that seems less important given the increased possibility of arrest due to federal, state, and local law enforcement crackdowns on hate- and patriot-related activity. Second, newly passed state legislation aimed at curbing militia and common law court activity have sent the message that hate and patriot crimes will be punished more severely. Third, many members from both movements have retired from active duty and instead retreated to the Internet where the SPLC recorded 263 active patriot sites in 1999. Fourth, the increased use of civil courts to force members of hate groups to assume financial liability for preaching and teaching hate has put some organizations out of business as well as greatly diminished the outreach of others.

Does this mean that the right-wing extremist movement is going away? According to organizations that closely monitor these groups, those who remain in the right-wing extremist movement still pose a great danger to American society for several reasons:

- Those who persist in the movements are among the most violent, avid, and absolute believers in their hate and/or patriotic cause.
- Some of those who have left the movements have begun to take what law enforcers often refer to as the "lone wolf" approach.

- Some who have left have increasingly gravitated to newer ideologies (see Chapter 7).
- Many have adopted a political mainstreaming strategy by running for elected office and supporting political parties.

Clearly, the right-wing extremist factions in American society are not disappearing. Rather, by the end of the twentieth century, most had learned to adapt to and capitalize on the political, social, economic, and ideology realities of the time. What the future may hold for these groups is the subject of Chapter 7.

DISCUSSION QUESTIONS

1. Describe and discuss the teachings of Christian Identity. How have various hate and patriot-militia groups adopted these teachings?
2. What are some arguments for and against the inclusion of patriot-militia groups and hate groups in a discussion of domestic terrorism?
3. What are some commonalties and differences between and among white supremacists, black separatist, other racial-religious orientations and patriot-militia groups?
4. The Ku Klux Klan experienced intense factionalism and the tendency to divide into ever-smaller groups. What roles do you believe these characteristics play, if any, in the viability and stature of the Klan groups?
5. It has been stated that the patriot-militia movement lacks central leadership and adheres to a leaderless resistance organizational structure for the purposes of carrying out criminal actions. What problems are created by this organizational structure? Do you believe these groups

pose a serious threat to the U.S. government? Why or why not?
6. Why do you think there is a resurgence of active recruitment into hate groups?
7. What role do you think the media (television, print) play in either strengthening or weakening the ideologies–causes of white supremacist groups?

STUDY QUESTIONS

1. The ADL states that the National Alliance's dramatic growth is significant because it comes at a time when other neo-Nazi organizations, as well as groups like the KKK, are becoming weaker and more fragmented. Moreover, the National Alliance does not appear to be siphoning members from these declining groups, but actually recruiting a fresh cast of educated, middle-class individuals. What evidence, including hard data, can you find supporting this statement?
2. According to the SPLC, women on the radical right are increasingly reexamining their position in the world of white supremacy. It is a similar debate that took place in the late 1960s when radical left-wing groups like The Weathermen, which originally relegated women members to supporting their male counterparts, began to consider more active roles for women. The Weathermen changed its name to the Weather Underground, and many of the female members were using guns. First, what are some of the traditional views of women held by various radical-right groups (e.g., Aryan Nations, Knights of the Ku Klux Klan)? Examine the available literature and determine whether women are in fact assuming more varied roles within these groups. Which groups appear more

receptive to women? Should one's gender define one's role in a racist organization?

3. The FBI, through the Uniform Crime Report system, collects data on hate crimes as part of its mandate. First, how does the FBI define "hate group"? What elements of a definition of terrorism are included in their definition of hate? What are the current figures on the level of activity for these right-wing domestic terrorists groups? How does the FBI data compare with the data recorded and published by the ADL and the SPLC? Are the activities of these hate groups either overrepresented or underrepresented in any of these datasets? If so, how would you explain the discrepancies?

4. Examine the FBI data on right-wing domestic terrorism. What trends reveal themselves, particularly during the 1990s? Did any one year stand out in terms of the number and severity of terrorist acts? If so, which group was responsible and what resulted from government actions?

5. What is the legal status of militias? Do states have laws against organized armed groups operating without state sanction? If so, describe these laws.

6. Louis Beam has a long history of involvement in the patriot–militia movement. Do a biographical search on Beam and discuss his role in promoting hate in America. Is he, as Dees (1996) argues, far and away the most dangerous and most radical of the racist leaders?

7. Research the existence of extremists or militia groups in your region. Do they present a concern for public safety in the community?

8. Describe and discuss the role of conspiracy theories in the patriot–militia movement. Who are the leading spokespersons suggesting the presence of a government conspiracy? What credence do you put in these theories?

REFERENCES

Abanes, Richard: *Rebellion, Racism and Religion: American Militias.* Downers Grove, IL: Inter-Varsity Press, 1996.

Anti-Defamation League: *Paranoia as Patriotism: Far Right Influences and the Militia Movement.* New York: Author, 1996.

——: *Vigilante Justice: Militias and 'Common Law Courts' Wage War Against the Government.* New York: Author, 1997.

——: World Church of the Creator. *Backgrounder.* New York: Author, 1999a.

——: Nation of Islam. *Backgrounder.* New York: Author, 1999b.

Beam, Louis: *Leaderless Resistance. Special Report On the Meeting of the Christian Men Held in Estes Park, Colorado, October 23, 24, 25, 1992: Concerning the Killing of Vickie and Samuel Weaver by the United States Government.* LaPorte, CO: Scriptures for America, 1992.

Bender, David, Leone, Bruno, Barbour, Scott, and Stalcup, Brenda (Eds.): *The Militia Movement.* San Diego, CA: Greenhaven Press, 1997.

Blee, Kathleen M.: *Women of the Klan: Racism and Gender in the 1920s.* Berkeley, CA: University of California Press, 1991.

Cotter, John M.: Sounds of hate: White power rock and roll and the neo-Nazi skinhead subculture. *Terrorism and Political Violence, 11* (2): 111–140, Summer 1999.

Dees, Morris (with James Corcoran): *Gathering Storm: America's Militia Threat.* New York: HarperCollins, 1996.

Durham, Martin: Preparing for Armageddon: Citizen Militias, the Patriot Movement and the Oklahoma City Bombing. *Terrorism and Political Violence, 8* (1): 65–79, Spring 1996.

Federal Bureau of Investigation: *Project Megiddo–A Threat Analysis for the New Millennium.* Washington, DC: The Domestic Terrorism Analysis Unit (NS-70), October 1999.

George, John, and Wilcox, Laird: *Nazis, Communists, Klansmen and Others on the Fringe.* Buffalo, NY: Prometheus Books, 1992.

Hamm, Mark S.: *American Skinheads: The Criminology and Control of Hate Crime.* Westport, CT: Praeger, 1993.

Hoffman, Bruce: Terrorism in the United States during 1985. *TVI Journal:* 4–8, 1986.

Kaplan, Jeffrey: Right-wing violence in North America. *Terrorism and Political Violence,* 7 (1): 44–95, 1995.

——: Leaderless resistance. *Terrorism and Political Violence, 9* (3): 80–95, Autumn 1997.

Laqueur, Walter: *The Age of Terrorism.* Boston: Little, Brown, 1987.

——: *The New Terrorism: Fanaticism and the Arms of Mass Destruction.* New York: Oxford University Press, 1999.

Levin, Brian: The Patriot Movement: Past, Present, and Future. In Kushner, Harvey W. (Ed.): *The Future of Terrorism–Violence in the New Millennium.* Thousand Oaks, CA: Sage, 1998, pp. 97–131.

Pitts, William L., Jr.: Davidians and Branch Davidians. In Wright, Stuart (Ed.): *Armageddon in Waco: Critical Perspectives on the Branch Davidian Conflict.* Chicago, IL: University of Chicago Press, 1995, pp. 20–42.

Poland, James M.: *Understanding Terrorism: Groups, Strategies and Responses.* Englewood Cliffs, NJ: Prentice-Hall, 1988.

Ross, Loretta: White Supremacy in the 1990s. In Berlet, Chip (Ed.): *Eyes Right! Challenging the Right-wing Backlash.* Boston: South End Press, 1995, pp. 166–181.

Schwartz, Alan M. (Ed.): *Danger Extremism: The Major Vehicles and Voices on America's Far Right Fringe.* New York: Anti-Defamation League, 1996.

Shinbaum, Myrna: *Press Release.* New York: Anti-Defamation League, May 16, 1996.

Smith, Brent L.: *Terrorism in America: Pipe Bombs and Pipe Dreams.* Albany, NY: State University of New York Press, 1994.

Southern Poverty Law Center: *False Patriots: The Threat of Antigovernment Extremists.* Montgomery, AL: Southern Poverty Law Center, 1997.

——: William Pierce: A political history. *Intelligence Report 93:* 14–15, 1999.

——: Active Hate groups in the U.S. in 1999. *Intelligence Report 97:* 30–39, Winter 2000.

——: Snarling at the white man. *Intelligence Report 100:* 16–23, Fall 2000.

Sprinzak, Ehud: Right-wing terrorism in a comparative perspective: The case of split delegitimization. *Terrorism and Political Violence, 7* (1): 17–43, Spring 1995.

Stencel, Sandra (Ed.): Muslims in America (Special Issue). *CQ Researcher, 3* (16): 363–383, 1993.

Stern, Jessica: *The Ultimate Terrorists.* Cambridge, MA: Harvard University Press, 1999.

Stern, Kenneth S.: *A Force Upon the Plain: The American Militia Movement and the Politics of Hate.* New York: Simon & Schuster, 1996.

Stuebner, Stephen: True Gritz: Will the real Bo Gritz please stand up. *Intelligence Report, 12:* 10–15, Fall 1998.

Vetter, Harold J., and Gary R. Perlstein: *Perspectives on Terrorism.* Pacific Grove, CA: Brooks/Cole, 1991.

Wade, Wyn Craig: *The Fiery Cross: The Ku Klux Klan in America.* New York: Simon & Schuster, 1987.

Chapter 5

SPECIAL-INTEREST EXTREMISTS AND TERRORISTS

Many experts identify three broad categories of domestic terrorist groups: left-wing, right-wing, and special-interest (Mullins 1997). While Chapters 3 and 4 discussed the first two categories, our focus herein will shift to special-interest terrorist groups. These groups are committed to a specific cause and focus on the resolution of particular issues. While the causes themselves are not illegal, committing terrorism is illegal.

This chapter is divided into two sections: the first discusses special-interest groups that have been involved in both extremist and terrorist actions, and the second discusses special-interest groups that have only espoused extremist philosophies but have not yet stepped over the ideological line into terrorist activities.

EXTREMIST AND TERRORIST GROUPS

While there are many special-interest groups that espouse extremist rhetoric as well as been involved in some sort of terrorist activity, we have confined our discussion to four of the most prominent movements oper-

ating over the past twenty years: ecological resistance (environmentalists), anti-environmental, animal rights, and anti-abortion.

Ecological Resistance Movements

The tenets of ecological terrorism are rooted in the philosophy of ecological consciousness, which is the belief that humans have to change themselves to repair human destruction of nature (Mullins 1997). The ecological resistance groups that are part of the radical environmental movement carry out their political campaigns to state their contempt for the manner in which the current system handles environmental policies.

They have struggled against a number of issues including logging of the old-growth redwoods that provided habitat for the threatened northern spotted owl, whaling, drift-net fishing, and the wearing of fur. A variety of terms have been applied to these resistance movements including ecoterrorism, environmental terrorism, ecological terrorism, ecotage, and monkey-wrenching. Whatever the term, some of their activities involve the use or threatened use of criminal violence, the targeting of innocent victims or property that are symbolic in nature and meant to reach a large audience for environmental-political purposes. As Eagen (1996) notes, these groups have three important elements in common in that they

1. argue that due to environmental necessity, an uncompromising position is needed;
2. spend their time and money on direct action to achieve this goal, rather than on lobbying government and industry; and
3. typically are grass roots organizations with little or no pay, perks, or hierarchical structure (pp. 2–3).

In addition, many individuals involved in these resistance movements do adhere to a firm position and engage in activities that range from acts of civil disobedience to acts of terrorism.

The conflict for many in the environmental movement revolves around the issue of whether the natural world is a place to manage or a place to revere. Eagan (1996) also suggests that historically, once a cause becomes mainstream—as environmentalism has—extremists find themselves pressed to articulate even more radical ideas. This section will discuss the origins and philosophies of two major ecological groups: Earth First! and Earth Liberation Front.

Earth First!

Earth First! (EF!), considered the most active and notorious homegrown radical environmental group in the United States, grew out of the lobbying by environmental groups in the late 1970s. David Foreman, one of the founders, was chief lobbyist for the Wilderness Society in Washington, D.C., in the 1970s and quit in 1979 when the Wilderness Society's management changed. Two trends in the late 1970s came into conflict and served as an impetus for people like Foreman

to move in a new direction to advocate on behalf of environmental interests (Lee 1995):

1. The recognition that successful lobbying required considerable financial resources, specialized knowledge of government functions, and an active presence in government.
2. The increase in the number of local or grassroots activity in the environmental area and the development of a more militant lobbying elite (pp. 26–27).

Lee also suggests that the publication of Edward Abbey's novel *The Monkey Wrench Gang* in 1975 coincided with these shifting trends in environmental lobbying. The book describes the exploits of four individuals (one woman and three men) who decide to defend the wilderness by any means necessary. Abbey described monkey-wrench terrorism as a form of low-technology sabotage of equipment; EF! has since defined it as ecotage (Mullins 1997). The primary importance of this fictional novel was that it probably helped shape the ideas and values that Earth First! espouses.

In Abbey's book, in the early 1970s, a group known as the Eco-Raiders used unconventional and illegal tactics, such as burning billboards, vandalism, and decommissioning bulldozers, to slow the growth of the suburbs near Tucson, Arizona (Lee 1995). The Monkey Wrench Gang traveled across the American Southwest pulling survey stakes, disabling or destroying bulldozers, ruining oil well drilling equipment, and plotting to explode several bridges, with their ultimate goal to demolish Glen Canyon Dam (Scarce 1990).

Another important turning point for the environmental movement began in 1977 and continued through 1979 when the U.S. Forest Service evaluated the 80 million acres of wilderness under its control and opted to keep only 15 million completely off-limits to timber, mining, and tourism interests (Eagan

1996). The decision to give this small percentage of eligible land a wilderness designation was a tremendous disappointment to the environmental movement and compounded its dissatisfaction (Lee 1995). To Foreman, it represented the inability of the traditional political system to effectively address the environmental crisis. Foreman identified this decision, known as the Roadless Area Review Evaluation (RARE II), as the primary impetus for the creation of Earth First!.

In April 1980, after assuming the position as the Wilderness Society's southwestern representative in New Mexico, David Foreman, along with four other friends with experience in the environmental area, went on a hike in the Pinacate Desert of Mexico: Ron Kezar, a longtime member of the Sierra Club as well as a seasonal worker for the National Park Service; Bart Koehler, who had worked for the Wilderness Society in Wyoming and left after RARE II; Mike Roselle, a veteran member of several radical left-wing groups; and Howie Wolke, the Wyoming representative for the Friends of the Earth.

As they were returning to the United States, they were "ranting and raving about the emasculated mainstream and fantastic talk of a group that would fight to set aside multi-million acre ecological preserves in Ohio, South Texas, and other forsaken places across the nation" (Scarce 1990: 61). They discussed setting up a massive system of ecological land preserves in every bioregion in the United States. Foreman called out "Earth First," and the organization was created. The exclamation point was added later that year.

Foreman stated that the main reason for Earth First! was to create a broader spectrum within the environmental community and specifically, to add a radical wing of the environmental movement: "The people who started Earth First! decided there was a need for a radical wing that would make the Sierra Club look moderate. Someone needs to say

what needs to be said, and do what needs to be done, and take the strong actions to dramatize it" (as quoted in Eagan 1996: 6).

Earth First!'s belief system is rooted in a philosophy known as deep ecology (Lee 1995). In its most basic form, deep ecology demands that human beings re-evaluate their relationship with the environment in such a way as to acknowledge that both human and non-human life have an intrinsic moral worth.

Organizationally, Earth First! consisted of autonomous groups that shared the same beliefs. There was no bureaucracy, no lobbyists or spokesperson, just a group of devoted, unpaid, grassroots activists (Scarce 1990). Lee (1995) also suggests that at its founding, Earth First! was well-organized, and that a number of close friends of the group of five who traveled to Mexico were also influential in its creation and activities.

Earth First! activism emerged with the avowed purpose to raise the level of confrontation between the mainstream environmental movement and its countermovement, corporations, and the state (Ingalsbee 1996). EF!ers rejected the mainstream environmental movement's resource-mobilization model of activism and instead advocated "no compromise in defense of Mother Earth" (Ingalsbee 1996: 264). Initially, they engaged in activism including nonviolent civil disobedience, strategic property destruction, and other forms of direct action.

In addition, beginning on July 4, 1980, they held annual Round River Rendezvous' to bring Earth First!ers together to show solidarity, celebrate achievements, serve as a forum to conduct business, and share speeches, poetry readings, and musical performances. Sometimes rendezvous attendees would sit in a circle and perform an exercise called a Council of All Beings, originated by Australian activist John Seed (Parfit 1990). At a Council, each individual chose a nonhu-

Box 5.1
Deep Ecology

Arne Naess coined the phrase deep ecology in 1973 to distinguish between two forms of environmentalism (shallow and deep ecology) and provide a philosophical framework for social transformation. The shallow ecology movement is designed to fight against pollution and resource depletion. Its central objective is the health and affluence of people in developed countries. The deep ecology movement argues that humans are part of the whole, not the master of it (Naess 1973, Stark 1995). Two core values guide deep ecology:

1. Self-realization extends the environmentally conscious individual's perception beyond the traditionally accepted aspects of the self to include the environment as a whole.
2. Ecocentrism (or biocentrism) embraces the ethical stance that everything in nature possesses inherent or intrinsic worth or value (Scarce 1990: 35–36).

[Note: biocentric philosophy is actually an ancient worldview, new only to westerners; it has been part of indigenous and traditionalist cultures for thousands of years.]

Citing from earlier writings of Arne Naess, Stark (1995) describes Naess's ecosophical premises that serve as a platform for deep-ecological theory and practice:

- The flourishing of human and nonhuman life on earth has intrinsic value. The value of nonhuman life forms is independent of the usefulness these may have for narrow human purposes.
- Richness and diversity of life forms are values in themselves and contribute to the flourishing of human and nonhuman life on earth.
- Humans have no right to reduce the richness of diversity, except to satisfy vital needs.
- Present human interference with the nonhuman world is excessive, and the situation is rapidly worsening.
- The flourishing of human life and culture is compatible with a substantial decrease of human population. The flourishing of nonhuman life requires such a decrease.
- Significant change of life conditions for the better requires change in policies. These affect basic economic, technological, and ideological structures.
- The ideological change is mainly that of appreciating *life quality* (dwelling in situations of intrinsic value) rather than adhering to a high standard of living. There will be a profound awareness of the difference between big and great.
- Those who subscribe to the foregoing points have an obligation, directly or indirectly, to participate in the attempts to implement the necessary changes (p. 261).

Thus, deep ecology recognizes the interrelatedness of all life, the equality of all organisms as part of an overall system, the rejection of human-centered arguments, the concept of the intrinsic value of nature, and the goal of humanity as a fundamental aspect of nature. It demands that individuals understand the world in biocentric terms, which advocates a respect for all species and a dedication to maintaining the full biodiversity of the earth (Lee 1995). Radical environmentalists believe that adherence to other than this philosophy allowed and created environmentally disastrous behaviors.

man form of life and meditated upon that form—a mouse, tree or stem of grass—until that individual seemed to be that stem or mouse. Then each person would tell others in the circle about lawn mowers or traps and how it felt to be oppressed by humans.

The early rendezvous of 1980 and 1981 were loosely organized gatherings, but later meetings scheduled workshops, speeches, and forums to share concerns to feature as many events as possible (Lee 1995). Earth First! published its own newsletter as a means of sharing its message with its members and others interested in its cause. In the fall of 1981, Foreman and Koehler also inaugurated the Earth First! Road Show to publicize their cause, revitalize the movement's disparate local groups, and seek new members. Over the first three months of the road show, Foreman and Koehler brought EF!'s message to audiences that ranged from 20 to 2,000 people (Lee 1995).

Eventually, some members of EF! felt activism was not enough to get their message across to the American public. Consequently, EF! adopted ecotage as its new strategy. Thereafter, its goal was to "block environmentally destructive projects, to increase the costs of such projects and thereby make them economically unattractive, and to raise public awareness of the taxpayer subsidized devastation of biological diversity occurring in the world" (Lee 1995). As it rose to power, EF! focused its efforts toward generating public support and hurting its opponents economically.

Monkey-wrenching, one of the first tools in such efforts, included pulling up survey stakes or putting sand in the crankcases of bulldozers. Foreman issued guidelines that monkey-wrenching should be purposeful, rather than for vandalism's sake. They would be nonviolent, targeted, and simple. Foreman and Haywood's 1985 book *Ecodefense: A Field Guide to Monkey Wrenching* provides instruc-

tions on how to lay spikes to give logging trucks or off-road vehicles flat tires and to remove signs and markers from snowmobile trails.

EF!'s first action of ecotage took place in spring 1981 when approximately 75 people gathered near the Glen Canyon Dam to spread their message about the necessity of allowing the Colorado River to run free, unhindered by a dam. Six members ultimately let a roll of black plastic unwind down the face of the dam, creating the impression of a three-hundred foot black rift in the wall (Eagan 1996). Since 1981, EF! has been engaged in a variety of other acts of civil disobedience, ranging from blockades of logging roads, to sit-ins in forest superintendents' offices, and placing members in treetops 80 feet in the air. While they were involved in many wilderness disputes all over the United States, they were most active in the West, where they initiated their efforts to protect old-growth forests.

In 1984, EF! began to employ violence with the introduction of "tree spiking" (Eagan 1996: 6). This process involves driving long metal spikes into trees scheduled for harvesting on public lands. Although the spikes do not harm the trees, they can be lethal to a logger when they come into contact with either a chain saw or mill blade. Earth First! formally renounced the use of tree spiking in 1990, but several renegade groups that are not officially associated with EF! have continued to use the tactic. As Earth First! grew in size, it also grew in diversity and some of the new followers challenged the founders' belief system. Consequently, the movement became unstable and eventually split into two factions (Lee 1995):

- The first faction remained focused on biodiversity but became philosophically apocalyptic—concerned only with events and earthly conditions leading up to the apocalypse, the climactic and dramatic event that they believe would soon bring about the end of human history. Its adherents were not interested in the postapocalyptic future, but were primarily concerned with preserving wilderness prior to the biological meltdown.

- The second faction emphasized both social justice and environmental issues, and it developed a doctrine that was philosophically millenarian–envisioning a salvation that is imminent, ultimate, collective, this-worldly and miraculous. Individuals in this faction hoped to convert as many adherents as possible to their cause in order to create a just and ecologically sensitive community (p. 142).

These two factions coexisted in the late 1980s, although internal bickering and external pressures often characterized the movement. Foreman was concerned that the group was moving away from its origins and that biodiversity would no longer dominate EF!'s agenda. He also felt that if the movement continued to grow, it would be forced to completely abandon its radical political stance. In late 1988, Foreman began the process of withdrawing from Earth First! (Lee 1995).

Several other events occurred in 1989 that were setbacks for the movement. First, Judi Bari and Darryl Cherney, members of a Northern California chapter of EF! who were coordinating a massive protest effort known as Redwood Summer, were injured when a motion-activated pipe bomb exploded in Bari's car. Local law enforcement officials insisted that Bari and Cherney placed the bomb in their car so that they could illustrate their accusations that law enforcers were harassing EF! members. However, a lawsuit filed by Bari and Cherney and upheld in the San Francisco Bay Area courts indicate that the bomb may have been planted by law enforcement or that law enforcement knew

about the bomb in advance and did nothing to prevent its detonation.

Shortly thereafter, David Foreman and four others were arrested and indicted for plotting to bomb Arizona's Palo Verde and California's Diablo Canyon nuclear power plants and Colorado's Rocky Flats nuclear weapons plant. Although Earth First! was not named directly, at least 15 people in several states were subpoenaed by a federal grand jury in Phoenix that heard evidence on the Evan Mecham Eco-Terrorist International Conspiracy (EMETIC) to which Foreman was linked. EMETIC was apparently jokingly named after a conservative car dealer who was elected governor of Arizona.

The FBI had investigated the EMETIC for over two years, using 50 agents. By the operation's conclusion, it had amassed over 1,300 hours of secret recordings (through the use of a FBI infiltrator in a small, tightly-knit cell). Foreman and his codefendants all changed their pleas to guilty when their claims of entrapment were denied by the judge. Under an unusual plea bargain, Foreman's sentencing was delayed for five years, when a guilty plea to lesser charges would be entered (Eagan 1996). Foreman formally resigned from Earth First! in the summer of 1990.

Earth First! expanded the range of the environmental debate in the United States and continues to challenge public and private policies that members believe are destructive to the environment. Today, they are considered extremists in many circles, while in others, they are still regarded as terrorists. Although EF!ers have abandoned violent practices, the value, perhaps, of such an organization is that it raises the public's awareness of fundamental policy questions and ethical issues into the arena of public discourse. It can also be argued that when EF! engaged in illegal and destructive activities, it made other environmental groups look more moderate.

Earth Liberation Front

Earth First! members who refused to abandon criminal acts as a tactic when others wished to "mainstream" Earth First! founded Earth Liberation Front (ELF) in Brighton, England, in 1992. Members advocated destruction of property to take action against corporations and companies they thought were hurting the environment. Evidence regarding their presence in the United States is difficult to obtain. What little we know suggests that ELF is not really a group like Earth First! but is a covert, underground group without a central organization and involves individual people working by themselves or in small groups.

ELF came to the public's attention in October 1998 when the group took responsibility for the most destructive act of environmental terrorism in U.S. history—the fire and property destruction at Vail resorts in Colorado that caused more than $12 million in damage by burning three buildings and damaging four ski lifts. ELF claimed it torched the buildings to protest the ski resort's controversial 880-acre expansion, and to protect the lynx, an endangered animal to be reintroduced into the wild in Colorado during the winter of 1998–99. As one ELF member explained, the expansion in Vail would ruin the last, best lynx habitat in the state. The organization could not tolerate putting profits ahead of Colorado's wildlife.

The area around Vail, Colorado, is prime lynx habitat. Katie Fedor, spokeswoman for the ELF, responded to the condemnation of these actions by mainstream environmental groups (including members of Earth First!) by stating that:

> Those groups should understand that in order to effect social change we're limited to certain tactics. These environmental groups had actually already tried to have a lawsuit to stop the expansion and it was thrown out of federal court. That's a perfect example of how that didn't work. But decreasing profits by destroying property has been very effective for both the ELF and Animal Liberation Front (ALF) in the past. (Eddy and Lipsher 1998: 13)

The ELF has links with the ALF, a group discussed later in this chapter. Collaboration between these groups usually occurs where animal-rights beliefs intersect with concern for ecosystems and species survival (Taylor 1998). In September 1993, a communiqué published by ELF and the ALF declared their solidarity of action. Several actions for which these groups take joint responsibility include the following:

- arson of a corral used to round up wild horses for slaughter in 1997 in Oregon;
- arson of U.S. Department of Agriculture Animal Damage Control building near Olympia, Washington, in June 1998 where animals were allegedly euthanized; and
- release of approximately 100 wild horses from the Bureau of Land Management's wild-horse corrals in Rock Springs, Wyoming, in September 1998.

Anti-Environmental Movement

In response to the more extreme efforts of environmental organizations, an anti-environmental movement emerged that argued that environmentalists were running the government and influencing national policy. Its position is that too much land is set aside and protected, that this limited-use policy has economic consequences, and that the rights of property owners are being denied. These anti-environmentalists believe that ranchers, for example, should be able to use their land in any way they see fit. The major organization in the movement is Wise Use.

Box 5.2

ELF AND VAIL

In 1992, a group of Wall Street investors gained control of Vail Resorts and subsequently expanded the resort areas, reorganized the company, replaced longtime local managers with outsiders, and took the company public. Several years later, Vail Resorts announced its desire to begin work on its Category III (Cat III) ski-area expansion–the third phase of the ski-company's master plan to develop a 2,200-acre area of Vail's backcountry, including 700 acres of old-growth forest and the prime habitat for elk and the endangered Canadian lynx.

Almost immediately, environmental activists began filing lawsuits on behalf of the lynx, but Forest Service officials decided in favor of the development, thus leaving only the Eagle County Commission to decide its fate. In March 1998, the Commission met with 300 environmentalists, locals, and animal-rights activists to debate the plan. Lawyers for Vail argued that Cat III was about improving snow quality and extending the ski season. Environmentalists charged that Cat III had nothing to do with skiing, but rather that it was about real estate development and profit. Some locals–representing a few of the 3,000 residents who signed a petition favoring the expansion–touted its economic advantages. In April, the Commission unanimously decided to support the project.

On Sunday, October 18th, shortly after construction crews had begun to clear trees in the disputed areas, a fire was deliberately set and caused $12 million in damages. Two days later, an e-mail was sent and signed by the ELF claiming responsibilities for the fires and threatening further action if the Cat III construction continued:

"Putting profits ahead of Colorado's wildlife will not be tolerated. This action is just a warning. We will be back if this greedy corporation continues to trespass into wild and unroaded areas. For your safety and convenience, we strongly advise skiers to choose other destinations until Vail cancels its inexcusable plans for expansion" (Dejevsky 1998: 2).

The results of ELF's actions were disastrous for the environmental movement. Not only did they destroy four ski lifts and two skiing lodges much beloved by skiers–both local and tourist–they had sent a clear message that the target of the attack was not just the ski company, but every skier in Vail. Public opinion dramatically turned against ELF, environmental activists in general, and every activist opponent of CAT III.

Source: Eddy & Lipscher 1998.

Wise Use

Wise Use is an anti-environmental movement that takes its name from an early twentieth century conservationist and first chief of the U.S. Forest Service Gifford Pinchot who said in 1907:

The first duty of the human race on the material side is to control the use of the earth and all that therein is. Conservation means the wise use of the earth and its resources for the lasting good of men. Conservation is the foresighted utilization, preservation, and/or renewal of forests, waters, lands, and minerals, for the greatest good of the greatest number for the longest time (as quoted in Echeverria and Eby 1995: 47).

Pinchot worked to limit private development of federal forests in the West. His message was initially interpreted as a call for conservation of our natural resources but has been refocused by the Wise Use movement in recent years. The modern coalition of anti-environmentalists began in the 1970s when a loose confederation of far-right groups formed in opposition to federal management of public lands (e.g., limits on mining and lumbering or the enforcement of the Endangered Species Act). Many advocates of this position argue that federal lands properly belong to localities. They are dedicated to attacking the environmental movement and promoting unfettered resource exploitation (Burke 1995).

The movement drew a lot from the Sagebrush Rebellion, which refers to the efforts of conservative western state legislators during the late 1970s and early 1980s to transfer control of federally managed public land to state government. Many had privatization as their ultimate goal (Ramos 1995). Adherents claim their actions support traditional American values, including the right to life, liberty, and the pursuit of happiness or individual rights to appropriate wealth from nature (Helvarg 1994).

There are two basic tenets that serve as the foundation for the Wise Use movement:

1. All constraints on the use of private property should be removed. They argue that the "taking" clause of the fifth amendment which states that "nor shall private property be taken for public use, without just compensation" must be enforced and that regulations that restrict an owner's use of his or her land is a taking.[44]
2. Access to public land should be unrestricted for logging, mining, drilling, motorized recreation, and all commercial enterprise. Their position supports the multiple use of public lands (Helvarg 1994: 9).

"Taking" has been a hot issue of debate within the country's law schools and legal journals. The property-rights movement is rooted in the ideology of Richard Epstein, a law professor at the University of Chicago. He argued in his 1985 book *Takings* that the fifth amendment to the Constitution requires public financial compensation for virtually all reduction in the use or value of private property due to regulatory action. The private-property-rights strategy, which seeks to protect private land from "government land grabs" or "unconstitutional takings" appeals strongly to rural landowners and small businesspeople, sectors of society that fear economic change, and heavy-handed environmental reforms (Burke 1995: 141).

Ron Arnold, Executive Vice President of the Center for the Defense of Free Enterprise (CDFE), has carried the message of the Wise Use movement. Arnold and CDFE are considered by many to be the founding and main strategy-setting forces in the grassroots anti-environmental movement. Alan Gottlieb, also of the CDFE, compiled *The Wise Use Agenda*, which delineates the goals of the movement and is touted as both the citizen's guide to environmental issues and a task-force report to the George H.W. Bush administration by the Wise Use movement. The agenda items range from dramatic changes in

---

[44] This clause is the basis for the concept of eminent domain, which allows government entities to take land for public projects by paying property owners the land's fair-market value.

wildlife management that allow for commercial development of all kinds, to measures that appear to promote preservation. They clearly set out specific actions to be taken in furtherance of the "wise use" of our natural resources. There is also a strong stripe of Christian fundamentalism, property-rights protectionism, and solid ties to the gun lobby and the motorized-recreation lobby (Snow 1996).

In 1999, the Clearinghouse on Environmental Advocacy and Research (CLEAR), a part of the public-interest group Environmental Working Group, published a strategic analysis of the Wise Use movement. *The Wise Use Movement: Strategic Analysis and Fifty State Review*, available on the Internet, provides a summary of the message, strategy and tactics of the Wise Use movement.[45] In summary, the report outlines three distinct messages Wise Use employs to reach different audiences crucial to the maintenance and growth of the movement:

1. The vanguard message is the central precept of the movement's organizers, and posits that human values, culture, and tradition are more important than living creatures and that economic activity should not be damaged to protect nature. This message is used to bring in and keep core right-wing activists and money allied with the movement.
2. The conspiracy message argues that big environmental groups, big government, an insensitive bureaucracy, and the powerful news media are all in cahoots to take away our basic rights. It is used as a tool to organize at the local level or to convince people already involved in local Wise Use groups of the need for a national movement.

3. The mainstream message argues that man and nature can exist in productive harmony; man is the preeminent species and nature exists for man; science, technology and our own ingenuity can solve our environmental problems; and the best government is the government that governs the least. It is often the most prominent communication in a given community that promotes stewardship and husbandry and reaffirms the morality of rural life (CLEAR 1999: 4–7).

CLEAR indicates that the basic strategy of the national Wise Use movement is well known and was delineated in Ron Arnold's book *Ecology Wars* (1987). Arnold's seven-point roadmap identifies the strategies to promote the Wise Use Movement:

1. Rewrite American law.
2. Use the courts to uphold the agenda.
3. Elect officials who will promote "wise use."
4. Press administrative agencies to regulate according to the agenda.
5. Develop public support.
6. Shape public opinion.
7. Govern permanently (p. 49–62).

The Wise Use movement leaders stress the importance of grassroots organizing and developing a strong, local base of support for the movement. Arnold and Gottlieb publish Wise Use books and newsletters, own a radio station, and maintain a web site for interested parties. Their message has appeal and has attracted grassroots members who are cattlemen, loggers, miners, private-property owners within national forests, off-road vehicle users, and other users of natural resources (Rousch 1995). Corporations bankroll much

---

[45] www.ewg.org/pub/home/clear/by_clear/Fifty_III.html.

Box 5.3
The Wise Use Agenda

Gottlieb identifies the following twenty-five goals of the movement, which were drawn from participants at a multiple-use strategy conference in 1988:

1. Initiate a public education project to demonstrate how Wise Use of the national forests and federal lands can reduce the federal deficit.
2. Develop the petroleum resources of the Arctic National Wildlife Refuge in Alaska.
3. Advocate the passage of an Inholder Protection Act, giving broader property rights to inholders (persons who hold land within the borders or tangent to federal or state lands).
4. Support the Global Warming Prevention Act that seeks to increase the young stands (i.e., removal of old-growth stands) in National Forest lands.
5. Increase harvesting of timber in the Tongass National Forest in Alaska.
6. Open all public lands to mining and energy production under Wise Use technologies.
7. Assert states' sovereign rights in matters pertaining to water distribution and regulation.
8. Commemorate the one hundredth anniversary of the founding of the Forest Reserves by calling attention to the commodity use of forests and the homestead settlement of these areas in the early years of the Service.
9. Increase harvesting of trees in national forests to promote "rural, timber-dependent community stability" through the Rural Community Stability Act.
10. Create a national timber harvesting system that allows for greater harvesting of timber on public lands.
11. Reorganize the National Park Service. This includes the implementation of Mission 2010, a 20-year construction program that would maximize concession stands and accommodations in national parks, remove entry limits and bring in private firms experienced in people moving, such as Walt Disney, to manage the parks.
12. Expand the window of time that a patent protects companies and individuals who develop new pest-control products by excluding the time spent testing the product.
13. Create the National Rangeland Grazing System to open more federal lands for grazing.
14. Open all wilderness areas to motorized wheelchair access.
15. Support the enactment of a national Industrial Policy Act requiring all Federal actions—legislative and regulatory—to include an economic impact statement.
16. Require greater specificity in the costs associated with actions by federal agencies.
17. Allow property owners to recover easements on property taken for railroad construction once the railroads have been abandoned.
18. Amend and weaken the Endangered Species Act. The amendment would exclude "relic species in decline before the appearance of man," such as the California Condor.
19. Require parties that unsuccessfully challenge any development or economic action in court to pay damages to the developer.

Box 5.3 *Continued*

20. Strengthen the claims to private rights on federal lands for mining, grazing, harvesting timber, etc.
21. Press for the enactment of the Global Resources Wise Use Act, which calls for the adoption of a pro-industry consideration in natural resource–use decisions.
22. Change the National Wilderness Preservation System to allow for commercial uses. Reorganize areas so that some are designated for partial development while others are allowed more extensive development.
23. Allow Wise Use groups standing to sue on behalf of industries that are threatened or harmed by environmentalists.
24. Use monies from the federal gasoline tax to create trails for off-road motorized vehicles.
25. Discontinue the Forest Service's policy of allowing some naturally occurring fires to burn, and introduce an active prevention system (Gottlieb 1989: 5–18).

---

of the movement, but they do not dictate its values (Ramos 1995).

Public Employees for Environmental Responsibility (PEER) make the monitoring of the Wise Use movement one of their major priorities because of the documented incidences of violence and threats of violence directed toward public employees. PEER constantly monitors the attacks that have been committed against public employees.[46] Several documented incidents (as of November 1999) include the following:

- August 4, 1995, a bomb detonated outside the home of a Forest Service district ranger in Carson City, Nevada, destroying the family van.
- November 25, 1995, someone fired two shots from a .45-caliber handgun into a Forest Service building in Alaska, causing $2,000 worth of damage.
- March 15, 1996, a Forest Service ranger in Arizona was harassed, threatened, forcibly thrown out of a public meeting of the local cattle association, and then beaten by several attendees.
- February 25, 1997, a pipe bomb was left at the Washington, D.C. office of the Army Corps of Engineers.
- July 31, 1997, an EPA employee in the Ozarks region of Missouri was beaten, bound with tape, and abandoned in her vandalized vehicle by suspected pro-mining activists.
- March 1998, a National Park Service ranger at Organ Pipe Cactus Monument in Arizona was run over by a moving vehicle driven by an anti-government landowner that had claimed ownership of federal land.

Helvarg (1994) cited a number of incidents of intimidation, vandalism, assault, arson, rape, and violence directed against grassroots environmental activists. He refers to them as "casualties of war." A member of an environmental-based group in Santa Fe re-

---

[46] peer.org/wise_use/violence.html

ceived death threats, a female member of a group trying to clean up her community received a single stab wound from a switchblade knife, and a New Mexico Navajo activist, part of an anti-logging group on the reservation, was killed.

Animal Rights

The 1970s witnessed the beginning of the present-day animal-rights movement that has grown in both size and importance. This worldwide movement now numbers dozens of organizations and millions of members. Its beginnings, however, can be traced back to England when the British Parliament in 1822 passed the first law aimed at preventing cruelty to animals. In 1824, the Society for the Prevention of Cruelty to Animals (SPCA) was formed in England, and the American equivalent was formed in 1866. However, it was not until 1966 that the United States Congress enacted the Animal Welfare Act, the first federal law regulating the treatment of animals.

Animal experimentation has been intrinsic to scientific and medical progress for more than 200 years. The anti-vivisection movement was born out of the perceived abuse of animals used in experiments. Anesthetics were not given in the late eighteenth century because none were available. Today's rules on the use of animals recognize the animals' distress. The federal government requires universities and other research centers to review most animal studies to ensure that as few animals as possible are used, that animals experience no unnecessary discomfort, and that substitute methods be considered. Regulations also favor the use of some species over others—mice or pigs rather than dogs or monkeys, for instance. The preference is largely determined by cultural attitudes.

Recent public opinion polls show broad support for parts of the animal-rights agenda,

including the movement's campaigns against wearing fur, eating veal, or using animals to test cosmetics and other consumer products (Masci 1996). The animal activism movement has three distinct types of organizations:

- animal-welfare organizations, which advocate better treatment of animals by humans;
- animal rightists, which may be grassroots in orientation and involve a level of non-passive activism, such as picketing to protest human uses of animals; and
- animal liberators, who may engage in legal and illegal protests against using animals for human ends (Scarce 1990: 116).

The animal-liberation movement in the United States was largely influenced by the publication of Peter Singer's 1975 book, *Animal Liberation: A New Ethics for Our Treatment of Animals*. Singer, an Australian philosopher, argued that discrimination based on difference of species, or speciesism, was as immoral as racism or sexism. Singer's book provided the intellectual spark that lit the animal rights flame in the United States (Masci 1996).

There are four main issues within the animal-rights movement:

1. Vivisection—performing medical experiments, especially surgery, on living animals for the purpose of studying organs and disease.
2. Animal-based agriculture—using animals for food and clothing.
3. Trapping and hunting—trapping and hunting fur-bearing species that are not raised on farms.
4. Animals in entertainment—using animals in films, zoos, circus animals and the like (e.g., exotic-animal auctions, private hunting reserves).

A key figure in the animal liberation movement was a New York activist named

Box 5.4

Peter Singer's *Animal Liberation*

"If we have learned anything from the liberation movements, we should have learned how difficult it is to be aware of the ways in which we discriminate until they are forcefully pointed out to us. A liberation movement demands an expansion of our moral horizons, so that practices that were previously regarded as natural and inevitable are now seen as intolerable" (Singer 1990: 220).

Singer's work, which inspired the animal-rights movement, is rooted in the principle of equality. Singer examines the early work of Jeremy Bentham, the founder of the reforming utilitarian school of moral philosophy, who incorporated the essential basis of moral equality into his system of ethics: each to count for one and none for more than one. Singer also suggests that the leading figures in contemporary moral philosophy support a similar requirement to Bentham that gives everyone's interests equal consideration. He then argues that this principle of equality implies that our concern for others and our readiness to consider their interests ought not to depend on what they are like or on what abilities they possess. The basic element, taking into account the interests of the being must, according to the principle of equality, be extended to all beings, black or white, human or nonhuman. The proposition that all creatures that can suffer pain have an equal interest in avoiding it, is the essence of Singer's morality (Monaghan 1997).

The topics covered in Singer's book include the ethics of animal liberation, animal research and experimentation, speciesism, factory farming, arguments for ethical vegetarianism, and objections to animal liberation. Singer's ethical position was that if a person suffers, there can be no moral justification for refusing to take that suffering into consideration and, indeed, it must count equally with the like suffering of any other being, including animals. He posits the philosophy that speciesism has contributed to the problems surrounding the treatment and handling of animals. Speciesism allows researchers to regard the animals they experiment on as items of equipment, laboratory tools rather than living, suffering creatures (Singer 1990).

Singer sees a parallel between racism, sexism and speciesism:

• Racists violate the principle of equality by giving greater weight to the interests of members of their own race when there is a clash between their interests and the interests of those of another race.
• Sexists violate the principle of equality by favoring the interests of their own sex.
• Speciesists allow the interests of their own species to override the greater interests of members of other species.

The core of the book is the claim that to discriminate against beings solely on account of their species is a form of prejudice, immoral and indefensible in the same way that discrimination on the basis of race is immoral and indefensible (Singer 1990). Singer then states that if you take morality seriously, you should try to eliminate speciesist practices from your own life, and oppose them elsewhere.

Henry Spira who wanted to build bridges between the traditional animal-welfare movement and animal-liberation philosophy (Scarce 1990). Beginning in the 1970s, he sought to change people's thinking in perhaps a revolutionary way–to consider that animals are not edible and that animals are not lab tools. He challenged Revlon® to reconsider its use of animals to test cosmetics, and because of Spira's challenge, money was given to Rockefeller University to find nonanimal alternatives to testing cosmetics on the eyes of rabbits. Spira was instrumental in bringing to an end a series of experiments that involved examining the sexual behavior of mutilated cats (Scarce 1990; Singer 1998). Many agree that Spira made a difference in the treatment of animals.

Spira will be remembered for his efforts to move beyond talking philosophy, setting plans, and taking action. When Spira was asked by Singer to sum up what he thought he had achieved, he said:

> I've pushed the idea that activism has to be results-oriented, that you can win victories, that you can fight city hall, and that if you don't like to be pushed around and you don't like to see others pushed around, you can have an impact. . . . It's like this guy from the *New York Times* asked me what I'd like my epitaph to be. I said, "He pushed the peanut forward." I try to move things on a little. (as quoted in Singer 1998: 198)

Beyond individuals like Henry Spira, there are numerous animal rights organizations worldwide. We will focus on the origins and activities of the Animal Liberation Front.

Animal Liberation Front

The Animal Liberation Front (ALF) consists of small autonomous groups of people all over the world that carry out direct actions against animal abuse in the form of rescuing animals and causing financial loss to "animal exploiters," usually through the damage and destruction of property. The organization derived from the ALF in England in 1972 with the formation of a new group calling itself the Band of Mercy. The members "began to feel that action should also be taken to save animals in laboratories and factory farms and not just on behalf of animals hunted for recreation" (Monaghan 1997: 109).

Since its emergence in the United States in the late 1970s, ALF has claimed responsibility for destroying or damaging over 100 animal labs and farms around the nation (Masci 1996). The damage has run into the millions of dollars and they have removed thousands of creatures from facilities to set them free or place them in less-harmful environments. Because ALF actions are against the law, activists work anonymously, either in small groups or individually, and do not have any centralized organization or coordination. ALF is more of a loose connection of like-minded people who see a need for action (Masci 1996). This fact also contributes to the difficulty of gathering information about this organization.

The ALF action guidelines (Animal Liberation Front 1999) are the following:

- TO liberate animals from places of abuse, i.e., laboratories, factory farms, fur farms, etc., and place them in good homes where they may live out their natural lives, free from suffering.
- TO inflict economic damage to those who profit from the misery and exploitation of animals.
- TO reveal the horror and atrocities committed against animals behind locked doors, by performing non-violent direct actions and liberations.
- TO take all necessary precautions against harming any animal, human and nonhuman (p. 1).

Box 5.5
Henry Spira—Ten Ways to Make a Difference

Singer (1998) examines the ten ways that Spira made a difference, drawing on several articles written by Spira. It is important to examine these methods because of the role that Spira played in the animal rights–animal liberation movement. As Singer (1990) notes, in twenty years "Spira's unique campaigning methods have done more to reduce animal suffering than anything done in the previous fifty years by vastly larger organizations with millions of dollars at their disposal" (p x–xi).

1. Try to understand the public's current thinking and where it could be encouraged to go tomorrow. Above all, keep in touch with reality.
2. Select a target on the basis of vulnerabilities to public opinion, the intensity of suffering, and the opportunities for change.
3. Set goals that are achievable. Bring about meaningful change one step at a time. Raising awareness is not enough.
4. Establish credible sources of information and documentation. Never assume anything. Never deceive the media or the public. Maintain credibility, don't exaggerate or hype the issue.
5. Don't divide the world into saints and sinners.
6. Seek dialogue and attempt to work together to solve problems. Position issues as problems with solutions. Presenting realistic alternatives best does this.
7. Be ready for confrontation if your target remains unresponsive. If accepted channels don't work, prepare an escalating public awareness campaign to place your adversary on the defensive.
8. Avoid bureaucracy.
9. Don't assume that only legislation or legal action can solve the problem.
10. Ask yourself, "Will it work?" (Singer 1998: 12).

Basically, you must ask yourself the question "Will it work?" at the outset of any campaign. If you can't see a realistic account of the ways in which the plans will achieve the stated objectives, then change the plans.

ALF's short-term goal is to save as many animals as possible and directly disrupt the practice of animal abuse. Their long-term goal is to end all animal suffering by forcing animal-abuse companies out of business. Since animals cannot defend themselves, humans must recognize their clear moral duty and take on the responsibility of advocating and ensuring animal rights (Monaghan 1997).

While ALF's guidelines and web page indicate that it should achieve its goals by "all lawful means possible,"[47] ALF has become increasingly unlawful and violent in its actions.

---

[47] www.hedweb.com/alfaq.htm

- During the 1980s, ALF members broke into farms and laboratories, released animals, or took them to hiding places where they could be cared for. Equipment was smashed, and in some cases, the homes of experimenters were painted with slogans or vandalized (Singer 1998). Letter bombs progressed from the targeting of property to the targeting of individuals.
- In 1984, the ALF released a hoax statement concerning the alleged alteration of Mars Bars with rat poison.

More recently, ALF has been involved in the following activities:

- In March 2000 in Sonoma County, California, the Farm Bureau was ransacked after posting a $50,000 reward in connection with the firebombing of two area meat-processing plants and an egg farm that occurred in February.
- In early 2000, the ALF firebombed trucks at B&K Universal breeding company in Fremont, California; attempted arson at Primate Products in Redwood City, California; and smashed windows at Neiman Marcus in San Francisco, California—with estimated total damages of $500,000.
- The Los Angeles chapter of ALF placed a "Most Wanted" section on its Web site. It lambasts Fur Commission USA executive Teresa Platt as "scum," and gives detailed directions to her house along with the note, "Now you know where to find her! Please feel free to use this vital information in any way to further the liberation of all animal beings."

ALF continues to secure the release of penned animals, including minks, and engage in related acts of vandalism. In addition, the tactics used by some members of this group have continually escalated—the tactic of breaking and entering laboratories and destroying equipment has been replaced by the sending of poster-tube bombs containing hypodermic needles and the planting of car bombs (Monaghan 1997). The effort is also focusing more on animal agriculture, the raising of animals for food and clothing.

We discussed the collaboration between the ALF and radical environmentalists, yet there are some profound differences. Radical environmentalists promote an ecosystem and species-focused ethics while animal liberationists focus more on the well-being of individual animals. Taylor (1998) indicates that this will continue to cause tensions between these groups and reduce the occasions for their collaboration and mutual influence.

Anti-Abortion Activists

In 1973, the United State Supreme Court in *Roe v. Wade* 410 U.S. 113 issued a decision that recognized the right of a woman to choose a legalized abortion during the first trimester of pregnancy. Supreme Court Justice Harry A. Blackmun wrote the opinion legalizing abortion and was the target of dozens of death threats and hate mail (Risen and Thomas 1998). It is this decision which the anti-abortion forces—who call themselves pro-life advocates—are seeking to reverse. While most anti-abortion activists are legitimate, law-abiding individuals, others espouse violence, threaten to use violence, or actually resort to violence. These fundamentalists seek the realization of religious values through political action, social manipulation, as well as through personal transformation (Blanchard and Prewitt 1993).

All abortion foes want to ban all abortion and most are generally motivated by the belief that because a fetus is a person, abortion is murder. The extremist fringe of the anti-abortion movement engages in protests and civil disobedience, while more extreme factions of the movement bomb abortion clinics and assassinate doctors performing abortions.

Several examples of their activities include picketing abortion clinics, displaying pictures of aborted fetuses, vandalizing clinics and cars of clinic employees, posing as patients and chaining themselves to the table and/or tossing stink bombs into waiting rooms, fire-bombing clinics, and murder.

The concern and protests against the decision began almost immediately after the Supreme Court made its ruling. By the mid-1970s, the pro-life picketers stationed themselves outside small clinics, stand-alone businesses operated by medical professionals, or chains run by groups like Planned Parenthood. Such facilities were becoming the nation's primary abortion providers as hospitals and other large health care facilities dropped abortion services under political pressure. Clinic arsons and bombings became more common and more serious by the early 1980s (Risen and Thomas 1998). By the 1990s, certain fringe members began assassinating physicians who performed abortions, as well as committing arson and attempted arsons, sniper attacks, butyric acid attacks, bombings, and various hoaxes. To gain a better understanding of these groups, two of the most active extremist movements are explained next—The Pro-Life Action Network and Operation Rescue—as are the activities of anti-abortion terrorists.

Pro-Life Action Network

One of the more active anti-abortion groups has been the Pro-Life Action Network (PLAN), a nationwide coalition of anti-abortion activists and organizations whose goal is to shut down clinics and persuade women not to have abortions. John O'Keefe, a member of that organization, was an early advocate of nonviolent direct action. Yet, ever since those early days in the 1970s when he was organizing sit-ins, small debates within

the organization began questioning the kinds of physical resistance that were permissible. O'Keefe continually emphasized that his guiding principle was nonviolence and passive resistance and that no one should fight back, damage equipment, or resist arrest in any way other than by going limp on the floor or sidewalk (Risen and Thomas 1998).

By the mid-1980s, O'Keefe wanted to venture into new territory of creating huge sit-ins that would result in large numbers of arrests in order to spread the message about abortion. The focus of PLAN's activities shifted, however, when Michael Bray became involved in the organization. A pastor in Maryland and editor of *Capital Area Christian News,* he provided the theological justification for clinic violence. He was more prone to engage in violence and ultimately served time in prison for conspiring to bomb ten clinics in the Washington, D.C. area.

The Dallas (Texas) PLAN engaged in very visible direct action, which became popular in the 1990s. Its initial efforts included gathering information about and conducting surveillance on twenty doctors who worked at nine Dallas abortion clinics. Two of PLAN's earliest targets, Drs. Clay Alexander and Norman T. Tompkins, received ultimatums: stop performing abortions or face the consequences. At first, both refused to cooperate with PLAN and, as promised, faced grim consequences:

- Dr. Alexander's office was flooded with leaflets picturing dead fetuses and advertising his home address, and members appeared at his house; and
- PLAN made thousands of "wanted-style" posters of Dr. Tompkins and he ultimately began wearing a bulletproof vest.

Dr. Alexander finally agreed to sign a letter on his own stationery saying he would never perform another abortion, and Dr.

Box 5.6
Roe v. Wade

An unmarried pregnant woman who wished to terminate her pregnancy by abortion instituted an action in the United States District Court for the Northern District of Texas, seeking a declaratory judgment on the alleged unconstitutionality of the Texas criminal abortion statutes. In Texas, abortions were prohibited except those procured or attempted by medical advice for the purpose saving the life of the mother.

In the opinion, Justice Blackmun acknowledged that the court was aware of the sensitive and emotional nature of the abortion controversy, of the vigorous opposing views even among physicians, and of the deep and seemingly absolute convictions that the subject inspires. One's philosophy, one's experiences, one's exposure to the raw edges of human existence, one's religious training, one's attitudes toward life and family and their values, and the moral standards one establishes and seeks to observe, are all likely to influence and to color one's thinking and conclusions about abortion.

Blackmun, expressing the views of seven members of the court, held that:

- The pregnant, unmarried woman had standing to sue.
- States have legitimate interests in seeing to it that abortions are performed under circumstances that ensure maximum safety for the patient.
- The right to privacy encompasses a woman's decision whether or not to terminate her pregnancy.
- A woman's right to terminate her pregnancy is not absolute, and may to some extent be limited by the state's legitimate interests in safeguarding the woman's health, in maintaining proper medical standards, and in protecting potential human life.
- The unborn are not included within the definition of person as used in the Fourteenth Amendment.
- Prior to the end of the first trimester of pregnancy, the state may not interfere with or regulate an attending physician's decision, reached in consultation with his patient, that the patient's pregnancy should be terminated.
- From and after the end of the first trimester, and until the point in time when the fetus becomes viable, the state may regulate the abortion procedure only to the extent that such regulation relates to the preservation and protection of maternal health.
- From and after the point in time when the fetus becomes viable, the state may prohibit abortions altogether, except those necessary to preserve the life or health of the mother.
- The state may proscribe the performance of all abortions except those performed by physicians currently licensed by the state (410 U.S. 113; 93 S.Ct. 705).

The privacy right involved was found not to be absolute and must be considered against important state interests (i.e., to protect health, medical standards, and prenatal life). The state's important and legitimate interest in potential life begins at viability—where the fetus presumably has the capability of meaningful life outside the mother's womb.

Tompkins filed suit against PLAN and ultimately lost staff members and income from the daily harassment.

Operation Rescue

A new breed of militants emerged in the late 1970s and early 1980s with the founding of Operation Rescue (OR). It built on the actions of the Pro-Life Action League, established in Chicago in 1980 by Joe Scheidler. It was in essence a youth movement, which was right-wing, male dominated, and fundamentalist (looked directly to the Bible for their faith, rather than a formal church structure). Randall Terry, its founder, was able to create a national campaign that put the issue of anti-abortion in the public eye. In January 1986, Terry and six others carried out their first rescue mission, locking themselves in one of the inner rooms of an abortion clinic before personnel arrived. They were arrested, convicted and fined.

To justify these actions, Terry used the "doctrine of necessity," a belief that violence is permissible as a last resort to stop or prevent greater violence, in this case abortions (Ginsburg 1998). OR made national news when it descended on Atlanta abortion clinics during the 1988 Democratic National Convention, beginning five months of protest called the "Siege of Atlanta." Over 1,300 were jailed for trespassing between July and October.

Other activities of OR include these four:

1. In early 1989, the first OR-sponsored National Day of Rescue resulted in the arrest of 2,631 persons in thirty-two cities, nineteen states, and Canada; an additional 2,019 people risked arrest; and another 5,443 people provided "Prayer Support Columns." By the end of 1989, about 20,000 people had been arrested in similar rescue operations.

2. In 1990, OR created "Operation Goliath" to unite all pro-life and rescue forces into "one mighty army."
3. In 1992, Randall Terry launched a nationwide effort that targeted physicians who perform abortions. The goals were to make targeted doctors a liability to everyone they encounter.
4. In 1993, OR organized six "Cities of Refuge" where mothers could come for help rather than seeking an abortion. The idea was based upon Deuteronomy, Chapter 9, where the Lord commanded Israel to build six cities to which an innocent man could run "lest innocent blood be shed."

Terry sees his battle against abortion as nothing less than a crusade to save the nation from God's judgment, which he believes will bring down immense suffering on Americans as punishment for their continued tolerance of abortion (Costa 1996). OR eventually became the biggest social-protest movement since the antiwar and civil rights campaigns of the 1960s, accomplishing more than 60,000 arrests at protests across the nation before it collapsed in the early 1990s (Risen and Thomas 1998).

In December 1990, Terry declared OR an underground organization and named Keith Tucci as head of an unincorporated above-ground organization called Operation Rescue National. It was originally located in South Carolina but Tucci's successor, the Reverend Flip Benham, moved the offices to Dallas, Texas. The organization was now more decentralized with loosely connected rescue groups throughout the country (Ginsburg 1998). OR continues to promote politically-extremist ideology and extremist political goals. As such, it has been involved in and possibly responsible for many acts of disruption and direct action, but not terrorism, at abortion clinics.

Box 5.7
Congressional Actions and Other Responses to Anti-Abortion Violence

The anti-abortion violence of the 1990s, including the killings of abortion providers and a renewed wave of bombings and arsons, forced Congress to pass the Freedom of Access to Clinic Entrance (FACE) Act. The law allows the FBI to arrest and charge people who impede clinic access. The result was that the potential punishment went from a few days in jail to years in a federal prison. It played a significant role in eliminating acts of civil disobedience.

Congress has had eighty-one votes to limit reproductive choice, ten of which have passed. While the Supreme Court upheld the basic right to abortion in 1992 (*Planned Parenthood of Southeastern Pennsylvania vs. Casey* 503 U.S. 957), it imposed a number of restrictions. Consequently 12 states have passed mandatory waiting periods for abortions. Thirteen have added mandatory parental consent or notice laws for minors, and nine have approved restrictions or bans on late-term abortions.

More abortion-clinic providers and women's groups have increasingly used class-action lawsuits against anti-abortion protesters and groups. A precedent was set in April 1998 in Chicago when a federal grand jury ruled that anti-abortion protest organizers used threats and violence to close down clinics. The lawsuit, filed in 1986 by the National Organization for Women, was refiled in 1994 under the Racketeer Influenced and Corrupt Organizations Act (RICO). The jury found that anti-abortion activist Joseph Scheidler and two associates engaged in twenty-one acts of extortion to shut down clinics and that two anti-abortion organizations—the Pro-Life Action League and Operation Rescue—were part of the scheme. The three activists and two organizations were ordered to pay about $258,000 to two abortion clinics in Milwaukee and Wilmington, Delaware. A number of other clinics are currently filing for class-action damages under the verdict.

Terry has expanded his scope from abortion to a broader concern in bringing conservative Christian values into the public sphere and is involved with the United States Taxpayers Party (USTP), a far-right group with operations in forty states (Ginsburg 1998). He also has been organizing Christian leadership institutes to train militants and activists for a new era.

Anti-Abortion Terrorists

In March 1993, an anti-abortion protester murdered obstetrician David Gunn as Dr. Gunn walked into an abortion clinic. Prior to Dr. Gunn's death, anti-abortion activity had been mired in a public debate about whether such activities constituted moral, ideological actions that were justifiable harassment, or whether they involved politically-violent procedures that posed real, terroristic threats to the government.

In one of the most comprehensive studies of abortion-clinic violence undertaken in the 1990s, the Feminist Majority Foundation surveyed the level of violence experienced in the first seven months of 1998 by 351 clinics and doctors' offices in forty-seven states and the District of Columbia. Almost one-fourth of clinics faced severe anti-abortion violence in 1998. Indeed, 22.2 percent of the clinics surveyed reported one or more types of severe violence including death threats, stalking, bomb threats, bombings, arson threats, arsons, blockades, invasions and chemical attacks (Jackman, Onyango, and Gavrilles 1999).

Not only have incidents of violence been growing, but also potentially-violent anti-abortion rhetoric has appeared with some regularity on the Internet. Perhaps one of the best known was "The Nuremberg Files." Created by anti-abortion advocate Neal Horsley, a fifty-four-year old computer consultant, the pages were rimmed with a pattern showing body parts and blood dripping on the print. Its goal was to compile lists of physicians, abortion-clinic staff, and security and law enforcement personnel who guard the clinics. It urged like-minded people to find more personal information on these targets, as well as submit new targets with their social security numbers, automobile-tag numbers, names and birthdates of spouses, children, and friends, and photos of the abortionist.

In January 1998, Planned Parenthood won a $107-million-dollar judgment against several groups of anti-abortion extremists by arguing that information like that in the Nuremberg Files was terroristic. Consequently, the Web site is no longer available as originally constructed.

Since 1995, at least two trends characterized abortion-clinic violence in the United States:

1. *Continued use of terrorist tactics by anti-abortion groups that target abortion clinics and their providers.* Statistics from the Department of Justice illustrate a growing trend in the use of violence during the 1990s—especially violence that kills and maims. Annually,

from 1993 through 1995, a total of sixteen arsons and bombings occurred across the nation. In 1996 alone, seven such actions were completed, including several attempts. In January 1998, a bomb exploded in a Birmingham, Alabama, clinic, killing an off-duty police officer and a nurse. The FBI received a letter from the "Army of God" claiming responsibility for the nation's first fatal bombing of an abortion clinic. The group also claimed responsibility for the Atlanta bombing.

2. *Continued commission of violence against clinics and individuals by a few extremist lone individuals.* For instance, in 1993, an Oregon housewife, Shelley Shannon, tried to assassinate Kansas Dr. George Tiller. On July 29, 1994, Paul Hill, the head of Defensive Action (a small anti-abortion group founded by Hill in 1994) shot and killed Pensacola doctor John Britton and clinic escort James Barrett; on December 30, 1994, John Salvi shot and killed two receptionists in clinics in Brookline, Massachusetts; in December 1996, a Baton Rouge, Louisiana, doctor was stabbed by an anti-abortion advocate; and in October 1998, an upstate New York doctor was shot and killed in his home.

SPECIAL-INTEREST EXTREMIST GROUPS TO WATCH

By the end of the twentieth century, there were at least two extremist groups that many law enforcement experts felt needed to be watched: Greenpeace and People for the Ethical Treatment of Animals. These groups have been involved in activities that might be

---

[48] For specific information, see www.greenpeacecanada.org

Box 5.8
Warriors of the Rainbow

The Indian legend and its prophecies are as follows:
There would come a time, predicted an old Cree woman named Eyes of Fire, when the earth would be ravaged of its resources, the sea blackened, the streams poisoned, the deer dropping dead in their tracks. Just before it was too late, the Indian would regain his spirit and teach the white man reverence for the earth, banding together with him to become Warriors of the Rainbow.

Together, using the symbol of the rainbow, all the races of the world would band together to spread the great Indian teaching and go forth as Warriors of the Rainbow to bring an end to the destruction and desecration of sacred Earth (Hunter 1979; Lee 1995).

---

more properly described as direct actions, sometimes bordering on the illegal, but not terroristic.

Greenpeace

In 1969, a small group of peace activists and members of the Sierra Club in Vancouver, British Columbia, formed a group called the Don't Make A Wave Committee. The Committee's aim was to protest the testing of nuclear weapons by the United States at Amchitka Island in the Aleutians (Scarce 1990). Amchitka is a small island off the west coast of Alaska, near the tip of the Aleutian Islands. The island was not only the last refuge for 3,000 endangered sea otters, home to bald eagles, peregrine falcons, and other wildlife but is situated in one of the most earthquake-prone regions in the world.[48]

The Committee changed its name in 1971 to Greenpeace, a combination of green for ecology and peace, literally for peace. They adopted the philosophy of "bearing witness" from the Quaker religion, which means that by drawing attention to an environmental abuse, one can register one's opposition. Sim-

ilar to many radical environmentalists, Greenpeace's founders came together because the moderate tactics and goals of mainstream environmental organizations frustrated them.

When it was announced that the U.S. Atomic Commission would conduct a nuclear test at Amchitka in early autumn 1971, the members made their plans and rented a boat, the *Phyllis Cormack,* and renamed it *Greenpeace.* This boat, along with another ship, traveled to the site, hoping that their actions would both raise public awareness of the issue and prevent the test itself (Lee 1995). Journalist Ben Metcalfe, one of the 12 men onboard, reported from the ship on September 16, 1971 (Greenpeace: "Hero's Welcome" 1999):

> Our goal is a very simple, clear and direct one—to bring about a confrontation between the people of death and the people of life. We do not consider ourselves to be radicals. We are conservatives, who insist upon conserving this environment for our children and future generations of man. (p. 9)

According to some, those aboard the ship read a book of North American Indian legends. Greenpeacers became the Warriors

---

Box 5.9
Greenpeace Politics

Greenpeace occupies a precarious position between two opposing camps. Many environmentalists see Greenpeace as too radical and its direct actions, which include positioning activists between harpooners and whales, parachuting from the tops of smokestacks, and floating a hot-air balloon into a nuclear test site, as too confrontational. They believe that these actions create more resentment rather than sympathy toward Greenpeace's efforts. Militant environmentalists, by contrast, see Greenpeace as not radical enough. Greenpeace's direct actions, such as banner hanging, merely advertise certain environmental threats but do not do anything about them. Their position is that these direct actions do not affect or change the structures of power, which create and support environmental destruction. The result is that many people begin to believe that merely knowing about environmental abuse will go a long way toward stopping it.

Wapner has confidence in the political efficacy of Greenpeace's work. He suggests that militant environmentalists misunderstand the nature of Greenpeace's actions and the political consequences of its work. Greenpeace's actions, like banner hanging, directly engage structures of power. Their efforts are designed to change structures that govern the way people think about the world and they count on the efficacy of this, in itself, to change the way vast numbers of people act with reference to the environment (Wapner 1995).

---

of the Rainbow and later their ship became the *Rainbow Warrior*. The ships were not successful in stopping the detonations. They did, however, get extensive media coverage in Canada and the United States, and by the time the second ship arrived home thousands of people had joined Greenpeace in opposition (Wapner 1995). Shortly after the Greenpeace protest in 1972, the United States decided to halt its plans to test nuclear weapons in Amchitka.

Greenpeace started off as an antinuclear group and evolved over the years into an organization concerned with environmental issues. Greenpeace now considers itself an independent campaigning organization that uses nonviolent, creative confrontation to expose global environmental problems and to force solutions that are essential to a green and peaceful future. They operate on Gand-

hi's philosophy of nonviolent civil disobedience and direct action.

It is virtually impossible to list all the actions taken by Greenpeace followers throughout the world. The types of actions taken include letter campaigns regarding endangered species, blocking of ships and shipments, scaling buildings to bring attention to a specie, and other forms of nonviolent civil disobedience. In the United States, "Greenpeace has protested, demonstrated, and sabotaged nuclear testing, fought against toxic waste dumping, worked actively on ocean ecology issues and protested for atmosphere and energy issues" (Mullins 1997: 231).

Greenpeace is a global organization with offices in over 30 countries. They are an independent, nonpartisan and nonprofit organization that concentrates on the marine environment. Their activities now extend beyond their nonviolent direct actions that they believe raise awareness and bring public opinion to bear on decisionmakers. Specifically, they conduct scientific, economic, and political research, publicize environmentally-sound recommendations, and lobby for change.

Greenpeace has been involved in the creation and passage of numerous international treaties and conventions of the United Nations and other international bodies on issues including toxic trade, ozone depletion, climate change, biodiversity, and endangered species. They took the lead in developing an ozone-safe refrigerator and have been involved in the certification of clear-cut free logging operations.

A very recent "victory" for Greenpeace occurred on July 9, 1999. In response to a lawsuit filed by Greenpeace and other organizations, Judge Thomas Zilly of the U.S. District Court in Seattle ruled that the federal government had failed to take the necessary action to protect the endangered Steller sea lion from becoming extinct ("Judge Rules in Favor" 1999: 5). The trawl-fishing industry in the North Pacific, which the National Marine Fisheries Service manages, jeopardizes the Steller sea lion. They were also successful in convincing The Home Depot to stop selling wood products from environmentally-sensitive areas, including redwood found in California and cedar, which can be found in the Great Bear Rainforest in British Columbia.

People for the Ethical Treatment of Animals

People for the Ethical Treatment of Animals (PETA) was incorporated on July 21, 1980. The two founders were Alex Pacheco and Ingrid Newkirk. PETA is the largest animal-rights organization in the world and is dedicated to establishing and protecting the rights of all animals. "PETA operates under the simple principle that animals are not ours to eat, wear, experiment on, or use for entertainment" (People for the Ethical Treatment of Animals 1999: 1). The organization focuses its attention on four areas where the largest numbers of animals suffer: factory farms, laboratories, fur trade and entertainment industry. Their message is spread through a campaign of public education, research, animal rescue, legislation, special events, celebrity involvement, and direct action.

PETA cofounder Alex Pacheco first uncovered the abuse of animals used in experiments in the 1980s when he compiled evidence of shocking neglect and maltreatment of monkeys used in experiments at the Institute for Behavioral Research in Silver Springs, Maryland (Singer 1998). His actions resulted in the first arrest and conviction of an animal experimenter in the United States on charges of cruelty to animals, the first confiscation of abused laboratory animals, and the first U.S. Supreme Court victory for animals in laboratories. The case sharpened public awareness of the nature of animal experimentation and made PETA one of the major animal-rights organizations in the United States.

On their Web site, PETA indicates that it has been responsible for such breakthroughs as the closure of the largest horse slaughterhouse in the United States and a military laboratory in which animals were shot. Their undercover investigation of a cosmetic-testing laboratory resulted in more than 550 cosmetic companies eliminating their testing products on animals. Their other projects involve getting Hollywood stars and models to pose for campaign ads (e.g., "I'd Rather Go Naked Than Wear Fur" campaign) and provide their talents for animal rights albums. Finally, they actively engage in educational campaigns and Ingrid Newkirk has written a how-to book for animal rights activists, along with a child's version.

As noted earlier, PETA has a relationship with ALF that Scarce (1990) suggests "exemplifies the mutually-supportive mix of organization/bureaucracy and decentralization/anarchy within the Animal Liberation Front" (p. 121). PETA has even acted on ALF's behalf to publicize findings from laboratory raids that show animal mistreatment (Masci 1996). Their position appears to be that ALF's raids provided evidence of horrific cruelty that would not have been discovered or believed otherwise. ALF's discoveries also resulted in the filing of criminal charges against laboratories, citing of experimenters for violations of law, and in some cases, closure of labs for abusive actions.

SUMMARY

Both categories of special-interest groups discussed herein–extremist and terrorist groups, and extremist groups–have engaged in various forms of direct action. Their respective actions range on a continuum from legal forms of civil disobedience to illegal forms of activity including firebombing, arson, vandalism, and up to and including, murder. Many of the key philosophers and advocates in these movements like Peter Singer, Arne Naess, Henry Spira, and Randall Terry, see the necessity to turn one's beliefs into action. For them, to merely adhere to a certain philosophical or ethical position is both inadequate, to a certain degree immoral, and sometimes in conflict with biblical mandates. According to these activists, one has an obligation to take action to remedy wrongs. In terms of those groups who are primarily extremist but have sometimes resorted to terrorism, we can make the following summary comments:

- The environmental movement, as represented by groups like Greenpeace and the Sierra Club, is well established. Yet there are individuals who continue to use more violent means to bring about environmental change. These "fringe" individuals frustrate the organizations attempting to bring about change through legal channels. In fact, some ecoterrorists argue that because their focus is to financially cripple an enterprise, they are not terrorists. Ecoterrorists frustrate law enforcement investigations by hitting remote targets, often at night, and leaving little evidence but charred ruins.

- The Wise Use movement has made inroads in terms of changing the government's policy on the handling of our natural resources. Fringe members are also implicated in criminal actions including the use of pipe bombs, car bombs, harassment, and physical violence. Their mainstream message has wide appeal because it promotes individual rights and a positive perspective on the "wise use" of the environment. Organizations that monitor their activities indicate that their appeal will grow but there are extremist aspects of their activities that need to be watched.

- The animal-rights movement is characterized by the presence of people like Henry Spira who for the most part set out to make changes in treatment of animals through campaigning, letter writing, politicking, and nonviolent civil disobedience. He was successful in moving the discussions and dialogues about animal rights into the mainstream. Spira's ethical position on the treatment of animals became more than words—he put his beliefs into action so that they had an impact on the world. In contrast, there are groups such as the highly decentralized Animal Liberation Front that engage in illegal actions at laboratories and farms. Some feel that while ALF's actions are well motivated, they will lead to a backlash against animal rights causes (Masci 1996). The group's activities give the bio-medical research and farming communities ammunition in their efforts to paint the an-imal-rights movement as a dangerous, fringe element in society.

In addition, there has emerged a pattern among these perpetrators of violent acts. Anyone who commits an act of environmen-tal terrorism and claims credit on behalf of the Animal Liberation Front (ALF) or the Earth Liberation Front (ELF) or other under-ground group becomes a "member." There are no membership rosters and no board of directors; just a collective sentiment that is enough to inspire certain people to commit life-threatening crimes against society.

The animal-rights movement is moving, however, from a position outside the main-stream to a point where the public at-large is taking them more seriously. Some animal ad-vocates and scientists are working quietly to reduce the use, discomfort, and death of mil-lions of creatures used for science. Groups like PETA are working with companies to explore alternatives to animal testing of products. They also conduct extensive educational cam-paigns to inform the public regarding the use and abuse of animals. Yet, there are still small groups of individuals engaging in illegal acts (Taylor 1998).

- The anti-abortion movement that was very active in the 1970s and 1980s still makes it presence known ("Unsolved Arson/Bomb-ing" 1999). There are the more-extreme fringe members who assassinate physicians and commit arson. Even with their avenue for certain activities curtailed by federal legislation (i.e., FACE), picketers confront facilities performing legal abortions and many individuals working in these clinics are concerned by the potential for renewed violence.

As stated earlier, Greenpeace and PETA remain committed to engaging in direct ac-tions that keep their respective messages in the public arena. While some actions may be illegal in a benign way, they do not at this time constitute terroristic acts.

DISCUSSION QUESTIONS

1. Radical environmentalism is out of the mainstream of social movements, in part because of members' engagement in vio-lent actions. In your opinion, have their activities in any way changed your views about the environment? Do you condone their use of illegal and/or violent actions to spread their message?

2. Bron Taylor (1998) argues that most rad-ical environmentalists refuse to use strategies that risk injury to humans or foster "terror" among the general popu-lace. Is the logical conclusion to this ar-gument that we should not include these individuals or groups in a discussion of domestic terrorism? Do their actions fit within the FBI or others' definition of ter-rorism?

3. Cecil Andrus, a former secretary of the interior, was critical of David Foreman and his early tactics and suggested that Foreman just wanted to sell books and make money. Based on what you know about the environmental movement and its activities, would you agree with this statement? In light of the philosophy of deep ecology, would you take a different position based on what you know about the resource-management approach adopted by government and industry?

4. Wapner suggests that Greenpeace, as an organization committed to environmen-tal change, is effective in spreading its message and bringing about structural

and political change without resorting to violence. Can you think of other organizations that have been successful in accomplishing its goal of change without the use of violence?

5. In 1998, the International Whaling Commission cleared the way for the Makah Indians to revive their tribal tradition of whaling. The Commission authorized the capture of up to five gray whales a year—more specifically, up to 20 whales over the next four years for "subsistence or ceremonial purposes." The gray whales that migrate from Mexico to the Bering Sea were driven to the edge of extinction by commercial whaling by the 1920s. The Makah Indians, who live at the very northwestern tip of Washington states, relied on the whales for a large part of their diet but stopped hunting the grays. The whale population recovered and now numbers at least 25,000. Consequently, the Makah decided to review their tribal tradition of whaling, around which many ceremonies, legends, and songs were built. In mid-May 1999, the Makah's harpooned and then shot a 30-ton female whale. Since 1986, there has been a worldwide ban on commercial whaling. This was the first U.S. kill outside Alaska since that time. (Sources: Hawley 1999; Verhovek 1999.) Some environmental groups, torn between a desire to protect the whales and respect for the ancient Indian traditions invoked by the Makah, took no position on the May 1999 whale hunt. Others said the whales' real enemy was not the Makah but commercial whalers in other parts of the world. Still others expressed outraged that the Makah were allowed to kill "an innocent sentient creature in such a bloody and untraditional way" (i.e., use of a .50-caliber assault rifle) (Verhovek 1999: 2). When do the rights of an in-

digenous population supercede the wishes of people who oppose killing the whales considered part of a protected class? Does the fact that the gray whale is apparently not endangered influence your decision in any way?

6. The mainstream message of the Wise Use movement has strong appeal. What, in your opinion, are the strengths of this message? Do you detect any contradictions in the core arguments underlying the mainstream message? Can you reconcile these beliefs with those of the environmentalists? Do you believe that wildlife deserves protection from the enterprises of man? If you worked in a resource-dependent industry (e.g., construction, oil drilling), would you feel any differently about the protection of wildlife and other natural resources?

7. What is your position on the use of animals for experimentation and research designed to test medicines and improve surgical processes for human beings? Do you feel that the public support for the use of animals in biomedical research will continue because most people know someone who has had a life-threatening disease? Is there any instance, in your opinion, when such experimentation is immoral or unethical?

8. Many laboratory animals are bred and raised for experimental purposes. Does this fact influence your attitude towards the use of animals in experiments?

9. For many years, animals were used as part of cosmetic testing. Is testing of animals truly necessary for achieving our consumer purposes? Are these purposes genuinely important?

10. The U.S. Supreme Court's decision in *Roe v. Wade* continues to be discussed and debated. What aspects of the court's decision are you in agreement with and what aspects of the decision concern you?

11. In your opinion, how should our government deal with people who climb trees or form barricades to protect trees from being cut down?

STUDY QUESTIONS

1. Several local affiliates of Earth First! have engaged in different forms of civil disobedience and in some cases, illegal activities. Conduct a search of the Internet and other available sources to determine what has occurred, who was responsible and what was the outcome (e.g., arrest). Are these environmental terrorists resorting to deadly attacks against humans rather than property? Where in the United States are most Earth First!-affiliated activities occurring?

2. Paul Watson is head of the Sea Shepherd Conservation Society, which sometimes calls itself the 'navy" of Earth First! and is best known for sinking whaling ships. The Sea Shepherd has claimed credit for sinking or scuttling five whaling vessels. This activist organization advocates the search-and-destroy method when it comes to ships that are violating an international ban (e.g., Norwegian whaling vessels *Senet* and *Brenna*). Watson argues that his is a law-abiding organization that recognizes the importance of laws of ecology over protection of corporate interests. Conduct research on this group's origins, philosophies and activities. What are its ties to Earth First!? Are their philosophies consistent and compatible with other environmental-resistance movements? If not, what impact does that have on the selection of strategies and targets?

3. What state and federal laws have been passed that either create or strengthen penalties against attacks by these "domestic terrorists"? Describe these laws. Are these new laws making it more difficult for individuals to protest within the law? Based on your research, have these new and/or stiffer penalties had any impact, including serving as a deterrent, on those wishing to express their opposition?

4. According to Helvarg, anti-environmentalism as a cause has flourished among right-wing politics and/or politicians and the right-wing movement. Can you find evidence to document this statement? If so, are you persuaded of its reliability and validity?

5. Wise Use advocates have been active and in many cases, successful in changing public opinion and translating their support into political and legislative action. What tools (e.g., economic boycotts, amendments to congressional laws) have they used in recent years to promote their philosophy? In your opinion, have they been successful?

6. Identify and describe the parallels between the justifications that white settlers used to expropriate land from the Native Americans in our early history and the rationale used by Wise Use advocates to support their position.

7. Identify and describe federal laws that set standards for the care and handling of animals used in research, and in zoos and circuses. Are handlers required to provide special accommodations, including giving drugs to eliminate pain and suffering? What organizational modifications are required, including the creation of oversight committees? Are experiments monitored? If so, what happens if violations are observed? Are there new reporting requirements?

8. In November 1999, approximately 88 scientists around the country received letters booby-trapped with razor blades and ordering them to release all research

monkeys or face violence. An animal-rights group called the "Justice Department" put a list on the Internet of scientists it singled out. The letter received by one University of California at Davis professor warned that "this is a drop in the bucket compared to what you will experience if you don't stop doing research on primates, and that they will do something much worse next time" (Schevitz 1999: A15). David Barbarash, listed on the Web site as a press contact, said he was a member of the Animal Liberation Front and not affiliated with the so-called Justice Department. However, he confirmed that the group had sent the letters. What law enforcement and legal actions were taken in response to this action? Do we know now the existence and/or membership of the group calling itself the Justice Department? Have there been any further incidences attributed to this group?

9. There is a group called the Animal Rights Militia (ARM) that holds similar views to that of the ALF but it differs with respect to attitudes on the use of violence directed at people (Monaghan 1997). They claimed responsibility for several bomb attacks on scientists' homes and car bombs, reinforcing their commitment to violence against people. Some writers have questioned whether ARM is actually a new distinct group or members of ALF. What information is available on this group? Have they claimed responsibility for extremist–terrorist actions in support of animal rights? If so, describe those actions. Have any ARM members been arrested and convicted?

10. The year 2000 was a watershed year for the animals-rights legal movement. The first textbook on animal law was published. Recent lower-court decisions have broadened the rights of pet owners by recognizing the human suffering caused by the loss or injury of a pet. Some believe that eventually the courts will extend certain rights to animals–changing their status from simply property to something more. Such a shift could give new protections to laboratory animals. Conduct legal research to determine the nature of animal protections upheld by the courts. Is there case law that protects laboratory animals?

11. What case law has emerged in the 1990s and beyond that deals with the rights of clinic patients to seek abortion services and the rights of abortion opponents to express their opinions?

12. Eric Rudolph, who has been accused of several abortion-clinic bombings and the Olympic bombing in Atlanta, Georgia, is a fugitive and has perhaps been hiding out in the North Carolina Mountains since early 1999. What efforts have law enforcement and other government officials initiated to capture this man? Could Rudolph's rationale for the Olympic bombing be to draw attention to his anti-abortion beliefs? Has he been caught and if so, what has been the outcome of any criminal proceedings?

13. Describe and discuss the history, organization and activities of the group calling itself Army of God.

14. The *Anti-Abortion Violence Watch* is compiled by the staff of the Feminist Majority Foundation and is published monthly. It reports on domestic terrorism against women's health clinics and is part of their ClinicWatch project. Review several years of these publications. Do you see any trends in the attacks against women's health clinics? Is there increased use of any particular strategy, whether it is arson, bombing or assassination?

15. In January 1994, a court held that RICO (Racketeer Influenced and Corrupt Or-

ganizations Act), that outlaws certain racketeering activity by or in relation to an enterprise, does not require that the enterprise be economically motivated. The Supreme Court concluded that RICO could be brought against those who, with a moral or religious motivation, conspire to shut down abortion clinics through a pattern of racketeering activity. How many federal racketeering cases have been filed in the 1990s and beyond? What was the outcome of these cases? Do you believe that this is an avenue for responding to anti-abortion violence?

16. There is some evidence to suggest that Ted Kaczynski was a member of Earth First!. Is there documentation that confirms this statement? If so, did this group in any way influence Kaczynski's involvement in bombings, etc.?

REFERENCES

Abbey, Edward: *The Monkey-Wrench Gang.* New York: Avon, 1975.

Animal Liberation Front (ALF): Frequently Asked Questions. Available online: http://www.hedweb.com/alffaq.htm. Northern American A.L.F. Supporters Group. Retrieved October 1999.

Arnold, Ron: *Ecology Wars—Environmentalism as if People Mattered.* Bellevue, WA: The Free Enterprise Press, 1987.

Blanchard, Dallas A., and Prewitt, Terry J.: *Religious Violence and Abortion: The Gideon Project.* Gainesville, FL: University Press of Florida, 1993.

Burke, William Kevin: The Wise Use Movement: Right-wing Anti-Environmentalism. In Berlet, Chip (Ed.): *Eyes Right! Challenging the Right-wing Backlash.* Boston: South End Press, 1995, pp. 135–145.

Clearinghouse on Environmental Advocacy and Research (CLEAR): *The Wise Use Movement: Strategic Analysis and Fifty State Review.* Retrieved on Nov. 24, 1999 at www.ewg.org/pub/home/clear/by-clear/fifty-iii.html

Costa, Marie: *Abortion: A Reference Handbook,* 2nd ed. Santa Barbara, CA: ABC-CLIO, 1996.

Dejevsky, Mary: Eco-terrorist burn ski resort. *The Independent,* October 23, 1998. Retrieved Oct. 26, 1999 at www.millennium-debate.org/ind23oct5.htm

Devall, Bill, and Sessions, George: *Deep Ecology: Living as if Nature Mattered.* Salt Lake City, UT: Gibbs Smith, 1985.

Drengson, Alan, and Inoue, Yuichi (Eds.): *The Deep Ecology Movement: An Introductory Anthology.* Berkeley, CA: North Atlantic Books, 1995.

Eagan, Sean P.: From Spikes to Bombs: The Rise of Eco-Terrorism. *Studies in Conflict and Terrorism, 19* (1): 1–18, 1996.

Echeverria, John D., and Eddy, Raymond Booth (Eds.): *Let the People Judge—Wise Use and the Private Property Rights Movement.* Washington, D.C.: Island Press, 1995.

Eddy, Mark, and Lipscher, Steve: Vail Fires Ruled Arson. *Denver Post,* October 28, 1998. Available online: http://www.denverpost.com/stories/0,1002,25,00.html. Retrieved October 1999.

Epstein, Richard: *Takings—Private Property and the Power of Eminent Domain.* Cambridge, MA: Harvard University Press, 1985.

Faux, Marian: *Crusaders: Voices from the Abortion Front.* New York: Carol Publishing, 1990.

Foreman, David, and Haywood, Bill (Eds.): *Ecodefense: A Field Guide to Monkey Wrenching.* Tucson, AZ: N. Ludd, 1987.

Ginsburg, Faye: Rescuing the Nation: Operation Rescue and the Rise of Anti-Abortion Militance. In Solinger, Rickie (Ed.): *Abortion Wars: A Half Century of Struggle, 1950–2000.* Berkeley, CA: University of California Press, 1998, pp. 227–250.

Gottlieb, Alan (Ed.): *The Wise Use Agenda.* Bellevue, WA: The Free Enterprise Press, 1989.

Greenpeace: A Hero's Welcome: Greenpeace Flashback October 30, 1971. *Greenpeace Magazine* 29: p. 29, Fall 1999.

Greenpeace Canada: *History of Greenpeace Canada.* Available online: http://www.greenpeacecanada.org/e/home.html. Retrieved October 1999.

Hawley, Chris: Makah hunt costs shadow on whaling meeting. *The Montreal Gazette 8:* E8, May 24, 1999.

Helvarg, David: *The War Against the Greens.* San Francisco, CA: Sierra Club Press, 1994.

Hunter, Robert: *Warriors of the Rainbow.* New York: Holt, Rinehart & Winston, 1979.

Ingalsbee, Timothy: Earth First! Activism: Ecological Postmodern Praxis in Radical Environmentalist Identities. *Sociological Perspectives, 39* (2): 263–277, 1996.

Jackman, Jennifer, Onyango, Christine, and Gavrilles, Elizabeth: *1998 National Clinic Violence Survey Report.* Feminist Majority Foundation, http://www.feminist.org/research/cvsurveys/1998/finaldraft.html. Retrieved June 15, 2000.

Judge Rules in Favor of Greenpeace and Steller Sea Lions: *Greenpeace Magazine, 5:* p. 5, Fall 1999.

Lee, Martha F.: *Earth First! Environmental Apocalypse.* Syracuse, NY: Syracuse University Press, 1995.

Masci, David: Fighting Over Animal Rights. *CQ Researcher, 6* (29): 673–696, 1996.

Monaghan, Rachel: Animal Rights and Violent Protest. *Terrorism and Political Violence 9* (4): 106–116, Winter 1997.

Mullins, Wayman C.: *A Sourcebook on Domestic and International Terrorism: An Analysis of Issues, Organizations, Tactics, and Responses,* 2nd ed. Springfield, IL, Charles C Thomas, Publisher, 1997.

Naess, Arne: The Shallow and the Deep, Long-Range Ecology Movement: A Summary. *Inquiry* (16): 95–100, 1973.

Parfit, Michael: EarthFirst!ers Wield a Mean Monkey Wrench. *Smithsonian 21* (1): 184–200, 1990.

People for the Ethical Treatment of Animals: About PETA–Our mission and history. Available online: http://www.peta-online.org/about/mission/html and http://www.peta-online.org/about/history.html. Retrieved October 1999.

Ramos, Tarso: Wise Use in the West: The Case of the Northwest Timber Industry. In Echeverria, John D., and Eby, Raymond Booth (Eds.): *Let the People Judge–Wise Use and the Private Property Rights Movement.* Washington, DC: Island Press, 1995, pp. 82–118.

Risen, James, and Thomas, Judy L.: *Wrath of Angels: The American Abortion War.* New York: Basic Books, 1998.

Roush, Jon: What We Can Learn from the Wise Use Movement. In Echeverria, John D., and Eby, Raymond Booth (Eds.): *Let the People Judge–Wise Use and the Private Property Rights Movement.* Washington, DC, Island Press, 1995, pp. 1–10.

Scarce, Rik: *Eco-Warriors: Understanding the Radical Environmental Movement.* Chicago: The Noble Press, 1990.

Schevitz, Tanya: Threats, Blades Mailed to Animal Researchers. *The Sacramento Bee,* pp. A-1 and A-15, October 22, 1999.

Singer, Peter: *Ethics into Action: Henry Spira and the Animal Rights Movement.* Lanham, MD: Rowman and Littlefield Publishers, 1998.

——: *Animal Liberation,* 2nd ed. New York: Review of Books, 1990.

——: *Animal Liberation: A New Ethics for Our Treatment of Animals.* New York: Avon Books, 1975.

Snow, Donald: The Pristine Silence of Leaving it All Alone. In Brick, Philip D., and Cawley, R. McGreggor (Eds.): *A Wolf in the Garden: The Land Rights Movement and the New Environmental Debate.* Lanham, MD: Rowman and Littlefield Publishers, 1996, pp. 27–38.

Solinger, Rickie (Ed.): *Abortion Wars: A Half Century of Struggle, 1950–2000.* Berkeley, CA: University of California Press, 1998.

Stark, Jerry A.: Postmodern Environmentalism: A Critique of Deep Ecology. In Taylor, Bron Raymond (Ed.): *Ecological Resistance Movements.* Albany, NY: State University of New York Press, 1995, pp. 259–281.

Taylor, Bron: Religion, Violence and Radical Environmentalism: From Earth First! to the Unabomber to the Earth Liberation Front. *Terrorism and Political Violence 10* (4): 1–42, 1998.

Taylor, Bron Raymond (Ed.): *Ecological Resistance Movements.* Albany, NY: State University of New York Press, 1995.

Unsolved Arsons/Bombing 97–99. *Anti-Abortion Violence Watch, 1,* p. 1, September 1999.

Verhovek, Sam H.: Old Tradition, A New Furor. *New York Times,* p. 2, May 23, 1999.

Wapner, Paul: In Defense of Banner Hangers: The Dark Green Politics of Greenpeace. In Tay-lor, Bron Raymond (Ed.): *Ecological Resistance Movements.* Albany, NY: State University of New York Press, 1995, pp. 300–314.

Chapter 6

CASE STUDIES IN DOMESTIC TERRORISM AND POLITICAL EXTREMISM

The case studies in this chapter were selected for a number of reasons: representation of various manifestations of political extremism and domestic terrorism, level of complexity, contemporary nature, and popular appeal. Of the six case studies, two involve political extremism (Ruby Ridge and Waco) and four represent domestic terrorism. The events portrayed in the cases include the following:

- armed altercations with individuals suspected of firearms violations, including the stockpiling of weapons and those considered armed separatists;
- bombings of public (i.e., government) and/or private buildings;
- standoffs between private individuals and local/state/federal law enforcement officials; and
- murder and bombings to respond to "the industrial-technological system."

In order of presentation, we will examine the following cases:

1. Randy Weaver and the incident in Ruby Ridge, Idaho, in August 1992;
2. Federal assault on the Branch Davidian Complex in Waco, Texas, on February 28–April 19, 1993;
3. World Trade Center bombing in New York on February 26, 1993;
4. Bombing of the Federal Building in Oklahoma City on April 19, 1995;
5. Standoff with the Freemen of Montana from March 25 to June 13, 1996; and
6. Unabomber case.

The perpetrators in the Ruby Ridge, Oklahoma City, and Freemen of Montana incidents adhere in varying degrees to far-right anti-government philosophies, racist and anti-Semitic agendas, and the belief in the rights of individuals to bear arms. The persons convicted in the bombing of the World Trade Center believe in the tenets of Islamic Fundamentalism and oppose Western ideology and the role of the United States in the Middle East. Finally, the Unabomber is one individual who opposed technological changes and, through his actions, "terrorized" potential targets for seventeen years.

RANDY WEAVER AND RUBY RIDGE

On August 21, 1992, a six-man team from the Special Operations Unit of the U.S. Marshals Service, dressed in full camouflage and armed with silenced automatic weapons, moved onto Randy Weaver's (a federal fugitive) 20-acre property known as Ruby Ridge, located in Northern Idaho. Their intent was a "nonaggressive mission" designed simply to gather intelligence about the terrain and its inhabitants for possible future action. The eleven-day siege of Weaver's home by federal law enforcement authorities ended with his surrender on August 31, 1992. During the siege, Weaver's wife Vicki and 14-year old son Samuel were killed, as well as one U.S. deputy federal marshal.

Background

Randy and Vicki Weaver adhered to a belief system based on apocalyptic prophecy, a deep distrust of government, and anti-Semitic/racism. In the early 1980s, the Weavers (including wife Vicki, two daughters Sara and Rachel, son Samuel and family friend Kevin Harris) moved from Iowa to Northern Idaho to be in the mountains because "God said they should move there" to prepare for Armageddon and to be among those who would endure the time of tribulations.

They came to adopt their version of Christian Identity beliefs, which included an intense interest in conspiracy theories, or convictions that tight, highly organized, and influential groups or conspirators gather all power in their hands to make life miserable for poor or middle-class people. The Weavers stockpiled guns—according to their testimony, for self-defense purposes only. In addition, after arriving in Idaho, Randy Weaver associated with members of the Aryan Nations (Vizzard 1997).

The incident that triggered the federal response at Ruby Ridge was Randy Weaver's arrest on January 17, 1991, on federal weapons charges. In October 1989, Weaver allegedly sold two sawed-off handguns to a Bureau of Alcohol, Tobacco and Firearms (ATF) informant. The informant was offered clemency for his gunrunning charges if he could sign up more people to do undercover work or arrange more busts. Weaver was short of money at this time and the informant said he could make some money selling guns. The informant then solicited Weaver to saw-off the barrels of a couple of shotguns, a modification illegal under federal firearm law.

As Gerry Spence would argue later when defending Weaver in court on other matters, Weaver had never owned an illegal firearm and was not engaged in the manufacture of illegal weapons. Vizzard (1997) states that the ATF was not interested in Weaver himself, but in using him as an "unwitting agent" to conduct an underground investigation of other militant separatists.

Eight months after the sale of the two sawed-off shotguns, ATF agents approached Weaver and told him he could avoid arrest for the shotgun charge by agreeing to spy on the Aryan Nations in Hayden Lake. Weaver refused to become a government spy and instead phoned the Aryan Nations to warn them that federal agents were trying to infiltrate the organization. In December 1990, Randy Weaver was indicted on federal firearms charges. After his arrest on January 17, 1991, Weaver appeared in court on the misdemeanor federal weapons charges and was released on bond. While the original court date was set for February and later changed to March 20th, there is conflicting evidence regarding Weaver's knowledge of the actual court date. After Weaver failed to appear in court, a warrant was issued for his arrest.

Another element of this case involved the FBI's expansion of its operations in Northern Idaho where it was believed that the white supremacist phenomenon posed a threat. The Aryan Nations organization located in Hayden Lake, Idaho, was becoming a mecca for white supremacists, some of whom advocated the creation of a separate white nation in the northwest portion of the United States, including Idaho.

The Federal Approach and Resulting Standoff

Since Weaver's failure to appear on federal weapons charges, federal officials put him under surveillance for 16 months. On August 21, 1992, six federal deputy marshals ascended Ruby Ridge to observe possible locations for surveillance/security teams for the proposed undercover operation. They encountered Randy Weaver, Kevin Harris, Weaver's son Samuel, and their dog. After calling out, "Stop. U.S. Marshals," gunshots were exchanged between the marshals, Kevin Harris, and the Weavers. While the testimony provided by all the agents during congressional hearings, as well as the court testimony of Randy Weaver and Kevin Harris, leave room for questions, several facts are known: the dog, Samuel, and one U.S. marshal were dead.

On the following day, August 22, over 100 federal, state, and local law enforcement officers and members of the National Guard surrounded the cabin. An operations plan, which included special rules of engagement, were sent to FBI headquarters and the U.S. Marshals Service for review. Eugene Glenn,

former Special Agent in Charge, Salt Lake City, Utah, FBI office, provided testimony before Congress regarding the Rules of Engagement that allowed for the use of deadly force if any adult in the compound was observed with a weapon:

> During the briefings I received, Randall Weaver was described as a violent and well-known individual who was a former Green Beret and explosives expert. Information indicated that Weaver had a large cache of arms. . . . He had stated that he wanted a showdown or last stand with the Federal Government. . . . I learned from the Marshal Service representatives that Deputy Degan had identified himself to those who shot him before he was shot. Thus, I concluded that Randy Weaver and those at his cabin knew that they had killed a deputy U.S. marshal. (Committee on the Judiciary of the U.S. Senate 1997: 474)

On the afternoon of August 22, Randy Weaver, his daughter Sara, and Kevin Harris went to the guest shed on the property where Sam's body had been placed. Federal agents fired, hitting Randy Weaver in the shoulder and seriously wounding Kevin Harris. Additionally, Vicki Weaver was shot in the doorway of the house while holding their ten-month-old baby. In the days that followed, the family members prepared to defend themselves, while sympathizers gathered outside the compound to lend support to the Weavers. These sympathizers included Aryan Nation followers, Identity adherents, Skinheads, and local residents who believed the government was wrong in its actions.

The federal forces surrounding the cabin made efforts to establish contact and communications with Randy Weaver. They shouted through the walls of the cabin and used bullhorns. There was no response. An armored vehicle brought a phone to the cabin's porch and Weaver was encouraged to contact FBI

Box 6.1
Federal Rules of Engagement

When FBI tactical teams, such as Hostage Rescue Team (HRT), are deployed and confrontations are a possibility, Rules of Engagement are commonly established. Rules of Engagement are instructions to deployed units or individuals that clearly indicate what action should be taken when confronted, threatened, or fired on by someone. They are intended to provide a context within which decisions about the use of deadly force are to be made. They serve two purposes:

1. Restrict the application of the standard FBI deadly force policy (i.e., deadly force is only allowed when someone "poses a threat of serious physical harm, either to the officer or others . . . and possesses an immediate threat to the safety of others"); or
2. Heighten the awareness of tactical personnel regarding the threat level of individual situations.

Formulation and approval of the Rules of Engagement are the responsibility of the on-scene commander.

The need for special Rules of Engagement for the Ruby Ridge crisis was discussed and agreed on early in the incident when Richard Rogers, commander of the HRT, and assistant director of the FBI, Larry Potts, had a series of conversations to discuss the situation. The revised Rules of Engagement provided that: "If any adult in the compound is observed with a weapon after the surrender announcement is made, deadly force can and should be used to neutralize this individual. If any adult male is observed with a weapon prior to the announcement, deadly force can and should be employed, if the shot can be taken without endangering any children." At that time, it was not clear whether FBI headquarters approved these revised Rules of Engagement. However, in subsequent proceedings, such was revealed (Bock 1995).

---

hostage negotiators to end the situation peacefully.

Bo Gritz, a former Green Beret who agreed to act as a negotiator, offered to talk with Weaver "solder to soldier." Gritz was driven to the cabin in an armored vehicle and although Randy Weaver didn't allow him into the cabin, they did converse through the plywood wall. Weaver said he wasn't ready to leave the cabin but that he would be willing to negotiate with Bo Gritz or with Vicki's brother, Lanny Jordison. Several days later, Gritz, Chuck Sandelin—a local Baptist

minister—and Jackie Brown—Vicki Weaver's closest friend—approached the cabin. When Jackie was allowed in, a medic was also allowed to approach the cabin, ask questions, and offer some advice for temporary first-aid measures for Kevin Harris. Apparently, the Weaver family was reluctant to leave the cabin because they feared that federal agents would never let them leave the cabin alive and that they would not get a fair trial.

On Sunday, August 30th, Gritz and others were allowed into the cabin, and the decision was made to take Kevin Harris out to a medical tent at the federal staging area. Harris was given first aid and then flown to a hospital in Spokane, Washington, where he remained for two weeks. Gritz and Jackie Brown then removed Vicki Weaver's body from the cabin and turned it over to the county coroner.

The following day, Weaver informed Gritz that after reading scriptures with Sara, they felt that the proper day for them to come out of the cabin was September 9th. After more discussions, and assuring Sara in particular that the government would keep its end of the bargain, Gritz was able to convince them to end the confrontation. Randy Weaver and his three children then walked out of the cabin together. Randy was transferred to Boise where he received a medical check-up before he was taken to the county jail. Sara, Rachel, and Elisheba were placed in the custody of their mother's parents, Jeane and David Jordison.

The Aftermath

On September 1, 1992, Randy Weaver, accompanied by attorneys Gerry Spence and Chuck Peterson, appeared in federal court to answer charges. Weaver pleaded not guilty to the original charge of selling illegal weapons and failure to appear. The prosecution filed an additional charge of assault on a federal officer, stemming from the gun battle and standoff. Weaver returned to court to enter a plea on the assault charge. Kevin Harris, who was still in the hospital, was charged with first-degree murder of a federal officer. His attorney, David Nevin entered Harris's not guilty plea.

As the preliminary hearing began, the lead prosecutor convened a federal grand jury to consider an indictment against Weaver and Harris. After the grand jury delivered the indictment—ten counts, including murder, aiding and abetting murder, conspiracy, and assault—the judge stopped the preliminary hearing, ruling that filing the indictment ended the necessity for a preliminary hearing.

Prior to the closing arguments, the defense presented a motion to dismiss all charges or to order a directed verdict of acquittal on all charges. Both Gerry Spence and David Nevin argued, for their respective clients, that the prosecution had failed to prove any aspect of the case against Randy Weaver and Kevin Harris. The judge dismissed two counts and reserved the right to dismiss a third count. He ruled that the remaining seven counts would be presented to the jury. The lawyers presented closing arguments, and the case was sent to the jury. The Weaver–Harris jury deliberated for twenty days before reaching a verdict on the remaining seven counts.

The government received a $10,000 fine during the trial for misconduct after it admitted staging photographic evidence of bullets found on Weaver's land (Abanes 1996). According to Abanes, the court also fined the government $1,920, declaring that the FBI had shown a complete lack of respect for the court and a callous disregard for the court, for the defendants' rights, and for the interests of justice.

The jury returned its verdicts on July 8, 1993: Kevin Harris was acquitted of all charges; Randy Weaver was acquitted of the original weapons charge and of all serious charges—murder, conspiracy, aiding and abetting—arising from the siege and standoff and found guilty of two minor charges arising from the original arrest—failure to appear and violating the terms of his bail. Weaver, who was sentenced to eighteen months in prison, was released from prison in December 1993.

In August 1994, Gerry Spence, David Nevin, and Chuck Peterson filed two civil lawsuits on behalf of Randy Weaver and Kevin Harris:

- A civil wrongful death suit against more than a dozen named and unnamed federal agents, which sought civil damages for the deaths of Vicki Weaver and Sam Weaver. In August 1995, the Department of Justice (DOJ) announced that it had agreed to pay $3.1 million to the Weaver family: $1 million to each of the three surviving Weaver children, and $100,000 to Randy Weaver. DOJ maintained that the settlement reflects the loss to the Weaver children of their mother and brother. The DOJ stated that it was not admitting wrongdoing or legal liability to the Weavers.
- A suit against the federal government for violating the constitutional rights of Randy Weaver, Kevin Harris, and the remaining Weaver family members. At the time of this writing, this suit was still pending.

Immediately following the jury's verdicts, Senator Larry Craig of Idaho, a conservative Republican, called for a federal investigation into the conduct of federal officials. Attorney General Janet Reno directed the U.S. Justice Department's Office of Professional Responsibility to inquire into the FBI's conduct at Ruby Ridge. According to a *New York Times* story on November 24, 1993, Deputy Attorney General Philip B. Heyman, who was supervising the inquiry, described it as a top-to-bottom review of the entire case, including whether officials failed to consider less aggressive tactics and later closed ranks to avoid scrutiny of their actions. The Justice Department inquiry was completed in April 1994.

Although the final report has not been made publicly available, various representatives of the media have reported seeing parts of the report and concluded the following:

- Senior officials violated standard FBI policies and the U.S. Constitution when they promulgated the Rules of Engagement for Ruby Ridge.
- FBI did not act with malice but misjudged the threat that Weaver posed to federal agents.

In early 1995, FBI Director Louis Freeh disciplined twelve FBI personnel in connection with the Ruby Ridge standoff, including suspensions and censure. Although he said that the shooting of Vicki Weaver was not intentional, Freeh admitted that those disciplined had "demonstrated inadequate performance, improper judgment, neglect of duty, and failure to exert proper managerial oversight" (Abanes 1996: 61). The FBI's standard rules of engagement, which "forbid the use of deadly force except in instances of imminent threat to human life and safety" were wrongfully replaced by shoot-on-sight orders (Abanes 1996: 48).

In September 1995, the Subcommittee on Terrorism, Technology, and Government Information of the Committee of the Judiciary began its hearings on what happened at Ruby Ridge, Idaho, in August 1992. The opening statement of Senator Arlen Specter set the stage for the hearings:

> This is an American tragedy with the killing of a U.S. marshal, William Degan, and the killing of Mrs. Vicki Weaver and young Sam Weaver, age 14. Those consequences have reverberated around the country with focal questions being posed on why the FBI changed the rules of engagement for the use of deadly force in the midst of this proceeding; and as conceded by the FBI itself, why the FBI records were destroyed in an effort to cover up what had happened. (Committee on the Judiciary of the U.S. Senate 1997: 2)

In over 1,100 pages of testimony taken at the Senate hearings, the Subcommittee was highly critical of the following:

1. Weaver's failure to appear in court for trial, holding that his compliance with the arrest warrant could have prevented the tragedy.
2. The ATFs' exaggerated report of Weaver as a dangerous fugitive who had a criminal record and had been linked to bank robberies, and of its subsequent failure to correct this report.
3. The FBI's Rules of Engagement, approving that deadly force can and should be used during the siege. The Subcommittee found that these rules were in violation of constitutional guidelines and of the FBI's standard policy on deadly force.

They also concluded that the second shot that killed Vicki Weaver was "a tragic and senseless mistake." The Subcommittee made suggestions for reform and questioned the duplication of efforts and possible mistakes that result from having multiple investigative agencies with overlapping responsibilities. However, the fallout from Ruby Ridge was not over yet.

In October 1996, E. Michael Kahoe, former chief of the FBI's Violent Crimes Section, pleaded guilty to obstruction of justice after admitting in federal court that he destroyed an internal FBI report criticizing the Bureau's handling of the 1992 siege at Ruby Ridge. As part of his plea, Kahoe agreed to cooperate with federal prosecutors who were looking into the possibility that other FBI officials were involved in the cover-up of the actions that took place during the nine-day standoff. He was sentenced to eighteen months in prison, fined $4,000, and placed on probation for two years after his release from federal prison. The DOJ announced in August 1997 that no criminal charges would be filed against senior FBI officials in connection with the Ruby Ridge incident because of lack of evidence. However, the department stated that this does not preclude the imposition of disciplinary sanctions against these individuals or other FBI officials.

On June 14, 2000 a federal appeals court refused to revive the criminal prosecution of an FBI sniper who killed Vicki Weaver. The 9th U.S. Circuit Court of Appeals, upholding a 1997 ruling by a trial court in Idaho, said agent Lon T. Horiuchi could not be charged with involuntary manslaughter for making what the circuit court's majority characterized as a reasonable law enforcement judgment call. The court stated that "Given the circumstances at the time, Horiuchi made an objectively reasonable decision" to shoot, though "today, all must regret the tragic result" (Cooper 2000: A4).

On June 5, 2001, the 9th U.S. Circuit Court, on a 6:5 decision reversed the 2000 ruling by the three judge panel of the same court. The Court stated that the FBI sharpshooter can be tried on state charges of manslaughter. The Boundary County prosecutor, however, announced he would not try the FBI sniper because it would be difficult to try the case.

Discussion Questions

1. At what point do the rights of civilians to bear arms conflict with the responsibility of federal law enforcement to keep the peace and uphold federal gun-related legislation?
2. Do the federal actions taken in this incident represent a justified use of force or an abuse of power?
3. If it is in the best interest of all American society, is it okay for the government to infringe on the rights of a few? Why or why not?
4. Some law enforcement experts argue that the verdicts in this case should cause federal agencies that shadow "fringe" groups and individuals to question their tactics and philosophies. Do you agree or disagree with this statement?

5. According to several sources, there were hours and hours of surveillance videotape that had been taken in and around the Weaver house prior to the siege. These tapes showed that all the adults in the household carried weapons whenever they came out of the cabin, and the older children carried weapons most of the time when outside as well. Given this information, can you justify the revised Rules of Engagement endorsed by the hostage response team? Why or why not?

6. In your opinion, do you think the issue of entrapment influenced the jury's decision to find Randy Weaver not guilty of the original weapons charge?

7. Are there some laws that simply cannot be enforced without abuse?

Study Questions

1. What policies and procedures were modified and adopted by the ATF and the FBI as a result of departmental inquiries and congressional hearings?

2. What was the nature of the relationship between the FBI and the U.S. Attorney's office in Idaho? Did their relationship in any way affect the events that occurred at Ruby Ridge?

3. The Weaver incident has been cited frequently as one of the principal events leading to the formation of militia groups. What evidence can you find to support this belief?

4. Investigate why Bo Gritz agreed to negotiate for the government with Randy Weaver. What has been Gritz' experience with right-wing extremists since 1996?

FEDERAL ASSAULT ON THE BRANCH DAVIDIAN COMPLEX IN WACO, TEXAS

The siege at the Branch Davidian Complex in Waco, Texas lasted from February 28, 1993 through April 19, 1993. During that period, agents of the ATF and the FBI attempted to execute arrest and search warrants and eventually resolve a standoff between federal agents and the Branch Davidians. This federal siege was reported to be one of the largest civilian law enforcement actions in U.S. history.

The facts in the Waco episode are complicated. The discussion that follows will address the precipitating factors that led to the arrival of federal agents at Mt. Carmel and will present as objectively as possible the facts as were revealed in government documents and personal accounts. Reavis (1995) notes that determining what happened at Mt. Carmel is difficult because of conflicting sources of information. Thus, the reader/researcher must weigh both a government and an anti-government point of view.

Several factors offered by federal authorities for the siege at Mt. Carmel and the urgency for resolving the standoff were allegations of extensive child abuse by David Koresh and the Branch Davidians, and a belief that sanitary conditions and the quality of life inside the facility were deteriorating. In several public statements, Attorney General Janet Reno raised the specter of child abuse and indicated that they had information that babies were being beaten. Although the federal government has no jurisdiction over such matters, Attorney General Reno repeatedly referred to the child-abuse allegations as a justification for her order to attack the community compound.

Specifically, the allegations included severe corporal punishment, sexual abuse, psychological abuse, and material deprivation. Many of those making the allegations were

---

Box 6.2
Davidians and Branch Davidians

The history of the Davidians can be traced back to 1929 when they emerged in Los Angeles as a movement calling for reform within the Seventh-Day Adventist Church (see Pitts 1995: 20–42). Victor Houteff, founder of this movement known as the Davidian Seventh-Day Adventists (Davidians), published *The Shepherd's Rod* and proclaimed himself the true messenger. He and his followers moved to central Texas in 1935 and established a community of about seventy people. Mt. Carmel, near Waco, Texas, eventually became the headquarters for the Davidians. They focused on expanding their self-sufficiency and using their land to produce as much food, lumber, and fuel as possible. The Davidians also produced their own money system, only to be used at Mt. Carmel. The money carried two logos: the lion of Judah representing the Davidic kingdom, and the eleventh-hour clock, a reminder of the impending end-time.

The Davidians adopted some of the teachings of the Seventh-Day Adventists, including the expectation of the second advent or coming of Christ, the appearance of prophetic voices and apocalyptic visions, observance of the Saturday Sabbath, opposition to serving as combatants in a war, and a strong emphasis on health. Houteff interpreted the Bible in terms of prophecy and fulfillment.

Victor Houteff died in 1955 and his wife, Florence, assumed the leadership role. Houteff believed that the end of time was near and that his mission in life was to prepare the church for the Second Advent of Christ, which was to occur in 1959. When this did not happen, the organization split into two: Davidians and Branch Davidians. Davidians scattered and Branch Davidians occupied the Mt. Carmel property under the leadership of Ben Roden, his wife Lois, and son George. Lois Roden took over as the "prophet" in 1978, although her son George, insisted on his divine appointment as the true prophet. When Vernon Howell (later known as David Koresh) arrived in 1981, Lois Roden attempted to groom him as her successor.

What distinguished the Branch Davidians was their communal social structure and the extraordinary spiritual and temporal authority vested in David Koresh. Indeed, individual and personal loyalty to Koresh became the basic building block of the community. Koresh initiated several recruitment campaigns to rebuild the membership base, which grew from about two dozen to 100 adherents by 1989. Several members indicated Koresh's prophetic qualities and charisma partially explained their attraction to the Branch Davidians.

He further ensured his role as leader and messiah by legally changing his name from Vernon Howell to David Koresh in 1990. In biblical language, Koresh–the Hebrew word for Cyrus, the Persian king who defeated the Babylonians 500 years before the birth of Jesus–is "a," as opposed to "the," messiah, one appointed to carry out a special mission for God. His first name, David, asserts a lineage directly to the biblical King David, from whom the new messiah would be descended.

Drawing on the Book of Revelation, Koresh asserted that in his role as a messiah, he became the perfect mate of all the female adherents. Central to his messianic mission was the creation of a new lineage of God's children from his own seed. Thus, all of the female

Box 6.2 *Continued*

Branch Davidians potentially became spiritual wives to Koresh. This claim, through the establishment of what Koresh called the House of David, produced the single most significant restructuring of the Davidian community during the Koresh era. Koresh believed that the way to salvation was the creation of a new spiritual lineage that could only be initiated by him acting in his messianic role.

The Branch Davidians believed the end of the world was near, that the world would end in a cataclysmic confrontation between themselves and the government, and that they would thereafter be resurrected. As Koresh began to prepare the community for the apocalypse, the group adopted survivalist tactics such as stockpiling large amounts of dried food, weapons and ammunition, and acquiring a large storage tank of propane gas. Koresh actually renamed the Mt. Carmel community "Ranch Apocalypse" in 1992. Tensions increased with the larger society during this time:

- intrafamily conflicts developed when some members defected while others remained loyal;
- arranged marriages of domestic and foreign adherents raised questions regarding immigration;
- Koresh's sexual innovations caused some to defect; and
- Koresh's actions of inducting young women who were legally minors into the House of David raised other issues.

All of these factors created a pool of potential allies for federal agencies and created the basis for legal action against the group. Ultimately, these practices strengthened the resolve of the coalition of individuals and groups opposed to Koresh and began the course of events that led to the destruction of the Mt. Carmel complex on April 19, 1993.

Sources: Barkun 1994; Bromley and Silver 1995; Pitts 1995.

members who defected from the community. In a press conference, President Clinton reiterated that federal officials had reason to believe that the children who were still inside the compound were being abused significantly as well as being forced to live in unsanitary and unsafe conditions.

One source of empirical information concerning the allegations of harsh physical punishment at Mt. Carmel was a 1992 investigation of the Branch Davidians by the Children's Protective Services (CPS), a division of the Texas Protective and Regulatory Services.

After three separate trips to the community, an interview with Koresh, the children, and other adults, and physical examinations of the children, CPS decided to terminate the investigation after two months. There was some evidence, however, to suggest that Koresh harshly disciplined the children, including hitting the children with a wooden spoon or withholding food for up to one day.

The evidence supporting the allegations regarding child sexual abuse appears somewhat stronger than the evidence supporting the other allegations against Koresh. Koresh had sexual relations with female minors, the full extent to which is unknown. Koresh acknowledged on a videotape sent out of the compound during the standoff that he had fathered more than twelve children by several wives who were as young as 12 or 13 when they became pregnant (Tabor and Gallagher 1995). Finally, questions were raised about the lack of indoor plumbing and the strict regulation of children's food consumption. Physicians who examined the children released prior to the fire found them to be healthy and fit.

An additional allegation was that the community at Mt. Carmel was amassing weapons. The ATF office in Austin, Texas was notified in May 1992 that a United Parcel Service (UPS) agent had delivered shipments to the Branch Davidian community of firearms worth more than $10,000, inert grenade casings, and a substantial quantity of an explosive known as black powder. A formal investigation into potential violations of federal gun laws by Koresh and his followers was initiated. Grenades are on the list of destructive devices prohibited by federal firearms law.

Warrants for the arrest of David Koresh and search of the premises of the Mt. Carmel compound for illegal weapons were issued by a magistrate judge on February 25, 1993. The affidavit in support of the request for the warrants was based partially on the recollection of former community members about the situation in the compound and information gleaned during undercover operations of the Branch Davidians by ATF agents. At the conclusion of the standoff, 300 firearms were recovered from the Branch Davidian compound, a number of live grenades and more than 300 grenade components, as well as hundreds of thousands of rounds of ammunition.

The ATF investigation also included an undercover agent's infiltration into the compound and the establishment of an observation post that could watch the compound (Vizzard 1997). The agent, Robert Rodriguez—who went to the compound regularly and talked with Koresh regarding religion and biblical teachings—was assigned to investigate and collect tactical intelligence (Vizzard 1997). Rather than make a show of force against the Davidians, ATF developed a plan to serve search and arrest warrants on the compound.

On February 28, 1993, ATF agents attempted to execute arrest and search warrants against David Koresh and the Branch Davidian compound. Two-thirds of the search warrant was in response to the child-abuse allegations and one-third was in response to allegations of illegal weapons. This initial operation involved approximately eighty federal agents, armed with semiautomatic and automatic weapons. After the failed siege, in which at least six residents of the compound and four ATF agents died and sixteen ATF agents were wounded, a fifty-one day standoff began. David Koresh was also injured during the shootout with federal agents. The FBI then became the lead agency, and advance units of the FBI's Hostage Rescue Team (HRT) arrived and negotiations were initiated.

In the early part of the standoff, the FBI's strategy was to negotiate a settlement, no matter how long it took. On March 1, ten children were sent out of the compound. FBI agents in armored vehicles secured the perimeter of the compound and cut the phone lines except for outgoing calls to the negotiators. Koresh initially agreed to surrender but then retracted his statement by saying that God had spoken to him and had told him to wait. At the end of the first week, the negotiations appeared to be at an impasse and the FBI acknowledged frustration while attempting to negotiate with Koresh.

During the second week of the standoff, members of HRT stated they saw weapons in the windows of the compound, and firing ports cut in plywood placed in the windows. The FBI shut off the power to the compound. According to one justice official, this was intended to challenge Koresh's control of the situation, to raise the level of stress within the compound, and to force more departures. In addition, the FBI began to illuminate the compound with bright lights to disrupt sleep, to put additional pressure on those inside, and to increase the safety of the hostage negotiators.

On March 25, the FBI issued an ultimatum that ten to twenty people must leave by 4 P.M. or action would be taken. At 4 P.M., armored vehicles moved into the compound and removed motorcycles. Another ultimatum was issued on March 26, with no response from Koresh or his followers.

Preliminary plans to use tear gas to get Koresh and his followers out of the Branch Davidian compound were discussed in early April and finalized on April 9. The plan was to insert gas in one area of the compound so that people could exit through uncontaminated portions. Attorney General Reno met with Delta Force commanders to review the tear gas plan. It was clear to federal officials that the Branch Davidians had sufficient water, food, and other provisions to withstand a prolonged siege. Reno approved the tear-gas plan on April 17th, President Clinton was briefed and concurred. On April 19th, the Davidians were notified of the imminent tear-gas assault. The tear gas was inserted into the compound in the early hours of the morning. The FBI's armored vehicles punched in the walls of the compound to insert the gas.

FBI Director Louis Freeh acknowledged in September 1999 that federal agents used incendiary devices in the raid (i.e., two pyrotechnic tear-gas canisters), which were fired at the compound. High winds dispersed much of the gas, which seemed to have little effect on the adult occupants during the six-hour assault. There were shots fired from the compound and by federal agents. Simultaneously, fires erupted at three or more different locations within the compound. The flames consumed Mt. Carmel, and the site was eventually bulldozed.

Of the approximately 80 individuals who died when the fire erupted, 25 were children. The medical examiners indicated that many of the Branch Davidians died from asphyxiation when the intense fire raced through the compound. Others, particularly women and children who huddled under wet blankets in a concrete chamber, were fatally injured when debris collapsed on them during the fire. Still others were shot to death and were either suicide or homicide victims.

In early 1994, eleven surviving Branch Davidians were tried in federal court in San Antonio on charges of conspiracy to murder federal agents, aiding and abetting murder of four federal agents who were killed in the raid, and on a number of lesser charges. When presenting their case, the prosecutors argued that the defendants willingly belonged to the Branch Davidians ("this revolutionary organization") and that they stayed even when there was talk of war against outsiders.

On February 26, 1994, the jury acquitted all of the defendants of the most serious charge of murder and conspiracy to commit murder. They acquitted four defendants of all charges and convicted five defendants of aiding and abetting the voluntary manslaughter of federal officers, which the judge defined as "acting in the sudden heat of passion caused by adequate provocation." The jury also convicted one defendant of possession of a grenade and one of conspiracy to manufacture and possess a machine gun and aiding and abetting possession of a machine gun. Five of the defendants were given forty years, and the remaining Davidians received lesser sentences, ranging from three to twenty years (Abanes 1996).

After the FBI raid at Waco, the symbolic date of April 19th became the rallying cry for scores of armed paramilitary groups throughout the United States. This is especially so among the most radical members.[49] The FBI refers to April 19 as the "Date of Doom" and the Montana militia leaders call it "Militia Day" (Hamm 1997: 29).

Discussion Questions

1. What limits may and should the government place on our ability to own weapons?
2. The effect of the FBI and ATF actions was the destruction of a religious community. Should this concern us? Why or why not?
3. Stuart Wright in *Armageddon In Waco*, states that the events of Waco provide evidence for two predominant themes of his book (1995: x):
   a. First, that marginal religions and their members are accorded diminished human and social value, largely tied to disparaging stigmas and widespread stereotypes ("brainwashed cultists") that recall some of the most vicious racial, ethnic and religious prejudices of our nation's past; and
   b. Second, that minority religions are more likely to be victimized by extreme efforts of social control, most

notably by government, but hastened and incited by selected interest groups.
   • Based on your life experiences and pursuit of knowledge, what aspects of Wright's statements ring true for you and why? What aspects of his statements concern you?
   • Has the government victimized minority religious groups in recent times? If yes, do you believe this victimization was justified? Why or why not?

4. Were the federal actions taken against David Koresh and the Branch Davidians, including the type and level of force used, proportionate to the alleged crimes? One critic stated that no one should doubt that Waco was terrorism, only committed by the federal government. Do you agree or disagree with this statement?
5. What effect would the availability of the Internet have on the nature and extent of media coverage?
6. Do you believe that the government has the right to set limits on how one practices one's religion, including amassing weapons and adopting survivalist tactics (e.g., stockpiling food, water)?
7. Did the federal agencies "construct an enemy" out of David Koresh and the Branch Davidians? If yes, in your opinion, did this enemy status justify the level of force?
8. Apparently, bullets killed 18 or 19 of the Branch Davidians. What does this suggest to you?
9. Based on what you know about this incident and the standoff at Ruby Ridge,

---

[49] When Timothy McVeigh was arrested after a routine traffic stop, a search of his car turned up a self-authored manuscript entitled "Revenge for Waco." The selection, in fact, of a calendar date as an ideological justification for terrorism comes from a scene in *The Turner Diaries* where The Order declares a given day as the "Day of the Rope." On this day, somebody from the news media must be hanged, preferably a Jew.

Idaho, has your confidence in federal law enforcement been altered in any way?

10. Attorney General Janet Reno assumed office just shortly before this incident (approximately 23 days on the job). The head of the FBI William Sessions was also leaving his post. What effect might these leadership changes have had on the course of events?

Study Questions

1. Review the second amendment to the U.S. Constitution and examine scholarly and legal analyses of this amendment. Respond to the following questions:
   a. What guidelines does the Second Amendment provide in terms of one's right to bear arms and specifically, stockpile weapons?
   b. Are there any restrictions placed on our right to bear arms based on the nature of the weapon?

2. There were and may continue to be political and other responses to the Waco incident. Identify and describe these responses including but not limited to congressional hearings, public statements by relevant federal agencies (e.g., FBI, ATF), internal agency investigations, reactions by civil rights and religious organizations, and coverage and commentaries by print and television media.
   a. What criminal and civil actions were taken against any ATF or other federal agent? Describe the charges, evidence, and resolution.
   b. On July 14, 2000, a five-member jury in Waco, Texas decided the government did not use excessive force in its attempt to serve search and arrest warrants. They also decided the government's actions on April 19th were not negligent and did not contribute to the deaths of

the Davidians. However, U.S. District Judge Walter Smith didn't have to follow the jury's advice. What was the final decision in this case?
   c. Did any of the federal agency reports indicate errors made by federal officials in the handling of the Branch Davidians? If so, describe these errors.
   d. ATF rules require that a mission be stopped if compromised. Did Agent Rodriguez, who was infiltrating the group, call ATF prior to the first assault to inform them that Koresh knew of the pending attack? If so, what response did ATF have to these allegations?

3. "To appreciate the tragedy of Waco we need to see it as a part of a long history of communal formation based on biblical prophecy and belief and the failure of law enforcement officials to know about that heavenly science" (Fogarty 1995: 18). What is Fogarty referring to and what evidence does he use to support this statement?

4. The print and television media were present during the entire incident. How did they portray David Koresh, the Branch Davidians, and the federal agents? What was the nature of the relationship between the media and federal agents in charge? Describe the level of coverage by both the print and television media. Are there any discernable differences in the type of coverage between the two mediums? Which entity do you believe presented the most objective, factual coverage of the Waco incident?

5. What was the nature of the relationship between the FBI and ATF, and the federal law enforcement agencies and local law enforcement?

6. Is there any evidence to suggest that the Delta Force was involved in this incident beyond just consulting with Attorney General Reno? If so, was this involvement consistent with their mission and responsibility as delineated under federal law?

7. What do the surviving Davidians say regarding David Koresh and their beliefs?
8. Do you think Koresh controlled the situation that occurred at Waco? If yes, how did he do this?

WORLD TRADE CENTER BOMBING

America's long-standing belief that our country was invulnerable to a terrorist attack changed in February 1993. The bombing of the World Trade Center in New York City was at the time one of the most significant and devastating acts of domestic terrorism in the 1990s. What made this incident even more troubling for many was the fact that the perpetrators were individuals with ties to international terrorists who wanted to retaliate against the United States for perceived wrongs to Islamic fundamentalist interests.

On February 26, 1993, at 12:18 P.M. on the B-2 level of the parking garage, a twelve hundred-pound bomb exploded in one of the 110-story twin towers of the World Trade Center in New York City. It consisted of explosives, composed of agricultural fertilizer (with ammonium nitrate) and was enhanced with compressed hydrogen to magnify the blast, and sodium cyanide to create a poisonous cloud after the explosion. The bomb was placed in a yellow Ford Econoline E-350 van, which was rented in New Jersey from the Ryder Truck Rental Company. The FBI determined that the bomb was the largest homemade device ever seen in the United States.

The bomb exploded with a velocity of over 15,000 feet per second and created a crater 150 feet in diameter and five stories high. The explosion killed six, injured over 1,000 innocent bystanders, and caused massive devastation to buildings and cars in the surrounding area. Property damages were estimated at $600 million. Of those injured,

only fifteen were hurt by the blast; the rest suffered smoke inhalation.

Both the main and backup power generators of the World Trade Center went off-line as a result of the blast, thus shutting off the complex's exhaust system and compounding the number of smoke-related injuries. Six levels of the parking garage were perforated by the blast and cars three or four stories below and 600 feet away from the center of the explosion were destroyed. The 22-story Vista Hotel, located directly above the blast, took much of the force of the explosion and was badly damaged.

On March 5, 1993, the *New York Times* received a letter claiming responsibility for the bombing by a group known as "Liberation Army, Fifth Battalion." The letter claimed the bombing was in retaliation for "American political, economical and military support to Israel, the state of terrorism, and to the rest of the dictator countries in the region" (FBI 1993: 3). The letter also warned that unless the United States severed its ties to Israel, military and civilian targets in the United States would be hit by "more than a hundred and fifty suicidal soldiers" of the "Liberation Army." The FBI later linked the letter to one of the suspects.

There were many agencies involved in the investigation. Federal agencies included two ATF National Response Teams (NRT), the FBI, Secret Service, Customs Office, the Department of State, and the Department of Defense. State agencies included the New York City Police Department, the New York City Transit Police, the Port Authorities of New York and New Jersey, and the New York and New Jersey State Police. In addition to the overlapping jurisdictions and responsibilities of so many agencies, the investigation faced two difficulties:

- *Dangers posed by* the structural integrity of building; the need to ensure area safe to

Box 6.3
Islamic Fundamentalism

The United States's support of Israel and its role as peacemaker in that region has generated much of the terrorism against American facilities overseas and now on American soil. The United States has been viewed as an appropriate target for Islamic militants due to its support for their "enemies." Islamic fundamentalist ideology assumes that the very existence of the secular West is an insult to Islam. A number of countries, including Iran, support Islamic fundamentalist groups, although many are also part of a loose confederation of terrorist groups that lack centralized command. Fundamentalism and religion unite these militants.

Islamic fundamentalist ideologues believe that non-Muslim regions and the West are corrupt and must be crushed and punished. The question, then, logically arises about whether or not Islamic fundamentalism poses a threat to American society. Amos Perlmutter, professor of political science and sociology at American University, argues in the affirmative. In contrast, Moorhead Kennedy, a former Foreign Service Arabist who spent 444 days as a hostage in Iran in 1979–80, argues in the negative.

Perlmutter, responding to the question whether the World Trade Center bombing was in fact an act of terrorism, stated: "Not only was it a terrorist act, but it was a terrorist act complete with symbolic overtones, a characteristic Islamic fundamentalist penetration, probably inspired by the exiled Egyptian Sheik Omar" (Perlmutter and Kennedy 1993: 377). Perlmutter presents the argument that the target was ripe with symbolism as an example of everything fundamentalists' preaching sees as evil in the West. New York was the site because it is viewed as "Western monster incarnate, dominated by Jewish Zionist devils, who manipulate the levers of grand capitalism" (Perlmutter and Kennedy 1993: 377).

Kennedy argues that equating Islamic fundamentalism with terrorism closes minds at a time when the American public badly needs to understand this important world movement, Islam. This is important because a version of it is increasingly visible and influential in our own African American community. In its various manifestations, Islam will become, before long, the second largest American religious group after Christianity. Kennedy suggests that we need to understand that Islamic fundamentalism is not only a faith but also a political system, a legal system and a way of life.

It is significant to note that in the wake of the bombing of the federal building in Oklahoma City, the media reported a Middle-Eastern connection. In fact, several counterterrorism experts were heard on television and radio saying the bombing looked like the work of Middle East terrorists and possibly those connected with the World Trade Center bombing. Before any evidence on the identity of the bombing suspect was revealed by the FBI, some blamed "Middle Easterners," "Islamic radicals," or "Muslim fundamentalists" and warned that American cities have become a battleground for Islamic terrorism. It is this "quick to blame it on fundamentalist Islamic terrorist groups" attitude which concerns Kennedy and many others (Perlmutter and Kennedy 1993).

conduct forensic analysis; dust and carcinogens deposited in air by the explosion; falling debris rupturing the freon tanks of the building's air conditioning system; flooding due to broken water mains; raw sewage and rotting food; and fires intermittently erupting throughout the garage from gas or fuel leaks.

- *Complexities caused by* 4,000 tons of rubble; thousands of photographs; numerous documents and vehicles seized; and thousands of fingerprints processed.

Early in the investigation, NRT members, working with a New York City Police Department bomb squad investigation team, uncovered a key piece of evidence–a vehicle identification number from a van that had been rented and reported stolen the day prior to the explosion. The FBI arrested Mohammed A. Salameh in Jersey City, New Jersey, as he tried to collect his $400 cash deposit on the van. He had earlier reported the van stolen. After a search of Salameh's home, the FBI found Abdul Yasin who led them to the group's bomb factory. Yasin fled to Jordan the next day.

The authorities also learned that Nidal Ayyad had rented cars to case the trade center. Ahmad Ajaj, who had arrived with Ramzi Yousef in New York using a phony passport, was arrested along with Ayyad. Mahmud Abouhalima, who had fled to Saudi Arabia after the bombing, was arrested in Egypt and returned to the United States. Finally, Bilal Al-Kaisi was arrested, a man who was identified as being present at the Jersey City address where the FBI determined the bomb had been assembled. One key suspect, Ramzi Yousef, was on a plane to Karachi, Pakistan, within 12 hours after the blast. He had been seen in the van with Salameh. Until his February 1995 arrest, Yousef became one of the world's most wanted fugitives, with a $2 million bounty on his head. Another suspect, Eyad Ismoil, also

fled the country the night of the bombing and was seized in Jordan in 1995.

On March 17, 1993, Salameh and Ayyad were initially indicted by a federal grand jury and charged with "unlawfully, willfully and knowingly, and with malice, aiding and abetting the damage and destruction of, by means of fire and an explosive, a building in interstate and foreign commerce and death did result" (FBI 1993: 6). Abouhalima was indicted the following week on the same charges as Salameh and Ayyad. Al-Kaisi was also charged with the same crimes as the three earlier defendants. Ajaj was charged with conspiring to damage and destroy, by means of fire and explosive, a building used in interstate commerce. All of these defendants pleaded not guilty and were ordered to be held without bail.

On May 26, 1993, a federal grand jury returned an indictment charging Salameh, Ayyad, Abouhalima, Al-Kaisi, Ajaj, and Yousef with a total of seven counts relating to the bombing:

> Damage by means of fire or an explosive; transport in interstate commerce of an explosive; destruction of motor vehicles or motor vehicle facilities; penalty of death or life imprisonment when death results; aiding and abetting; destruction by fire and explosives to the buildings and vehicles; and commission of a crime of violence through the use of a deadly weapon or device. Ajaj and Yousef were charged with an additional count of interstate and foreign travel or transportation in aid of racketeering enterprises. (FBI 1993: 7–8).

Salameh, Ayyad, Abouhalima, and Ajaj were convicted and sentenced to life in prison. Yousef, believed to be the mastermind behind the bombing, was sentenced to 240 years behind bars in solitary confinement. Additionally, he was sentenced to life in prison for smuggling a bomb hidden in a watch aboard a Philippines Airlines plane in December 1994 that detonated, killing a Japanese man and injuring ten others. Eyad Ismoil, arrested earlier and tried at the same time as Yousef, was accused of being the driver of the van used in the blast and was found guilty of all ten counts brought against him.

The FBI was also alerted that yet another group was planning an even more extensive rampage to include attacks against the United Nations, the Lincoln and Holland Tunnels, and other New York landmarks. Emad Salem, a former Egyptian army colonel who had done some work for the FBI as an informant in the investigation of the 1990 murder of Jewish extremist Rabbi Meir Kahane, provided the FBI with tape-recorded conversations that were used to identify these other perpetrators. Although the Bureau had fired him earlier because he was difficult to work with and untrustworthy, they needed him because of his contacts within the Islamic community.

Salem offered extensive intelligence and evidence that the New Jersey-based group was purchasing explosives, detonators, and other supplies necessary to make large bombs. He indicated that the leader was Abdel-Rahman, an Egyptian cleric who was an outspoken critic of Cairo's pro-Western stance and who was viewed by many as the man responsible for issuing the *fatwa* (religious decree) ordering the assassination of Egyptian President Anwar Sadat in 1981.

Abdel-Rahman and nine men were eventually charged with seditious conspiracy, which does not require that the accused be linked to any specific acts of terrorism but rather can be implicated by his statements (e.g., his public statements against the enemies of Islam). In fact, Abdel-Rahman was never connected directly with the design and construction of the bombs. The trial, one of the longest terrorist trials to date, took eight months and resulted in convictions of all defendants.

Discussion Questions

1. A key defendant in the bombing was Sheik Omar Abdel-Rahman, the blind Muslim cleric who entered the United States fraudulently by claiming political asylum and then proceeded to preach at the mosques in New Jersey and Brooklyn that the United States was an enemy of the Islamic World. Should the federal government place limits on immigration and/or requests for political asylum if the individuals making the request have anti-American beliefs? Would you change your view if the individual belonged to a group identified by the United States as a terrorist organization but had not personally been involved in an act of terrorism?

2. Using the charge of seditious conspiracy, a prosecutor can argue and a jury can convict an individual for that individual's thoughts and statements, not actions. Many legal experts are concerned that this particular application of the law may open the door to prosecuting people for simply harboring inflammatory beliefs–"If you think it, then you are guilty." What do you think?

3. Does the fact that the defendants in the seditious conspiracy charge case (i.e., plans to blow up New York landmarks) were encouraged in their plot by a government informer concern you?

4. What concerns, if any, do you have regarding government use of informants? Are there any differences (e.g., practical, legal, and ethical) between the use of infiltrators versus informants?

Study Questions

1. What federal legislation was discussed and passed following this incident? Do you believe the new laws will reduce any fear Americans have about the potential for terrorist threats in our country? Are there

any civil liberties implications present in these new laws?

2. Is there any evidence to suggest that Islamic radicals are establishing a base in the United States through providing logistical support (e.g., housing, community support) to arrange strikes from across the Atlantic? Is there evidence to support the belief that these potential terrorists are dangerous because they are now blending into Western societies where they have established personal and community roots?

3. Select three or four major periodicals (e.g., *Christian Science Monitor, New York Times*). Find articles written about Middle Eastern people and culture, including stories on Islam. Do you find the presentations to be balanced? How and why?

4. The World Trade Center bombing heightened anti-immigrant sentiments among the American public. Did the U.S. Department of Justice offer any proposals to restrict immigration and/or to deport suspected terrorists following this incident? If so, do you believe these proposals threaten the civil rights of immigrants?

5. The convicted bombers were intent on bringing down one of the twin towers. They also represented an ad hoc grouping of like-minded individuals who shared a common religion, worshiped at the same religious institution, had the same friends, and were linked by family ties as well. This presents a new pattern for terrorism—where terrorist groups were once recognizable as distinct organizational entities, we now see people with like-interests and beliefs coming together on an ad hoc basis to commit terrorist acts. What problems do the experts believe these new "groupings" pose for future acts of domestic terrorism, in terms of lethality and targets? Do you agree with their conclusions?

BOMBING OF THE ALFRED P. MURRAH FEDERAL BUILDING IN OKLAHOMA CITY, OKLAHOMA

The photographs of little Baylee Amon's listless body, wrapped in the arms of a fireman, will forever be a symbol of the horror of the blast that destroyed the Alfred P. Murrah Federal Building in Oklahoma City on April 19, 1995. The facts are unambiguous but there are a number of significant issues, including timing and motive, which will be discussed to more fully present the entire picture of the events prior to and following the bombing.

On the morning of Friday, April 19, a Ryder rental truck loaded with approximately 5,000 pounds of explosives was parked in front of the Oklahoma City federal building. At exactly 9:02 A.M., the bomb was detonated by remote from an unknown location. The street-level bomb blast knocked out smaller columns supporting the beams of the nine-story structure, eliminating the support for the larger columns on top and causing huge chunks of the building to rumble to the ground. One hundred sixty-eight people perished in the blast, including nineteen children. Over 500 people were injured. As the dust began to settle, hundreds of victims and their families, and people in the vicinity of the building during the blast, and emergency response personnel pulled people from the wreckage, bandaged wounds, and searched for other survivors. The bombing is considered one of the worst terrorist attacks on U.S. soil.

Approximately two and one-half hours after the blast, the rear axle housing of what was later identified as a Ryder truck was found one block west of the federal building. A partial vehicle identification number was retrieved and the truck was traced to Miami, Florida. Authorities learned that the truck was at a body shop in Junction City, Kansas. After interviewing several employees, a composite drawing of the person who rented the truck was prepared by FBI artists.

It was learned that a man in a Ryder truck, later identified as Timothy McVeigh, had been a guest at a local motel. Federal agents conducted an NCIC (National Crime Information Computer) inquiry on McVeigh and found he had been arrested in Perry, Oklahoma, and was being held in the Noble County jail. His arrest occurred 90 minutes after the blast when an Oklahoma Highway Patrol trooper stopped McVeigh because the vehicles' license plate wasn't clearly visible, and subsequently arrested him on firearm charges. The next day, federal authorities released sketches of suspects John Doe No.1 and John Doe No. 2. On April 21, federal authorities arrested McVeigh hours before he was expected to make bail on the firearms charges. Terry Nichols, an army buddy of McVeigh's surrendered to police in Herrington, Kansas, after learning that law enforcement was looking for him in connection with the bombing.

A federal grand jury issued an indictment containing 11 counts, including three counts for conspiring to use a weapon of mass destruction to kill people and destroy federal property. The eight remaining counts were for killing federal law enforcement agents. The indictment alleged that McVeigh alone set off the bomb that destroyed the federal building. Michael Fortier, a friend of McVeigh's and Nichols's was also charged with firearms violations, lying to a federal agent, and prior knowledge of a felony.

Fortier pleaded guilty to the charges but was not sentenced until after he testified against Nichols and McVeigh. In his testimony before the court, Fortier contended that on December 16, 1994, while en route from Arizona to Kansas to take possession of some firearms, McVeigh and Fortier entered the Murrah building and identified it as the target of a future bombing. A federal judge in a hearing in October 1999 sentenced Fortier to 12 years in prison for failing to notify authorities about plans for the bombing. The judge noted that "the bombing was widespread and far more serious," but the judge also acknowledged Fortier's cooperation with federal prosecutors when he reaffirmed his earlier sentence of 12 years (Talley 1999: 310).

Attorney General Janet Reno granted prosecutors permission to seek the death penalty against Nichols and McVeigh. A change of venue was ordered and the trial was moved to Denver, Colorado, because of the intense media coverage in Oklahoma" and the possibility that McVeigh and Nichols could not receive a fair and impartial trial in Oklahoma. He also granted separate trials based on the fact that Nichols had given investigators lengthy statements incriminating McVeigh, but that McVeigh's attorneys would not be able to question him about those statements without violating Nichols's right not to incriminate himself. The judge also had to balance the interests of the defendants who have a right to a fair trial considering the heated emotions of bombing victims. Thus, he banned cameras and limited the scope of comments by attorneys outside the courtroom.

The McVeigh trial lasted 28 days and the jury found him guilty on 11 counts, including conspiracy to use a weapon of mass destruction, use of a weapon of mass destruction, destruction by explosive, and eight counts of first-degree murder. Testimony began in the sentencing phase of the trial as witnesses recounted their stories of April 19, 1995. The jury condemned McVeigh to death by lethal injection, which was carried out in Terre Haute, Indiana on June 14, 2001.

The Nichols trial lasted approximately six weeks and he was found guilty of conspiracy to use a weapon of mass destruction and eight counts of involuntary manslaughter in the deaths of eight federal employees. He was

Box 6.4
Similarities between *The Turner Diaries* and the Oklahoma City Bombing

The bombing of the Alfred P. Murrah federal building was clearly modeled after one of the missions that Earl Turner and his fellow patriots had accomplished:

Similarity	The Turner Diaries	Oklahoma City Bombing
Target	FBI's national headquarters downtown	A federal building housing FBI offices downtown
Bomb	A little under 5,000 pounds	Slightly less than 5,000 pounds
Explosive	Ammonium nitrate fertilizer and fuel oil	Ammonium nitrate fertilizer and fuel oil
Timing	9:15 A.M.	9:02 A.M.
Vehicle	A delivery truck	A Ryder moving truck

(Abanes 1996)

acquitted on the destruction by explosive charge. The convictions of conspiracy and involuntary manslaughter (i.e., unlawful killing of a human being with malice) suggest that the jury found Nichols was a junior, rather than an equal partner in the bombing. The Denver jury deadlocked after spending two days deliberating Nichols's sentence. The judge dismissed the jury, a decision that essentially removed the possibility of a death sentence. Finally, the local district attorney in Oklahoma City indicated that he would pursue 160 murder charges against Nichols and McVeigh in state court for the nonfederal employees' deaths in the bombing.

The case itself presents a number of issues:

• *Timing:* The bombing occurred two years to the day from the 1993 Branch Davidian siege in Waco, Texas. Indeed, some argue that April 19th is a symbolic date for the radical right.

• *Philosophical shift:* Traditionally, terrorist attacks were direct, intended to produce a political effect through injury or death, and excluded innocent bystanders as victims.

By the 1990s, anyone could be a victim of terrorism.

• *Target:* The bomb targeted a governmental building in the heartland of the United States with an architectural design that contributed to the high casualty count.

• *Motive:* Perpetrators had links to the militia movement. The FBI stated that McVeigh was extremely upset about the federal government's assault on the Branch Davidian compound. He apparently held strong right-wing political views and his two visits to Waco solidified his deep-seated resentment against the government (Hamm 1997).

• *Bomb material:* Simple ingredients, primarily ammonium nitrate fertilizer, was used and is readily available. This was combined with flammable material (diesel fuel) and a few sticks of dynamite for detonation. A high level of sophistication was not required to build and detonate the bomb.

What these issues suggest is that to fully understand the event, one must isolate the significant elements of the case and determine the role each issue had in terms of providing motive, access, and opportunity for the perpetrators.

Discussion Questions

1. What impact did and will this bombing have on the victims, their families, and the public at-large?
2. Fire personnel, medical technicians, and other emergency service personnel were dispatched to Oklahoma City from many cities around the United States. In your opinion, why was there such an immediate response to what appears to be an unsolicited call for help? Would you agree that while the event was limited to one relatively small location, it created a "national need to help"? If so, do you believe that Americans in general have short memories or will this desire to help have more long-lasting effects?
3. Are you concerned that membership in paramilitary groups preaching armed resistance to the federal government propels people into acts of violence and terrorism? If yes, to what degree are these groups then liable for the actions of the individual?
4. Our first amendment of the Constitution provides for freedom of speech. Certain individuals have used this constitutional right to publish and personally profit from books and other materials that describe, for example, how to build bombs and use these bombs against the government. Should the government censor these publications in the name of public safety?
5. Christian Identity is a theology that attempts to rationalize the blessing of God to the racist cause. Do individual citizens retain their right to freedom of religion if it advocates racism and violence against our government or specific individuals? Is there any role for government intervention?

Study Questions

1. There was extensive media coverage of the bombing and other related events including the first anniversary of the bombing. After examining the available data on media coverage, explore the following questions:
   a. How would you describe the initial coverage of the bombing? If you were there at that time, what impressions were you left with regarding this incident?
   b. Were there any particular aspects of the coverage that concern you? If yes, please describe them.
2. Hatred and distrust of government are running so deep that many militia members believe that federal agents exploded the Oklahoma City bomb and murdered innocent children to discredit the militia movement and to facilitate passage of an anti-terrorist crime bill (Dees 1996). Can you find any evidence to support this statement?
3. What federal proposals were initiated after the bombing? Specifically, what issues were they designed to deal with? Among other things, assess these initiative's impact on the public's perceptions of vulnerability and sense of security.
4. McVeigh made numerous anti-government statements and was alleged to have promoted the book *The Turner Diaries* prior to the April 1995 bombing. What role do scholars and experts believe this fictional account of the violent overthrow of the government plays, if any, in McVeigh's decision to bomb the federal building?
5. For many, a very disturbing aspect of this case is the evidence that some people in the federal government had prior knowledge of the impending disaster in Oklahoma City. Is this the case? Describe and discuss the evidence on which you base

your opinion. If you believe, based on the evidence, that the government had prior knowledge, what could or should have been done to protect those in danger?

6. Timothy McVeigh and Terry Nichols were army buddies. Were the seeds for the destructive blast planted when the two were together in the army? What are the similarities and differences in their backgrounds that provided the motivation and justification for their involvement in the bombing?

7. Compare and contrast the events at Waco and Oklahoma City. Identify and describe similarities and differences in terms of the people involved, the terrorist act, the response, and the aftermath.

8. Research and describe the various actions taken by individuals and groups to acknowledge the victims in this tragedy.

THE FREEMEN OF MONTANA

On a ranch foreclosed by creditors in November 1994, at least 21 people calling themselves Freemen refused to leave following the arrest of two of their members and claimed their ranch as sovereign territory. Called Justus Township, the 960-acre wheat farm and sheep ranch is located 30 miles northwest of Jordan, Montana. In December 1994, five Freemen members sent a document to local officials threatening deadly force against anyone who tried to repossess the property, including the federal judge overseeing the foreclosure.

A December 1995 indictment charged these five and seven other Freemen with fraud and illegal possession of weapons and ammunition. In March 1996, when the two Freemen leaders, LeRoy Schweitzer and Daniel E. Petersen, were arrested while off the ranch, the other residents of Justus Township refused to

leave. Thus began the standoff between the FBI and other law enforcement agencies, and the residents of Justus Township.

The Freemen of Montana consider the government illegitimate and have declared themselves exempt from its laws, regulations, and taxes. The Freemen are part of the common law court movement that denies the legitimacy of the government, supports issuing "warrants" for the arrest of public officials to be tried in the Freemen's "court," and produces false financial documents (e.g., bogus liens and money orders). Their beliefs also include the Christian Identity doctrine that Jews are the offspring of Satan and nonwhite races are subhuman.

An investigation conducted in 1996 by the ADL revealed evidence of activity linked to the Montana Freemen in at least 18 states: Arizona, California, Colorado, Florida, Kansas, Michigan, Minnesota, Montana, Nebraska, New Mexico, North Carolina, Ohio, Oklahoma, Oregon, South Dakota, Texas, Utah, and Wyoming. The ADL report also described how followers of this movement declare themselves exempt from America's laws, regulations and taxes, conduct seminars laced with racial and religious bigotry, and promote their own brand of mob rule.

Following the arrest of Schweitzer and Petersen on March 25, 1996, in connection with fraudulent check and money-order schemes, the other adults on the ranch refused to leave. Schweitzer and Petersen were indicted by a federal grand jury on May 19, 1995. Another ten members of the Freemen had been indicted nearly a year earlier on check and money-order fraud. Vowing not to repeat the errors made in the raids at Waco, Texas, and Ruby Ridge, Idaho, the FBI sought a peaceful solution to the standoff. U.S. Attorney Sherry Matteucci made a "personal promise to the people on the property that if they do turn themselves in voluntarily, they will be safe" (CNN 1999: 1). Six people were allowed to leave the farm and were not arrested. The other Freemen who remain in the compound were armed.

After surrounding the compound, the 100 FBI agents and other U.S. marshals and deputies attempted to persuade the people inside to come out. On the sixth day of the standoff, Richard Clark, one of ten fugitive members of the Freemen group wanted on conspiracy and fraud charges, turned himself in to federal authorities. He was arraigned on 55 federal counts, including conspiracy to commit fraud, armed robbery, and threatening to kill a federal judge. On the eighteenth day, two other wanted Freemen surrendered and were taken into custody.

Several attempts to negotiate with the Freemen were made by Montana State Representative Karl Ohs, John Connor, chief prosecutor of the Montana state Department of Justice, former Army Green Beret Col. James "Bo" Gritz, and former Arizona police officer Jack McLamb. During this siege there was also a "call to arms" over the Internet that brought militia members from all over the country to the compound.

On the 39th day, Freemen leaders rejected a FBI proposal to meet face-to-face away from their ranch to discuss terms for their surrender. The FBI backed its offer with a threat of action. At the same time, the Freemen released a video reiterating their desire to end the standoff. Then, on the 53rd day, the Freemen, FBI representatives, and Colorado State Senator Charles Duke held talks at the ranch for the first time. Failing to resolve their differences, the FBI cut the power to the Freemen's ranch on June 3, 1996, 71 days into the standoff. Several members left the compound over the next several days and finally on the 81st day of the standoff, the last 16 members of the Freemen group surrendered.

The Freemen were charged with hundreds of criminal counts and most were de-nied bail pending trial. The defendants boycotted the proceedings and refused to cooperate with their lawyers. They yelled objections to the American flag in the courtroom and made rambling statements about their own beliefs. Two members of the original group entered guilty pleas at the beginning of the trial. There were partial verdicts returned that included a number of convictions against the remaining 12 Freemen defendants. The jury members were unable to agree on the central part of the prosecution's case–which stated that the Freemen, despite their fiercely anti-government rhetoric, were really a group of con artists engaged in "epic fraud" against the banking system.

LeRoy Schweitzer was found guilty on 21 of 30 counts, most of them involving forged checks and money orders. The jury also found Schweitzer and three other Freemen members (Daniel Petersen, Richard Clark, and Rodney Skurdal) guilty on two counts of threatening to kill U.S. District Court Judge Jack Shanstrom.

Discussion Questions

1. Would you agree or disagree that the FBI had a legitimate interest in pursuing the Freemen? Did the FBI and other law enforcement officials properly handle the standoff? What, if anything, could they have done differently to end the standoff sooner?

2. How did the FBI's handling of the Freemen compare and contrast with its involvement at Ruby Ridge?

Study Questions

1. Given your knowledge of militia groups gained from earlier readings and after conducting additional research on militia groups, do the Freemen as a group repre-

sent a "typical" militia organization? What characteristics suggest they are similar and what characteristics suggest they are different from other militia groups?

2. The increased availability and use of the Internet make it easier for these "anti-government" groups to share their message. Do the Freemen of Montana have a web site? If yes, what is the essence of their message?

3. Jack McLamb, the retired Arizona police officer who offered to help in the Freemen negotiations, is the founder of Police Against the New World Order, a right-wing group of current and former police officers. Search the Internet for information about McLamb and his organization. What is its goal? How successful has McLamb been in recruiting other law enforcers to his cause? Why would law enforcers be interested in Lamb's organization or beliefs?

THE UNABOMBER

Theodore John Kaczynski, eventually charged and convicted as the Unabomber, was successful in eluding authorities for 17 years. During that time, he killed three people and injured 33 in 16 bombings in eight states. The name Unabomber—un (university), a (airlines), bomber—was crafted because the first targets were universities and airlines.

The Unabomber believed that he must receive a wide audience for his message: that "the industrial-technological system" in which we live is a social, psychological and environmental "disaster for the human race" (Sale 1995: 306). His antitechnology message and general arguments against industrial society and its consequences buttresses his belief that there are many evils associated with modern technology, including the potential for mass suffering resulting from a machine-dominated world.

The reign of bombing terror perpetrated by the person authorities called the Unabomber began on May 25, 1978, extended to April 24, 1995. In each of the 16 bombings, an improvised explosive and/or incendiary device was used. The explosive devices were delivered to the victim either by physical placement or by the United States Postal Service. The mailed devices had similar packaging. The locations of the incidents are similar in that the devices were mailed to or from, or placed in Chicago, Salt Lake City, Sacramento, or the San Francisco Metropolitan Bay Area.

The UNABOMB task force, headquartered in San Francisco, California, assigned 150 agents to the case. FBI agents, joined by ATF agents and postal inspectors, worked the case full-time in San Francisco, Sacramento, Salt Lake City, Chicago and Newark, New Jersey. Eight of the 16 devices bore a personal identification mark consisting of the initials FC located either inside the devices or contained in the letter sent to the *New York Times* on April 24, 1995, claiming credit for several devices. FC is variously cited as the initials for Freedom Club or Freedom Collective, although it is popularly thought to stand for a vulgar comment about computers.

A major break in the case occurred when on June 24, 1995, the *New York Times* and *The Washington Post* received a request from FC, identified by the FBI as the Unabomber, to publish a 35,000-word manifesto. The manuscript described the harmful effects of technology and science, and was replete with footnotes to books and publications. He said that if either company published the entire document within three months, he would not bomb again with the intent to kill.

About the same time, *Scientific American* also received a letter from the Unabomber that similarly focused on the negative physi-

Box 6.5
Unabomber Chronology

- May 25, 1978: University of Illinois, Chicago. A package was found in the Engineering Department parking lot at the Chicago Circle Campus. The parcel was opened by a police officer who suffered minor injuries when the bomb detonated.
- May 9, 1979: Northwestern University, Evanston, Illinois. A disguised explosive device that had been left in the university's Technological Institute slightly injured a graduate student when he tried to open the box.
- November 1, 1979: Chicago, Illinois. An explosive parcel mailed from Chicago detonated in the cargo compartment of American Airlines Flight 444, forcing the plane to make an emergency landing at Dulles Airport. Twelve people were treated for smoke inhalation.
- June 10, 1980: Lake Forest, Illinois. A parcel was mailed to a United Airlines president at his home. He was injured in the explosion.
- October 8, 1981: University of Utah, Salt Lake City. An explosive device was found in the hall of a classroom building and rendered safe by bomb squad personnel.
- May 5, 1982: Vanderbilt University, Nashville, Tennessee. A wooden box containing a pipe bomb detonated when a secretary in the Computer Sciences Department opened it. The secretary suffered minor injuries. The package was initially mailed from Provo, Utah on April 23, 1982, to Pennsylvania State University and then forwarded to Vanderbilt.
- July 2, 1982: University of California, Berkeley. A small metal pipe bomb was placed in a coffee break room of Cory Hall. A professor of electrical engineering and computer science was injured when he picked up the device.
- June 13, 1985: Auburn, Washington. A parcel bomb was mailed to the Boeing Company Fabrication Division. After employees opened it, bomb squad personnel rendered the device safe.
- May 15, 1985: University of California, Berkeley. A bomb detonated in a computer room at Cory Hall. A graduate student in electrical engineering lost partial vision in his left eye and four fingers from his right hand. The device was probably placed in the room several days prior to detonation.
- November 15, 1985: Ann Arbor, Michigan. A package was mailed to the home of a University of Michigan professor from Salt Lake City. A research assistant was injured when he opened the package.
- December 11, 1985: Sacramento, California. A device was left near the rear entrance to a computer rental store. Owner Hugh Scrutton was killed when he picked it up and it exploded.
- February 20, 1987: Salt Lake City. An explosive device was left at the rear entrance to CAAMs Inc. (computer store). The bomb exploded and injured the owner when he tried to pick up the device.
- June 22, 1993: Tiburon, California. A parcel was mailed from Sacramento to the home of a geneticist, Dr. Epstein, who was severely hurt when he tried to open the parcel and it exploded.

Box 6.5 *Continued*

- June 24, 1993: Yale University, New Haven, Connecticut. A parcel was mailed from Sacramento to a professor/computer scientist (David Gelernter) at Yale. When he tried to open it, the parcel exploded, severely injuring him.
- December 10, 1994: North Caldwell, New Jersey. A package was mailed from the San Francisco area of California to Thomas Mosser, a New York advertising executive. He was killed when the package exploded while opening it.
- April 24, 1995: Sacramento, California. A package bomb addressed to William M. Dennison, former president of the California Forestry Association (CFA), was opened by Gilbert Murray, current president of the CFA. He was killed instantly.

Source: U.S. District of Montana, April 3, 1996.

---

cal consequences of scientific advances, negative social consequences of technological progress, and the author's position that the harm caused by technological progress was now sufficiently apparent that to continue to promote it was grossly irresponsible. The letter stated it was from the terrorist group FC.

The Unabomber, perhaps feeling outdone both in headlines and sheer mayhem in April 1995 by the Oklahoma City bombers, threatened to return to "wild nature" and kill again if his message wasn't shared with the public. On September 19, 1995, at the request of Attorney General Janet Reno and the FBI, the *New York Times* and *The Washington Post* jointly published the 35,000-word manifesto, titled *Industrial Society and its Future.*

Theodore Kaczynski's brother David, a youth-shelter social worker who lived in Schenectady, New York, read the article and believed that the manifesto mirrored some of his brother's angry writings. While cleaning out his mother's home in Chicago in anticipation of her move to Schenectady, David found hundreds of letters from his brother that "brimmed with the same disturbing rhetoric" that he had read in the manifesto. It wasn't just the rote denunciations of technology, but the fact that Ted and the Unabomber

shared other certain phrases, such as "Eat your cake and have it too."

David Kaczynski contacted a Washington lawyer to intervene on his behalf with the FBI. Seeking assurances that his name and family would be kept confidential and that the federal government would not seek the death penalty if Ted were the Unabomber, David turned over the documents he had found in his mother's home. David persistently urged the federal government to consider not only that his brother may be guilty of heinous crimes, but that he was also deeply mentally ill and, therefore, should not be executed.

The FBI also conducted a consensual search of Ted's mother, Wanda Kaczynski's home. Later, the FBI did a comparative analysis of Theodore Kaczynski's essay and letters and the Unabomber manuscript. Over 160 examples of similarities were found.

The UNABOMB task force began surveillance in Lincoln, Montana, in March 1996. One month later on April 3, 1996, armed with a search warrant obtained by Attorney General Janet Reno, the FBI SWAT team knocked on Theodore Kaczynski's remote 13x13-foot cabin door and detained him as the Unabomber suspect. Within two weeks, federal law enforcement officials found the original typewritten manuscript of the Unabomber's manifesto, along with an original of a letter he sent to the *New York Times.*

On April 30, 1996, following his arrest, Ted Kaczynski asked the Supreme Court to order a hearing on his effort to have the government barred from prosecuting him. He claimed that the government's right to prosecute him was effectively forfeited when federal law enforcement officials denounced him in the national media before charging him officially with any Unabomber crime.

On June 18th in Sacramento, California, Kaczynski was indicted by a federal grand jury on charges involving the deaths of Gilbert Murray and Hugh Scrutton, and the injuries of Yale professor Gelernter and Dr. Epstein, the geneticist from Tiburon, California. He also faced ten counts of transporting, mailing, and using bombs. On June 25th, he entered a plea of "not guilty" in federal court in Sacramento.

Attorney General Janet Reno requested the death penalty for Kaczynski, despite pleas for mercy from his mother and brother. Although he potentially faced other charges (e.g., attacks in Michigan, Utah, and Tennessee between 1986 and 1992), the government decided to try him first in California, where, if convicted, he could face the death penalty. On October 1, 1996, a federal grand jury in Newark, New Jersey, indicted Kaczynski for mailing the bomb that killed Thomas Mosser in 1994. The 22,000 pages of documents seized by investigators from Kaczynski's Montana cabin were the backbone of the government's case. In addition, federal prosecutors had forensic evidence linking bomb fragments to items found in the cabin and a typewriter found there had "ties into a lot of Unabomber correspondence and mailing labels on the bombs" (U.S. District of Montana 1996: 38).

During the trial, the defense filed a motion to suppress virtually all of the evidence seized in Kaczynski's Montana cabin. The judge denied such motions and also ruled that Kaczynski could be executed if convicted of using a bomb to kill someone, rejecting the defense's argument that a capital sentence was "cruel and unusual punishment." In early January 1998, Kaczynski halted his trial before it got under way, asking to make a statement to the judge in private. He reportedly protested his brother David's presence in the courtroom.

A few weeks later, just a day before opening statements were set to begin, attorneys for both the government and defense agreed that Kaczynski had the right to represent himself in court as he requested. One of Kaczynski's concerns was his defense team's desire to pursue a mental health defense. Several defense mental health experts asserted that Kaczynski suffered from paranoid schizophrenia, an illness marked by delusions and a potential for violence. The judge eventually denied his request to represent himself.

Finally, on January 22, 1998, Kaczynski pleaded guilty to thirteen federal charges covering five bombings, including two deaths in Sacramento and one in New Jersey. The agreement resolved all federal charges against Kaczynski, who admitted his role in the Unabomber attacks for which he had not been charged. The plea came on the day the jury was finally to be sworn in and opening statements were to begin. He was sentenced to life in prison without parole. He also must forfeit any future earnings from the bombing campaign, including books, movies, and memorabilia.

The FBI, which for nearly twenty years mounted the most intensive manhunt in bureau history to catch the Unabomber, gave a $1 million reward to David Kaczynski for turning in his brother. David indicated that most of the money, except the portion needed to pay off the family's legal bills resulting from the Unabomber case, would go to the victims' families.

Discussion Questions

1. Facing the same pressures as the *New York Times* and *The Washington Post*, would you have published the Unabomber manifesto? What are the ethical issues inherent in either the decision to print or the decision not to print?
2. David Kaczynski was troubled by the similarities in content and tone of the Unabomber manifesto and his brother's writings and was torn between familial obligations and the protection of the public. "I regret every day my decision to turn in my brother, but there was nothing else I could do" (Claiborne 1998: 2). What would you have done?
3. What factors contributed to the lengthy investigation until a suspect was arrested?
4. Did the judge's order for juror anonymity in the Kaczynski trial infringe on the public's First Amendment rights of access to the trial?
5. Kaczynski allegedly tried to hang himself in his jail cell with his own underwear (January 8, 1998). Under those circumstances, how could a judge find him competent to stand trial? Competency to stand trial requires a finding that the defendant understands the nature of the charges and can assist in the defendant's defense.
6. Defense counsel wanted to pursue a mental health defense and Kaczynski opposed that strategy. If ordered to abandon this rebuttal to the charges, what ethical obligations would cause defense counsel to seek to withdraw from representation?
7. Kaczynski might argue that his actions, to some degree, saved the world from the evils of technological and scientific progress. Do you agree or disagree?

Study Questions

1. Read the full text of the Unabomber's manifesto. What is his message?
2. There is a lot of scholarly research and other writings describing and discussing Ted Kaczynski's early life and schooling. Following a review of that material, what aspects of his early childhood and academic career might have explained or motivated him to engage in a seventeen-year bombing and killing spree?
3. Have we heard anything from Ted Kaczynski during his confinement in federal prison? If yes, describe these communications.

SUMMARY

The cases described in this chapter are examples of the various manifestations of political extremism and domestic terrorism in the United States: threats, stockpiling of weapons, federal gun violations, bombings, and murders. The motivations and justifications for the actions taken by the perpetrators varied: orientations ranged from an anti-government stance, opposition to American Western culture and U.S. interests overseas, to survivalists, adherents to religious teachings, and finally, to a lone individual highly frustrated with our technological developments and their impact on our lives.

The bombing of the federal building in Oklahoma demonstrated the potential violence that can be perpetrated by domestic terrorists in our own country who want to get their message across to the American public. The World Trade Center bombing, in contrast, raised the specter of international terrorists retaliating against the United States by attacking Americans within their own boundaries. The Ruby Ridge incident, the Branch Davidian siege at Waco, and the standoff with the Freemen of Montana show us what can happen when individuals and/or groups, believed to be "extremist" or "terroristic in their activities," take a stand against federal, state, and local law enforcement efforts to contain them.

We still have much to learn about these incidents. Federal agencies, congressional leaders, and local law enforcement officials continue to examine what happened at Waco and Ruby Ridge. These cases generate some troubling questions about individual liberties and the federal government's role in suppressing alleged acts of domestic terrorism. They also suggest the need to reexamine America's vulnerability to acts of terrorism, whether perpetrated by its own terrorists or individuals carrying out the directives of international terrorists seeking revenge against Americans and American interests.

REFERENCES

Ruby Ridge

Abanes, Richard: *American Militias: Rebellion, Racism and Religion.* Downers Grove, IL: InterVarsity Press, 1996.

Bock, Alan W.: *Ambush at Ruby Ridge: How Government Agents Set Randy Weaver Up and Took His Family Down.* Irvine, CA: Dickens Press, 1995.

Cavanagh, Suzanne, and Teasley, David: *The Randy Weaver Case at Ruby Ridge, Idaho: A Chronology.* Washington, DC: Congressional Research Service, 1995.

Committee on the Judiciary of the United States Senate: *The Federal Raid on Ruby Ridge, ID. Hearings before the Subcommittee on Terrorism, Technology, and Government Information of the Committee on the Judiciary of the U.S. Senate*

(September 6, 1995). Washington, DC: Government Printing Office, 1997.

Cooper, Claire: Federal Court Rejects "Ruby Ridge" Appeal. *The Sacramento Bee,* p. A4, June 15, 2000.

Spence, Gerry: *From Freedom to Slavery: The Rebirth of Tyranny in America.* New York: St. Martin's Press, 1993.

Vizzard, William J.: *In the Crossfire: A Political History of the Bureau of Alcohol, Tobacco and Firearms.* Boulder, CO: Lynne Rienner Publishers, 1997.

Walter, Jess: *Every Knee Shall Bow: The Truth and Tragedy of Ruby Ridge and the Randy Weaver Family.* New York: Harper Paperbacks, 1995.

Branch Davidians

Abanes, Richard: *American Militias: Rebellion, Racism and Religion.* Downers Grove, IL: InterVarsity Press, 1996.

Barkun, Michael: Millenarian Groups and Law Enforcement Agencies: The Lessons of Waco. *Terrorism and Political Violence 6*(1): 73–95, 1994.

Bromley, David G., and Silver, Edward: The Davidian Tradition: From Patronal Clan to Prophetic Movement. In Wright, Stuart (Ed.): *Armageddon in Waco: Critical Perspectives on the Branch Davidian Conflict.* Chicago: University of Chicago Press, 1995, pp. 43–72.

Cavanagh, Suzanne, and Teasley, David: *The Branch Davidian Siege at Ranch Apocalypse Near Waco, Texas: A Chronology.* Washington, DC: Congressional Research Service, 1995.

Fogarty, Robert S.: An Act of Wisdom, An Age of Foolishness. In Wright, Stuart (Ed.): *Armageddon in Waco: Critical Perspectives on the Branch Davidian Conflict.* Chicago, IL: University of Chicago Press, 1995, pp. 3–19.

Hamm, Mark S.: *Apocalypse in Oklahoma.* Boston: Northeastern University Press, 1997.

Pitts, William L., Jr.: Davidians and Branch Davidians 1929–1987. In Wright, Stuart (Ed.): *Armageddon in Waco: Critical Perspectives on the Branch Davidian Conflict.* Chicago, IL: University of Chicago Press, 1995, pp. 20–42.

Reavis, Dick J.: *The Ashes of Waco: An Investigation.* Syracuse, NY: First Syracuse University Press, 1995/98.

Tabor, James D., and Gallagher, Eugene V.: *Why Waco? Cults and the Battle for Religious Freedom in America.* Berkeley, CA: University of California Press, 1995.

U.S. Department of Treasury: *Report of the Department of the Treasury of the Bureau of Alcohol, Tobacco and Firearms Investigation of Vernon Wayne Howell, Also Known as David Koresh.* Washington, DC: Government Printing Office, 1993.

U.S. Department of Justice: *Report to the Deputy Attorney General on the Events at Waco, Texas, February 28 to April 19, 1993.* Washington, DC: Government Printing Office, 1993.

Vizzard, William J.: *In the Crossfire: A Political History of the Bureau of Alcohol, Tobacco and Firearms.* Boulder, CO: Lynne Rienner Publishers, 1997.

Wright, Stuart A. (Ed.): *Armageddon in Waco: Critical Perspectives on the Branch Davidian Conflict.* Chicago, IL: University of Chicago Press, 1995.

World Trade Center

Blumenthal, Ralph: Tapes Depict Proposal to Thwart Bomb Used in Trade Center Blast. *New York Times,* October 28, 1993.

Dowell, William, and Waller, Douglas: The Imaginary Apocalypse. *Time Magazine* 146: 16, October 16, 1995.

Federal Bureau of Investigation: *Bombing of the World Trade Center, New York City, February 26, 1993.* Washington, DC: Department of Justice, July 27, 1993.

Fritz, Sandy: The Blast Heard "Round the World." *Popular Science 243* (3): 66, September 1993.

Nacos, Brigitte L.: *Terrorism and the Media: From the Iran Hostage Crisis to the World Trade Center Bombing.* New York: Columbia University Press, 1996.

Perlmutter, Amos, and Kennedy, Moorhead: Does Islamic Fundamentalism Pose a Threat to American Society? *CQ Researcher 3* (16): 377–378, April 30, 1993.

Oklahoma City Bombing

Abanes, Richard: *American Militias: Rebellion, Racism and Religion.* Downers Grove, IL: Inter Varsity Press, 1996.

Bea, Keith, Cavanagh, Suzanne, and Doyle, Charles: *Oklahoma City Bombing: Underlying Federal Response Authorities.* Washington, DC: Congressional Research Service, 1995.

Cavanagh, Suzanne, and Teasley, David: The *Oklahoma City Bombing Investigation: A Chronology.* Washington, DC: Congressional Research Service, 1996.

Dees, Morris (with James Corcoran): *Gathering Storm: America's Militia Threat.* New York: Harper Collins Publishers, 1996.

Hamm, Mark S.: *Apocalypse in Oklahoma: Waco and Ruby Ridge Revenged.* Boston: Northeastern University Press, 1997.

Hoffman, David: *The Oklahoma City Bombing and the Politics of Terror.* Venice, CA: Feral House, 1998.

Talley, Tim: Bomb Figure Resentenced. *The Sacramento Bee,* p. B10, October 9, 1999.

The Final Report of the Oklahoma County Grand Jury. Available online: http://www.kwtv.com/news/bombing/grand-jury.htm. Retrieved September 1999.

Freemen of Montana

Anti-Defamation League Fact Finding Department: *The Freemen Network: An Assault on the Rule of Law.* New York: Anti-Defamation League, 1996.

Schwartz, Alan M. (Ed): *Danger Extremism: The Major Vehicles and Voices on America's Far Right Fringe.* New York: Anti-Defamation League, 1996. CNN: *Calendar of Events During the Standoff.* Available at www.cnn.com/us/freemen/index.html. Retrieved September 1999.

Unabomber

Many Internet sites contain the full text of the manifesto, *Industrial Society and Its Future.* See, for example, http://www.washingtonpost.com/wp-archives/front.htm, Retrieved September 1999.

Claiborne, William: FBI Gives Reward to Unabomber's Brother. *The Washington Post,* p. A2, August 21, 1998.

Sale, Kirkpatrick: Unabomber's Secret Treatise: Is there Method in His Madness. *The Nation, 261* (9): 305–312.

U.S. District of Montana: *Affidavit of Assistant Special Agent in Charge–Terry D. Turchie,* April 3, 1996. Available online: http://www.cs.umass.edu/~ehaugsja/unabom/docs/affidavit.html. Retrieved September 1999.

Chapter 7

THE CHANGING CHARACTER OF
DOMESTIC TERRORISM

As Part Two has illustrated, domestic terrorism has become increasingly diverse. Thus, in the twenty-first century, the tendency to view terrorism in black-and-white terms with easily identifiable enemies may become obsolete as the diversity of participants increases and as the lines between terrorism, extremism, and freedom fighting become further blurred (Simon 1994). Some experts postulate that one of the greatest changes will be "seamless terrorism" where the line between foreign and domestic terrorists operating in the United States may become unclear (Sloan 1997:10). Yet another factor that signals change and obscures a clear understanding of contemporary terrorists is that groups do not claim credit for their violent exploits as they did in the past. Indeed, we have new adversaries with new motivations, some who embrace amorphous religions and who do not seek notoriety (Hoffman 1997).

The manner in which terrorists carry out their acts is also changing. Technological advancements in weaponry and tactics create potentially more lethal and deadly incidents and increase the number of potential targets. Advancements in communication provide ready access to the information needed to carry out an act of terrorism. While the numbers of terrorist incidents vary year-by-year, the lethality of the acts has the potential to be far greater than we have seen in the past.

Finally, as the twenty-first century unfolds, we are witnessing a new merger of extremist ideologies from young people on both the extreme left and extreme right of the political spectrum who believe their world views overlap in several areas. These "Third Positionists" are adamantly opposed to the centralizing forces of globalism, as well as the capitalist system that concentrates wealth into the hands of a few, makes people and economies more alike, and threatens to turn the planet into a bland and materialistic "Mc-World."

This chapter focuses on the changing character of terrorism by examining trends in four specific areas: the ideologies and activities of right-wing and special-interest terrorist groups; the burst of international terrorist links; new and different terrorist tools and tactics; and the new ideological stance adopted by some extremists–advocates of the Third Positions.

THE IDEOLOGIES AND ACTIVITIES OF RIGHT-WING AND SPECIAL-INTEREST TERRORIST GROUPS

There is a general consensus among terrorist experts that while historically the United States has been relatively immune to large numbers of terrorist acts within its borders, the new millennium raises the possibility and probability that we may experience more terrorist threats—especially from right-wing extremists. As we enter the twenty-first century, it appears that some right-wing extremists may

- continue to believe in right-wing causes, but some may leave the movement and begin to act alone, as individuals, rather than as members of a larger movement;
- try to secure a mainstream image and political influence as they seek to have their ideas incorporated into existing political parties;
- shed the beliefs and activities of the "old guard"—the KKK, Aryan Nations, Christian Identity, common law courts—in favor of new organizations and belief systems like Odinism (see Chapter 4);
- become more divorced from rational thought, less likely to calculate the risks and benefits of using weapons of mass destruction (WMD), and more certain that divine intervention or messianic leadership obliges them to commit violence in the name of their cause;
- attempt to develop biological weapons, nurture an interest in attacking basic infrastructure systems, and demonstrate a propensity to engage in indiscriminate violence in order to achieve their goals;
- continue to create sophisticated communications networks via the Internet that are linked to like-minded but geographically dispersed groups;

- adopt an apocalyptic view, believing that we are entering the final period of warfare between the forces of good and evil that signal the second coming of Christ, as written in the New Testament's Book of Revelation. Such extremists believe the government is an arm of Satan that is persecuting them and that they are religious martyrs who have a biblical mandate to take part in the coming battles; and
- adopt a millenarian ideal, believing that the present age is corrupt and that a new age, the millennium, will emerge after an apocalypse. These individuals believe in the existence of powerful enemies—conspirators, the Antichrist, Satan, the unbelievers, Jews, Americans, and Western imperialism—who have secret plans to conquer the world.

Additionally, many of the right-wing groups in general are

- continuing to increase in numbers or at least remain steady. Those who gravitate to and remain in the right-wing movement will become the "true believers"—the most hard-core proponents of their hateful and/or patriot philosophies;
- upgrading their recruitment efforts to target a "higher class of person," as evidenced by the example of the National Alliance in Box 7.1;
- moving away from the traditional, hierarchical, and structured organizations of the past and creating more fragmented, less cohesive, leaderless organizations where individuals and small groups act with autonomy; and
- become more international in organization and scope such as the current efforts of National Alliance leader William Pierce in establishing an international white-power music scene dominated by "national socialist black metal."

Along with an increase in the number of right-wing extremist groups, experts also see

---

Box 7.1
Right-Wing Recruiting Strategies

Several right-wing extremist groups have announced new recruiting strategies that target universities and colleges to increase their membership roles. By the late 1990s, Matt Hale of the World Church of the Creator began recruiting middle- and upper-class white youth at various postsecondary education institutions in Illinois. By the turn of the century, National Alliance membership coordinator Billy Roper told the *Intelligence Report* (2000) that he was looking for "a higher class of person" (p. 5). To accomplish this, Roper began sending bulk quantities of William Pierce's white-power music magazine, *Resistance* "to white college students," especially to "the fraternities and sororities of as many universities and colleges as possible. . . . With this age group, the more radical the material we put out, the more buzz we create and the cooler it becomes" (p. 5).

---

an increase in activities by special-interest groups, particularly the "fringe" militants within the ecological/environmental, anti-abortion and animal-rights movements. The breadth and depth of violence perpetrated by special-interest terrorists is just beginning to be understood and documented. Since this unique form of terrorism just emerged in the 1980s and 1990s, its potential for various forms of violence has yet to be realized.

INTERNATIONAL TERRORIST LINKS

Simon (1994) offers another view on the potential for terrorism within U.S. borders. He suggests the pool of potential terrorists is likely to increase with the expected surge in immigration by people escaping the many ethnic-nationalist conflicts of the 1990s. Yet Simon also reiterates that as long as terrorists find an abundance of American symbols to hit overseas, the number of incidents on domestic soil will be limited.

Over the past several decades, the FBI has been concerned about anti-American ter-

rorist groups and individuals who oppose U.S. policies or U.S. involvement overseas and have representation throughout the world, including the United States. Although an international terrorist act in the United States is a rare occurrence and terrorist groups remain reluctant to strike here, their contingency plans for a possible action continue to progress. Support infrastructures are being upgraded and group members are receiving training in terrorist boot camps throughout Sudan and Afghanistan (Kushner 1998). What is particularly disturbing to Kushner is the fact that many of these international terrorist groups are in communication with one another in the United States. The vast improvement in modern technology, including the Internet, faxes, and cellular phones, eliminate any communication barriers and make it more plausible for terrorists to stay in contact.

Perhaps the greatest fear that international terrorists will perpetrate acts of terrorism on American soil concerns the actions of Islamic militants. For these militants, acts of terrorism against the United States are largely a reaction to U.S. policies and actions in the Middle East. Intelligence agents and law enforcement officials have discovered that militant Islamic extremists have established extensive networks throughout the United States and now pose the greatest threat of domestic terrorism in the United States (Emerson 1998).

The location of the radical groups span the entire United States and include cities like Chicago, Dallas, Boston, Los Angeles, New York, Washington, D.C., Tampa, Oklahoma City, New Jersey and Arizona. Some of the sites contain offices of Islamic militant groups that raise funds, recruit new members, disseminate propaganda, provide military training, and in some cases, recruit terrorists (Emerson 1998).

Jacobs (1998) states that the possibility of U.S. involvement in an international dispute with so-called rogue or pariah states should produce a heightened awareness of the possibility of nuclear, biological, or chemical attacks by terrorists or other countries. Libya (Qaddafi) was suspected of producing chemical weapons that the CIA feared would be given to terrorist groups like an anti-Arafat Palestinian splinter group (Barnaby 1990). Yet, countries such as Libya, Cuba, and North Korea, formerly engaged in supplying terrorists with training, weapons, or funds, have reportedly renounced this role (Stern 1999). In contrast, Iran remains deeply involved in acts of terrorism committed by its own agents or by surrogate groups. Sudan and Syria have been implicated in several bombings overseas in the mid-1990s and are known to support terrorist camps in their countries.

Terrorist access to chemical and biological weapons is also a growing threat to the international community. Iraq is a state known to sponsor terrorism and it is developing chemical and biological weapons and, in fact, has used chemical weapons against its own citizens (Stern 1999). While some of Iraq's nuclear, biological, and chemical weapons infrastructure was destroyed during the Gulf War in the early 1990s, significant parts of the nuclear and biological infrastructure survived (Falkenrath, Newman, and Thayer 1998: 255). Questions remain about their ability to maintain or reconstitute the capability to use weapons of mass destruction.

A final dimension of international links between extremists and terrorists in America and Europe is related to the music scene. In the 1980s, neo-Nazi Skinheads were linked throughout the world by rock bands that spewed the racist lyrics of "oi" music. It was just around the same time that the international white-power music scene also ushered in another new genre of racist music–Black Metal.

Black Metal became popular when the British band Venom began singing about anti-Christian themes that were interspersed with Satanic messages. The movement gained some notoriety in Britain, but was most popular in Scandinavia. In the early 1990s, the Black Metal music theme was further influenced by pagan themes, a frightening music combination initially encouraged by the Norwegian band Mayhem. Its leader formed a group called the Black Circle that believed that Christianity should be violently expelled from Norway and replaced with a new hybrid mixture of Satanism and paganism.

Beginning in 1991, Black Circle was blamed for a series of church burnings in Norway, and in neighboring countries, similar crimes were linked to the Black Metal scene. Black Metal took another turn in 1994 when one of the Black Circle members went to prison and began to urge his followers to add a new dimension to the music–National Socialist racism and anti-Semitism. Thereafter the neo-Nazi-type music–now called National Socialist Black Metal (NSBM)–became extremely racist and violent and subsequently was banned throughout Europe and consigned to the black market. Since then, NSBM has become an extremely lucrative criminal enterprise, commanding about 3 to 4 million dollars annually in sales.

National Alliance leader William Pierce stepped into this enterprise in 1999 when he bought America's largest racist music label, Resistance Records, along with its magazine, *Resistance*. At the same time, Pierce expressed interest in expanding into NSBM, an interest he discussed in the spring 1999 issue of *Resistance* under the title, "Is Black Metal a White Noise?" Long a leader in establishing international relations between European and American neo-Nazis, Pierce has begun to use his music company and magazine to further those endeavors (SPLC Fall 2000). For a sampling of national socialist, racist, Odinist, and other white-power music, see the following Internet sites: www.nsbm.com; www.black-metal. com; and www.burzum.com.

NEW AND DIFFERENT TERRORIST TOOLS AND TACTICS

While Part One postulated that terrorism was more of an evolutionary rather than revolutionary phenomenon, it also emphasized that new technological advances in terrorist tools and tactics made terrorism appear to be revolutionary. This section focuses on two of these technological advances that have been adapted by a wide variety of terrorist groups: cyberterrorism and the Internet, and weapons of mass destruction.

Cyberterrorism and the Internet

Cyberterrorism poses another potential threat to the United States. Computer hackers continue to use the Internet to try to break into sensitive American military and civil sys-

tems. The main weapons in this new kind of warfare are the following:

1. Computer viruses, programmed to damage software;
2. Logic bombs, set to detonate at a certain time and destroy or rewrite data; and
3. High-energy radio frequency guns that disable electronic targets through high-powered electromagnetic impulses affecting all electronic components in the vicinity (Laqueur 1999:75).

Laqueur states that a large percentage of the government's and private sector's transactions are online. This exposes enormous vital areas of national life to sabotage by any computer hacker. If the new terrorism directs itself toward information warfare, its destructive power will be exponentially greater than any it wielded in the past (Laqueur 1999).

In January 2000, then President Clinton called for increased spending and new programs to protect the country against cyberterrorism. The recently released report of the President's Commission on protecting the nation's digital infrastructure makes it clear that the country has a long way to go in addressing computer security needs. Given the complex and evolving nature of the problem, only continued attention can keep the focus where it belongs. Many experts believe that cyberterrorism threats and vulnerability will increase as more and more of the nation's critical systems become dependent not just on computers, but on connected networks between them.

Weapons of Mass Destruction

Nuclear, biological, and chemical weapons share three terrible characteristics. The first is immense lethality: a single weapon can kill thousands of people. The second is portability, which allows them to be easily delivered

Box 7.2
World Wide Web and the Internet

The Internet is a collection of computers connected through networked communications. Access to the Internet is through a browser that allows users from virtually any type of computer to connect with any computer on the "net." It allows an individual to reach a large dispersed audience with information that is almost instantly available at any time. The World Wide Web is a graphic environment that can use typography, graphics, music, and even video to present information. Web sites can be linked so that material stored on one computer can be reached from another by pressing a key or clicking a mouse. This makes information more accessible while simplifying its preparation, storage, and distribution.

The Anti-Defamation League (ADL) and the Southern Poverty Law Center (SPLC) indicate that many right-wing groups maintain Internet Web sites. For example, the SPLC in its Winter 2000 edition of *Intelligence Report* indicated that since the first hate Web site was put up by former Klansman Don Black in 1995, Web hate sites have been added almost weekly. The Intelligence Project found that the number of sites went from 163 at the end of 1997 to 254 by the end of 1998, and increased to 305 by early 2000. Included in that total is a more than doubling of Klan and neo-Nazi sites. This number may be conservative because it does not include pages that are anti-Semitic or pages created by patriot groups.

The low cost of entry and the relative ease of Internet publishing help to expand the number of lesser-known individuals espousing an extremist message. Thus, we can expect that more and more individuals or groups promoting hate will go online with their message, potentially reaching an audience of millions.

As the number of neo-Nazi, white supremacist, and other hate-group Internet sites increase, women are also establishing their own web sites. The focus of these sites range from discussions on the role of women in the racist movement to recipes and parenting tips for white mothers. Many of the web sites also offer links to similar sites, including articles "of and for the women in the White Racialist Movement" (SPLC 1999: 17).

Another Internet technology that allows for more personalized propagandizing and recruiting is Usenet. The Usenet is a collection of public bulletin boards or community discussion groups. In these newsgroups, people write letters to the entire community of readers who come to that particular newsgroup. According to ADL, some of the more enterprising and energetic extremists have decided that the newsgroups can be used effectively to recruit new members. Tag lines at the end of the messages direct the interested to the Web sites of various extremist groups. E-mail is then used to communicate with those whose postings indicate possible support for the extremist position; it is the primary technology for private communication.

Many believe the Web represents the future of communications. The number of people who use the Internet is expected to increase and it is very likely that the Web will become an increasingly important information source. Consequently, ADL expects that it and the rest of the Internet will become an even more significant part of the propaganda arsenal of extremist groups. (Source: Schwartz 1996; SPLC Summer 1999.)

against civilian populations and unprepared military forces. And the third is accessibility, which means that they may fall into hostile hands, despite the best efforts at prevention. (Falkenrath, Newman and Thayer 1998: 1)

From the mid-1990s, there have been more discussions and greater speculation regarding the potential use of weapons of mass destruction by individuals and groups carrying out acts of terrorism. It is the potential use of these weapons that generates a high level of fear among the public and government authorities. As Foxell (1999) notes, "mass-destructive-capability weapons are inherently the quintessential devices of terror, and their likely widening availability in coming years will greatly escalate the menace of terror" (p. 96).

A well-executed chemical-weapon attack would kill several thousand people and a single nuclear weapon could easily kill over 100,000 people if detonated in a densely populated urban area (Falkenrath, Newman and Thayer 1998). Yet most experts agree that the actual probability of chemical or biological attacks remains low compared to other less risky terrorist tactics. At the same time, however, the potential impact in terms of property damage and death can be far greater. Falkenrath, Newman and Thayer (1998) argue that terrorist organizations are reluctant to inflict mass casualties because they do not want to risk stronger government countermeasures and fear provoking widespread public revulsion.

The sarin attack in Japan on March 20, 1995, by Aum Shinrikyo (Aum Sect of Truth), a religious group founded by Shoko Asahara in 1987, alerted security officials worldwide that the deployment of biological or chemical warfare agents into a populated area is not beyond the capabilities of terrorists. The attack killed 12 and injured about 5,000. It was perhaps the most successful and most publicized terrorist use of weapons of mass destruction

to date (Stern 1999). This attack also marked a significant historical watershed in terrorist tactics and weaponry; it clearly demonstrated that it is possible, even for ostensibly amateur terrorists, to execute a successful chemical terrorist attack (Hoffman 1997).

Before this incident, as Chapter 1 indicated, other terrorists had attempted or threatened to use chemical or biological agents, but they were usually on such a small scale that no one noticed or the threats were never carried out. The single case involving the actual use of biological agents in the United States occurred in 1984 when members of the Rajneeshee cult in Oregon poisoned salad bars with *salmonella typhimurium* (Stern 1999).

According to Falkenrath, Newman and Thayer (1998), the range of extremists-terrorists that possess the technical capacity to obtain and use WMD is increasing. The diffusion of increasingly sophisticated knowledge of the nuclear, biological, and chemical sciences is increasing the number and range of individuals who could assist terrorists in carrying out a violent act using a WMD. The United States, as the world's only superpower, is increasingly endangered because of the rise of fanatical groups determined to harm those they see as their enemies (Foxell 1999).

Some experts suggest that if terrorists acquire WMD in the near future, they are likely to opt for chemical rather than biological or nuclear weapons (Barnaby 1990). Chemical terrorism is of concern because of the ease with which information and chemicals are acquired. Several international uses of chemical weapons include Iraq's use of nerve gas and mustard gas against Iranian military forces in the late 1980s and Iraq's use against its Kurdish civilians in March 1988.

Disseminating a chemical agent in an enclosed environment and contaminating food are probably two of the easiest ways to use WMD. Biological agents can be delivered to a target in a variety of ways, some which re-

Box 7.3
Weapons of Mass Destruction (WMD)

There are four types of weapons of mass destruction: biological agents, chemical agents, radiological weapons, and nuclear weapons. Biological agents are living organisms or infective material derived from them that could cause death and which depend for their effects on their ability to multiply in the person attacked. Biological agents tend to die quickly unless in a precisely suitable environment. They can include bacteria, viruses, fungi, toxins, and rickettsia (e.g., typhus). Bacteria are genuine living organisms capable of surviving outside the host and include anthrax and plague. Viruses, which cannot live outside the host, include encephalitis and yellow fever.

There is a broad spectrum of chemical agents causing damage to living organisms. Those substances affecting only humans can be classified into five categories: incapacitating agents, blister agents, choking agents, blood agents, and nerve agents. Police and other forces for riot control mainly use the incapacitating agents. They cause violent vomiting, which is induced very rapidly. The agents include chloracetophenon (CN) and diphenylchloroarsine. The blister agents include such products as distilled mustard or nitrogen mustard. They affect the eyes and skin as well as the lungs and other internal tissues. Choking agents, such as phosgene or CG as it is designated by the military, is a common industrial chemical and affects respiratory organs and can result in death.

Blood agents are mainly cyanide-based compounds. Hydrogen cyanide is a blood agent that has a lethal dose slightly higher than that of phosgene but is less effective due to its rapid rate of evaporation. Nerve agents can disrupt the nervous system and cause paralysis and death. There are two main groups: G-agents that cause death mainly by inhalation and V-agents that can be absorbed through the skin. They include sarin, tabun, soman, and others. Sarin, for example, is a fatal chemical weapon that was developed by Nazi Germany during World War II. In general, they are hundreds to thousands of times more lethal than blister, choking, and blood agents.

Radiological materials include radioactive isotopes that can be found in a number of diverse facilities, including hospitals and industrial plants, and in waste from nuclear power plants. These weapons are now generally called radiation-dispersal devices (RDD). They are commonly confused with nuclear weapons, however they disperse radioactive substances but do not produce a nuclear explosion. Nuclear weapons require uranium and plutonium, which are fissionable radioactive materials. The basic nuclear weapon is the fission bomb, or atomic bomb (A-bomb). A fission chain reaction is used to produce a very large amount of energy in a very short time, roughly a millionth of a second, and therefore a very powerful explosion.

One final note—international treaties ban biological, chemical, and nuclear weapons whereas radiological weapons are not banned.

Sources: Barnaby 1990; Laqueur 1999; Simon 1994; Sloan 1997; Stern 1999.

quire minimal technical skills (e.g., in a building's ventilation system or dispersal of bacterium spores by high-powered rifle). Cultivation of a biological agent does not require expensive equipment or a large space. They can also be obtained through the mail or Internet.

Stern (1999) states that detonation of a nuclear device is the least likely form of terrorism involving WMD. There has not been a single instance of nuclear terrorism since the end of World War II, yet nuclear materials and technology are vulnerable to various forms of diversion and may become accessible to terrorists. The proliferation of fissile materials from the former Soviet Union and emergent illicit market in nuclear materials is surfacing in eastern and central Europe (Hoffman 1997).

Thus far, chemical agents have been used in warfare by at least one nation as an instrument of terrorism from above (in the Iran-Iraq war), and by one fanatical religious group as an agent of terrorism from below. The contemporary fear is that for at least three reasons, "terrorists might escalate violence to the chemical weapons threshold" (Joyner 1993: 121):

1. In their long struggle against the state or society, some terrorists may see a resort to chemical weapons as an easy and effective means to accomplish their end.
2. As the public becomes more indifferent to terrorist violence, terrorists might feel compelled to use greater violence to achieve greater public attention.
3. The same states that sponsor terrorist causes are known to be those very states that have recently acquired chemical weapons; thus they are capable of supplying such weapons to terrorists as well as training them to inflict mass casualties.

Many experts have examined the potential use of nuclear bombs by terrorists (Clark 1980; Leventhal and Alexander 1987; Laqueur 1999). Some argue that since the mid-1970s, when information became easily available for designing nuclear bombs, it has been increasingly possible for any proficient terrorist group to obtain fissionable material, create a nuclear device, and detonate it (David 1985; Livingstone and Arnold 1986; Laqueur 1999). Others cite the fact that although nuclear-bomb technology is readily available and is not appropriately protected from theft, no terrorist group has yet used nuclear technology as a weapon of terror (Jenkins 1975; Stohl 1983). Still others have asserted the controversial but plausible thesis that "real nuclear terrorism" has already been committed, not by terrorists operating from below, but by those operating from above, those who orchestrated Hiroshima and used terrorism as an instrument of war" (Stern 1999: 14).

By the end of the 1990s, however, many experts believed that nuclear terrorism was a distinct threat for the future: too much enriched fissionable material had disappeared; too many people had access to readily available information about how to construct a sizable nuclear weapon; and the cost of producing a nuclear bomb had sharply decreased. Additionally, as Laqueur (1999) explains, in the 1970s, a considerable number of "luggage nukes"–small nuclear devices built in the form of a suitcase and easily transported by one person–were produced by the Soviet military industry for the KGB. In 1997, President Yeltsin's former security adviser reported that several of these singular weapons were unaccounted for. It is also believed that some small nuclear devices have been produced in the Ukraine, Belarus, and Kazakhstan.

In the final analysis, although many experts recently have pointed to the increasing interest in WMD–especially chemical and nuclear–by terrorist groups operating from below, many are in agreement that the real threat is the danger they pose, rather than the probability that they would use such weapons. As Laqueur (1999) has noted, for most terrorist groups, their use is unnecessary:

> so chances are slim that a state or a terrorist group would deploy them. Why use complicated and risky arms if traditional weapons can bring about the same result? Their use may be considered only if the intention is to destroy rather than just defeat the enemy, or if the power of the enemy is so great that there is no hope of victory with conventional arms. The use of weapons of mass destruction is unlikely, but the dangers involved are immense even in the remotest possibility. (p. 247)

Unfortunately, as Lifton (1999) illustrates in his study of Aum Shinrikyo, the precedent has been set and we cannot ignore its implications.

> A threshold has been crossed. . . . Aum stepped over a line that few had even known was there. Its members can claim the distinction of being the first group in history to combine ultimate fanaticism with ultimate weapons in a project to destroy the world. . . . We can no longer pretend that such a line does not exist, that another group, even a small one, might not be capable of similar world-ending zealotry. . . . It could even be inspired by the Aum model, determined to supersede it. For that model is now abroad in the world, available to the perverse imaginations of every sort. (pp. 343–344)

Third Position

The Third Position gained some momentum across Europe in the mid-1990s with support from young people on the extreme left and right end of the political spectrum who believed that their worldviews overlapped in several areas. By the end of the decade, the movement began to find support in the United States where its members favor a social revolution that will

- stimulate the return of family-owned businesses and workers' cooperatives;
- redistribute the wealth in a way that supports widespread property ownership;
- outlaw the use of animals for scientific testing;
- encourage respect for the environment that has been destroyed by corporate agriculture and urbanization; and
- devolve political power down to the lowest possible level.

In short, Third Positionists support a wide array of special issues that spread across both extreme ends of the political spectrum—abortion, the abuse of animals and the environment, the abuses of capitalism and globalism. Third Positionists are, however, firmly entrenched within the right-wing in terms of their racism and anti-Semitism. Almost all Third Positionists see their major enemy as the "multiculturalist Jew," with their hatred of blacks and immigrants falling close behind.

Over the past few years, the SPLC has monitored the activities of several organizations as well as Web sites that have openly advocated a Third Positionist perspective. Foremost among them is the American Front (AF). According to its Web site (www.americanfront.com), the American Front

> is a political movement which seeks National Freedom and Social Justice. It is a way beyond Left and Right; beyond capitalism and communism. It is a progressive new outlook which addresses the political, social and economic issues which affect our daily lives. The American Front offers a real alternative for the Peoples of North America.
>
> The People's of every Nation have an unalienable right to self-determination—to pre-

serve their own culture and traditions and have control over their future and the future of their children. We believe that European (White) people represent distinct Nations in America, Canada, and Quebec, linked by ties of culture and history. Common ancestry is the main determining factor in Nationhood. We feel that culturally mixed societies cannot form a true Nation and are inherently unstable. No one race or culture is "superior" to others, but they are all different. Racial integration threatens all Peoples. Humane efforts towards separation and self-determination are better for us than endless repression, tension, and racial violence. We believe in equal opportunity for all but unearned privilege for none.

We believe the opportunity of every citizen to own one's own home and have a decent and rewarding job is the right of all our People. We believe every citizen should have a hand in the production and distribution in their place of work, for the good of family stability and for the best use of national resources. Therefore, we promote the following practices in order to regain our economic freedom:

- Family owned businesses, since the family is the basis of any healthy society.
- Partnerships between individuals jointly owning an enterprise.
- Producer cooperatives.
- Profit sharing and worker representation.

We hold the environment in trust for future generations. Pollution of land, sea, and air, and our bodies through radiation and toxic chemicals threatens our very existence. We believe in a return to natural family farming methods, a ban on harmful food additives, the outlawing of "animal-testing," and the charging of corporations with the clean-up of all toxic waste.

The system of "representation" is a fraud. Party rule is a cloak for dictatorship of big business and media bosses. Government must be in the hands of the People, who through new information technology and the election of delegates, can be recalled at any time, to carry out the wishes of the community.

Power must be devolved to the lowest level possible so that the government is structured from the bottom up and not the top down. People must learn to take charge of their own lives through participation rather than leave affairs up to distant officials and faceless bureaucrats.

We do not believe that the police or the military should have a monopoly on firearms, as this is the first step towards dictatorship. The right to self-defense belongs to all responsible citizens.

These changes cannot be brought about by tinkering within the System, or by relying on the System's own institutions. They can only spring from a National Revolution. This revolution must begin in the hearts and minds of individuals, then spread by example to involve whole communities in alternative structures such as local councils and schools, neighborhood anti-crime patrols, health care and self-help groups. Once we cease to depend on the old State, it can be swept aside.

SUMMARY

Terrorist groups and terrorists themselves are different today than what we saw in the 1960s and up to the early 1990s. In the past, terrorist organizations were somewhat recognizable by their organized structure and ideological beliefs, and many terrorists were engaged full-time in their attacks and in some cases, were under the direct control or acting at the behest of a foreign government (Hoffman 1997). Today, these more traditional and familiar organizations are joined by an evolving group of terrorists who are less organizationally cohesive, often act alone, and usually adhere to religious, millenarian, or pagan beliefs. They represent a diverse and potentially more lethal threat than the more traditional terrorists of the 1960s and 1970s (Hoffman 1997 and 1999; Laqueur 1999; Stern 1999).

The reasons for terrorism's increasing lethality are complex and include growth in the number of terrorist groups motivated by a religious imperative; proliferation of amateurs involved in terrorist acts; and the increasing sophistication and operational competence of professional terrorists (Hoffman 1997 and 1999). Right-wing extremists who follow anti-government, racist, religious ideologies may, in fact, feel displaced by the rapid changes occurring in the U.S. culture. They may be seeking some sort of personal affirmation.

The Skinhead movement, far more mature than the earlier days when rebellious but ideologically unsophisticated teens formed in bulk, is producing more political violence than it has in years (SPLC 2000). According to the SPLC, the Hammerskin Nation, the largest coalition of neo-Nazi Skinheads in the world, absorbed a number of smaller Skinhead groups and added about 70 percent more chapters in 1999 (SPLC 2000).

Many individuals prone to terrorist violence are adopting Odinism as their belief system and justification for violence. The lack of structure within this movement creates a greater potential for violent actions by lone offenders and/or leaderless cells. Many factions of the right-wing, including militias and Identity followers, maintain multiple memberships. A person could be a member of more than one group or move from one to the other.

ADL (1997) discusses the ever-increasing cross-fertilization between right-wing anti-government extremists. This increased level of cooperation (e.g., attending each other's training, dual memberships) creates an environment in which ideology can easily spread and law enforcement efforts to monitor are challenged because there are no distinctive borders between groups' ideology.

The fact that no terrorist organization has, to date, employed a nuclear or radiological device in an act of terrorism is not to be taken as an indication that this state of affairs will continue indefinitely (Jacobs 1998). Yet terrorism experts are deeply divided over this issue (Hoffman 1999). The difficulties in assessing both the threats and potential threats regarding the use of WMD are compounded by the relative paucity of academic analyses on this issue. It was not until the 1995 Tokyo nerve-gas attacks that terrorism experts and scholars began to reexamine the issue.

The potential for international terrorists perpetrating acts of violence on American soil concerns law enforcement because of their growing presence in the United States and the offices of Islamic militant groups that raise funds, recruit new members, and provide military training. While most experts see a greater potential for right-wing extremist violence in the next millennium, they do not discount the future potential of international terrorists carrying out their acts in America.

DISCUSSION QUESTIONS

1. Do the threats posed by white supremacists and patriot-militia groups concern you? If so, what specific aspects of their ideology or actions are most troublesome?
2. Describe and discuss the many potentials for spreading a group's message and recruiting new members on the Internet.
3. What elements of the terrorism expert's projections about the character of future terrorism ring true for you and why?
4. In the past, terrorist groups would claim credit for their attacks. A key component of a definition of terrorism includes the desire to publicize one's agenda, and claiming credit for an attack can do this. What can we imply by this trend? Can this lead to a higher level of lethality?

5. Do domestic terrorist activities tend to be supported by the American public or alienate the terrorist group?
6. Why do right-wing groups pose a new threat to the United States?

STUDY QUESTIONS

1. The U.S. Department of Justice and the FBI collect data on domestic and international terrorist incidents. Review the data for a two-year period. What trends are revealed?–for example, are the perpetrators predominantly "home-grown" or "foreign-based"? Is the proportion of people killed in terrorist incidents rising or falling? Are there in fact links between domestic and international terrorist groups? Are the terrorist groups expanding their networks, improving their sophistication, and working to stage more spectacular acts?
2. The SPLC and its co-founder Morris Dees filed a lawsuit on behalf of Victoria Keenan and her son Jason. The case went to trial in August 2000 but stems from an incident in July 1998 when Aryan Nations security members allegedly shot at and accosted Ms. Keenan and her son whose car backfired near the Aryan Nations compound. They had stopped to retrieve a wallet that had fallen out of the car window. In September 2000, the judge ruled the Aryan Nations was negligent of its security force. The jury awarded compensatory and punitive damages to the Keenans. Describe and discuss the impact of this decision on the Aryan Nations? Have watchdog groups like the SPLC or ADL made any public statements about this case? If so, what is the nature of those comments?
3. Federal and state law enforcement agencies have gathered information that many right-wing extremist groups are stockpiling

weapons such as automatic rifles with laser-sighting devices, clips, and other rifles designed as sniper weapons. Is there evidence to document this statement? If so, describe in detail the types of weapons stockpiled and by whom.
4. Research the owners of Resistance Records. Who owns the company, who are they drawing in (i.e., identify the bands or groups that they produce records for), and what is the message of the music produced by Resistance Records?
5. A number of scholars and terrorism experts have written about the 1995 sarin attack in Tokyo's subway system and about the Japanese cult called Aum Shinrikyo and its leader, Shoko Asahara (see Watanabe 1998). Review the available literature and provide a description of the religious cult and its leader. What are the cult's religious beliefs and how did it provide justification for this act of terrorism? Where is it now and does it continue to pose a threat?
6. Describe the various international treaties and conventions that govern the use of biological, chemical, radiological, and nuclear weapons.
7. What is the current assessment of the potential threat for biological, chemical, or nuclear acts of domestic terrorism? Which groups pose the greatest threats, who are their potential targets, and when will these events occur? Be sure to use both government documents and scholarly studies (e.g., Foxell 1999 article).

REFERENCES

Anti-Defamation League: *Vigilante Justice: Militias and "Common Law Courts" Wage War Against the Government.* New York: Author, 1997.

Barnaby, Frank: *Weapons of Mass Destruction: A Growing Threat in the 1990s?* London, Research Institute for the Study of Conflict and Terrorism, October/November 1990.

Cilluffo, Frank J., and Gergely, Curt H.: Domestic Right-wing Terrorism: An Analysis of the Threat. *Intelligence Report, 85:* 12–13, Winter 1997.

Clark, Richard C.: *Technological Terrorism.* Old Greenwich, CT: Devin Adair, 1980.

David, Steven R.: *Defending Third World Regimes from Coups d'etat.* Lanham: University Press of America, 1985.

Dees, Morris (with James Corcoran): *Gathering Storm: America's Militia Threat.* New York: Harper Collins, 1996.

Emerson, Steven: Terrorism in America: The Threat of Militant Islamic Fundamentalism. In Kushner, Harvey W. (Ed.): *The Future of Terrorism: Violence in the New Millennium.* Thousand Oaks, CA: Sage, 1998, pp. 33–54.

Falkenrath, Richard A., Newman, Robert D., and Thayer, Bradley A.: *America's Achilles' Heel: Nuclear, Biological, and Chemical Terrorism and Covert Attack.* Cambridge, MA: MIT Press, 1998.

Foxell, Joseph W., Jr.: The Debate on the Potential for Mass-Casualty Terrorism: The Challenge for U.S. Security. *Terrorism and Political Violence, 11* (1): 94–109, Spring 1999.

Hoffman, Bruce: The Confluence of International and Domestic Trends in Terrorism. *Terrorism and Political Violence, 9* (2): 1–15, Summer 1997.

——: *Terrorism and Weapons of Mass Destruction: An Analysis of Trends and Motivations.* Santa Monica, CA: RAND, 1999.

Jacobs, Stanley S.: The Nuclear Threat as a Terrorist Option. *Terrorism and Political Violence, 10* (4): 149–163, Winter 1998.

Jenkins, Brian H.: *International Terrorism: A New Mode of Conflict.* Los Angeles, CA: Crescent, 1975.

Joyner, Christopher C.: Chemoterrorism: Rethinking the Reality of the Threat. In Oan, Henry H. (Ed.): *Political Violence: Limits and Possibilities of Legal Control.* New York: Oceana, 1993, pp. 115–125.

Kushner, Harvey W.: The New Terrorism. In Kushner, Harvey W. (Ed.): *The Future of Terrorism: Violence in the New Millennium.* Thousand Oaks, CA: Sage, 1998, pp. 3–20.

Laqueur, Walter: *The New Terrorism.* New York: Oxford University Press, 1999.

Leventhal, Paul, and Alexander, Yonah (Eds.): *Preventing Nuclear Terrorism: The Report and Papers of the International Task Force on Prevention of Nuclear Terrorism.* Lexington, MA: Lexington Books, 1987.

Levin, Brian: The Patriot Movement: Past, Present, and Future. In Kushner, Harvey W. (Ed.): *The Future of Terrorism: Violence in the New Millennium.* Thousand Oaks, CA: Sage, 1998, pp. 97–131.

Lifton, Robert J.: *Destroying the World to Save It: Aum Shinrikyo, Apocalyptic Violence and the New Global Terrorism.* New York: Metropolitan Books, 1999.

Livingston, Neil C., and Arnold, Terrell (Eds.): *Fighting Back.* Lexington, MA: Heath, 1986.

Olson-Raymer, Gayle: Personal Notes. Arcata, CA, 2000.

Schwartz, Alan M. (Ed.): *Danger Extremism: The Major Vehicles and Voices on America's Far Right Fringe.* New York: Anti-Defamation League, 1996.

Simon, Jeffrey D.: *The Terrorist Trap: America's Experience with Terrorism.* Bloomington, IN: Indiana University Press, 1994.

Sloan, Stephen: The Future of Terrorism in the United States. *Intelligence Report, 85,* 10–11, Winter 1997.

Smith, Brent L., and Damphousse, Kelly R.: Two Decades of Terror: Characteristics, Trends and Prospects for the Future of Terrorism. In Kushner, Harvey W. (Ed.): *The Future of Terrorism: Violence in the New Millennium.* Thousand Oaks, CA: Sage, 1998, pp. 132–154.

Southern Poverty Law Center: Women on the Web. *Intelligence Report, 94:* 16–17, Summer 1999.

——: The Year in Hate. *Intelligence Report, 97:* 6–7, Winter 2000.

Stern, Jessica: *The Ultimate Terrorists.* Cambridge, MA: Harvard University Press, 1999.

Stohl, Michael (Ed.): *The Politics of Terrorism,* 2d ed. New York: Marcel Dekker, 1983.

Watanabe, Manabu: Religion and Violence in Japan Today: A Chronological and Doctrinal Analysis of Aum Shinrikyo. *Terrorism and Political Violence, 10* (4): 80–100, Winter 1998.

Part Three

INTELLIGENCE GATHERING AND EMERGENCY RESPONSE INCIDENT MANAGEMENT TO TERRORISM

Jeffrey O. Whamond

The first seven chapters focus on the historical roots of domestic terrorism and follow examples of Americans becoming victims of a contemporary right-wing terrorist movement. Combating and defeating this terrorist movement have been possible through a combined approach of effective criminal intelligence-gathering and the implementation of terrorism incident management strategies. These strategies lessen the impact of a terrorist event while rapidly reestablishing order and confidence in the government's ability to bring terrorists to justice.

Chapter 8 develops an understanding of a complex and interrelated system of collecting criminal intelligence information on terrorist enterprises while reinforcing the concepts of due process and privacy rights. The prevention of a terrorist act clearly begins with intelligence gathering that identifies the overt or conspired acts of a domestic terrorist. This is a simplified approach to promoting an understanding of the investigative techniques used to combat terrorism.

Chapter 9 focuses on terrorism incident management strategies for prevention techniques, threat assessment, domestic preparedness, and tactics for a unified national response to a conventional or a weapon of mass destruction incident. The organizational management strategies of handling terrorism investigations and incidents are a top-down philosophy in which the highest priority is prevention. In its simplest terms, the U. S. counterterrorism policy considers terrorists as criminals. Not since World War II have federal, state, and local governments joined so effectively with private industry to apprehend these criminals who are singularly focused on the destruction of American democracy.

Chapter 8

THE GATHERING OF CRIMINAL INTELLIGENCE: POLICY AND PRACTICE

The specter of Timothy McVeigh's unanticipated terrorist attack against the Alfred P. Murrah Federal Building in Oklahoma City continues to be a powerful reminder of the threat posed by domestic terrorism. To circumvent future attacks, it is imperative to understand how intelligence is gathered about domestic terrorism and how law enforcement coordinates to combat domestic terrorism. Thus, this chapter will develop an understanding of the goals in gathering criminal intelligence, the relationship between intelligence gathering and the right to privacy, the responsibility of the FBI, and sources and process(es) of criminal intelligence.

CRIMINAL INTELLIGENCE GATHERING GOALS

If terrorists are to be stopped, they must first be recognized, and criminal intelligence gathering is the first step in identifying potential domestic terrorists. Criminal intelligence is the "product resulting from the collection, evaluation, analysis, integration and interpretation of all available information which concerns one or more aspects of criminal

activity . . ." (Wright 1998: 2). It involves collecting information (e.g., obtaining criminal history records, financial statements, telephone toll records, surveillance operations, etc.) on individuals or organizations whose background, activities, or associations identify them with organized criminal activity with the purpose of preventing and/or prosecuting a criminal act (Fact Sheet 1998).

To recognize the relationship between criminal intelligence gathering and domestic terrorism prevention, consider the following scenario:

Law enforcement receives information suggesting the existence of a terrorist cell. Surveillance of individuals suspected to be affiliated with the cell reveals the suspects illegally purchased detonation cord and explosives. A search warrant is obtained and executed at the suspects' residences. During the search, law enforcement officials discover plans for an attack against a federal building and explosive material necessary to execute the attack. Based on the information gathered both by surveillance and through the search warrant, local law enforcement arrests the suspects and, in conjunction with federal enforcement, develops security protocols to prevent similar terrorist attacks.

Clearly, stopping domestic terrorism begins with intelligence gathering.

Before law enforcement officials can undertake a criminal intelligence gathering operation pertaining to domestic terrorism, they must identify overt acts or conspired acts of domestic terrorism. The resultant investigation is directed toward a known, or suspected, criminal enterprise and not at particular individuals. Focusing on the organization rather than the individual is significant because it provides greater protection to the public than an investigation of an individual and it permits law enforcement to gather information without violating an individual's right to privacy (Federal Bureau of Investigation 1999; Struve 1994).

In gathering criminal intelligence, law enforcement is guided by three goals:

1. To prevent the terrorist act and to bring those who conspire or commit these acts to justice.
2. To determine if the individuals threatening terrorist activity are capable of executing their threat.
3. To develop an operational plan to forestall the threatened terrorist activity consistent with available law enforcement resources quickly enough to be effective (FBI 1999: 85–86).

To realize these goals, law enforcement gathers both strategic and tactical intelligence. *Strategic intelligence* aids law enforcement in anticipating potential terrorist attacks and consists of information that pertains to a long-term plan or event. One form of strategic intelligence is to identify and track dates for significant terrorist activity to recognize any patterns indicating possible future terrorist activity. An example of such strategic intelligence might be to recognize that the Oklahoma City bombing occurred on the first anniversary of the burning of the Branch Da-

vidian compound in Waco, Texas. Recognizing this correlation, law enforcement might decide to enhance security at all state and federal buildings on the following anniversary.

In contrast, *tactical* intelligence collects information to assist immediate law enforcement needs and to support immediate and short-range planning. An example of unintentional tactical intelligence gathering was the unexpected resistance that the ATF agents faced when they attempted to serve a search warrant at the Branch Davidian compound. The tactical reassessment of the Branch Davidian resistance required ATF to develop a new operational plan.

RELATIONSHIP OF PRIVACY RIGHTS TO THE GATHERING OF CRIMINAL INTELLIGENCE

As already discussed, criminal intelligence gathering is a necessary and legitimate law enforcement activity. However, criminal intelligence gathering is problematic because it can potentially impinge upon an individual's right to privacy. Both the legislature and the judicial branch have attempted to balance law enforcement's need to gather information with an individual's right to privacy (Joseph F. Barbara personal interview, January 5, 2000).

The right to privacy is deeply ingrained into the American conception of inalienable rights. Indeed, many incorrectly believe that the right to privacy is guaranteed in the Constitution. The historical development of the concept of a constitutional protection of privacy rights began in 1890 when law student Louis O. Brandeis wrote in the *Harvard Law Review* for the need to protect individual privacy. As a champion of privacy rights, Justice Brandeis has had a lasting effect on the U.S.

Supreme Court's interpretation of the Constitution, especially through decisions such as *Olmstead v. The United States* (see next paragraph). Because the Supreme Court enjoys the immense power of judicial review, the Court's most recent decisions have all but guaranteed the individual's right to privacy by ruling that the right to privacy is *implied* throughout the Bill of Rights.

Olmstead v. The United States (1928) 277 U.S. 438 was the first case that the Court accepted that centered on the broad question of whether individual privacy is guaranteed in the U.S. Constitution. In particular, the case concerned whether law enforcement's use of wiretaps to listen and record telephone conversations violated Olmstead's individual right to privacy. Chief Justice Taft wrote the majority opinion in which he argued that the right to privacy is not constitutionally guaranteed, and hence, the argument was moot. However, writing the dissenting opinion, Justice Louis O. Brandeis argued that the right to privacy is implicit in the fourth amendment of the Constitution and that the police had violated Olmstead's constitutional right to privacy.

Almost 40 years later, the U.S. Supreme Court revised its initial assertion that the right to privacy is not constitutionally guaranteed. In the case of *Griswold v. Connecticut,* 381 U. S. 479 (1965), the issue before the court was the right to marital privacy. Griswold, the Executive Director of the Planned Parenthood League of Connecticut, and its medical director Dr. Buxton, a licensed physician, were convicted for giving married persons information and medical advice on how to prevent conception and, following a medical examination, prescribing a contraceptive device. Justice Douglas delivered the opinion of the Court holding that

1. Griswold had standing to assert the constitutional rights of the married people (see also *Tileston v. Ullman,* 318 U.S. 44 p. 481 [1943]); and
2. The Connecticut statute forbidding use of contraceptives violates the right of marital privacy, which is within the penumbra of specific guarantees in the Bill of Rights.

While the Constitution does not explicitly guarantee the right to privacy, according to California State Attorney Joseph F. Barbara, the right to privacy has been successfully argued in cases involving the first, third, fourth, fifth and fourteenth amendments. In *Boyd v. United States,* 116 U.S. 616, 630 (1886) "the Court held that as a protection against all government invasions of the sanctity of a man's home, the Fourth and Fifth Amendments insure the privacies of life." In *Mapp v. Ohio,* 367 U.S. 643 (1961) the Court held that "the fourth amendment creates a right to privacy no less important than any other right reserved for the people" (Joseph F. Barbara personal interview, January 5, 2000).

The public's concern over law enforcement's infringement on an individual's right to privacy accelerated during the late 1960s and early 1970s. During this period, a growing public mistrust in government combined with concerns over privacy issues resulted in numerous lawsuits against the government—both state and federal. These lawsuits alleged that governmental agencies were acting without cause in their invasion of privacy solely because individuals were exercising their first amendment rights. Specifically, these agencies were accused of using improper collection procedures, the storage of noncrime-related information, and infiltration into noncriminal organizations (Luca 1998).

In 1972, California voters amended art. 1, sec. 1 of their state Constitution to read: "All people are by nature free and independent and have inalienable rights. Among these are enjoying and defending life and liberty, acquiring, possessing and protecting property, and pursuing and obtaining safety, happiness, **and privacy** (emphasis added)." The addition of the term "privacy" to the California Constitution as well as twenty-four other state constitutions is consistent with the U.S. Supreme Court's interpretation of privacy as a constitutional right (Joseph F. Barbara personal interview, January 5, 2000). The states' constitutional amendments underscore the need to balance law enforcement's need to conduct criminal intelligence gathering with an individual's right to privacy. Consequently, at least four other privacy-related issues must be understood in relation to the gathering of criminal intelligence: privacy rights within the context of criminal intelligence gathering; public access to information gathered by law enforcement; Privacy Act implications; and criminal intelligence filing procedures.

Gathering criminal intelligence information is a legitimate law enforcement function; however, a balance must be struck between law enforcement's need to conduct criminal intelligence gathering and the individual's right to privacy. Thus, as a policy, the gathering of criminal intelligence information has to have a predicate or nexus to a crime or crime-related activity; it cannot be based upon an individual or a group's exercise of the first amendment.

During the 1960s and 1970s, the FBI and other law enforcement agencies came under intense criticism for infiltrating into various organizations that were actively protesting the Vietnam War. Because of congressional pressure that threatened to substantially limit the FBI's investigative powers, the sitting Attorney General Edward Levi promulgated strong guidelines that would strike a balance between the need to protect both society and individual privacy. These Attorney General guidelines have been revised under Attorney General's William French Smith and Richard Thornburgh. The FBI continues to follow the Attorney General guidelines established by Dick Thornburgh.

To establish a *criminal predicate*, a trained law enforcement officer must have sufficient factual evidence to suggest a "reasonable possibility" that an individual or organization is engaged in a criminal enterprise or activity (28 CFR 23.20(c)). When establishing a criminal predicate, law enforcement conducts a preliminary investigation before employing an investigative technique; an important consideration is whether the information could be obtained by timely and effective, but less intrusive, means. To judge the intrusiveness of an investigative technique, law enforcement considers to what extent the technique impinges on a person's privacy and to what extent the technique will damage a person's reputation (Thornburgh 1989).

As a matter of policy, law enforcement begins with the least-intrusive viable intelligence gathering methods such as searching the federal and state criminal history databases for any pertinent information. Having exhausted less-intrusive methods, law enforcement may escalate the intrusiveness of their methods to gather even more useful and specific information. These more highly intrusive methods of gathering criminal intelligence information require a court order and include wiretapping and the executing of search warrants. (See the section on "Sources and Processes of Intelligence Information" for additional examples of intelligence gathering techniques.)

Understandably, the Supreme Court has had to rule on these more aggressive criminal intelligence gathering techniques. However, despite its tendency to protect an individual's right to privacy, in the case of the *United States v. Aguilar,* 883 F. 2d 662, 705 (9th Cir. 1989), the Court found in favor of the U.S. argument that the use of an informant or an undercover agent was not necessarily a "highly intrusive investigative technique" (as quoted in Luca 1998: 35). The Court found that the first amendment does not forbid the infiltration of an organization where the investigation is conducted in good faith. Although the Court's decision upheld law enforcement's proactive use of informants and undercover agents, it also found that the qualification that such investigations must be conducted in "good faith" provides ample ground for appeal. In each case, it is important to note that a criminal investigation has to be based on a legitimate law enforcement function and be predicated upon an individual or a group's execution of first amendment freedoms.

Public Access to Information Gathered by Law Enforcement

In a discussion of criminal intelligence gathering, it is important to note that the Federal 1967 Freedom of Information Act (FOIA) 5 U. S. C. Sec. 552 greatly enhanced the public's access to previously restricted information. The policies concerning law enforcement use of the information are of particular interest. FOIA law opened for inspection broad ranges of document files held by federal agencies while exempting law enforcement from having to disclose records compiled for an ongoing law enforcement investigation. Perhaps the most significant effect of the FOIA was to open closed federal, state, and county records to the public. Due to its effectiveness at striking the delicate balance between law enforcement's need to conduct criminal investigations and the public's right to be aware of these investigations insofar as they directly impinge upon the right to privacy, the FOIA would become the blueprint for later laws regarding the public dissemination of information.

Another law that affected the policy and practice of using information was the 1974 Federal Privacy Act, 5 U. S. C. 552. Furthering the right to privacy, this act requires government to keep secure all information it collects from unwarranted access. Sec. 552a(e)(7) of this Act provides that each agency shall "maintain no record describing how any individual exercises rights guaranteed by the First Amendment . . . unless within the scope of an authorized law enforcement activity." Thus, the Federal Privacy Act effectively furthers the right to privacy by strictly controlling and limiting what information law enforcement agencies can collect and store in their files.

The FOIA and the Federal Privacy Act were the key issues in a case heard by the 5th Circuit Court of Appeals. In the case of *Williams v. Superior Court* (1993) 5 C. 4th 337, South Coast Newspapers, Inc. petitioned the court to compel the San Bernardino Sheriff's Department to release the report of a disciplinary proceeding against two of its deputy sheriffs. The issue before the Court was that the information requested by South Coast was part of an investigation with a concrete and definite prospect of an enforcement proceeding.

The 5th Circuit Court of Appeals ruled that California Government Code Sec. 6254(f) should not be interpreted as incorporating provisions of the 1967 FOIA. This ruling provided that the public's right to know applies only to federal information expressly enumerated in Sec. 6254(f) of the California Records Act. The Court upheld the "intelligence information" exemption barring the disclosure of personal identifiers, confidential sources, and confidential information regarding criminal activity. The Court's ruling greatly altered the interpretation of the FOIA. In particular, while the materials requested by South Coast might be nonexempt from FOIA, they became exempt when they were included in the investigatory file, and this exemption could continue far longer than the actual investigation.

Privacy Act Implications: Cases Relating to the Maintenance and Dissemination of Criminal Intelligence Information in California

In 1982, The American Civil Liberties Union (ACLU) brought a case against California State Governor George Deukmejian. In *ACLU v. Deukmejian* (1982) 32 Cal.3d 440, the ACLU petitioned for access to 100 index cards that were maintained by the California Department of Justice to determine if the cards contained information required to be accessible under the law. Denying the ACLU's petition, the California Supreme Court ruled that the California Public Records Act Government Code Section 6250 et seq. exempts confidential sources of information, personal identifiers, and confidential information relating to criminal activity from mandatory public access. Thus, the California Supreme Court established the importance of a clear policy regarding the maintenance and dissemination of criminal intelligence information.

Further altering the provisions surrounding the dissemination of criminal intelligence was the 1984 ruling of the 3rd District Court of Appeal. In the *South Coast Newspapers, Inc. v. Oceanside* (1984) 160 Cal. App. 3d 261c, the petitioner challenged California Government Code Sec. 6254(f) for unnecessarily limiting access to criminal investigative records. The court upheld the challenge and ruled that all investigative records must be disclosed unless disclosure would

- interfere with law enforcement proceedings;
- deprive a person of a fair trial;
- constitute an unwarranted invasion of privacy;

- disclose the identity of a confidential source;
- disclose secret investigative techniques and procedures; and
- endanger the safety of law enforcement personnel.

South Coast Newspapers, Inc. v. Oceanside was an especially significant case pertaining to the dissemination of criminal intelligence records because it was seen as exempting all investigative records from disclosure. This decision stood for only nine years until it was set aside by the *Williams v. Superior Court* decision of 1993.

The concept that individual privacy rights extend to the disclosure of information that is not otherwise exempted (i.e., personal identifiers, confidential sources of information, and confidential information relating to criminal activity) is also held within the 1974 Federal Privacy Act. Another exemption to the release of information is the concept of the states' secret privilege, as found in *Ellsberg v. Mitchell* (D.C. Cir. 1983) 709 F.2d 51, 56. In a motion to the U.S. Supreme Court, the Attorney General of the United States argued that individual rights of discovery in the case before the court were less important than the security of the nation. The court responded in its decision "that it is now well established that the United States, by invoking its States secrets privilege, may block discovery in a lawsuit of any information that, if disclosed, would adversely affect national security" (as quoted in Luca 1998: 35). This ruling broadened the exemptions for disclosure of information by placing the greater importance on national security over the individual right to privacy and the ability of an individual to obtain information held by the government.

Further complicating the relationship between an individual's right to privacy and the rights of law enforcement to gather and maintain criminal information was the case of *Rubin v. City of Los Angeles* (1987) 190 C. A. 3d at p. 577. Rubin petitioned for the release of specific information gathered by Los Angeles law enforcement. In response, the City of Los Angeles argued that the release of criminal intelligence information would adversely affect their security and asserted a privilege similar to the privilege of "states secret." The court held that only the federal government may assert the privilege of state's secrets or national security.

Criminal Intelligence Filing Procedures

The laws, statutes, and regulations that address privacy rights in the context of gathering criminal intelligence information in domestic terrorism cases, as with general criminal intelligence files, do not dictate whether public information should be kept in separate files. In gathering criminal intelligence information in domestic terrorism cases, public information is maintained as supportive documentation of an organization's activity. The collecting and maintaining of publicly available information consistent with the Privacy Act is not prohibited. The U.S. Attorney General's guideline on domestic terrorism investigation suggests a conservative approach to the storing of first amendment public-domain materials (newspaper articles, books, magazine articles) that can be obtained by any citizen. Also called "open source materials" (Thornburgh 1989: 3), these materials are perhaps best indexed and stored in a case subfile and not in the main criminal case file because they could be subject to disclosure. By separating the open-source information from law enforcement sensitive information, there is less risk of the inadvertent release of controlled and exempted information.

THE FBI LEAD AGENCY RESPONSIBILITIES

The FBI's lead agency responsibilities are explicit:

> In cases that involve terrorist activities or acts in preparation of terrorist activities within the statutory jurisdiction of the United States, the FBI has primary investigative jurisdiction. This authority includes the collection, coordination, analysis, management and dissemination of intelligence. Should another federal agency identify individuals who are engaged in terrorist activities or in acts in preparation of terrorist activities, that agency is requested to notify the FBI. (28 U.S.C. 524(c)(1)(L))

Thus, the FBI is expressly tasked with combating terrorism and receives federal funding to enable it to train specialized units to deal with terrorists' threats. The FBI 1999–2000 fiscal budget contained a request to increase funding of their Joint Terrorism Task Force (JTTF) operations in additional geographical areas. This funding would increase the total number of specialized task forces of federal, state, and local law enforcement officers to 29 JTTF's strategically located in metropolitan areas throughout the United States. The FBI exercises lead agency responsibility in investigating all crimes for which it has primary or concurrent jurisdiction. The FBI in its investigation of terrorism divides domestic terrorism into three classifications:

1. terrorist incidences;
2. suspected terrorist incidents; and
3. terrorist prevention (FBI 1997: 189–190).

A terrorist incident is a violent act, or an act dangerous to human life, in violation of the criminal laws of the United States or of any state, to intimidate or coerce a government, the civilian population, or any segment thereof, in furtherance of political or social objectives. Example:

On February 26, 1993, a bomb exploded at the World Trade Center in New York City, causing millions of dollars in damage as well as serious disruptions in international trading. Six persons were killed in the blast and approximately 1,000 others were injured. In 1994, four of the six persons responsible for this act were convicted and sentenced to 240 years in prison, in addition to a $250,000 fine.

A suspected terrorist incident is a potential act of terrorism; however, responsibility for the act cannot be attributed to a known or suspected terrorist group or individual(s). Assessment of the circumstances surrounding an act will determine its inclusion in that category. Moreover, additional information through investigation can cause a redesignation of a suspected terrorist incident to terrorist incident status. Example:

On January 17, 1993, a fire occurred at the Serbian National Defense Council (SNDCA) in Chicago, Illinois. Subsequent investigation determined that three molotov cocktails had been placed inside the building through a large window that was broken. SNDCA employees advised investigators that the office had received threatening telephone calls. In addition, in both September and December of 1992, the office had been the target of anti-Serbian vandalism. This incident appears to be an attempt to use force or violence in an effort to intimidate or coerce the target of furtherance of the perpetrators' political goals. However, because no claims of responsibility were made, nor were the specific objectives stated by the perpetrator(s), this incident was designated as a suspected incident of terrorism.

Terrorism prevention is a documented instance in which a violent act by a known or suspected terrorist group or individual(s) with the means and a proven propensity for violence is successfully interdicted through investigative activity. Example:

During the period of June 24 through June 30, 1993, nine suspects were arrested on conspiracy charges while constructing several bombs. These bombs were to be used at several locations in New York City, including the United Nations Building; 26 Federal Plaza, which houses the FBI's New York field office; and the Lincoln and Holland Tunnels. The arrests of these individuals prevented a disastrous event from occurring, which could have resulted in death and injury to countless numbers of persons and an indeterminable amount of property damage. (FBI 1997: 189–190)

The Investigation Potential and Actual Terrorist Acts

Attesting to the efficacy of the FBI in stopping terrorist activity, Jeffrey Simon (1994) in his book *The Terrorist Trap* notes that a number of "potential terrorist acts have been thwarted in the United States, . . . through law enforcement efforts" (p. 386). Post-incident investigations and the use of tactical intelligence gathering by FBI's JTTF have also resulted in the arrest and conviction of domestic terrorists. The Oklahoma City bombing case in April 1995 is one of the best examples of a post-incident investigation. In this case, fire, and public works emergency responders assisted the law enforcement agencies in locating, protecting, and collecting evidence that turned out to be critical in the development of a criminal case. Another successful post-incident investigation was the World Trade Center investigation, "where the terrorists tried to obtain a refund on the rental van that carried the explosives into the trade center" (Simon 1994: 386). The terrorists' attempt to obtain a refund allowed JTTF to identify and arrest suspects throughout the terrorist organization.

The use of strategic intelligence gathering helps to protect the public by preventing the terrorist act and bringing those who conspire or commit these acts to justice. Examples of the importance of strategic intelligence gathering include the following:

- In 1986, in Chicago, members of the street gang El Rukn were arrested for planning terrorist acts within the United States with funding from Libya (Simon 1994: 386).
- In 1987, law enforcement arrested Japanese Red Army terrorist Yu Kikumura before he could initiate a series of bombings (Simon 1994).
- In 1993, Islamic militants were arrested for plotting to blow up the United Nations headquarters and other targets in New York City.
- In 1999, a JTTF investigation in Sacramento, California, resulted in the arrest of two militia members for conspiring to blow up a television tower, an electrical substation, and two 12-million-gallon propane storage tanks. The suspect's goal was to create such chaos on or around January 1st 2000 that President Clinton would declare martial law, giving militant groups the opportunity to overthrow the government (Lorch and Murr 1999: 32).

In April 1995, the Oklahoma City bombing forced America to realize that law enforcement agencies had to address domestic terrorism. In June 1995, the White House addressed the lack of strategic criminal intelligence information prior to the Oklahoma City bombing by issuing Presidential Decision Directive 39 (PDD-39) "United States Policy on Counter-terrorism." PDD-39, which is designed to reduce America's vulnerability to domestic- and foreign-based ter-

rorist attacks on American soil, initiated a policy of deterrence and response to terrorist acts and strengthened the federal government's capabilities to prevent and manage the consequences of nuclear, biological, and chemical (NBC) weapons, including WMD. PDD-39 discusses crisis management and consequence management, which was the first time these management concepts were included in federal policy.

The gathering of criminal intelligence information and the investigation of domestic terrorists or domestic terrorist incidents require a national coordination and an organizational structure. The FBI, in fulfilling its lead agency role, provides a national coordination of law enforcement's efforts into the investigation and gathering of criminal intelligence information related to domestic terrorism. The investigation of individuals and groups to prevent terrorist incidents is a cornerstone in the FBI's counterterrorism policy. As of June 10, 1999, the FBI's "Ten Most Wanted" list included the names of Osama Bin Laden as an international terrorist and Eric Robert Rudolph as a domestic terrorist. The names of violent domestic terrorism fugitives Joanne Deborah Chesimard, Elizabeth Anna Duke, Victor Manuel Gerena, and William Guillermo Morales, while not on the infamous top ten list are actively being sought by the FBI for their involvement in bombing incidents.

As a lead agency in the JTTF, the FBI is responsible for the analysis of criminal intelligence information leading to the investigation and arrest of domestic terrorists. In cases where there is little information about the suspected terrorist or organization, the FBI is supported by several field support units that are located at the FBI Academy in Quantico, Virginia. The following units assist with investigative and support functions as a component of the Critical Incident Response Group (CIRG)–an FBI support group of

---

Box 8.1
PDD-39–The Policies

General: Terrorism is both a threat and a criminal act to our national security. The administration has stated that it is the policy of the United States to use all appropriate means to deter, defeat, and respond to all terrorist attacks on our territory and resources, whether these acts are towards people and/or facilities.

Lead Agency Responsibilities: PDD-39 validated and reaffirmed existing federal lead agency responsibilities for terrorism and counterterrorism, which were assigned to the Department of Justice. The Attorney General delegated to the FBI lead agency responsibility for the investigation of threats or acts of terrorism within the United States. Following PDD-39 were two additional Presidential Directives: PDD-62 and PDD-63 (PDD's 39, 62 and 63 related to emergency response will be discussed in more detail in Chapter 9, Terrorism Incident Management: Strategies and Tactics.) All three directives combined strengthened the FBI's lead agency responsibilities for crisis management and response to threats or acts of terrorism within the United States, its territories, or in international waters when a foreign vessel is not involved. PDD-62 provided a framework for interagency cooperation under the coordinating authority of the FBI. This directive also appoints the FBI as lead agency for operational response to WMD incidents. PDD-63 provides objectives and goals for the United States in protecting the critical infrastructures of our Nation.

Crisis Management: During crisis management, the FBI is to coordinate closely with local law enforcement authorities to provide successful resolutions to the incident.

Consequence Management: PDD-39 states that the Federal Emergency Management Agency (FEMA) shall ensure that the Federal Response Plan (FRP) is adequate to respond to the consequences of terrorism. It shall be FEMA's responsibilities to use FRP structures to coordinate all federal assistance to state and local governments for consequence management.

Source: PDD-39, June 1995.

---

technical advisers available to make recommendations during the crisis management phase of a domestic terrorist incident–as well as provide law enforcement with an enforcement-oriented behavioral science and data-processing center where research can be consolidated:

- The National Center for the Analysis of Violent Crime (NCAVC).
- The Criminal Investigative Analysis (CIA) program.

- The Arson Bombing Investigative Services (ABIS).

Then Attorney General Janet Reno reports, "the FBI endeavors to initiate investigations as early in the chain of conspiratorial events as possible" (Reno 2000: 116). These support units can be critical in assisting investigators in prevention cases when little information may be available about an individual, the group's members, or the criminal investigation.

Box 8.2

Of the criminal intelligence information submitted to NCAVC, some, but not necessarily all, of the following areas may be addressed in a typical profile:

- Age range
- Sex
- Race
- Intelligence level
- Lifestyle
- Work habits
- Marital status/adjustment
- Pre- and postoffense behavior

- Social adjustments
- Personality or characteristics
- Emotional adjustment
- Employment history or adjustment
- Prior criminal arrest history
- Sexual adjustments and perversions
- Location of residence

An Investigative Support Unit

The analysis of the information gathered in a criminal intelligence investigation of suspected domestic terrorists is more difficult when law enforcement knows little about suspects who have no criminal record, or about the membership, goals, and motivations of the suspected terrorist organization. The FBI in fulfilling its responsibilities as the lead agency in domestic terrorism investigations can call upon NCAVC for their assistance in reviewing all of the intelligence information gathered pertaining to the suspects and their organization.

By analyzing the way the crime was committed, the NCAVC behavioral scientists can often identify the major personality and behavioral characteristics of an individual. NCAVC has noted that generally a person's basic patterns of behavior, exhibited in the commission of a crime, will be present in that person's lifestyle. Thus, a criminal investigative analyst may be able to determine the type of person who committed the crime and that person's possible motive(s).

No two domestic terrorists or terrorist organizations are identical and therefore, the offender may not show common traits that fit neatly into each category of the analysis. Whenever possible, NCAVC team members travel to the scene to access all of the available data for a more complete and timely profile of the terrorist. The NCAVC also evaluates both strategic and tactical intelligence information and conducts a threat assessment of a suspected terrorist organization that allows law enforcement professionals to identify, assess, and manage the risk of targeted violence and the potential terrorists.

In conducting its assessment, the NCAVC evaluates anonymous written or verbal communications to determine authorship and/or whether the author has the means to carry out any stated threat. A behavioral description of the author may be provided to assist in the author's identification and apprehension. Identified offenders who make threats or appear to pose a danger may similarly be assessed for potential dangerousness given appropriate and sufficient background data.

Attorney General Guidelines on General Crimes, Racketeering Enterprise, and Domestic Security Terrorism Investigations

The Attorney General (AG) guidelines direct law enforcement officers as they investigate crimes or crime-related activities. Based on the establishment of a criminal predicate, these guidelines specify when FBI agents, and law enforcement officers working with the FBI as members of the JTTF's, can gather intelligence information, the type of information that can be gathered, and acceptable methods for gathering criminal intelligence information.

The AG guidelines articulate some general principles, which state that preliminary inquiries and investigations are conducted to prevent, detect, or prosecute violations of federal and/or state law. According to the guidelines "these investigations shall be conducted with as little intrusion into the privacy of individuals as the situation permits. Based on the information discovered, if a reasonable factual predicate is found, a criminal intelligence investigation can proceed" (Thornburgh 1989: 5).

In law enforcement's efforts to be proactive when investigating crimes, it is sometimes necessary to anticipate criminal conduct to prevent crime. According to the AG guidelines, it is important that such activities are not based solely on activities protected by the first amendment or on the lawful exercise of any other right secured by the Constitution of the United States. When, however:

> statements advocate criminal activity or indicate intent to engage in criminal acts or a crime of violence, an investigation may be warranted. These investigations are often referred to as "general crimes" or "criminal intelligence investigations" and should be terminated when all logical leads have been

exhausted and no legitimate law enforcement interest justifies their continuance. (Thornburgh 1989: 5)

Nothing in the AG guidelines prohibit maintenance of information that could be found in a public library.

Domestic terrorism is defined by the AG guidelines as: unlawful use of force or violence, committed by a group(s) of two or more individuals, against person or property to intimidate or coerce a government, the civilian population, or any segment thereof, in furtherance of political or social objectives. For example: The Pedro Albizu Campos Revolutionary Forces (PACRF) is a domestic terrorist group that directs its terrorist activities at the United States and receives no foreign direction or financial assistance. PACRF is a violent Puerto Rican separatist group dedicated to achieving total Puerto Rican independence from the United States. In the 1990s, this group was credited with committing four terrorist incidents in Puerto Rico (Thornburgh 1989).

Like racketeering-enterprise investigations, terrorism investigations are concerned with the investigation of entire enterprises rather than an individual participant. The FBI's investigative terrorism goal is to prevent terrorist acts and arrest everyone in the terrorist organization, not just ones assigned to carry out the criminal act. The AG guidelines, therefore, authorize intelligence investigations to determine the structure and scope of the enterprise, as well as the member's relationship to that organization (Thornburgh 1989).

In determining whether an investigation should be conducted, investigators are to assess the following: (1) the magnitude of the threatened harm, (2) the likelihood it will occur, (3) the immediacy of the threat, and (4) the danger to privacy and free expression posed by the investigation (Thornburgh 1989: 12, also see http://www.lectlaw.com/files_ p_/cjs03.htm). Attorney Joseph F. Barbara notes: "It should be remembered that before employing an investigative technique, start with the least intrusive means of collecting information first, and always consult with the prosecuting attorney at the beginning of a terrorism investigation" (Joseph F. Barbara personal interview, January 5, 2000).

The scope and collection of information for domestic terrorism investigations should focus on overt criminal acts. By following the finances of the criminal enterprise, the activities of the members, mail correspondence, and telephone activity, other people associated with the criminal act can be further identified. The goals of the terrorist enterprise are an equally important area on which to gather intelligence. Information gathered during the early stages of the investigation should address the past and present activities of the enterprise to identify its goals and objectives. During the investigation of domestic terrorism, it may be determined that there is a state-sponsored link to the terrorist organization. In these types of cases, there are specific AG guidelines for the investigation of international terrorism.

> International terrorism as defined by the Attorney General is the unlawful use of force or violence, committed by a group(s) or individual(s), who is foreign based and/or directed by countries or groups outside the United States or whose activities transcend national boundaries, against persons or property to intimidate or coerce a government, the civilian population, or any segment thereof, in furtherance of political or social objectives. For example, an international terrorist group that has been active in the United States is the Mujahedin-E Khalq (MEK). The MEK is an Iranian terrorist group opposed to the current Iranian regime. This group is foreign based and its activities transcend national boundaries. On April 5, 1992, five MEK members forcibly entered and seized control of the Iranian Mission to the United Nations in New York, New York. No injuries resulted and all

five members were subsequently arrested. (Thornburgh 1998: 12)

Sources and Processes of Intelligence Information

The gathering of criminal intelligence information means the use of sources with a measurable history of accuracy. The types of intelligence sources used in an operation depend on the criminal predicate offense (28 CFR 23.20(C)) and the availability of resources (Luca 1998). The sources of information used in domestic terrorism investigations include the Internet, concerned citizens, law enforcement officers, criminal information indexes, and confidential informants. Additional publicly available information sources include the ADL, the SPLC, the Militia–Watchdog, and the *National Institute of Justice Journal*, a publication of the U.S. Department of Justice and Office of Justice Programs.

The 1974 Privacy Act [5 U.S.C. Sec. 552-(e)(7)] states, "public source information also called First Amendment Records (i.e., information that could be obtained at the public library) should not be placed in a file unless it is pertinent to and within the scope of an authorized law enforcement activity." The law enforcement exception granted within the Privacy Act permits retaining public source information when the information pertains to an authorized criminal investigation, intelligence investigation, or an administrative investigation.

INVESTIGATIVE TECHNIQUES

In gathering of criminal intelligence information and in the investigation of domestic terrorism cases, the employment of investigative techniques centers around three factors: (1) the timeliness of the information;

Box 8.3

Representative Investigative Techniques are Based on Level of Intrusiveness

Least Intrusive Techniques: Law enforcement criminal files and publicly accessible records combined with preliminary interviews.

1. Criminal history checks.
2. Review of public records.
3. Review of federal, state, and local records.
4. Interview of the complainant, previously established informants, and confidential sources.
5. Interview of the potential subject. This can be an effective way to lock a subject into a story early on in an investigation. However, consult with a prosecuting attorney and discuss a risk versus gain of this technique.
6. Interview of persons who should readily be able to corroborate or deny the truth of the allegation. This does not exclude pretext interviews (stating a false reason for the interview) or the interview of a potential subject's employer or coworkers unless the interviewee was the complainant.
7. Physical or photographic surveillance of any person.

Moderately Intrusive Techniques: The implementation of operational plans involving moderately intrusive techniques requires a criminal predicate and a likelihood of operational success. These techniques go beyond the requesting of documents and records, which are obtained through grand jury subpoenas or court orders.

1. Informants and confidential sources.
2. Undercover operations.
3. Undisclosed participation in the activities of an organization by an undercover officer or cooperating private individual.

Highly Intrusive Techniques: These techniques are warranted when a serious criminal predicate and less likelihood of success are used in a timely manner with any of the other techniques.

1. Mail covers. The photocopying of the face of an envelope or package showing the postal markings of addressee and return address.
2. Mail openings. The court-ordered mail openings most commonly occur in correctional facilities.
3. Nonconsensual electronic surveillance or any other investigative technique covered by Title 18 U.S.C. 2515.
4. Pen registers and trap and trace devices, the monitoring of telephone numbers and call times to and from a target phone number; Title 18 U.S.C. 3123.
5. Access to stored wire or electronic communications, Title 18 U.S.C. 2701-2710.
6. Consensual electronic monitoring.
7. Search Warrant: search and seizures.

Source: Thornburgh 1989.

(2) the effectiveness or likelihood of success of the technique; and (3) the intrusiveness of the technique. The accuracy of the information indicating a crime and the seriousness of the crime influence these three factors. The use of lawful but confidential investigative techniques may be used when other techniques are not likely to succeed (i.e., sting operations) (Thornburgh 1989).

In the mid-1980s, law enforcement agencies noted that some suspects were attempting to evade wiretaps by using pay phones or otherwise frequently changing phones, the location of which would not always be anticipated for inclusion in a wiretap application. In response, as part of the Electronic Communications Privacy Act of 1986, Congress enacted a limited exception to the particularity requirement for situations where the government makes a special factual showing, authorizing what are sometimes known as "roving taps." "In the case of wiretaps, the government must show, based on physical surveillance or other evidence, that the target is thwarting interception by changing facilities" (Dempsey 1997: 158).

Consequently, since the mid-1980s law enforcement has extended its wiretapping procedure to include roving taps. The standards for roving taps are found in Sec. 18 U.S.C. 2518(1)(b) and 2518(4)(b). (Also see the Electronic Communications Privacy Act of 1986, Senate Report 99-541, 99th Congress, 2d Session, United States Senate: 1986).

The Internet as an Intelligence Information Source

The Internet contains unverified information from international sources. When accessing the Internet and looking up information of suspected domestic terrorists, one must remember the freedom of speech issues and expectation of privacy issues that are addressed in the case law and statutes section of this chapter. Information on the Web pages and Usenet sites is available to the public and there is no expectation of privacy. However, electronic mail (e-mail), password protected Electronic Bulletin Board or Bulleting Board Services (BBS), Internet Relay Chat (IRC), and information secured by encryption, such as "Pretty Good Privacy" (PGP), contain an expectation of privacy and generally require a court order for law enforcement access.

When utilizing the Internet as an investigative tool, law enforcement agents should not research suspected criminal agents from an "uncloaked" office or home computer, unless they are willing to let others know who they are. However, when used properly, the Internet is a tool that can assist in the gathering of information. Like any tool, one must work with the Internet for some time to develop full proficiency in its use.

Sources of Criminal Intelligence Information and the Evaluation Process

The gathering of criminal intelligence information means the evaluation and classification of data the bulk of which may relate to unverified allegations or information. The worth and usefulness of this information depends on the evaluation process. Since World War II, the intelligence community has used a uniform set of criteria in the evaluation of intelligence information. The use of a uniformed system of evaluation and classification as part of the criminal intelligence gathering process protects sources, the investigation, and an individual's right to privacy. Therefore, before being retained as part of a criminal investigation, information has to be assessed for source reliability and content.

Box 8.4
Introducing the Internet

The Internet is accessed via an Internet Provider (IP) or an online service using a browser. The browser is simply a protocol to convert source codes into a computer language that can be displayed in images on a computer screen. The Internet is made up of computer applications as follows (Netscape 1999): The World Wide Web pages (WWW); Usenet Message Boards; Electronic Mail (e-mail); Internet Relay Chat (IRC); and Electronic Bulletin Boards (BBS).

Web pages are listed under specific addresses or "Universal Resource Locators" (URL). The URL is a group of characters that combine to form an Internet address. At the end of the URL is a suffix that indicates the type of site or country location you are accessing. U.S.-based URL sites will normally not show a country indicator. A two-letter state abbreviation is optional. If the site is a foreign-based site, you will see a two-letter designator that is country specific. U.S.-based suffixes are: .com (commercial "for profit venture"); .org (nonprofit organization); .net (communications Network); .gov (government entity); .mil (military service); and .edu (educational institution).

Example of a URL: http://www.aum-shinrikyo.com/
http:// (Hypertext Transfer Protocol Instruction)
www (World Wide Web)
Aum-shinrikyo (The Domain Name)
com (Top-Level Domain Extension)
Source: Netscape 1999, http://home.netscape.com
Additional references: http://www.ed.gov/pubs/parents/internet/whatis.htm
http://www.ed.gov/pubs/parents/internet/glossary.htm
http://www.internic.com
http://whois.arin.net/whois/arinwhois.htm
http://www.dejanews.com

The objective of gathering criminal intelligence information is to collect A-1 (Reliable and Confirmed) "information that law enforcement agencies can use to protect the public and suppress criminal operations" (Struve 1994: 1). As previously noted, information gathering techniques move from the least-intrusive to most-intrusive methods of collection. The most-intrusive methods of collection require warrants and include search warrants, wiretaps, pen registers, and trap traces. The use of these highly intrusive techniques requires a compelling circumstance to be justified when less-intrusive methods had been unsuccessful or have little likelihood of success (Thornburgh 1989).

SUMMARY

The most effective deterrent to domestic terrorism is the gathering of criminal intelligence information that can be used by law

---

Box 8.5
Source Reliability, Content Validity, and the Classification System

Source Reliability

1. *Reliable:* the reliability of the source is unquestioned or has been well tested in the past.
2. *Usually reliable:* the reliability of the source can usually be relied upon as factual. The majority of the source information provided in the past has proven to be reliable.
3. *Unreliable:* the reliability of the source has been sporadic in the past.
4. *Unknown:* the reliability of the source cannot be judged. Either experience or investigation has not determined its authenticity or trustworthiness.

Content Validity

1. *Confirmed:* an investigator or another independent, reliable source has corroborated the information.
2. *Probable:* the information is consistent with past accounts.
3. *Doubtful:* the information is inconsistent with past accounts.
4. *Cannot be judged:* the information cannot be judged. Either experience or investigation has not yet determined its authenticity.

Classification System

1. *Sensitive:* the highest classification used in (civilian) law enforcement cases is "sensitive." On an occasion where the sensitivity of the information requires a more limited dissemination of information, you may see a document marked "Sensitive–for Commander's Eyes-Only. DESTROY AFTER READING." The types of ongoing cases marked "sensitive" could be a significant criminal investigation, public corruption, information about informants, or criminal-intelligence reports.
2. *Confidential:* information that is for law enforcement use only and is not otherwise designated as being sensitive.
3. *Restricted:* when the intended recipient of a report is another law enforcement agency and the information is nonconfidential, it is generally regarded as restricted. Only the generating agency can further disseminate the information.
4. *Unclassified:* information from public sources that the public has, or had, access to in its original form is designated unclassified. Some of these types of sources include news media information, newspapers, magazines, periodical clippings, and videotapes of television broadcasts. Note: Federal Law Enforcement and Intelligence Agencies in addition to this system, use for National Security purposes, the classification system of: Top Secret, Secret, Confidential and For Official Use Only.

Source: Luca 1998.

enforcement to prevent a terrorist act. Criminal intelligence gathering is a proactive tool that, when used effectively, allows for the development of strategic or tactical operational plans that are consistent with the availability of resources.

Although in 1890, the Court did not uphold the individual's right to privacy, forty years later, in the case of *Griswold v. Connecticut,* the Court reversed its original finding and argued that the right to privacy is implicit throughout the Constitutional amendments. The Court's most broad interpretation of the Constitution as guaranteeing an individual's right to privacy resulted from the case *Mapp v. Ohio.* The Court found that "the Fourth Amendment creates a right to privacy no less important than any other right reserved for the people" (Barbara interview 2000). The debate on the individual's right to privacy versus law enforcement's right to gather information continued throughout the late 1960s and the early 1970s. This widespread concern led 25 states to amend their constitutions to specifically include the right to "privacy." Given the importance of an individual's right to privacy, law enforcement balances its intelligence gathering activities against an individual's rights.

The coordination of law enforcement efforts in the investigation of domestic terrorism requires clear lead agency responsibilities to ensure the proper collection, coordination, analysis, management, and dissemination of intelligence information. PDD-39 validated and reaffirmed existing Federal Lead Agency responsibilities for terrorism and counterterrorism with the Department of Justice. Consequently, the Department of Justice designated the FBI as the agency responsible for the investigation of threats or terrorist acts within the United States or on ships in international waters not under foreign flags. In case of a terrorist act, the FBI is in charge of crisis management for the incident.

The criminal intelligence system as described in Sec. 28, Code of Federal Regulations, Part 23, examines everything that is required to establish, operate, and maintain a criminal intelligence unit. Criminal intelligence gathering requires a criminal predicate or a reasonable suspicion. The gathering of this criminal intelligence information is governed by the balance between an individual's rights and law enforcement's ability to control criminal activity. Law enforcement agencies engaged in intelligence gathering are careful to utilize only those sources with a history of accuracy. The use of a uniform system of evaluation and classification as part of the criminal intelligence process protects sources, the investigation, and individual's rights.

The objective of gathering criminal intelligence information is to collect reliable and confirmed information that law enforcement can use to protect the public and to suppress criminal operations. Information gathering techniques used by law enforcement move from the least-intrusive to the most-intrusive methods of collection when less-intrusive methods of intrusion would have little likelihood of success.

DISCUSSION QUESTIONS

1. What are some of the arguments for and against the use of the Internet as an intelligence gathering tool?
2. Should law enforcement agencies be prohibited in using public-domain information in their intelligence and criminal case files?
3. Do first amendment rights preclude the use of undercover agents at assemblies where there is no expectation of criminal conduct?
4. Do you think law enforcement agencies should place undercover agents into suspected domestic terrorist organizations? Explain why or why not.

STUDY QUESTIONS

1. The gathering of criminal intelligence information is an excellent tool that can be used for lawful investigative purposes. Using the information provided in this chapter, establish the goals and objectives of a criminal intelligence gathering unit. Having established these goals and objectives, write your unit's criminal intelligence gathering policy.
2. Using the guide information provided in this chapter, develop a criminal intelligence information plan using the Internet in finding out all that is possible about the international terrorist group Aum Shinrikyo. Acting as an intelligence analyst, classify the intelligence information that you have gathered.
3. Select any suspected domestic terrorist group discussed in this text and research as much as possible about the group using Internet sources. Using the information from the AG guidelines, describe the type of information that you would have to develop to investigate fully your domestic terrorist group. Identify the predicate offenses (refer to the appendix terrorism statutes) necessary for your intelligence gathering unit to conduct its investigation. Develop an operational plan for the use of investigative techniques, when these techniques should be used, and what you think you can learn about the organizational structure and membership of the suspected terrorist organization through the investigative process.

TERRORISM STATUTES

1. Title 18, United States Code (USC), sec. 81, 113, 114, 1111, 1112, 1113, 1201 1363, 2111, 2241, 2244: Crimes Committed Within the Special Maritime Jurisdiction of the United States.
2. Title 18, USC, sec. 111, 351, 1114, and 1751: Crimes Against Selected United States Officials.
3. Title 18, USC, sec. 112, 878, 1116, and 1201(a)(4): Crimes Against Internationally Protected Persons.
4. Title 18, USC, sec. 32: Aircraft Sabotage.
5. Title 18, USC, sec. 33: Destruction of Motor Vehicles or Motor Vehicles Facilities.
6. Title 18, USC, sec. 35: Imparting or Conveying False Information.
7. Title 18, USC, sec. 37: Violence at International Airports.
8. Title 18, USC, sec. 43: Animal Enterprise Terrorism.
9. Title 18, USC, sec. 115: Crimes Against Family Members of a Federal Official.
10. Title 18, USC, sec. 175–178: Prohibition with Respect to Biological Weapons.
11. Title 18, USC, sec. 229 et seq.: Chemical Weapons.
12. Title 18, USC, sec. 231: Civil Disorders.
13. Title 18, USC, sec. 241: Civil Rights Conspiracies.
14. Title 18, USC, sec. 245: Federally Protected Activities.
15. Title 18, USC, sec. 247: Damage to Religious Property.
16. Title 18, USC, sec. 248: Freedom of Access to Clinic Entrances.
17. Title 18, USC, sec. 371 et seq.: Conspiracy.
18. Title 18, USC, sec. 831: Prohibited Transactions Involving Nuclear Materials.
19. Title 18, USC, sec. 844: Explosive Materials.
20. Title 18, USC, sec. 872–880: Extortion and Threats.
21. Title 18, USC, sec. 921–930: Unlawful Activity: Firearms.

22. Title 18, USC, sec. 952–970: Neutrality.
23. Title 18, USC, sec. 1074: Flight to Avoid Prosecution for Damaging or Destroying Any Building or Other Real or Personal Property.
24. Title 18, USC, sec. 1091: Genocide.
25. Title 18, USC, sec. 1117: Conspiracy to Murder.
26. Title 18, USC, sec. 1119: Foreign Murder of United States Nationals.
27. Title 18, USC, sec. 1203: Act for the Prevention and Punishment of the Crime of Hostage Taking.
28. Title 18, USC, sec. 1361: Government Property or Contracts.
29. Title 18, USC, sec. 1362: Communication Lines, Stations or Systems.
30. Title 18, USC, sec. 1364: Interference with Foreign Commerce by Violence.
31. Title 18, USC, sec. 1366: Destruction of an Energy Facility.
32. Title 18, USC, sec. 1367: Interference with the Operation of a Satellite.
33. Title 18, USC, sec. 1651–1661: Piracy and Privateering.
34. Title 18, USC, sec. 1956: Money Laundering as it Relates to Terrorism Offenses.
35. Title 18, USC, sec. 1958: Murder for Hire by Persons Who Travel or Use Facilities in Interstate or Foreign Commerce with the Intent to Murder.
36. Title 18, USC, sec. 1959: Violent Crimes in Aid of Racketeering Activity.
37. Title 18, USC, sec. 1991, 1992: Railroads.
38. Title 18, USC, sec. 2151, et seq.: Sabotage.
39. Title 18, USC, sec. 2271–2281: Destruction of Vessels.
40. Title 18, USC, sec. 2331–2332: Terrorist Acts Abroad Against United States Nationals.
41. Title 18, USC, sec. 2332a: Use of Weapons of Mass Destruction.
42. Title 18, USC, sec. 2332b: Acts of Terrorism Transcending National Boundaries.
43. Title 18, USC, sec. 233d: Financial Transactions.
44. Title 18, USC, sec. 2339A: Providing Material Support to Terrorists.
45. Title 18, USC, sec. 2339B: Providing Material Support or Resources to Designated Foreign Terrorist Organizations.
46. Title 18, USC, sec. 2340A: Torture.
47. Title 18, USC, sec. 2381 et seq.: Treason, Sedition, and Subversive Activities.
48. Title 18, USC, sec. 3286: Extension of Statute of Limitation for Certain Terrorism Offenses.
49. Title 22, USC, sec. 2712: Controls over Certain Terrorism: Related Services.
50. Title 26, USC, Subtitle E, Chapter 53: Machine Guns, Destructive Devices and Certain Other Firearms.
51. Title 42, USC, sec. 2011–2284: Atomic Energy Act.
52. Title 49, USC, sec. 46501–46507: Aircraft Piracy.
53. Title 49, USC, sec. 46314: Entering Aircraft or Airport Area in Violation of Security Requirements.
54. Title 49, USC, sec. 80501: Damage to Transported Property.

OTHER AUTHORITIES RELATING TO THE FBI'S INVESTIGATIVE JURISDICTION IN TERRORISM CASES

PDD 39: Outlines the FBI's lead jurisdictional responsibilities in relation to terrorism.

PDD 62: Provides a framework for interagency cooperation under the coordinating authority of the FBI. Also appoints the FBI as lead agency for operational response to a weapon of mass destruction incident.

PDD 63: Provides objectives and goals for the U.S. in protecting our nation's critical infrastructures.

REFERENCES

Dempsey, James X.: Statement Before the U.S. Senate Committee on the Judiciary, Washington, DC, May 24, 1995. In Musch, Donald J. (Ed.): *Terrorism: Documents of International and Local Control, 14.* New York, Oceana Publications, 1997, p. 158.

Fact Sheet: *United States Policy on Counterterrorism PDD 39.* Annapolis, MD: The White House Office of the Press Secretary, 1985.

Fact Sheet: Los Angeles Police Department, Intelligence Functions and Objectives, Organized Crime Intelligence Division, Summer 1998. In Wright, Dick (Ed.): *Guidelines for the Criminal Intelligence Function.* Sacramento, California: Attorney General's Office, 1998.

Fact Sheet: The National Advisory Committee on Criminal Justice Standards and Goals, 1976, Intelligence Gathering Goals. In Wright, Dick (Ed.): Guidelines for the Criminal Intelligence Function. Sacramento: Attorney General's Office, 1998.

Federal Bureau of Investigation: Terrorism in the United States 1994 and 1995. In Musch, Donald J. (Ed.): *Terrorism: Documents of International and Local Control, 13.* New York: Oceana Publications, 1997, pp. 161–214.

——: Terrorism in the United States–Counter Terrorism Threat Assessment and Warning. In Alexander, Yonah, and Musch, Donald J. (Eds.): *Terrorism: Documents of International and Local Control: U.S. Perspectives,18.* New York: Oceana Publications, 1999, pp. 84–112.

——: *Terrorism in the United States: 1991.* Washington, DC: Terrorist Research and Analytical Center, 1991.

Lorch, Donatella and Murr, Andrew: The Real Y2K Fireworks. *Newsweek,* December 20, 1999, p. 32.

Luca, Robert J. (Ed.): *Criminal Intelligence Program for the Smaller Agency.* Sacramento, CA: California Peace Officers Association, 1998, pp. 2–53.

Netscape: *Introduction To Communicator 4.* Mountain View, CA: Netscape Communications Corporation, 1999.

Reno, Janet: Statement of the Attorney General before the Subcommittee on Technology, Terrorism and Government Information Committee on the Judiciary and Selected Committee on Intelligence, The Threat of Chemical and Biological Weapons. In Alexander, Yonah, and Musch, Donald J. (Eds.): *Terrorism: Documents of International and Local Control, 17.* New York: Oceana Publications, 2000, pp. 113–136.

Simon, Jeffrey D.: *The Terrorist Trap: America's Experience with Terrorism.* Bloomington, IN: University Press, 1994.

Struve, David E.: *Criminal Intelligence Guidelines.* Sacramento, CA: Attorney General's Office, 1994.

Thornburgh, Dick: *The Attorney General's Guidelines on General Crimes, Racketeering, Enterprise and Domestic Security and Terrorism.* Washington DC: Office of the Attorney General, 1989, pp. 3–12 (Also see: http://www.lectlaw.com/files/cjs03.htm)

United States Senate: Electronic Communications Privacy Act of 1986. Senate Report 99-541, 99th Congress, 2nd Session. Washington, D.C.: U.S. Senate, 1986.

Wright, Dick (Ed.): *Guidelines for the Criminal Intelligence Function.* Sacramento, CA: California Attorney General's Office, 1998.

Chapter 9

TERRORISM INCIDENT MANAGEMENT: STRATEGIES AND TACTICS

While the rights of the individual are integral to American society, unfortunately, they provide a ready-made shelter for terrorists. Terrorism, whether it is internationally or domestically based, is a cost-effective means of committing political crime and psychological intimidation (Alexander and Musch 2000). Thus it was that the year after the bombing of the federal building in Oklahoma City, former President Clinton gave a speech that emphasized the American resolve to combat terrorist activities:

> The forces of destruction prey on all that divide us. They forget that, for all our differences, so much unites us. Here in America's heartland and all over the world, most people want the same things: to live in peace, to be treated with dignity, to provide for themselves and their families, and to build a life better than their parents had, and pass on an even better one to their children. The lesson of Oklahoma City is that even the most horrible acts of terror are no match for those simple dreams and for the human spirit. (Clinton 1997: 6–7).

In keeping with the President's message of hope, this chapter has several objectives:

- To illustrate the chief objectives of U.S. anti-terrorist policy: intercepting terrorists before they can execute their plan; and aggressively prosecuting in federal court those who commit acts of terrorism.
- To explain the two components that compose the government's general organization response to terrorism: crisis management, led by the Department of Justice through the FBI; and consequence management, coordinated by the Federal Emergency Management Agency (FEMA).
- To describe three specific terrorist incident management strategies–prevention, threat assessment, domestic preparedness–as well as the tactics employed to create a unified national response to a weapons of mass destruction (WMD) incident.

STRATEGIES TO PREVENT TERRORIST INCIDENTS

Of the different strategies for the prevention of terrorist incidents, the most effective strategy comprises two complementary elements: a comprehensive strategy to prevent terrorist incidents, which involves a partnership between federal, state, local, and the private sector partnership to protect the American infrastructure; and criminal intelligence gathering, which seeks to arrest terrorists for any crimes they may commit in preparing a terrorist assault.

Partnerships for Protecting the Infrastructure from Terrorist Attack

On May 22, 1998, President Clinton ordered the strengthening of America's defenses against terrorism by bringing together the management of the agencies that would be impacted by a terrorist attack. This managerial partnership brought what is termed a "program-management" approach to the U.S. counterterrorism efforts. Presidential Decision Directives (PDD) 62 and 63 provide a national strategic plan that, in the event of a terrorist attack, is designed to prevent and/or limit damage to the cities, the economy, governmental operations, and the critical cyber infrastructures.

Combating Terrorism Directive PDD-62 established a new and more systematic approach to preventing terrorism by expanding and solidifying the anti-terrorist missions of many government agencies. It also clarified the activities and goals of the U.S. counterterrorism programs from intelligence gathering and apprehension, to prosecution. PDD-62 reinforced PDD-39, the Federal Response Plan (FRP) for terrorist incidents, enhanced our national response capabilities to terrorist incidents by establishing a means of protecting the computer-based systems at the center of the U.S. economy, and established the Office of the National Coordinator for Security, Infrastructure Protection, and Counterterrorism.

Critical Infrastructure Protection Directive PDD-63 calls for the protection of the U.S.'s vulnerable and interconnected infrastructure. This directive mandates immediate federal government action to reduce exposure to a terrorist attack of our telecommunication systems, banking and finance, energy, transportation, and essential government services. PDD-63 stresses the strategic necessity of establishing a taskforce relationship between government agencies responsible for combating terrorism and private-sector representatives and creates the possibility of a coordinated defense of the U.S. infrastructure. PDD-63 immediately established a national terrorist warning and response center, increased security to government systems, and set 2003 as the deadline to establish a reliable, interconnected, and secure private-sector information-system infrastructure (Executive Summary 2000). PDD-63 comprises six strategic points relating to the U.S. response to a terrorist attack:

1. *The Increasing Potential for Vulnerability:* The United States has the world's strongest military and the largest economy. Our economy and our military power are mutually reinforcing and dependent. In addition, they are increasingly interdependent upon a cyber-based information system. Because of these interdependent relationships between the military and economy, safeguards must be implemented to protect both systems from the vulnerability to nontraditional attacks on our cyber system (White Paper 2000).

2. *The President's Intent:* It is the intent of PDD-63 that every necessary measure is carried out to protect our critical infrastructures from vulnerability to terrorist attacks, both physical and cyber, and to establish clear goals and deadlines for the implementation of protective measures (White Paper 2000).

3. *National Goals in the Advent of a Terrorist Attack:* The national plan to defeat terrorist

---

Box 9.1

The National Coordinator

To achieve this new level of integration in the fight against terror, PDD-62 establishes the Office of the National Coordinator for Security, Infrastructure Protection, and Counterterrorism. The National Coordinator oversees the broad variety of relevant policies and programs including such areas as counterterrorism, protection of critical infrastructure, preparedness, and consequence management for weapons of mass destruction. The National Coordinator also works within the National Security Council, reports to the President through the Assistant to the President for National Security Affairs, and produces an annual Security Preparedness Report. The National Coordinator also provides advice regarding budgets for counterterror programs and assists in the development of guidelines that might be needed for crisis management (Fact Sheet 2000a).

---

attacks comprises a three-fold set of goals to protect the federal government's ability to perform essential national security missions while at the same time ensure the general public's health and safety; ensure that state and local governments are able to maintain order and provide the minimum essential public services; and ensure the ability of the private sector to provide essential telecommunications, energy, financial, and transportation services (White Paper 2000).

4. *A Public-Private Partnership to Reduce Vulnerability to Cyberterrorism:* A terrorist attack on the critical cyber infrastructure would greatly affect the public, the economy, and governmental services. It would be impossible for the U.S. government to secure the infrastructure from cyberterrorism without the assistance and consent of the private sector. This partnership must avoid programs that increase government regulation or expand unfunded government programs to the private sector (Clarke 2000).

5. *Guidelines:* The protection of the critical infrastructures is a responsibility shared by the federal government and the private sector. As technology within the infrastructure

changes rapidly, the protective measures designed to guard the system must adapt. It is the federal government's responsibility to guide this adaptation by encouraging international cooperation in managing the international threat of terrorism. Key presidential mandates are the following:

- The Congress shall be consulted for their input on how to best protect the U.S. infrastructure.
- Regulations designed to protect the infrastructure shall be implemented only if the marketplace fails to protect the health, safety, or well-being of the American people.
- The full resources of the government shall be available to ensure that infrastructure protection is established and maintained.
- All critical infrastructure protection plans shall include the needs and responsibilities of state and local governments and first responders, agencies responsible for the initial response to terrorist activity (White Paper 2000).

6. *The Structure and Organization:* The agencies within the federal government charged with protecting U.S. infrastructure will be

organized around four components with a representative of the rank of Assistant Secretary or higher. This representative will coordinate dissemination of the information in accord with the following guidelines:

- *The Lead Agencies for Sector Liaison,* which depending on the location in the country and the infrastructure vulnerability for that geographical area, will come from one of fifteen different agencies. The Agency representative will serve as the Sector Liaison Official (SLO) and will be paired with a private-sector representative who will serve as the Sector Coordinator (SC).
- *The Lead Agency for Special Functions* serves as the Functional Coordinator for their agencies' area of responsibility. The agency coordinators are from national defense, foreign affairs, intelligence, and law enforcement. With their foreign counterpart, as well as state and local law enforcement and intelligence gathering counterparts, these coordinators represent the action arm of PDD-63.
- *Interagency Coordination* is accomplished by the SLOs and SCs coordinating their efforts with representatives from other relevant departments and agencies, including the National Economic Council, which will meet and confer on the implementation of this directive under the auspices of the Critical Infrastructure Coordination Group (CICG). The National Coordinator (NC) chairs the CICG for Security, Infrastructure Protection, and Counterterrorism. The NC will then report to the Assistant to the President for National Security Affairs, who in turn, reports to the President.
- *The National Infrastructure Assurance Council* comprises the Lead Agencies, the National Economic Council, and the National Coordinator who will meet

with infrastructure providers and state and local governmental officials appointed by the President (White Paper 2000).

Support and Structure of Presidential Decision Directive-63

Our defense systems, communications, transportation, banking systems and government services are all dependent on elaborate computer-driven systems. As computers become even more closely integrated into these systems, cyberterrorism becomes an increasingly significant threat. Contrasting the physical attacks associated with traditional terrorism, cyberterrorism denotes virtual attacks aimed at disrupting, damaging, or destroying technology. Most often, these attacks take the form of viruses and hacks of computer systems. Thus, a critical element of PDD-63 is the protection of the U.S.'s information infrastructure from cyberterrorist attacks. Although the physical acts of terrorism are more widely covered, the most probable, and most serious attack against the United States is not the terrorist intent to cause physical mayhem, but the cyberterrorist. A recent White House Executive Summary seeks to explain the threat posed by the cyberterrorist, "The threat to American security can be as simple as a lap top computer in the hands of an individual or group that has discovered a way of circumventing our cyber security and safeguard systems" (Executive Summary 2000: 62).

To address the threat posed by cyberterrorism, PDD-63 directs the executive branch to assess the cyber vulnerabilities of the nation's critical infrastructures, including information, communications, energy, banking, commerce, transportation, water supply, emergency services, and public-health systems, as well as all levels of federal, state, and local government. PDD-63 directs the federal government to develop critical infrastructure security systems that can serve as a model for public- and private-information security. Because the knowledge of our vulnerabilities to cyberterrorist attack is dynamic, the plan to protect from these must be similarly dynamic (White Paper 2000).

The most direct means of protecting the U.S. infrastructure from cyberterrorist attacks would be to restrict access to the cybersystem, the most obvious of which is the Internet; however, to do so is inconsistent with the civil liberties guaranteed in the first amendment to the Constitution. Because the United States values the rights of the individual so highly, the steps taken by antiterrorist organizations to prevent and defeat terrorist activity must not infringe on an individual's rights, especially the individual's right to privacy. Consequently, safeguarding systems that contain personal information is a very high priority. These systems cannot be placed at risk in exchange for assurances that security objectives will someday be designed to protect the information systems from identity theft. The lead agency responsible for the protection and investigation of identity theft is the United States Secret Service.

One of the more sensational forms of cyberterrorism is the unauthorized attempt to intrude, or "hack," into government and industrial computer networks. In the past, cyberterrorist hackers were not deemed a significant threat. However, "now the stakes have grown more serious as cyberterrorists have committed industrial espionage theft, have been revenge seekers, vandals, and extortionists" (Executive Summary 2000: 62). The FBI has investigated incidents of cyberterrorism committed by individuals ranging in age and scope from juveniles trying to prove themselves, to adults affiliated with organized-crime groups, including terrorist cells, potentially hostile militaries, and foreign government intelligence services. Because of the

significant threat to our information systems network, additional management tools to help identify systems' vulnerability have been established as part of the plan to protect this critical infrastructure (Executive Summary 2000).

Three additional management components are identified in PDD-63 to support the structure and organization of the infrastructure protection system:

1. National Infrastructure Protection Center (NIPC or IPC) is operated by the FBI as a full-scale operations center that provides threat assessment, warning, and continual identification and protection of areas of vulnerability.
2. Partner members of the IPC include the United States Secret Service (USSS), the Department of Defense (DOD), the Central Intelligence Agency (CIA), and members of other lead agencies as needed. The IPC provides a national focal point for collecting and managing the information gathered through implementing PDD-63. Additionally, the IPC provides the principal means for ensuring a coordinated response to an incident, mitigating attacks, investigating threats, and coordinating emergency response to a suspected WMD incident.
3. Information Sharing and Analysis Center (ISAAC). The National Coordinator, working with the Sector Coordinators, Sector Liaison Officers, and the Economic Council in coordination and consultation with the owners and operators of critical infrastructures, will create a private information sharing and analysis network.

Although the strategies for preventing terrorist acts did not begin with the issuing of PDD-62 and 63, the directives demonstrate the magnitude of the terrorist threat. The NIPC provides for rapid threat assessment while adhering to the laws that govern the

---

Box 9.2

The Central Intelligence Agency's (CIA) Role in Terrorism Prevention

In contrast with the FBI's role to prevent and pursue terrorist activity within U.S. borders, the CIA plays an important role in preventing foreign terrorist attacks. Whereas the FBI is tasked with general law enforcement, the CIA is mission oriented and, therefore, less restrictive in its operational approach to intelligence collection (Wittes 1996).

The National Security Act of 1947, which created the CIA, reflected the concerns of former President Truman and Congress, neither of whom wanted to create an American version of the dreaded Nazi "Gestapo." This act specifically precludes the CIA from having anything to do with law enforcement or internal security (50 U.S.C. 403-3(d)(1)). PDD-63 helps to bridge the gap created by the National Security Act intelligence information sharing and analysis by the federal government with local law enforcement. Under this directive, the CIA is included in the process as the lead agency for foreign intelligence information. However, the CIA, in accordance with public law, does not have a domestic operational mission.

---

collection and sharing of intelligence information. As discussed in Chapter 8, law enforcement's operational activities and rules are designed to protect the individual's rights.

Since the implementation of PDD-63, the IPC has evolved into a twenty-four-hour watch presence maintained by the FBI, the National Security Systems Agency, the Defense Intelligence Agency, and the Defense Information Systems Agency. The IPC builds and enhances close ties with state and local law enforcement. This bringing together of federal, state, and local law enforcement investigators in combating domestic terrorism has resulted in the operational concept behind the creation of the Joint Terrorism Task Forces (JTTF).

Louis J. Freeh, former Director of the FBI, on January 28, 1998, testified before the Senate Select Committee on Intelligence to address the topic of threats to U.S. national security: "Though the national security threat from cyber-related issues is of concern, the FBI, with its private-and-public sectors partners, is building a fire wall of protection between malevolent actors and the critical U.S. infrastructure systems" (Freeh 1999: 85). One component of this firewall is The National Plan for Information Systems Protection (see Box 9.3).

TERRORISM PREVENTION: PROACTIVE CRIMINAL INVESTIGATIONS

Since 1995, there has been a growth of domestic and international terrorism and a parallel increase in the terrorist threat to U.S. citizens, military personnel, and government officials both home and around the world (FBI 1999). Unfortunately, there is no single tactic to prevent terrorism. However, one key anti-terrorist tactic is proactive investigation of potential terrorist activity. U.S. anti-terrorism policy recognizes that terrorists are criminals and will be investigated and brought to justice for their overt criminal acts (FBI 1999). The various statutes and presidential decision directives that address terrorism

Box 9.3
Overview of the National Plan for the Information Systems Protection

The plan's goal is to achieve a critical information systems defense with an initial operating capability by December 2000 and a full operating capability by May 2003. When that systems defense is in place, the United States should have achieved the capability to ensure that:

"Any interruption or manipulation of these critical functions must be brief, infrequent, manageable, geographically isolated, and minimally detrimental to the welfare of the United States" (President Clinton in PDD-63).

To meet the ultimate goal established by former President Clinton for defending the nation's critical infrastructures against deliberate attacks by 2003, the current version of the Critical Infrastructure Plan was designed around three broad objectives into which ten programs have been created to help achieve each objective:

Prepare and Prevent: those steps necessary to minimize the possibility of a significant and successful attack on the U.S.'s critical information networks, and build an infrastructure effective in the face of such attacks.

Program 1: Identify Critical Infrastructure Assets and Shared Interdependencies and Address Vulnerabilities

Detect and Respond: those actions required identifying and assessing an attack in a timely way, and then to contain the attack, quickly recover from it, and reconstitute affected systems.

Program 2: Detect Attacks and Unauthorized Intrusions

Program 3: Develop Robust Intelligence and Law Enforcement Capabilities to Protect Critical Information Systems, Consistent with the Law

Program 4: Share Attack Warning and Information in a Timely Manner

Program 5: Create Capabilities for Response, Reconstitution, and Recovery

Build Strong Foundations: the things we must do as a Nation to create and nourish the people, organizations, laws, and traditions which will make us better able to prepare and prevent, and detect and respond to attacks on our critical information networks.

Program 6: Enhance Research and Development in Support of Programs 1–5

Program 7: Train and Employ Adequate Numbers of Information Security Specialists

Program 8: Outreach to Make Americans Aware of the Need for Improved Cyber Security

Program 9: Adopt Legislation and Appropriations in Support of Programs 1–8

Program 10: In Every Step and Component of the Plan, Ensure the Full Protection of American Citizens' Civil Liberties. Their Rights to Privacy and Their Right to the Protection of Proprietary Data (Executive Summary 2000).

may be reduced to two far-reaching mandates: the effective management of investigative resources, and the protection of life and property. These complementary mandates can best be achieved through prevention (FBI 1997).

To appreciate the imminent terrorist threat, consider that in 1998, the FBI reported seventeen domestic terrorist incidents, twelve of which it successfully prevented.[50] Of the remaining five incidents, three occurred in the U.S. Commonwealth of Puerto Rico. The two remaining incidents involved a bombing allegedly committed by Eric Robert Rudolph, which left one off-duty police officer dead and a nurse seriously injured. The remaining incident involved an arson fire in Vail, Colorado, that caused an estimated twelve million dollars in damage. Shortly after the arson fires, the Earth Liberation Front (ELF), an extreme environmental movement, sent an e-mail to local universities, newspapers, and radio stations claiming responsibility for the fires (See Chapter 5). The ELF message further warned skiers to "choose other destinations until the resort discontinued its expansion efforts" (FBI 2000: 4). This incident demonstrates that domestic terrorism is as dangerous as international terrorism, although the latter often receives more media coverage.

In 1998, the FBI prevented twelve incidents of terrorism that included assassinations, bombings, and robberies. The following four examples of prevention cases show the general patterns of criminal conduct associated with a bombing, a chemical attack, and a deployment of a biological agent.

Case Study One: Altogether, nine domestic-terrorism attacks with multiple targets were prevented in the following cities: Montgomery, Alabama; St. Louis, Missouri; East St. Louis, Illinois; Los Angeles, California; Centralia, Illinois; and New York, New York. Of these attacks, one is worth special mention. Six members of the Aryan Nations formed a white supremacist group named The New Order, was modeled after The Order, a white supremacist group formed in the 1980s by Robert J. Mathews who died in a shoot-out with law enforcement (See Chapter 4). The New Order (TNO) was dedicated to Mathews's principle of racial hatred denouncing Jews, African Americans, and other "nonwhite" racial groups. The TNO planned violent criminal acts to further their white supremacist and anti-government agenda.

Between May 1997 and February 1998, members of the TNO entered into criminal conspiracies to commit the following felonies, which indicate probable terrorist action by planning:

- to rob an armored car in St. Louis, Missouri;
- to assassinate Morris Dees of the Southern Poverty Law Center by firing an antitank weapon into the center's Montgomery, Alabama, office;
- to poison the water supply near East St. Louis, Illinois, as a diversionary attack to divert law enforcement resources away from the planned bank robbery;
- to rob and kill several individuals in California for criticizing the Aryan Nations;
- to bomb the Simon Weisenthal Center in Los Angeles;
- to kill an outspoken African American radio talk-show host believing that his murder would start a racial riot in Los Angeles;

---

[50] The FBI makes a distinction between actual terrorist incidents that are carried out, and those incidents that were planned but prevented. Thus, in 1998, five terrorist incidents actually occurred and twelve prevented from occurring.

- to murder a former TNO member they believed was planning to leave their group and divulge their secrets; and
- to attack the New York office of the B'nai B'rith, a Jewish social service organization.

Between February 23 and 26, 1998, all six members of the TNO who conspired to commit these violent criminal acts were arrested in Illinois and Michigan and charged with weapons violations. Subsequent additional search warrants of their residences revealed explosives, bombmaking material, firearms, hand grenades, and a pipe bomb. The six TNO members were convicted of the weapons violations and were given prison sentences ranging from 20 to 87 months (FBI 2000).

Case Study Two: Lawrence A. Maltz, a physicist with over 20 years experience and who was known to suffer from manic-depression, repeatedly threatened to assassinate the directors of the FBI, the U.S. State Department, the Internal Revenue Service, as well as members of Congress and the President using biological, chemical, and nuclear devices. Because of these threats, the Secret Service interviewed Maltz several times. When Maltz's threats demonstrated that he possessed sufficient knowledge to execute them, the FBI conducted an extensive investigation of his activity.

During this investigation, the FBI discovered that Maltz had conducted research on the production of chemical nerve agents such as sarin. The FBI also obtained and analyzed copies of Maltz's formulas to produce the sarin and concluded that Maltz had created a viable formula for the production of sarin. The FBI investigation also disclosed the following overt acts:

- Maltz had contacted chemical companies regarding the purchase of the precursors

and chemical agents necessary to produce the nerve agent sarin.
- Maltz was growing increasingly committed to violent action, and he had developed a means to execute his threats.

The FBI arrested Maltz on April 8, 1998, for violations of Title 18 of the United States Code (USC) 2332a (threat to use a weapon of mass destruction). In September 1998, Maltz pleaded guilty to a lesser charge of violation of Section 18 USC 875 (mailing threatening communications). Maltz was sentenced to 16 months of incarceration followed by three years of supervised release (FBI 2000).

Case Study Three: Members of the militia group Republic of Texas (RoT), a secessionist organization, planned a biological attack targeting government officials. Through criminal intelligence gathering and investigation, a Texas-based FBI JTTF discovered the overt acts of three RoT members who were constructing a device to disburse toxins, which they planned to use to infect various government officials. An FBI investigation of the three revealed the following criminal acts indicating probable future terrorist activity:

- The purchase and/or collection of blood tainted with the AIDS virus.
- The purchase of materials necessary to construct WMD.
- The purchase and/or collection of blood tainted with rabies.
- The plan to obtain weapons grade biological-agent anthrax from a foreign country.

The suspects were arrested based on a sealed criminal complaint (held from public release until after the service of the arrest warrants) for violation of 18 USC 2332a (a threatened use of a weapon of mass destruction). On October 29, 1999, a jury found two RoT members guilty of two counts of threatening to use WMD against federal agents and their families.

Case Study Four: In July 1998, an individual who expressed strong anti-government sentiments approached a technical-school student regarding the construction of an explosive device to be used against an unspecified target in Washington, D.C. When the student notified the FBI of the individual's request, the FBI initiated an investigation that led to the execution of a search warrant of the individual's residence for bombmaking components and instructional materials.

During the search, agents discovered a circuit board with a timing circuit and electronic components used to construct a triggering device, as well as instructions about building the explosive device. The individual was questioned by the FBI and gave a sworn statement detailing his plan to build a bomb as well as identifying his potential targets. The individual pled guilty to violation of 18 USC 373 (the solicitation of another to use an explosive device to damage or destroy a building owned by the United States). The individual sentence could carry a 36-month prison term and three years of formal probation (FBI 2000).

STRATEGIES FOR THREAT ASSESSMENT

Throughout history, bombs and hand-held weapons have been the first choice of terrorists and assassins. Fortunately, these weapons pose a limited threat, and their damage is generally confined to a small area or single building and produce relatively few casualties, notwithstanding the Oklahoma City bombing. In contrast, even an improvised chemical or biological attack tends to produce far more casualties. Fortunately, these attacks require a level of scientific under-

standing by the terrorist that varies on a scale from no knowledge to a high degree of sophisticated intelligence.

The most common examples of chemical weapons requiring little specialized knowledge are toxic industrial-chemicals such as chlorine, phosgene, and hydrogen cyanide. More specialized knowledge is required for only a few biological agents (e.g., plague and small pox), which are communicable and can be spread beyond those directly affected by the weapon or dissemination device (Government Accounting Office (GAO) 2000b). The multiplication of threats and the necessarily limited resources of antiterrorist agencies necessitate a means to evaluate and prioritize terrorist threats.

Threat and risk assessment are central programs if anti-terrorist efforts are to be successful because they provide law enforcement managers with a way to prioritize programs to combat terrorism. The importance of these programs is underscored by former President Clinton's Fiscal Year 2000 budget, which included "dollars for counterterrorism programs, which was a three-billion dollar increase over the Fiscal Year 1999. Of the ten billion dollars, $8.6 billion were earmarked for combating terrorism and $1.4 billion were for critical infrastructure protection" (GAO 1999a: 3).

The budgeted money is targeted for a variety of programs to combat terrorism. Yet, according to the GAO, not all of these programs are initiated with a sound threat and risk assessment (GAO 1999a: 3). A 1999 GAO report cites a program by the Department of Health and Human Services to establish a national pharmaceutical and vaccine stockpile that was initiated without the benefit of sound threat and risk assessment process (GAO 1999a: 3). According to the GAO, no studies were conducted to determine if the biological agents with the greatest probability of use by terrorists would be blocked by the vaccines. The omission of this crucial piece of information suggests that the study was ill-conceived and that the attendant plan may be similarly flawed.

FBI Threat Analysis

Threat assessment is the collaborative product of many people from different governmental agencies at the federal, state, and local levels. Clearly, the response to a terrorist threat or incident requires a highly coordinated and well-managed team approach. Threat assessment procedures are, according to the FBI, most applicable before a terrorist attack. However, they can also have validity in postreported attacks by determining if an alleged biological weapon was used or a natural outbreak has occurred. In the case of a natural outbreak, a group might be trying to capitalize on the event. The FBI's threat assessment process has three components:

1. Does the organization or individual have the behavioral resolve to carry out the threatened attack? If the terrorist group was not known to carry out its threats, the threat would receive a low priority.
2. Is the operational probable? If a small, underfunded terrorist cell threatens to mount a nuclear attack (a very expensive undertaking), the threat would also receive a low assessment.
3. Is it technically feasible? If a terrorist cell were to threaten to poison water reservoirs, but the pathogen would not survive the environment, the threat would also receive a very low assessment (Benwell-Legeune 2000).

PDD-39 establishes the FBI as the lead agency concerning terrorist activities within the United States. The following core federal agencies support the FBI (Dalich 1999):

- Federal Emergency Management Agency– Lead Agency for Consequence Management
- Department of Defense
- Department of Energy
- Environmental Protection Agency
- Department of Health and Human Service (pp. 132–133).

Department of Justice/Federal Bureau of Investigation

The Attorney General is responsible for ensuring the development and implementation of policies directed at preventing domestic terrorist attacks and for the criminal prosecution of terrorist acts. The Attorney General has charged the FBI with managing federal responses to terrorism incidents that occur within the United States, its territories, and U.S. flagged ships in international waters.

The FBI coordinates any federal operational response (crisis management) and acts as the federal on-scene commander that coordinates the federal response with state and local authorities. The FBI executes its operational duties by joining the multi-agency unified command structure with the primary responsibilities of investigating and collecting evidence necessary to bring the terrorists to justice. In other words, the FBI may form and coordinate the deployment of a Domestic Emergency Support Team (DEST) with other agencies, when appropriate, and seek appropriate federal support if warranted.

Federal Emergency Management Agency (FEMA)

FEMA ensures that the Federal Response Plan (FRP) is adequate to respond to terrorism directed against populations in the

United States, including terrorism involving WMD. As a result, a Terrorism Incident Annex has been added to the FRP. Although the Federal Response Team (FRT) was established to provide an effective and coordinated federal response to natural disasters, such as earthquakes, fires, and storms, the terrorism annex to the FRP ensures the same high-level response to a manmade incident. As the lead agency for consequence management, FEMA supports the FBI with the planning and execution of functions undertaken to respond to the consequences of a terrorist incident. Additionally, FEMA designates appropriate liaison and advisory personnel for the Strategic Information and Operations Center (SIOC) and deployment with the DEST, the Joint Operations Center (JOC), and the Joint Information Center (JIC). FEMA directs and coordinates any federal emergency response to coordinate federal support of state and local authorities.

Department of Defense (DOD)

In accordance with DOD Directives and the Chairman Joint Chiefs of Staff CONPLAN 0300-97, DOD provides military assistance and/or Federal Response Plan Emergency Support Function to primary agencies during all aspects of a terrorist incident on approval by the Secretary of Defense. Initial DOD assistance involves the transport of urban search-and-rescue teams activated as needed by FEMA. Additional support could include emergency medical and morgue assistance, threat assessment, DEST deployment, technical advice, tactical operations, support to civilian law enforcement authorities in the event of civil disturbances, transportation, and disposal of a WMD device.

Department of Energy (DOE)

DOE provides scientific-technical personnel and equipment in support of all aspects of a nuclear/radiological WMD terrorist incident. DOE assistance supports both crisis- and consequence-management activities with capabilities such as threat assessment, DEST deployment, technical advice, forecasted modeling predictions, and operational support to include direct support of tactical operations. Deployable DOE scientific-technical assistance and support includes such capabilities as:

- Search Operations
- Access Operations
- Diagnostic and Device Assessment
- Radiological Assessment and Monitoring
- Material Identification
- Federal Protective Action Recommendations Development
- Information Provisions on the Radiological Response
- Render Safe or (make safe) Operations
- Hazards Assessment
- Containment, Relocation and Storage of Special Nuclear Material Evidence
- Post-incident Clean-Up
- On-Site Management and Radiological Assessment to the Public, the White House, and Members of Congress and Foreign Governments.

All DOE support for a federal response is coordinated through a Senior Energy Official.

Environmental Protection Agency (EPA)

The EPA provides technical personnel and support equipment on all aspects of a WMD terrorist incident. EPA assistance may include threat assessment, DEST and regional emergency response team deployment, technical advice, and operational support. EPA assistance and advice includes consultation, agent identification, hazard detection and reduction, environmental monitoring, sample and forensic evidence collection/analysis, assessment and clean-up, identification of contaminants, onsite safety, protection, prevention, and decontamination activities.

Additionally, the EPA and the United States Coast Guard (USCG) share responsibilities for responding to oil discharges into navigable waters and releases of hazardous substances, pollutants, and contaminants into the environment under the National Contingency Plan (NCP). EPA provides the predesignated Federal On-Scene Coordinator for inland areas and the USCG for coastal areas to coordinate containment, removal, and disposal efforts and resources during an oil, hazardous substance, or WMD incident.

Department of Health and Human Services (DHHS)

The DHHS is the primary agency under the FRP for the provision of health, medical, and health-related social services. DHHS provides technical personnel and support equipment to the Lead Federal Agency (LFA) during all aspects of a terrorist incident. DHHS assistance could support threat assessment, DEST deployment, epidemiological investigation, pharmaceutical support operations, technical advice, as well as operational medical and mental health services to the public.

Technical assistance and advice includes identification of contaminants, sample collection and analysis, onsite safety, medical management plans, health and medical care, and mass-fatality management. The Public Health Service (PHS) would activate the National Disaster Medical System to support local and state authorities in delivering direct medical care in the form of prehospital treatment, hospital evacuation, and in-hospital care casualties (GAO 1999b).

Threat Assessment Trends

Threat assessment and response to a terrorist incident is practiced by all of the agencies involved in our counterterrorism efforts. Although most terrorist attacks involve traditional explosives and firearms, the possibility that terrorists might use biological or chemical weapons cannot be ignored and has been the focus of the Domestic Preparedness Program, which focuses particularly on the possibility of biological weapons. The CIA and other members of the U.S. counterterrorism community consider the use of biological warfare agents and weapons as only a modest risk (See Chapters 1 and 7). The end of the Cold War and the fall of the Soviet Union resulted in an increased ability for terrorists and the sponsors of terrorism to acquire biological-warfare agents and weapons, as well as the technology and specific expertise to use these agents as WMD.

In his study on terrorist organizations and the potential use of biological weapons, Mick Donahue (1999) identified seven motivational trends that could lead a terrorist organization to committing WMD attacks:

1. *Belief in political goals:* The terrorist believes his/her political ideology is the only correct ideology and his/her operations are designed to make the government capitulate.
2. *Undermine government authority:* The terrorist believes that he/she can polarize the people against the government by destroying normal lifestyles, producing fear in the populace, and creating economic uncertainty.
3. *Justification for religious beliefs:* The terrorist believes that his/her religion mandates ex-

treme, violent action usually to "purify" his/her race or his/her country, or as preparation for the end of the world.

4. *Attract publicity and attention:* The terrorist believes that his/her actions will either attract public support to his cause or turn public support against an enemy of the cause.

5. *Express/redress a grievance:* The terrorist believes that when the government is unsympathetic to the people's demands, he/she is justified in using terrorism in order to gain the government's attention.

6. *Free Colleagues:* The terrorist believes that he/she can affect the release of a colleague by committing terrorist acts, which often includes the trading of hostages.

7. *Obtain Money:* The terrorist believes that he/she can obtain the necessary money to purchase weapons, supplies, and equipment by demanding money to stop certain criminal activities. Occasionally, the terrorist commits crimes solely for financial gain (pp. 25–26).

As with military operations, the physical environment will often dictate the terrorist's target and the tactics. In 1998, The U.S. Department of State (DOS), Office of Intelligence and Threat Analysis, Bureau of Diplomatic Security, indicated there were 131 attacks worldwide that targeted Americans; 93 involved terrorist attacks that killed or severely wounded Americans (DOS 2000 and GAO 2000d). These attacks largely involved the use of relatively cheap homemade devices.

Just as the environment will dictate the target and tactics, the types of terrorist groups and their ability to obtain financing also determines the target selection. For example, state-sponsored terrorist groups tend to select transnational targets that oppose their governmental regime. Non-state-sponsored groups pose a broader and more complex threat because they choose their targets for a

variety of reasons. When conducting threat analysis of general patterns of terrorist violence, it is possible to extrapolate from past incidents to identify likely future targets and methods of attack. For example, militia groups tend to target governmental buildings, employees, and community infrastructures to include power and fuel sources. Racist groups usually target members of other racial groups. Religious extremists may target anyone outside their faith. If religious extremism is paired with racist notions, the number of potential targets becomes quite large indeed.

STRATEGIES FOR DOMESTIC PREPAREDNESS

Conventional explosives and firearms continue to be the primary weapons of choice for terrorists. However, the bombings of the World Trade Center in New York City in 1993 and the federal building in Oklahoma City in 1995, as well as the nerve-agent attack in the Tokyo subway in 1995 heightened concerns about terrorist attacks and the possible use of chemical, biological, radiological, and nuclear weapons (CBRN). Terrorists, however, are still more likely to use conventional weapons because it is difficult to produce biological and chemical weapons and because the results of the attacks are often unpredictable. The Tokyo subway incident is a good example of the difficulties in weaponization and predictability of deploying a chemical agent. Aum Shinrikyo had established chemical laboratories in their attempt to produce a lethal toxic agent, but their inability to transform the agent sarin into a weapon testifies to the difficulty of producing and employing a chemical weapon.

As they prepare to thwart terrorist activity, U.S. law enforcement and intelligence agencies have to continuously assess both for-

---

Box 9.4
Criteria for Evaluating a Terrorist Target

"Law enforcement counterterrorist specialists who track terrorists' attacks have discovered that terrorists often choose their targets around six subjective criteria, or CARVER—which are as follows—Critically, Accessibility, Recoverability, Vulnerability, Effect, and Risk."

- *How critical is the target?* Is its functioning key to the continued suppression of the terrorist's goals?
- *Is the target accessible enough to complete the attack?*
- Are there points of *vulnerability* to allow for maximum damage to the target and do those vulnerabilities match the weapons and skills the terrorists' possess?
- What will be the anticipated *effect* on the group because of the attack?
- Will the local authorities be frightened by the possibility of more attacks, or will the act be so horrendous that the international community will collaborate in their apprehension?
- With the exception of suicide bombers whose fate is decided, the terrorist must also *assess the risk of capture* when analyzing a target (Donahue 1999: 31)

---

eign and domestic terrorist threats within the United States. In the Oklahoma City federal building bombing, it was clear that "in seconds a terrorist incident could result in the loss of 168 lives, leave thousands seriously injured, 30 children orphaned, 300 businesses destroyed, and throw government services into the midst of chaos" (Simank 2000: 523). Immediately after the bombing, the unified Incident Command System (ICS) was established:

> The city mayor, chief of police, fire chief, and the local special agent in charge (SAC) of the FBI met and made decisions on how Oklahoma City should proceed. The FBI took charge of the crime scene, the Oklahoma City Police sealed off the perimeter and assisted with evidence recovery and the fire department took charge of rescue and recovery efforts. Federal resources from the Federal Emergency Management Agency (FEMA) were requested for immediate response (Simank 2000b: 524).

Approximately 15 hours later, the first two of ten Urban Search and Rescue (USAR) task forces requested by FEMA, arrived at the scene (Simank 2000). The USAR teams before this incident were established by FEMA to assist in normal recovery efforts resulting from natural disasters, such as tornadoes, floods, hurricanes, and earthquakes. These teams had not been trained to work in a crime scene. The FBI almost immediately began on-the-job training of rescue personnel "in crime scene identification and evidence preservation, to include the issuing of photo I.D. to control access into the scene" (Simank 2000: 524). This unified response demonstrates the effectiveness of the operational guidelines established in PDD-63.

Logistically, the government agencies that first responded to the scene were overwhelmed in hours. However, the response of the community to this disaster was inspiring. The Oklahoma Restaurant Association

(ORA), which set up a food operation in the Convention Center to feed rescue personnel 24 hours a day, estimated they served 100,000 meals over nine days. A national pizza chain set up cooking operations onsite and served over 9,000 pizzas a day. Local cellular telephone providers donated 1,056 cellular phones and $1,000,000 of airtime usage per day at no charge to rescuers (Comeau 1996).

The Oklahoma City bombing resulted in the development of a Terrorist Incident Response Component to the Federal Response Plan. What was learned from this tragedy was that the damage starts at the point of impact then spreads outward in all directions. Unlike a natural disaster, terrorist incidents are considered a crime scene and must be protected by law enforcement. The local responders to a terrorist incident are the first and only responders and will have to be self-reliant for many hours after the incident. Therefore, training and the proper equipment are essential for first-responders. Clearly, incident command issues, funding sources, and logistical concerns have to be anticipated well in advance of an incident and made part of the federal, state, and local emergency response plans.

Following the bombing in Oklahoma City, the initial federal efforts to develop plans for programs and training initiatives lacked input from state and local responders. However, it rapidly became apparent that since federal support to a terrorist incident would not be available for hours, joint-training exercises combining local firefighters, law enforcement, and emergency medical responders would be needed nationwide to increase domestic preparedness to a terrorist incident.

The Defense against Weapons of Mass Destruction Act of 1996 (Public Law 104-201), also known as the Nunn–Lugar–Domenici Domestic Preparedness Program, was created to address the problems learned from Oklahoma City and establish the highest-level training possible for domestic preparedness to a terrorist attack. The Act authorized federal agencies to provide resources, training, and technical assistance to state and local emergency management personnel who would respond to a WMD terrorist incident. The Act mandated that the United States enhance its capability to respond to domestic terrorist incidents involving nuclear, biological, chemical, and radiological weapons.

This legislation designated the DOD as the interagency lead to carry out a program to train and advise civilian personnel from federal, state, and local agencies regarding emergency responses to a use or threatened use of WMD or related materials. This interagency effort resulted in the establishment of the "train-the-trainer" program we call the Domestic Preparedness Program (DPP).

In the planning stages of this program, it was agreed that training priority would be given to the largest population centers of the United States. This translated into a program plan to provide initial training and preparedness assistance for domestic WMD response for the 120 largest (according to 1990 census data) cities in the United States.

Federal, state, and local responders have evaluated the DPP training as excellent, but note the need for more unified and comprehensive training. The DOJ and DOD components of the DPP work close together in order to obtain the desired efficiency of training and equipment supply operations. According to a recent GAO report to Congress, the aggressive fiscal expenditures on DPP resulted in emergency first-responders having been trained in WMD awareness, operations, EMS response, and incident command. Over 201 federal counterterrorism exercises were sponsored by 26 government agencies and conducted in strategically located cities (GAO 2000c).

The first-responders were challenged by both conventional and WMD scenarios designed to prepare the intergovernmental agencies and private organizations with a variety of possible situations. "Four of these exercises included foreign government participation directed at creating international cooperation and exchanges of methodologies in dealing with WMD incidents" (GAO 2000c: 202). In each test, the DPP-trained teams responded superbly.

TACTICS TO CREATE A UNIFIED NATIONAL RESPONSE TO WEAPONS OF MASS DESTRUCTION

The Domestic Preparedness Training and Equipment Funding Programs target the emergency response to a WMD incident. Training local, state, and federal emergency responders, as well as law enforcement officers, to coordinate their efforts and resources under a unified command structure minimizes the effects of a WMD incident. Past fears of a hazardous materials (HAZMAT) team responding to a WMD biological incident, and not knowing what to do, have been set aside by superior first-responder training. As a veteran HAZMAT officer stated at the conclusion of his WMD domestic preparedness training, "Biological incidents are nothing more than HAZMAT's with an attitude" (Anonymous 1999).

The possibility that a WMD could be deployed against a large civilian population is a growing concern. The break-up of the Soviet Union and news reports of missing weapons grade biologicals and backpack-size nuclear weapons suggest that terrorists may have access to these weapons. The thought that these weapons might be vulnerable to theft has attracted the attention of many concerned citizens, including members of the U.S. Congress. The 104th Congress, in response to

growing concerns of an increasing terrorist threat, passed the following anti-terrorism legislation:

> The Domestic Preparedness Program funded training for first responders from law enforcement, fire HAZMAT teams, medical emergency responders and dispatchers to respond to a terrorist incident. The additional funding measures provides the training and supplying of equipment to law enforcement investigators, so that they are in compliance with the Occupational Safety and Health Administration (OSHA) 29 CFR 1910.120 training standards in the Environmental Protection Agency (EPA) 40 CFR 311 Hazardous Wastes Operations and Emergency Response (HAZWOPER) standards. (Davis 1998: 188–189)

While these standards predate the DPP, law enforcement officers conducting investigations and collecting evidence are now deemed necessary because of the threat posed by WMD biological/chemical agents. Therefore, agents of the FBI and other law enforcement officers investigating WMD cases must establish and work under an Emergency Response Plan (ERP) when executing search warrants on sites where WMD biological and/or chemical agents are suspected to be present. These regulations also require the establishment of the Incident Command System and the appointment of a site safety officer. The ERP must also address the following eleven components:

1. Pre-emergency planning and coordination with outside parties.
2. Personnel roles, lines of authority, training and communication.
3. Emergency recognition and prevention.
4. Safe distances and places of refuge.
5. Site security and control.
6. Evacuation routes and procedures.
7. Decontamination.
8. Emergency medical treatment and first aid.

9. Emergency alerting and response procedures.
10. Critique of response and follow-up.
11. Personal protection equipment (PPE) and emergency equipment (Lesak 1999: 18).

The FBI and members of the JTTF have or are in the process of receiving up to 200 hours of safety scientific and management training to effectively respond to the threats presented by WMD biological or chemical agents. Adopted from the National Fire Academy (NFA), the FBI and law enforcement officers assigned to terrorist WMD investigations utilize an operational decision-making and management process known as GEDAPER. The seven steps in the GEDAPER process are as follows:

1. *G*ather information
2. *E*stimate potential course and harm
3. *D*etermine appropriate strategic goals
4. *A*ssess tactical options and resources
5. *P*lan of action implementation
6. *E*valuate the effectiveness of the plan
7. *R*eview the process (Lesak 1999: 41).

Military intelligence officers during World War II simply state that to assess and predict an enemy's battle strategies simply stated, "you must know your enemy." This saying equally applies to the use of WMD biological or chemical agents by terrorists. The management of a search warrant site or the emergency response to a WMD biological or chemical incident requires safety planning, a selection of appropriate protective clothing, consideration of appropriate decontamination and disposal processes, as well as the protection and maintenance of public health and safety. Therefore, knowing something about the characteristics of selected biological or chemical agents is a critical information component to an effective WMD credibility assessment and response. According to the GAO, the biological and chemical agents described in Box 9.5 were selected by experts in biological and chemical warfare, science, intelligence, law enforcement, and medicine as among those most likely to be employed in a terrorist attack (GAO 2000b):

Because this GAO report details the characteristics of selected chemical and biological agents and notes the likelihood of their use by terrorists, it is helpful in developing a risk assessment, establishing threat levels, as well as assessing the training and equipment requirements of the first-responders. Chemical and biological threat and risk assessments vary from city to city for environmental and other reasons. Therefore, Section 1404(A) of the National Defense Authorization Act for Fiscal Year 1999 provides that:

> The Attorney General, in consultation with the Director of the Federal Bureau of Investigation and representatives of appropriate federal, state and local agencies, shall develop and test methodologies for assessing the threat and risk of terrorist employment of WMD against cities and other local areas. The results of the test may be used to determine the training and equipment requirements under the program developed under section 1402. The methodologies required by this subsection shall be developed using cities or local areas selected by the Attorney General, acting in consultation with the Director of the Federal Bureau of Investigation and appropriate representatives of federal, state and local agencies. (Colgate 2000: 439–440)

This provision allows for necessary flexibility in assessing and responding to terrorist threats.

Biological Weapons

The Biological Weapons Convention (BWC) of 1972 has been signed by 140 state parties with another 12 additional nations having signed but not ratified the accord

Box 9.5
Characteristics of Selected Chemical Agents for Use by Terrorists

Choking Agents with Low Lethality

1. Chlorine (CL): An industrial product that does not require precursors. CL is a likely agent due to its availability as a commercial product.
2. Phosgene (CG): An industrial product that does not require precursors. CG is a likely agent due to its availability as a commercial product.

Nerve Agents with High Lethality

1. Tabun (GA): This product is not readily available. The precursors are available and with manufacturing instructions, it is relatively easy to manufacture. GA is a likely agent due to the availability of precursor chemicals and relative ease of manufacture.
2. Sarin (GB): This is a moderately difficult agent to manufacture. The precursor chemicals are covered by the chemical weapons convention (CWC). GB is a likely agent due to the demonstrated use by Aum Shinrikyo in the Tokyo subway incident.
3. GF: This is a moderately difficult agent to manufacture and the precursor chemicals are covered by the CWC. This agent is not likely to be used as an agent by terrorists.

Nerve Agent with Very High Lethality

1. VX: This product is difficult to manufacture. The precursor chemicals are covered by the CWC. This is not likely to be used by terrorists.

Blood Agents with Low to Moderate Lethality

1. Hydrogen Cyanide (AC): This is an industrial readily available chemical. The precursor chemicals are covered by the CWC. This chemical is likely to be used as a terrorist agent due to its availability as a commercial product. Precursor availability, however, may be a problem.
2. Cyanogen Chloride (CK): This product is not easily produced. It is available as a commercial product, although precursor availability may be a problem. This is a likely terrorist agent.

Blister Agents with Lethality Based on Dose

1. Sulfur Mustard (HD): This product is easy to synthesize. Large quantity purchases of the precursor chemicals would be very difficult without detection as they are covered by the CWC. It is not likely that a terrorist would choose this chemical agent.
2. Nitrogen Mustard (HN-2): This product is easy to synthesize. However, buying large quantities of the precursors would be very difficult because they are covered by the CWC. It is not likely that this agent would be used by a terrorist.
3. Nitrogen Mustard (HN-3): Same as HN-2.
4. Lewisite (L, HL): This product is moderately difficult to produce and very difficult to obtain the necessary precursor chemicals. It is not likely that this agent would be used by a terrorist.

Box 9.5 *Continued*

Characteristics of Selected Biological Agents for Use by Terrorists

Bacterial Agents

1. Inhalation Anthrax: This agent is difficult to obtain in a virulent seed stock and to successfully process and disseminate. The spores are very stable and resistant to sun, heat and some disinfectants. Lethality is very high and virtually always fatal once symptomatic. A vaccine is available but must be used shortly after exposure. This is a possible choice for a terrorist biological agent, but requires sophistication to effectively manufacture and disseminate to create mass casualties. Use of this agent could indicate state sponsorship.

2. Plague: Plague seed stock is very difficult to acquire, successfully process, and disseminate. The plague spores can be long lasting with a very high lethality rate. Heat, disinfectants and direct sun can render the spores harmless. This is a possible agent, but not a likely terrorist choice as it is difficult to acquire and very difficult to weaponize.

3. Glanders: Glanders seed stock is very difficult to acquire and moderately difficult to process. It is very stable with a moderate to high lethality. No vaccine is available. This is a potential agent but not a likely choice for a non-state-sponsored terrorist.

4. Tularemia: Tularemia is difficult to acquire and process. It is unstable and killed by mild heat and disinfectants. Antibiotics are very effective in early treatment. This is a potential agent but not a likely choice as it is unstable and effectively treated with a new drug (IND).

5. Brucellosis: Brucellosis is difficult to acquire and produce with long incubation periods and low lethality. While it is very stable in wet soil and food, it can be treated with antibiotics. This is not a likely choice as an agent for a terrorist.

6. Q Fever (Rickettisai Organism): Q Fever is very difficult to acquire, produce, and weaponize. It has a very low lethality when treated with antibiotics. This is not a likely choice as an agent for a terrorist.

Viral Agents

1. Hemorrhagic Fever (e.g., Ebola): The Hemorrhagic Fever viral agents are very difficult to obtain, process and very unsafe to handle. Lethality can be very high depending on the strain. This is a very unlikely choice agent for a terrorist.

2. Smallpox: The only sources for smallpox seed stock are known to be secured in the United States and Russia. It is very stable with a moderate to high lethality rate. Can be treated with limited effectiveness. This is a very high consequence agent. This is not a likely terrorist agent due to limited access to the pathogen.

3. Venezuelan Equine Encephalitis: This is a difficult to obtain viral agent that is easily processed and weaponized. As an agent, it is relatively unstable and can be destroyed by heat and disinfectants. It has a low lethality rate and a vaccination with an Investigational New Drug (IND) is available. It is not a likely terrorist agent.

Box 9.5 *Continued*

Toxins

1. Ricin: Ricin is made from the caster bean and is readily available. It is moderately easy to process but requires quantities for a mass casualty result. Ricin is stable and with a very high lethality rate. Ricin is the agent of choice for an assassination not a terrorist mass casualty agent.
2. Botulinum (Types A-G): Botulinum is not widely available in a high toxin state. It is not easy to process or weaponize. Without respiratory support, it is highly lethal. Treatment with antitoxin and respiratory support is an effective treatment. There is a very low likelihood that this would be a terrorist agent of choice due to its low lethality and lack of transmissibility.

   Note: This is not a complete list of all the chemical or biological agents that might be used by a terrorist (GAO 2000b: 430 and 435).

(Franz 2001). The BWC prohibited the development, production, and stockpiling of bacteriological (biological) and toxin weapons. If BWC were followed by the signatories, then the availability of WMD to domestic terrorist theoretically would be diminished. However, the U.S. government believes that Russia, Iraq, China, Syria, Iran, Egypt, and Libya have engaged in activity that violates some, if not all, parts of the BWC (Franz 2001).

Following the Gulf War, the United States and the United Nations Special Commission (UNSCOM) on Iraq were in an excellent position to conduct a BWC compliance inspection of Iraq as a 1972 signatory to the BWC. During the UNSCOM inspections, examiners gathered site data and compiled a clear picture of the direction and extent of Iraq's Biological Weapons Program. From the UNSCOM inspections, it was learned that Iraq had produced 90,000 liters of botulinum toxin, produced 8,300 liters of anthrax, and an agent that causes cancer; loaded Botulinum toxin and anthrax on SCUD missiles and aerial bombs; and conducted research on mycotoxins and infectious viruses (Franz 2001).

The past incidents of WMD biological terrorism in the United States have been centered on the actions of religious fanatic groups, neo-Nazi extremists and militia groups. Some recent incidents of biological terrorism are the following:

- *1993:* The Muslim fundamentalists who bombed the World Trade Center building had packed their bomb with cyanide in an attempt to spread the poison throughout the building. This was ineffective as the heat generated from the blast vaporized the cyanide.
- *1995:* Two members of the Minnesota Patriots Council, a right-wing militia organization, were convicted for planning to use ricin in their plot to violently overthrow the U.S. government.
- *1995:* Aum Shinrikyo members planned to launch a lethal sarin attack at Disneyland in California over a crowded Easter vacation weekend.
- *1995:* Larry Wayne Harris, a member of the white supremacist organization Aryan Nations was arrested for forgery and receiving stolen property after attempting to

obtain three vials of freeze-dried bubonic plague bacteria.

- *1995:* Thomas Louis Lavy, an Arkansas survivalist, was charged with attempting to smuggle 130 grams of ricin across the Alaska and Canadian borders.

In addition in 1997, the FBI investigated 73 cases involving suspected WMD threats, most of which were false reports. These reports involved the use of chemical and/or biological agents. False WMD reports pose a significant problem to government emergency services because a significant amount of human and other resources must be deployed to investigate each threat. In today's society, with public Internet access to scientific explanations of WMD technology, terrorists and other criminals can obtain sufficient technical information to force the FBI to classify their threat as high risk.

Because of PDD-39 and the Domestic Preparedness Program, these false reports trigger large, highly trained, equipped, and coordinated federal, state, and local responses under a unified-command system. The increase in false WMD reports and the expenditure of hundreds of thousands of dollars caused U.S. criminal law to include a provision for prosecuting threatened terrorist acts. Title 18 of the U.S.C. Section 2332(a) makes it a felony to threaten to use WMD. This section carries a ten-year prison term and has an eight-year statute of limitation. The primary investigative authority for cases involving the threatened use of a WMD is the FBI.

SUMMARY

The rich, interconnected U.S. infrastructure is susceptible to several forms of terrorist attack. Thus, the creation of any anti-terrorist policy must require coordination at all levels of U.S. government with state and local law enforcement agencies, as well as with private industry. In addition, anti-terrorist policies must also respect all citizens' civil liberties.

The chief objectives of the U.S. anti-terrorist plan are to intercept the terrorists before they can execute their plan and to aggressively prosecute in federal courts those who successfully implement a terrorist act. In the context of anti-terrorism objectives at least three policies are especially significant: PDD-39, which designates the FBI as lead agency for combating terrorism; PDD-62, which establishes a systematic approach to terrorism prevention; and PDD-63 which establishes the six key elements of U.S. anti-terrorism policy.

The federal response to terrorism is divided into two functional components: (1) crisis management led by the Department of Justice through the FBI; and (2) consequence management coordinated by FEMA. Under FEMA's coordination and support, state and local governments protect public health and safety and restore essential government services. FEMA also provides for emergency relief to governments, businesses, and individuals affected by the consequences of an act of terrorism (Reno 1999: 126).

Because anti-terrorist resources are limited, to defeat terrorist activity it is necessary that the FBI be able to ascertain the risk of each threat. To this end, the FBI has implemented a process to assess terrorist threats whereby it is able to deploy its resources more effectively. To defeat both traditional terrorist attacks as well as attacks employing WMD, government and local officials attend an extensive training program created under the DPP that has been largely successful.

Although bombing and assassination attempts continue to dominate terrorist threats, there is a growing concern about terrorists deploying WMD. However, the specialized knowledge required both to manufacture and to successfully deploy these devices mitigates threats of terrorists successfully deploying them. However, as the Aum Shinrikyo sarin attack in a Tokyo subway demonstrated, WMD attacks do constitute an increasing threat.

Ultimately, if anti-terrorism efforts are to be successful, they must remain flexible. To this end, the anti-terrorist policy is dynamic and able to adjust itself to respond to any terrorist act: cyber or physical, conventional weapons or WMD, individual or the work of a large, well-funded cell.

DISCUSSION QUESTIONS

1. Since the vast majority of past terrorist incidents in the United States have involved conventional weapons, why should the U.S. government spend billions of dollars for WMD Domestic Preparedness Programs?
2. Describe and discuss a likely WMD scenario employing a biological weapon.
3. Describe and discuss a likely WMD scenario employing a chemical weapon.
4. In the past, terrorist groups have not used WMD biological or chemical weapons for fear of losing public support, membership, and funding. Why would terrorist groups now be willing to use WMD?
5. Of state-sponsored, transnational, and domestic terrorism, what groups pose the greatest threat to the United States?
6. The prevention of terrorist acts and treating a terrorist as a criminal are the highest priorities in the U.S. counterterrorism policy. What could be done to strengthen U.S. policy against domestic terrorism?

STUDY QUESTIONS

1. The key provisions of the 1996 Antiterrorism Act states that members of named groups may not enter the United States, transact business, or solicit funds. In a free and open society, how do we prevent terrorists from raising money, recruiting supporters, and meeting with their followers? (Antiterrorism and Effective Death Penalty Act of 1996, Public Law No. 104-132)
2. In a free society, how far should the government go to defeat terrorists' objectives and to protect its citizens?
3. What are the State Department's selection criteria for generating a list of foreign terrorist organizations? Is the list fair and complete?
4. Given the threat that biological and chemical WMD pose to the United States, what is the importance of improved intelligence gathering and threat analysis?
5. Should U.S. anti-terrorism policies and capabilities regarding the prevention, determent, and response to biological and chemical WMD be changed? Please explain why or why not.
6. What are the strong points of U.S. anti-terrorism policy? What are its weaknesses?

REFERENCES

Alexander, Yonah and Musch, Donald: Preface. In Alexander, Yonah and Musch, Donald J. (Eds.): *Terrorism Documents of International and Local Control–U.S. Perspectives.* New York: Oceana Publications, 2000, pp. 1–2.

Anonymous: Personal statement (one of Jeff's trainees made the comment). October 1999.

Benwell-Legeune, Peter: Conference on Countering Biological Terrorism, Panel 3: Consequence Management. In Alexander, Yonah, and Musch, Donald J. (Eds.): *Countering Biological Terrorism in the U.S.: An Understanding of Issues and Status.* New York: Oceana Publications, 1999, pp. 327–356.

Clark, Richard A.: National Coordinator for Security, Infrastructure Protection and Counterterrorism, Message from the National

Coordinator. In Alexander, Yonah, and Musch, Donald J. (Eds.): *Terrorism: Documents of International and Local Control–U.S. Perspectives.* New York: Oceana Publications, 2000, pp. 56–60.

Clinton, William Jefferson: Defeating the Forces of Destruction: A National Security Priority, Oklahoma City, April 5, 1996. In Alexander, Yonah, and Musch, Donald J. (Eds.): *Terrorism: Documents of International and Local Control–U.S. Perspectives.* New York: Oceana Publications, 1997, pp. 3–7.

Colgate, Stephen R.: Department of Justice letter to Mark E. Gebicke, July 16, 1999. In Alexander, Yonah, and Musch, donald J. (Eds.): *Terrorism Documents of International and Local Control–U.S. Persepctives.* New York: Oceana Publications, 2000, pp. 439–440.

Comeau, Edward: *NFPA Fire Investigation Report: Rescue Operations Report, Oklahoma City, Oklahoma, April 19, 1995.* Quincy, MA: NFPA Fire Investigations, 1996.

Dalich, Michael J.: Statement Before the Subcommittee on National Security, International Affairs, and Criminal Justice Committee on Government Reform and Oversight, U.S. House of Representatives, October 2, 1998. In Alexander, Yonah, and Musch, Donald J. (Eds.): *Terrorism: Documents of International and Local Control–U.S. Perspectives.* New York: Oceana Publications, 1999, pp. 132–133.

Davis, Zachary S.: Weapons of Mass Destruction: New Terrorist Threat, January 8, 1997. In Alexander, Yonah, and Musch, Donald J. (Eds.): *Terrorism: Documents of International and Local Control–U.S. Perspectives.* New York: Oceana Publications, 1998, pp. 181–191.

Department of State: Political Violence Against Americans, 1998. In Alexander, Yonah, and Musch, Donald J. (Eds.): *Terrorism: Documents of International and Local Control–U.S. Perspectives.* New York: Oceana Publications, 2000, pp. 97–100.

Donahue, Mick: Terrorist Organizations and the Potential Use of Biological Weapons. In Alexander, Yonah, and Musch, Donald J. (Eds.): *Terrorism: Documents of International and Local Control–U.S. Perspectives.* New York: Oceana Publications, 1999, pp. 21–34.

Executive Summary: The White House, National Plan for Information System Protection: Defending America's Cyberspace. In Alexander, Yonah, and Musch, Donald J. (Eds.): *Terrorism: Documents of International and Local Control–U.S. Perspectives.* New York: Oceana Publications, 2000, pp. 61–94.

Fact Sheet: Combating Terrorism: PDD 62, The White House, May 22, 1998. In Alexander, Yonah, and Musch, Donald J. (Eds.): *Terrorism: Documents of International and Local Control–U.S. Perspectives.* New York: Oceana Publications, 2000a, pp. 19–20.

——: Funding for Domestic Preparedness and Critical Infrastructure Protection–Response to Terrorism, the White House Office of the Press Secretary, January 22, 1999. In Alexander, Yonah, and Musch, Donald J. (Eds.): *Terrorism: Documents of International and Local Control–U.S. Perspectives.* New York: Oceana Publications, 2000a, pp. 21–22.

Federal Bureau of Investigation: Policy and Guidelines–Terrorism in the United States. In Alexander, Yonah, and Musch, Donald J. (Eds.): *Terrorism: Documents of International and Local Control–U.S. Perspectives.* New York: Oceana Publications, 1999, pp. 85–86.

——: Terrorism in the United States, 1995. In Alexander, Yonah, and Musch, Donald J. (Eds.): *Terrorism: Documents of International and Local Control–U.S. Perspectives.* New York: Oceana Publications, 1997, pp. 193–214.

——: *Terrorism in the United States 1998.* Washington, D.C.: Counter-terrorism Threat Assessment and Warning Unit, National Security Division, 2000, pp. 5–7.

Franz, David: Lecture on Biological Weapons. Aniston, AL: *Center for Domestic Preparedness,* March 5, 2001.

Freeh, Louis J.: Statement for the Record Before the Senate Select Committee on Intelligence. In Alexander, Yonah, and Musch, Donald J. (Eds.): *Terrorism: Documents of International and Local Control–U.S. Perspectives.* New York: Oceana Publications, 1999, pp. 67–96.

Gebicke, Mark E.: Statement Before the Subcommittee on Oversight and Investigations House Transportation and Infrastructure Committee, U.S. House of Representatives, Hearing on

Preparedness Against Terrorist Attacks. In Alexander, Yonah, and Musch, Donald J. (Eds.): *Terrorism: Documents of International and Local Control–U.S. Perspectives.* New York: Oceana Publications, 2000, pp. 533–547.

General Accounting Office: *Combating Terrorism: Observations on Federal Spending to Combat Terrorism.* Washington, D.C. GAO/T-NSIAD/GGD-99-107, 1999a, p. 3.

——: Combating Terrorism–Federal Agencies Efforts to Implement National Policy and Strategy, September 1997, GAO/NSIAD-97-254. In Alexander, Yonah, and Musch, Donald J. (Eds.): *Terrorism: Documents of International and Local Control–U.S. Perspectives.* New York: Oceana Publications, 1999b, pp. 189–259.

——: Combating Terrorism–Issues to be Resolved to Improve Counter-terrorism Operations, GAO Report to Congress, May 1999. In Alexander, Yonah, and Musch, Donald J. (Eds.): *Terrorism: Documents of International and Local Control–U.S. Perspectives.* New York: Oceana Publications, 2000a, pp. 191–219.

——: Combating Terrorism–Need for Comprehensive Threat and Risk Assessments of Chemical and Biological Attacks, September 1999. In Alexander, Yonah, and Musch, Donald J. (Eds.): *Terrorism: Documents of International and Local Control–U.S. Perspectives.* New York: Oceana Publications, 2000b, pp. 408–440.

——: Combating Terrorism–Use of National Guard Response Teams is Unclear, GAO report to Congress May 1999. In Alexander, Yonah, and Musch, Donald J. (Eds.): *Terrorism: Documents of International and Local Control–U.S. Perspectives.* New York: Oceana Publications, 2000c, pp. 222–263.

——: Threat and Risk Assessment can Help Prioritize and Target Program Investments, April 1998, GAO/NSIAD-98-74. In Alexander, Yonah, and Musch, Donald J. (Eds.): *Terrorism: Documents of International and Local Control–U.S. Perspectives.* New York: Oceana Publications, 2000d, pp. 333–366.

Lesak, David M.: *Hazardous Materials Strategies and Tactics.* New Jersey: Prentice Hall, 1999.

Public Law 50 USC 403-3(d)(1). The Establishment of the CIA.

Reno, Janet: Statement Before the Subcommittee on Technology, Terrorism and Government Information on the Threat of Chemical and Biological Weapons, April 22, 1998. In Alexander, Yonah, and Musch, Donald J. (Eds.): *Terrorism: Documents of International and Local Control–U.S. Perspectives.* New York: Oceana Publications, 1999, pp. 113–130.

Simank, Ann: Testimony Before the House Subcommittee on Oversight, Investigations and Emergency Management, June 9, 1999. In Alexander, Yonah, and Musch, Donald J. (Eds.): *Terrorism: Documents of International and Local Control–U.S. Perspectives.* New York: Oceana Publications, 2000, pp. 523–531.

White Paper: The Clinton Administration's Policy on Critical Infrastructure Protection: Presidential Decision Directive 63, May 22, 1998. In Alexander, Yonah, and Musch, Donald J. (Eds.): *Terrorism: Documents of International and Local Control–U.S. Perspectives.* New York: Oceana Publications, 2000, pp. 3–16.

Wittes, Benjamin: Blurring the Lines between Cops and Spies. *Legal Times 20,* September 1996.

ADDITIONAL INFORMATION

United States Department List of Foreign Terrorist Organizations

1. Abu Nidal Organization
2. Abu Sayyaf Group
3. Armed Islamic Group
4. Aum Shinrikyo
5. Euzkadi Ta Askatasuna
6. Democratic Front for the Liberation of Palestine–Hawatmeh Faction
7. HAMAS
8. Harakat ul-Ansar
9. Hisbollah
10. Gamma'a al-Islamiyya
11. Japanese Red Army
12. al-Jihad
13. Kach

14. Kahane Chai
15. Khmer Rouge
16. Kurdistan Workers' Party
17. Liberation Tigers of Tamil Eelam
18. Manuel Rodriguez Patriotic Front Dissidents
19. Mujahedin-e Khalq Organization
20. National Liberation Army
21. Palestine Islamic Jihad–Shaqaqi Faction
22. Palestine Liberation Front–Abu Abbas Faction
23. Popular Front for the Liberation of Palestine
24. Popular Front for the Liberation of Palestine–General Command
25. Revolutionary Armed Forces of Columbia
26. Revolutionary Organization 17 November
27. Revolutionary People's Liberation Party/Front
28. Revolutionary People's Struggle
29. Shining Path
30. Tupac Amaru Revolutionary Movement

Trade and Foreign Assistance Legislation

- Foreign Assistance Act of 1961, as Amended
  Prohibited the provision of U.S. assistance to foreign countries whose governments support terrorism (22 U.S.C. 2371, as amended).
- Arms Export Control Act, as Amended (Formerly the Foreign Military Sales Act of 1968)
  Prohibited various transactions with foreign countries that support acts of terrorism, such as exports of any munitions items or the provision of credits, guarantees, or other financial assistance to those countries (22 U.S.C. 2780, as amended).

- International Financial Institutions Act (1977)
  Directed that the U.S. government, while participating in enumerated international financial institutions, shall seek to channel assistance to countries other than those whose governments provide refuge to individuals that commit acts of international terrorism by hijacking aircraft (Title VII, P.L. 95–118).
- 1978 Amendments to the Bretton Woods Agreements Act
  Required the U.S. Executive Director to the International Monetary Fund to oppose the extension of any financial or technical assistance to any country that supports terrorist activities (P.L. 95-435).
- Export Administration Act of 1979
  Listed compatibility with U.S. efforts to counter international terrorism as a factor in determining whether certain controls should be imposed for a particular export license on foreign policy grounds (P.L. 96-72, sec. 6).
- International Security and Development Cooperation Act of 1985
  Authorized the President to ban the import into the United States of any good or service from any country that supports terrorism or terrorist organizations (Part A of Title V, P.L. 99-83).
- Iraq Sanctions Act of 1990
  Classified Iraq as a terrorism-supporting foreign country and imposed U.S. export controls and foreign assistance sanctions (P.L. 101-513, sec. 586).
- Iran–Iraq Arms Non-Proliferation Act of 1992
  Suspended foreign assistance military and dual-use sales to any foreign country whose government knowingly and materially contributes to Iran's or Iraq's efforts to acquire advanced conventional weapons (Title XVI, P.L. 102-484).

- 1996 Amendment to Export-Import Bank Act
  Restricted the President from granting special debt relief regarding any Export-Import Bank loan or guarantee to any country whose government has repeatedly supported acts of international terrorism (P.L. 103-87, sec. 570).
- Middle East Peace Facilitation Act of 1994
  Allowed the President to suspend for six-month periods, until July 1995, any previously passed restrictions on U.S. assistance to the Palestinian Liberation Organization (Part E of Title V, P.L. 103-236).
- Spoils of War Act of 1994
  Prohibited the transfer of spoils of war in the possession of the United States to any country that the Secretary of State has determined to be a nation whose government has repeatedly supported acts of international terrorism (Part B of Title V, P.L. 103-236).
- Foreign Operations, Export Financing, and Related Programs Appropriations Act for Fiscal Year 1995
  Prohibited the direct funding of any assistance or reparations to certain terrorist countries such as Cuba, Iraq, Libya, Iran (Title V, P.L. 103-306).
- 1996 Amendments to the Foreign Assistance Act of 1961 and the Arms Export Control Act
  Removed certain restrictions on the manner in which antiterrorism training assistance could be provided (Chapter 3 of Title I, P.L. 104-164).
- 1996 Amendments to the Trade Act of 1974
  Required the President to withhold General System of Preference designation as a beneficiary developing country entitled to duty free treatment, if the country is on the Export Administration Act's terrorist list, or if the country

has assisted any individual or group that has committed an act of international terrorism (P.L. 104-295, sec. 35).
- Iran and Libya Sanctions Act of 1996
  Required the President to impose sanctions against companies that make investments of more than $40 million in developing Iran's or Libya's oil resources (P.L. 104-172, sec. 5).

State Department and Related Foreign Relations Legislation

- Act for the Protection of Foreign Officials and Official Guests of the United States (1972)
  Established as a federal crime the murder or manslaughter of foreign officials and official foreign guests (Title I, P.L. 92-539).
- Act for the Prevention and Punishment of Crimes Against Internationally Protected Persons (1976)
  Provided federal jurisdiction over assaults upon, threats against, murders of, or kidnapping of U.S. diplomats overseas (P.L. 94-467).
- Act for the Prevention and Punishment of the Crime of Hostage-Taking (1984)
  Imposed punishment for taking a hostage, no matter where, if either the terrorist or the hostage is a U.S. citizen, or if the purpose is to influence the U.S. government (Part A of Ch. XX, P.L. 98-473).
- 1984 Act to Combat International Terrorism
  Offered cash awards to anyone who furnishes information leading to the arrest or conviction of a terrorist in any country, if the terrorist's target was a U.S. person or U.S. property (Title I, P.L. 98-533).

- Omnibus Diplomatic Security and Antiterrorism Act of 1986

  Provided extraterritorial criminal jurisdiction for acts of international terrorism against U.S. nationals (Title XII, P.L. 99-399).

- Antiterrorism Act of 1987

  Prohibited U.S. citizens from receiving anything of value except information material from the Palestine Liberation Organization (PLO), which has been identified as a terrorist organization (Title X, P.L. 100-204).

- PLO Commitments Compliance Act of 1989

  Reaffirmed a U.S. policy that any dialogue with the PLO is contingent upon certain commitments, including the organization's abstention from and renunciation of all acts of terrorism (Title VIII, P.L. 101-246).

- Immigration Act of 1990

  Required the exclusion or deportation from the U.S. any alien who the U.S. government knows or has reason to believe has engaged in terrorist activities (P.L. 101-649, sec. 601 and 602).

- Federal Courts Administration Act of 1992

  Provided civil remedies for U.S. national or their survivors for personal or property injury due to an international terrorism act; granted U.S. district courts jurisdiction to hear cases (Title X, P.L. 102-572).

- Antiterrorism and Effective Death Penalty Act of 1996

  Established procedures for removing alien terrorists from the United States; prohibited fundraising by terrorists; prohibited financial transactions with terrorists (Title IV, P.L. 104-132).

Aviation Security

- Federal Aviation Act of 1958

  Authorized the Federal Aviation Administration (FAA) Administrator to prescribe such rules and regulations as necessary to provide adequately for national security and safety in air transportation; prohibited the air transportation of explosives and other dangerous articles in violation of FAA rule or regulation (P.L. 85-726, sec. 601 and 902).

- Anti-Hijacking Act of 1974

  Established a general prohibition against aircraft piracy outside U.S. special aircraft jurisdiction; allowed the President to suspend air transportation between the United States and any foreign state that supports terrorism (Title I, P.L. 93-366).

- Air Transportation Security Act of 1974

  Authorized screening of passengers and their baggage for weapons (Title II, P.L. 93-366).

- Aircraft Sabotage Act of 1984

  Prohibited anyone from setting fire to, damaging, or destroying any U.S. aircraft (Part B of Ch. XX, P.L. 98-473).

- Foreign Airport Security Act of 1985

  Required FAA to assess foreign airport security procedures and the security procedures used by foreign air carriers serving the United States (Part B of Title V, P.L. 99-83).

- Aviation Security Improvements Act of 1990

  Implemented many recommendations of the President's Commission on Aviation Security and Terrorism to improve aviation security and consular affairs assistance (Titles I and II of P.L. 101-604).

- Federal Aviation Reauthorization Act of 1996

    Mandated the performance of an employment investigation, including a criminal history record check, of airport security personnel (Title III, P.L. 104-264).

Other Legislation

- International Security and Development Cooperation Act of 1981

    Required the President to submit a report to Congress describing all legislation and all administrative remedies that can be employed to prevent the participation of U.S. citizens in activities supporting international terrorism (P.L. 97-113, sec. 719).
- Convention on the Physical Protection of Nuclear Material Implementation Act of 1982

    Prohibited a person from engaging in the unauthorized or improper use of nuclear materials (P.L. 97-351, sec. 2).
- National Defense Authorization Act for Fiscal Year 1987

    Required Department of Defense (DOD) officials to ensure that all credible, time-sensitive intelligence received concerning potential terrorist threats be promptly reported to DOD headquarters (P.L. 99-661, sec.1353).
- Undetectable Firearms Act of 1988

    Prohibited the import, manufacture, sale, and shipment for civilian use of handguns that are made of largely nonmetallic substances (P.L. 100-649, sec. 3).
- Biological Weapons Antiterrorism Act of 1989

    Prohibited a person from knowingly producing or possessing any biological agent or toxin for use as a weapon or knowingly assisting a foreign state or organization to do so (P.L. 101-298, sec. 3).

- National Defense Authorization Act for Fiscal Year 1994

    Required certain defense contractors to report to DOD each commercial transaction with a terrorist country; expressed the sense of Congress that FEMA should strengthen interagency emergency planning for potential terrorists' use of chemical or biological agents or weapons (P.L. 103-160, sec. 843 and 1704).
- Violent Crime Control and Law Enforcement Act of 1994

    Made it a federal crime to intentionally destroy or damage a ship or its cargo or to perform an act of violence against a person on board a ship (P.L. 103-322, sec. 60019).
- Antiterrorism and Effective Death Penalty Act of 1996

    Expanded and strengthened criminal prohibitions and penalties pertaining to terrorism; established restrictions on the transfer and use of nuclear, biological and chemical weapons, as well as plastic explosives (Titles II, III, V & VII, P.L 104-132).
- National Defense Authorization Act for Fiscal Year 1997

    Established the Domestic Preparedness Program (DPP) to strengthen U.S. capabilities to prevent and respond to terrorist activities involving WMD; authorized DOD to take the lead role and provide necessary training and other assistance to federal, state and local officials (Title XIV of P.L. 104-201, commonly known as Nunn–Lugar–Domenici).
- Omnibus Consolidated Appropriations Act (1997)

    Provided substantial funding for multiple federal agencies to combat terrorism, in response to the President's request (see individual agency appropriations acts within P.L. 104-208). Emergency Supplemental Appropriations for Additional Disaster Assistance, for Antiterrorism Initiatives, for Assistance in the Recovery From the Tragedy That Occurred at Oklahoma City, and Rescissions Act 1995. In response to the tragedy of the Oklahoma City federal building bombing, provided substantial emergency funding for various federal agencies to combat terrorism (Title III, P.L. 104-19).

Key to Abbreviations

ACIRG	Attorney Critical Incident Response Group
ATA	Antiterrorism Assistance Program
BC	Biological or Chemical
BWC	Biological Weapons Convention 1972
CBIRF	Chemical Biological Incident Response Force (USMC)
CBRN	Chemical Biological Radiological Nuclear
CIA	Central Intelligence Agency
CIRG	Critical Incident Response Group
CMU	Crisis Management Unit (FBI)
CNU	Crisis Negotiations Unit (FBI)
CDC	Centers for Disease Control and Prevention
CRT	Crisis Response Team (FBI)
CWC	Chemical Weapons Convention
DEST	Domestic Emergency Support Team
DHHS (DHHS)	Department of Health and Human Services
DOD	Department of Defense
DOE	Department of Energy
DOJ	Department of Justice
DOMS	Director of Military Support
DPP	Domestic Preparedness Program
EOC	Emergency Operations Center
EOD	Explosives Ordnance Disposal Group (USA)
EPA	Environmental Protection Agency
ERT	Evidence Response Team
FBI	Federal Bureau of Investigations
FEMA	Federal Emergency Management Agency
FISCAM	Federal Information System Controls Audit Manual
FRP	Federal Response Plan
GAO	General Accounting Office
HAZMAT	Hazardous Materials
HMRU	Hazardous Materials Response Unit (FBI)
HRT	Hostage Rescue Team (FBI)
IAFC	International Association of Fire Chiefs
ICC	Information Coordination Center
ICG	Senior Interagency Coordinating Group on Terrorism
ICS	Incident Command System
IND	Investigational New Drug
IST	Incident Support Team
JIC	Joint Information Center
JIISE	Joint Interagency Intelligence Support Element
JOC	Joint Operation Center
LFA	Lead Federal Agency
LLNL	Lawrence Livermore National Laboratory
MADU	Materials and Devices Unit
MMRS	Metropolitan Medical Response Systems
NASA	National Aeronautics and Space Administration
NBC	Nuclear, Biological or Chemical

NCAVC	National Center for Analysis of Violent Crime (FBI)	OPM	Office of Personnel Management
NCS	National Communications System	PDD	Presidential Decision Directive
NCSIPC	National Coordinator for Security, Infrastructure Protection and Counter-terrorism	RAID	Rapid Assessment and Initial Detection Team (National Guard)
		RST	Rapid Start Team (FBI)
NDPO	National Domestic Preparedness Office	SAC	Special Agent in Charge
		SBCCOM	Commander of Soldier and Biological Chemical Command
NFPA	National Fire Protection Association		
NIAC	National Infrastructure Assurance Council	SIOC	Strategic Information Operations Center
NIC	National Intelligence Control	TEU	Technical Escort Unit (US Army)
NIE	National Intelligence Estimate		
NIH	National Institute of Health	UNSCOM	United Nations Special Commission on Iraq
NIPC	National Infrastructure Protection Center	USAR	Urban Search and Rescue Task Forces
NLC	National League of Cities		
NMRT	National Medical Response Teams	USCG	United States Coast Guard
		WMD	Weapons of Mass Destruction
NSA	National Security Agency	WMDCU	Weapons of Mass Destruction Countermeasures Unit (FBI)
NSC	National Security Council		
NSD	National Security Division (FBI)	WMDICP	Weapons of Mass Destruction Incident Contingency Plan
NSP	National Strategic Plan		
NSP	National Strategic Plan	WMDOU	Weapons of Mass Destruction Operations Unit
OJP	Office of Justice Programs		
OMB	Office of Management and Budget		

NAME INDEX

A

Abanes, R., 129, 132, 177, 178, 184
Adams, J., 14
Alexander, Y., 212, 242
Arendt, H., 12
Arey, J., 28
Arnold, R., 149
Arnold, T., 6, 212
Avrich, P., 45

B

Bales, K., 22
Barbara, J. F., 222–24, 233, 238
Barkun, M., 182
Barnaby, F., 207, 211
Beam, L., 129
Bennett, D. H., 78
Bennett, J., 51
Biddle, W., 25
Blanchard, D. A., 156
Blee, K. M., 48, 49, 108
Bloom, J. M., 84
Bock, 176
Boyer, P., 77
Brodie, B., 24
Brodie, F. M., 24
Bromley, D. G., 182
Brown, R. M., 37, 82
Bullard, S., 38, 49, 50, 84
Burke, W. K., 148

C

Caputi, J., 10
Chaliand, G., 48
Chalk, F., 24

D

Chalmers, D. M., 49, 50, 78, 79
Chomsky, N., 6, 12
Claiborne, W., 201
Clark, R. C., 212
Clarke, R. A, 244
Clinton, W. J., 242, 248
Clutterbuck, R. L., 15, 68
Coates, J., 77
Cohn, N., 23
Colgate, S. R., 259
Comeau, E., 257
Cook, A., 81
Cooper, C., 178
Costa, M., 159
Cotter, J. M., 115
Crenshaw, M., 5, 10, 17, 18
Crotty, W. J., 20
Curtin, P. D., 22

D

Dahlke, H. O., 84
Dalich, M. J., 252
David, S. R., 212
Davies, K., 66
Davis, Z. S., 258
Dees, M., 128, 131, 194
Dejevsky, M., 147
Demos, J., 76
Dempsey, J. X., 235
Donahue, M., 256
Dugard, J., 10
Durham, M., 128
Duvall, R., 12

E

Eagen, S. P. ,141, 142, 144

Echeverria, J. D., 148
Eddy, M., 146, 147
Eddy, R. B., 148
Ekirch, A. R., 23
Emerson, S., 207
Eubank, W. L., 16

F

Falkenrath, R. A., 207, 210
Fanon, F., 58
Fields, R. M., 16
Ford, F. L., 38
Foxell, J. W., Jr., 210
Franz, D., 262
Freedman, L. Z., 17
Freeh, L. J., 247

G

Gallagher, E. V., 182
Gavrilles, E., 160
Gay, P., 39
George, A., 6
George, J., 109, 111, 112, 125
Georges-Abeyies, D. E., 16
Gerth, H., 12
Gilje, P. A., 81
Ginsburg, F., 160
Gottlieb, A., 149–51
Grabosky, P. N., 26
Gross, F., 46
Grosscup, B., 5
Gunter, M. M., 48
Gurr, T. R., 15, 26, 75, 93

H

Hacker, F. 15
Hamm, M. S., 10, 123, 185
Hammel, E., 26
Hanmer, J., 23
Harrigan, A., 26
Hee, K. H., 16
Helvarg, D., 148, 151
Herman, E. S., 6, 12
Hester, M., 23
Hoffman, B., 7, 105, 204, 210, 212, 214, 215
Honderich, T., 12

Huey, J., 16
Hunter, R., 163
Hutchinson, M. C., 58

I

Ingalsbee, T., 142
Ispahani, M., 25

J

Jackman, J., 160
Jacobs, S. S., 207, 215
Janowitz, M., 83
Jaszi, O., 20
Jenkins, B., 5, 26
Jenkins, B. H., 212
Joesten, J., 26
Jonassohn, K., 24
Jordan, W. D., 37
Joyner, C. C., 29, 212

K

Kaplan, J., 117
Kellen, K., 15
Keniston, K., 93
Kennedy, M., 188
Kirkpatrick, J., 12
Kohn, S. M., 81, 93
Kuper, L., 47
Kupperman, R., 27, 29
Kurz, A., 47
Kushner, H. W., 206

L

Laqueur, W., 5, 6, 10, 12, 18, 20, 45, 108, 135, 208, 211–14
Lee, M. F., 141, 142, 144, 145, 161, 163
Lesak, D. M., 259
Leventhal, P., 212
Lewis, B., 39
Lewis, J. D., 20
Libaridian, G. L., 39
Lifton, R. J., 18, 213
Lipsher, S., 146, 147
Livingstone, N. C., 6, 212
Loewen, J. W., 82, 83

Long, D. E., 10
Lorch, D., 229
Lovejoy, P. E., 22
Luca, R. J., 223, 225, 226, 233, 237
Lyman, S. M., 80

M

MacDonald, E., 16
MacFarlane, A., 23
Marable, M., 84, 85, 96
Masci, D., 152, 154, 166
McKnight, G., 16
McVey, P., 3
Merari, A., 47
Merkl, P. H., 17
Miller, B. H., 15
Miller, D. E., 47
Miller, L. T., 47
Miller, W., 46
Mills, C., 12
Monaghan, R., 153–56
Moorehead, C., 21
Moors, C. S., 4
Morgan, R., 16
Morris, A. D., 84
Mullins, W. C., 140, 141, 163
Murr, A., 229
Musch, D., 242

N

Naess, A., 143
Netanyahu, B., 6, 10
Newman, R. D., 207, 210
Newton, H., 95
Nissenbaum, S., 77

O

Oliver, R., 61
Olson, J. S., 78
Olson-Raymer, G., 16
Onyango, C., 160

P

Parfit, M., 142
Perdue, W. D., 6

Perlmutter, A., 188
Perlstein, G. R., 28, 39, 109
Perlstein, R. M., 12, 16
Phillips, W. D., 22, 27
Pitts, W. L., Jr., 181, 182
Plotnicov, L., 21
Poland, J. M., 109
Porta, D., 18
Post, J. M., 16
Prewitt, T. J., 156
Prunier, G., 66

Q

Quayle, E., 17, 18

R

Ramos, T., 148, 151
Reavis, D. J., 180
Reno, J., 263
Riley, K. J., 7
Risen, J., 156, 157, 159
Ross, L., 116
Rousey, D. C., 98
Rubenstein, R. E., 17
Russell, C., 15
Russell, J. B., 10, 22

S

Sale, K., 197
Saunders, S., 23
Scarce, R., 141–43, 152, 154, 161, 165
Schevitz, T., 169
Schmid, A., 5
Schwartz, A. M., 109, 112, 115, 118, 120, 209
Sellars, C., 85
Shain, Y., 23
Shinbaum, M., 114
Silver, E., 182
Simank, A., 256
Simon, J., 17, 228, 229
Simon, J. D., 204, 206, 211
Simpson, J., 51
Singer, P., 153–56, 164
Sloan, S., 204, 211, 214
Smith, B. L., 107
Snow, D., 149

Sobel, L. A., 26
Sprinzak, E., 115, 116, 118
St. John, P., 27, 28
Stampp, K. M., 37
Stark, J. A., 143
Stavrionos, L. S., 20
Stencel, S., 126
Stern, J., 136, 207, 210–14
Stern, K. S., 107, 118, 131, 133
Stock, C. M., 75, 80, 85–88, 91
Stohl, M., 6, 12, 212
Strentz, T., 15
Struve, D. E., 222
Stuebner, S., 132

T

Tabor, J. D., 182
Talley, T., 192
Taylor, B., 156, 166
Taylor, M., 17, 18
Ternon, Y., 48
Thayer, B. A., 207, 210
Thomas, J. L., 156, 157, 159
Thornburgh, R., 224, 227, 232, 234–36
Toynbee, A., 47
Trevor-Roper, H., 23
Tuden, A., 21
Turner, L., 16

U

Utter, J., 43

V

Vetter, H. J., 28, 39, 109
Vizzard, W. J., 174, 183

W

Wade, W. C., 49, 50, 82, 83, 111
Walter, E. V., 12
Wapner, P., 162, 164
Ward, R. H., 4
Wardlaw, G., 12
Weinberg, L., 16
Werner, J. M., 81
White, J. R., 5, 6, 9, 12., 44, 45, 61
Wilcox, L., 109, 111, 112, 125
Wilkinson, N. B., 25
Wilkinson, P., 47
Wright, D., 221

Z

Zinn, H., 88, 96

SUBJECT INDEX

A

Abortion
  activities against clinics and doctors, 157, 159
  clinic violence, trends toward, 160–61
  congressional responses to violence, 162
  Operation Rescue, 159–60
  organization and activities, 156–61
  Pro-Life Action Network, 157, 159
  Roe v. Wade, 156, 158
  terror events, 157, 160–61
Afghanistan
  Afghan civil war, 63–65
  Afghani state vs. Muslim community, 61–65
  ethnic, tribal, clan relations, 62–63
  historical overview, 61–65
  Islamic fundamentalism, 64–65
  Islamic revolution, 61–65
  jihad, 664
  Taelban, 61, 65
African Americans
  civil rights activists, 84–85
  enslavement, 22, 36–38, 81
  fear, hatred, intolerance, 81–85
  free black persons, 81
  Ku Klux Klan, 82–85 (*see also* Ku Klux Klan)
  urban riots, 82–84
  vigilante actions against, 81–85
  White Citizen Councils, 84
Alfred P. Murrah building, Oklahoma City, OK
  domestic terrorist bombing, 5, 27, 105, 191–93
Algeria, FLN, and FIS, 58–60
Allan, Ethan, 88
  Green Mountain Boys, 88 (*see also* Militias)
Allotment re Native Americans, 42
American Front, 213–14

American Nazi Party, 92
  platform for appeal, 92
  Rockwell, George L., 92
American slavery, 22, 36–38
  defense rationalizations, 37
  historical overview, 36–38
  Supreme Court decision (Dred Scott), 38
Anarchists
  bomb usage, 44–45
  Haymarket Square riots, 45
  political violence, 44
  propaganda by the deed, 44, 45
  Russian revolutionaries, 44–45
  terror vs. oppression, 44
Ancient times to 1800, terrorism overview
  American slavery, 36–38
  Assassins, Order of the, 38–39
Animal Liberation Front, 154, 165
  action guidelines, 154
  commercial losses, promote by terrorism, 154
  rescue operations, 154–55
Animal rights movement, 163–66 (*see also* People for the Ethical Treatment of Animals)
  animal experimentation protests, 152–54
  Animal Liberation Front, 154–56
  Animal Welfare Act, 152
  core issues, 152
  organizations and activities, 152–56
  overview, 152–54
  People for the Ethical Treatment of Animals, 163–65
  Singer, Pete, 152–54
  Spira, Henry, 154
  ten ways to make a difference, 155
Anti-abortion activists, 156–61, 166
  activities against clinics and doctors, 157, 159
  congressional responses to violence, 162

Operation Rescue, 159–60
organization and activities, 156–61
Pro-Life Action Network, 157, 159
Roe v. Wade, 156, 158
terror events, 157, 160–61
Anti-environmental movement, 146–52 (*see also* Environmental movement)
Wise Use, 147–52
Anti-terrorism
strategies and tactics, 3, 242–64
case studies, 249–51
critical infrastructure protection directive points, 243–45
information infrastructure protection strategies, 245–47, 248
partnerships for infrastructure protection, 243
proactive criminal investigations, 247–51
threat assessment, 251–52
weapons of mass destruction, 242–63
Argentina's covert dirty war, 51–54
historical overview, 51–54
human rights violations trials, 52–53
national reorganization, 51
Arizona Patriots, 134
organization and activities, 134
Armenian genocide and Turkey, 46–48
historical overview, 46–48
Armenian Secret Army for the Liberation of Armenia, 48
Arnold, Ron, 148
Ecology Wars, 149
Wise Use promotion strategies, 149
Arson
historical overview, 24–25
Arson Bombing Investigative Services, 230
Aryan Brotherhood, 120
hate targets, 120
organization and activities, 120
Aryan Nations, 119
hate targets, 119
organization and activities, 119
Asian immigrants
Alien Land Law, 81
Cable Act, 81
Chinese Exclusion Act, 80
Chinese immigrants, 79–80
immigration exclusion, 80
Immigration Act, 81

Japanese immigrants, 80
relocation camps, 81, 101
Korean immigrants, 80
socio-economic-political environment, 79–81
vigilantism, 79–81
Assassination
historical overview, 19–20
contemporary practices, 20
Greek and Roman tyrannicide, 20
Machiavelli, 20
terrorism from above and below, 19, 20
Assimilation re Native Americans, 42–43
Aum shinrikyo, 18, 210

B

Baader-Meinhof Gang, 15
Bacon, Nathaniel, 86–87
Bacon's Rebellion, 86 (*see also* Militias)
political violence as justifiable means, 85
racial radicalism re Indians, 86
Bacon, Roger and gunpowder, 25
Bakunin, Mikhail, 44
Banishment
historical overview, 23
Great Britain: criminal population, 23
American colonies, 23
Australia, 23
Greece: honorable exile, 23
Rome: exile or death, 23
Bari, Judi, 145
Baumann, Michael, 15
Beach, Henry, 117
Beirut, Lebanon Marine Barracks, 26
Biological weapons, 208–13, 260–63
incidents of use, 262–63
Biological Weapons Convention, 259–63
Black Circle, 207–8
Black Metal, 207–8
Black Liberation Army, 96–97
Cleaver, Eldridge, 96
militant violence, 96–97
Black Panthers, 95–97
core philosophy 96
Newton, Huey, 95
Seale, Bobby, 95
urban guerilla warfare tactics, 96–97
Black separatist groups, 108, 125–27, 135
Nation of Islam, 125–26

New Black Panthers, 126–27
Bombs
  historical overview, 25–27
    aircraft sabotage, 26–27
    anti-American bombing incidents, 26–27
      Beirut, Lebanon Marine barracks, 26
      U.S. embassies: Kenya, 26
      ————Tanzania, 26
      U.S. military installations: Dhahran, Saudi Arabia, 26
      ————Riyadh, Saudi Arabia, 26
      U.S.S. *Cole*, 27
    car bombs, 26
    dynamite, 26
    Gunpower Plot, 25–26
    Murrah Federal Building, Oklahoma, 5, 27, 105, 191–93
    nitroglycerin, 26
    timing devices, 26
  public infrastructure and sabotage, 27
  Unabomber case study, 197–200
Branch Davidians, Waco, TX: case study, 180–85
Bureau of Alcohol, Tobacco, and Firearms: case studies
  New York, NY and World Trade Center bombing, 186–90
  Ruby Ridge, ID and Randy Weaver, 174–80
  Waco, TX and Branch Davidians, 180–85
Burke, Edmund, 11, 14
Busic, Zvonko, 15
Butler, Richard, 119

C

Castro, Raoul and hijacking, 28
Catholic religion
  anti-Catholicism persecution, 77–79
    Know Nothings, 78, 98
    Ku Klux Klan, 78–79
    Order of the Star Spangled Banner, 78
  colonial America, 77
  Maryland colony, 77
  political restrictions, 77
  vigilantism, 77–79
Che Guevara (*see* Guevara, Che)
Chemical weapons, 208–13
Cherney, Darryl, 145
Christian Identity movement, 116–21

Aryan Brotherhood, 117, 120
Aryan Nations, 117, 119
core beliefs, 116–17
Covenant, Sword and the Arm of the Lord, 117, 120–21
hate targets 116
justified use of killing, 117
organization and activities, 116
Phineas Brotherhood, 117
Posse Comiatus, 117–18
second coming of White Aryan Christ, 117
SPLC observation of membership, 117
The Order, 117, 119–20
Civil Rights Movement
  violence toward
    Evers, Medgar, 85
    Freedom Riders, 84–85
    integration marchers, 84
    Mississippi Summer Project, 85
    Moore, William L., 85
    NAACP, 84
Clearinghouse on Environmental Advocacy and Research, 149
Colonial America, 17th century vigilantes, 74–91
Common Law Courts, 134–35
  arrest warrants, 134
  liens, 134–35
  state laws banning activities of, 135
Communist Manifesto, 44
Cosmetic companies and animal experimentation, 154
Counter-terrorist operations
  case studies, 249–51
    critical infrastructure protection directive points, 243–45
    information infrastructure protection strategies, 245–47, 248
    partnerships for infrastructure protection, 243
    proactive criminal investigations, 247–51
    threat assessment, 251–52
    weapons of mass destruction, 242–63
Covenant, Sword, and Arm of the Lord, 120–21
  hate targets, 120
  organization and activities 120
Covington, Harold aka Winston Smith, 112
Criminal Investigative Analysis, 230
Cuba, 9

Cyberterrorism and internet, 208
  digital infrastructure, 208
  high-energy radio frequency guns, 208
  logic bombs, 208
  viruses, 208

D

Dawes Severalty Act of 1887, 42–43
Day, Luke, 89
  Shays Rebellion, 89 (*see also* Militias)
Deep ecology, profile, 142, 143
  Greenpeace mission, 142
Defenders of the Christian Faith, 92 (*see also* Militias)
Definitions
  broad definition, 9
  categories, 5–6
    analytical re violence toward innocent victims, 5
    legal re criminal violence, 5
    simple re political change, 5
    state-sponsored re repression, terror for power, 6
    Western viewpoints, attack, 5–6
  characteristics, 8–9
  complexities, 3, 5, 6, 29–30
    criminal violence, 5
    force for political change, 5
    innocent victims, violence, 5
    power via repression, terror, 6
    Western influence retribution, 6
  FBI, 7–8
  government manipulation, 6, 12
  interpretation re political adversaries, 9–10
  motivations, 5–6, 10–11
  Omnibus Diplomatic Security and Antiterrorism Act, 9
  pejorative connotation, 6
  terrorism from above, 8, 10–13, 29–30, 35 (*see also* Terrorism from above)
  terrorism from below, 8, 10–13, 29–30, 35 (*see also* Terrorism from below)
  terrorism vs. terror terminology, 6, 8
Domestic terrorism, 3, 74–100 (*see also* U.S. terrorism)
  Alfred P. Murrah building bombing, 5, 105, 191–93
  changing character, overview, 204–15

colonialists
  core belief, 75
  extremists, 74–75
  terrorism as response to threat, 75
17th – 20th century America
  African Americans and vigilantes, 81–85
  Asian immigrants, 79–81
  Catholics and vigilantes, 77–79 (*see also* Catholic religion)
  witch hunts, 76–77 (*see also* Witch hunts)
modern era terrorism, 39
North American Indians, genocidal policies, 40–43
social and political constructs for terrorism, 39–40
socialist, anarchist influences, 43–45
Domestic terrorism, 21st century, 204–15
  cyberterrorism and internet, 208
    digital infrastructure, 208
    high-energy radio frequency guns, 208
    logic bombs, 208
    viruses, 208
  international links, 206–8
    access to weapons of mass destruction, 207
    Islamic militants, 206–7
    Middle East involvement, 206
    rogue nation's retaliation, 207
    technology facilitation, 206
  music, oi, 207–8
    Black Circle, 207–8
    Black Metal, 207–8
  right-wing extremists: principles and tactics, 205–6
    ideals, 118, 131, 205
    recruiting strategies, 206
  sarin attack, Japan, 18, 210
  weapons of mass destruction, 208, 210–13
    biological, 208–11
    chemical, 208–11
    nuclear, 208, 212
    profile, 211
    weapons use incidents
      Iran-Iraq war, 212
      salmonella typhimurium, OR
      sarin, Japan, 18, 210

E

Earth First!

deep ecology, 142, 143
disruption of commercial activities, 144–45
ecotage, 144–145
government's opening of protected lands, 141–42
law enforcement retaliation, 145
monkey wrenching, 141, 144
organization and activities, 141–45
Roadless Area Review Evaluation 142
Round River Rendezvous, 142
sabotage of commercial equipment, 141
tree spiking, 144
Earth Liberation Front, 146
organization and activities, 146
use of violence to achieve ends, 146
Vail, CO, ski area fires, 146, 147, 249
Ecological resistance movements, 140–47
anti-environmental movement, 146–52 (*see also* Wise Use)
core beliefs, 141
Earth First! 141–45
Earth Liberation Front, 146
organization and activities, 141–52
Ecotage, 144–145
Ellison, James, 120
Engels, Friedrich, 44
Enslavement and subjugation
constant social characteristic, 21
historical overview, 21–22
motivation: economics, politics, 21–22
slave societies, rise and fall of
Atlantic slave trade, 22, 36–38
European colonists, 22
Roman Empire, 21–22
peasantry of serfs, 22
racial hatred, intolerance, 22
Environmental activists movement, 140–45
anti-environmental movement, 146–52
Earth First! 141–45
Earth Liberation Front, 146
Epstein, Richard, 148
Evan Mecham Eco-Terrorist International Conspiracy, 145
Evolutionary vs. revolutionary, 19, 30, 35–68, 74
historical continuity (*see also* Historical continuity of terrorism)
ancient times to 1800, 36–39
17th century colonial vigilantes, 74–91

1800 to 1900, 39–45
1900 to 1950, 45–50
1950 to 1979, 50–60
1980 to 2000, 60–68
motivations, 35–36
Extremists, political, 173–200
left-wing extremist activities, 6, 92–99
right-wing extremists, 7, 127–37
special-interest extremists, 7, 140–66
Extremists, political: case studies, 173–200
commonalities, 173, 201–2
Freeman of Montana standoff, 195–96
Murrah Federal Building, Oklahoma City, OK, 191–93
Ruby Ridge, ID, 174–80
Unabomber, 197–200
Waco, TX, Branch Davidians, 180–85
World Trade Center, 186–90

F

Fanon, Franz, 57–58
Algerian Liberation Front, 57
freedom of man via terror, 57–58
political revolution views, 57–58
Farmer's Holiday Association, 91 (*see also* Militias)
Farrakhan, Louis, 125
Nation of Islam, 125
racist philosophies, 125
Fascist groups and militia activity, 91–92
Fawkes, Guy and Gunpowder Plot, 25–26
Fear, hate, intolerance, 10–11, 22, 76–85
different than white, 76
economic motivators, 76
racial, ethnic, religious differences, 76–85
motivators for terrorism, 10
external constraints absent, 11
opportunity available, 11
societal norms accepting violence, 11
17th – 20th century America
African Americans and vigilantes, 81–85
Asian immigrants, 79–81
Catholics and vigilantes, 77–79 (*see also* Catholic religion)
witch hunts, 76–77 (*see also* Witch hunts)
Fear in a social context, 10–13
Federal Bureau of Investigation
Attorney General guidelines on information

gathering, 232–33
  domestic terrorism, 232
  international terrorism, 233
definitions of terrorism (*see also* Definitions)
  differing re local law enforcement, 7–8
  terrorists, 6
evaluation process
  classification system, 227, 235, 237
  content validity, 235, 237
  source reliability, 235, 237
intelligence gathering, lead agency responsi-
    bility, 227–38
  domestic terrorism classifications, 227
  investigation of potential and actual acts,
    228–30
  investigative support units, 227, 231
    Joint Terrorism Task Force, 227
    National Center for the Analysis of Vio-
      lent Crime, 230–31
  investigative techniques, 233–37
    critical factors, 233–34
    internet sources, 235
Feminist Majority Foundation, 160
  survey of abortion clinic violence, 160
Force to bring about political change, 5
Foreign relations
  terrorist vs.freedom fighters, 9, 69
Foreman, David, 141–43
FIS (Islamic Salvation Front), 59–60
FLN (Front de Liberation Nationale), 13, 51,
    58–60
  activities, 13, 58–60
  organization, 58–60
Freedom fighters, 9, 69
Freeman of Montana, 129–30, 195–96
  case study, 195–96
Fundamentalists, 69

G

Gale, William Potter, 118
Gender status quo
  gender-related terrorism, 10
Genocide, 11, 23–24
  cultural, 23–23
    motivations, 24
  ethnic, racial, religious, 23–24
    motivation, 24
German Red Army, 15

German 2nd of June Movement, 15
Global terrorism, 4, 35–68
  historical overview, 35–68
  terrorism from above, 35
  terrorism from below, 35
Government repression/oppression, 12 (*see also*
    Terrorism from above)
  cycle of terror/violence, 12–13
  definitions
    covert terrorism, 10, 13, 51
    overt terrorism, 10, 13, 51
Great Britain, 9
Green Mountain Boys, 88 (*see also* Militias)
Greenpeace, 161–63
  antinuclear origination, 162
  bearing witness, 161
  environmental activists, 162–63
  organization and activities, 161–63
  profile, 164
Gritz, James "Bo" profile, 132
Guatemala's covert reign of terror, 54–55
  historical overview, 54–55
  human rights violations of Mayans, 54
  U.S. apology, 55
  U.S. complicity in covert war, 54–55
Guerilla warfare
  rural warfare, 56, 69
  urban warfare, 57, 69
Guevara, Che, 56–57
  political revolution views, 56
  rural guerrilla warfare, 56
Gunn, David, 160
Guns
  automatic assault rifles, 25
  gunpowder, 25
    Chinese development, 25
    Roger Bacon, Western development, 25
  historical overview, 25
  standoff weapons, 25
    grenade launchers, 25
    suitcase wire-guided missiles, 25
    surface-to-air missiles, 25
Guzman, Abimael and SL, 68
  guerilla warfare and Maoist goals, 68

H

Hale, Matt, profile, 121–23
Hardin, Ty, 134

Hate groups, 107–27 (*see also* specific group
    names)
  black separatists, 108, 125–27
    group listing, 108
  racial-religious orientation, 108, 121–24
    group listing, 108
  white supremacists, 108–21
    group listing, 108
Haymarket Square riot, 45
  McCormick Reaper Works strike, 45
Heinzen, Karl, 44
Hijacking
  historical overview, 27
    political asylum, 27–28
    skyjacking, 27
Historical continuity (*see also* Revolutionary vs.
    evolutionary)
  ancient times to 1800, 36–39
  1800 to 1900, 39–45
  1900 to 1950, 45–50
  1950 to 1979, 50–60
  1980 to 2000, 60–68
Hutu genocide of Tutsis, 65–68

I

Imprisonment, punishment, 22–23
  accusation terror, 23
  heretics, witches, Jews, 23
  Inquisition, 23
  religious hatred, fear, 22–23
  witch hunt trials, 22–23
Innocent targets of violence, 5
Intelligence gathering, 3, 219–41
  FBI responsibilities, 227–38 (*see also* Feder-
    al Bureau of Investigation)
  filing procedures, 227
  information gathering, 221–26
    goal guidelines, 222
    privacy rights, 222–25
      court cases determining, 223–25
      court order, 224
      search warrants, 224
      wiretapping, 224
      criminal predicate, establishing, 224
      public access, 225
        California determinations, 226
        court cases determining, 225–27
      strategic intelligence, 222

  dates of activity for patterns, 222
  skill building, 3, 219–64
International relations
  omitting re terrorist regimes, 9
  targeting re terrorist regimes, 9
International terrorism, 3
Interpretations of terror justification
  enemies of the people, 10
  freedom, self-determination, independence,
    10
  just war for freedom, 9
  state of emergency, 10
Iran, 9
Iraq, 9
Irish Republican Army, 25, 27
Islamic fundamentalism, 64–65
Islamic revolution, 61–65
Israel, 9

J

Japanese Red Army, 15
Jihad, 664
Justice Commandos for the Armenian Genocide,
    48

K

Kaczynski, Theodore J., Unabomber: case
    study, 197–200
Kahl, Gordon, 118
Kallinokos and Greek fire, 24
Kidnapping
  historical overview, 20–21
    American slavery, 22, 36
    Greek mythology, 20
    hostage taking, 21
    political usage, 20
  ransom organizations/professions, 20–21
  terrorism from above and below, 19, 20
Klassen, Ben, 121
  Church of the Creator, 121
  publications, 121
Klein, Hans J., 15
Know Nothings, 78, 98
Kropotkin, Peter, 44
Ku Klux Klans
  activities, 13, 48–50, 82–85,
    African Americans, activities, 82–85

anti-Catholic activities, 78–79
contemporary groups, 109–12
  Christian Knights of KKK, 109
  Federation of Klans, 111
  Invisible Empire, KKK, 111
  Keystone Knights of KKK, 111
  Knights of KKK (AR faction), 111
  Knights of KKK (LA faction), 111
  Knights of KKK (MI faction), 111
  United Klans of America, Inc., 109
First Klan, 108
historical overview, 48–50, 108–9
motivation(s), 108
1960s major terror events, 109
organization and activities, 48–50, 108–11
Second Klan, 108
Simmons, William J., 49
Third Klan, 108
vigilante movement, 48–50, 108–11
white supremacists, 108–21

L

Law enforcement
  influence of ethnic suppression, 98
  influence of racism, 98–99
  KKK activities, 98–99
  left-wing extremist activities, 98–99
Law enforcement officials
  local agencies, 3
    educational needs re extremists, 3
    educational needs re terrorists, 3
  specialized police forces, 4, 97
Left-wing extremism, 6, 92–99
  Black Liberation Army, 96–97
  Black Panthers, 95–97

  liberal extremes for political action, 6
  Students for a Democratic Society, 92–95
  Weather Underground, 92–95
Libya, 9

M

Mahler, Horst, 15
Malcolm X, 125
Mao Tse-Tung, 55–56
  people's war, 56
  political revolution views, 55–56

Red Terror, 56
Marighella, Carlos, 57
  urban guerrilla warfare, 57
Marx, Karl, 44
Mass destruction, weapons of, 28–29, 208, 210–13, 242–64
  biological weapons, 29, 208–13, 260–63
  ———use incidents, 262–63
  chemical weapons, 28–29, 208–13
  lethal gases, 28–29
  mustard gases, 28, 29
  nerve gases, 29
  nuclear weapons, 208, 212
Mathews, Robert J., 119
  Silent Brotherhood, 119
McGee, Michael, 126
McLaren, Richard, 130
McVeigh, Timothy, Oklahoma City bombing, 191–93
Mercedarians (religious order), 21
Messianic movements
  Assassins, Order of the, 38–39
Metzger, Tom, 122
Middle East
  rogue nations, 207
  role in facilitating domestic terrorism, 206–8
Militia of Montana, 133–34
  organization and activities, 133
  publications, 134
Militias, 75, 85–92 (*see also* Militias and patriot groups, contemporary)
  Colonial America, 86–89
    Bacon's Rebellion, 85–86
    Green Mountain Boys, 88
    New Jersey land rioters, 87
    Paxton Boys, 87
    South Carolina Regulators, 88
  core goals, 85
  extremists, terrorists, law enforcement responses, 97–100
  government as target, 98
  law enforcement, influence of racism, 98–99
  scapegoating vigilante terrorism, 97
  similiaries between historical periods, 97
  left-wing extremism, 92–99
    Black Liberation Army, 96–97
    Black Panthers, 95–97

Students for a Democratic Society, 92–95
Weather Underground, 92–95
1930 to 1950s
  fascist groups, 91–92
    American Nazi Party, 92
    Defenders of the Christian Faith, 92
    Silver Shirts, 92
  Farmer's Holiday Association, 91
post-Revolution, 89–92
  Molly Maguires, 90
  Shays' Rebellion, 98
  Whiskey Rebellion, 99
Militias and patriot groups, contemporary, 127–37
  militias, 130–34
    apocalypticism, 131
    Arizona Patriots, 134
    core beliefs, 131
    Militia of Montana, 132
    organization and activities, 131–34
  patriots, 127–30
    common law, 129
    core beliefs, 128, 129
    federal government antipathy, 128
    Freeman of Montana, 129–30
    leaderless resistance, 128, 129
    organization and activities, 128–30
    Republic of Texas, 130
Molly Maguires, 90 (*see also* Militias)
Monkey wrenching, 141, 144 (*see also* Environmental resistance groups)
Moral judgment disruption, 16
Muammar al-Qaddafi, 14
Muhammad, Elijah, 125
  black pride, 125
  Nation of Islam, 125
Muhammad, Khalid, 127
Murrah Federal Building, Oklahoma City, OK, 5, 27, 105, 191–93
Muslims and Order of the Assassins, 38–39
  Sunnis vs. Shi'ites, 38–39

N

Narcissism, 16–17
Nation of Islam, 125–26
  Elijah Muhammad, 125
  Farrakhan, Louis, 125
  hate targets, 125–26
  Islam, fundamentals, 126
  Malcolm X, 125
  organization and activities, 125–26
  publications, 125
National Alliance, 113
  organization and activities, 113
  publications, 113
  spillover from Christian Identity groups, 117
National Center for the Analysis of Violent Crime, 230–31
National emergency declarations, 14
National Socialist White People's Party, 112
  organization and activity, 112
National Socialist Vanguard, 113
  organization and activity, 113
Nationalists, 69
Native Americans, genocidal policies, 40–43
  constitutional interpretation of sovereignty, 40
  genocidal, federal policies, 41–43
    allotment and assimilation, 41, 42–43
    elimination, 41, 43
    removal, 41–42
    reservations, 41, 42
  Supreme Court decisions re sovereignty, 40–41
    Cherokee Nation v. Georgia, 41
    Johnson v. McIntosh, 41
    Marshall Trilogy, 41
    Worcester v. Georgia, 41
  treaties, 40–41
  tribal land-grab policies, 42–43
Nechaev, Sergey, 44
Neo-Nazi Skinheads, 113–16
  ADL observation of memberships, 116
  hate attitudes and violence, 10
  hate targets, 113, 116
  music, 115
  organization and activities, 113–16, 215
  profile, 113–16
    Racist, Neo-Nazi Skins, 113
    SHARPS, 113
    Trads, 113
Neo-Nazis, 112–13
  ADL observation of memberships, 112
  American Nazi Party, 113
  hate targets, 112–13
  organization and activities, 112–13
  National Socialist White People's Party, 112
  National Socialist Vanguard, 113

Netanyahu, Benjamin, 14
New Black Panther Party, 126–27
  organization and activities, 126–27
  organized response to racial violence, 127
  urban guerilla warfare, 126
Newkirk, Ingrid, 163
Nichols, Terry, 192–93
1900 to 1950 terrorism overview
  Armenian genocide, 46–48
  Bolshoi Terror, 46
  international terrorism, 45–46
  Ku Klux Klan, 46, 48–50
  Stalin, Joseph, 46
1950 to 1979 terrorism overview
  conventions of violence 51
  covert activities, 10, 13, 51
  Front de Liberation Nationale, 51
  revolutionary fevor, 51
  terrorisms justifications, 51
1980 to 2000 terrorism overview, 60–68
  ethnic hatreds, 60
  nationalism vs. religious nationalism, 61
  religious ideologies, 60–65
    Afghanistan's Taleban, 61
    Islamic fundamentalists, 60–65
Nobel, Alfred B., and dynamite, 26
North American Indians, genocidal policies, 40–43
  constitutional interpretation of sovereignty, 40
  genocidal, federal policies, 41–43
    allotment and assimilation, 41, 42–43
    elimination, 41, 43
    removal, 41–42
    reservations, 41, 42
  Supreme Court decisions re sovereignty, 40–41
    Cherokee Nation v. Georgia, 41
    Johnson v. McIntosh, 41
    Marshall Trilogy, 41
    Worcester v. Georgia, 41
  treaties, 40–41
  tribal land-grab policies, 42–43
North Korea, 9
Northern Ireland
  exposure to violence
    disruption of moral judgment, 16
Nuclear weapons, 208, 212 (*see also* Weapons of mass destruction)
  Hiroshima, Japan, 208, 212

threat of offensive use, 212

O

Odinism, 123–24
  Asatru, 123
  contemporary beliefs, 124
  hate targets 124
  neo-Nazi Skinhead participation, 124
  origination of religion, 123–24
Okamoto, Kozo, 15
O'Keefe, John, 157
Oklahoma bombing, 5
Operation Rescue
  organization and activities, 159–60
  terror events, 159
Operation Rescue National, 159
Oppression, 11
Order, the, 119–20
  organization and activities, 119–20
Order of the Star Spangled Banner, 78

P

Pacheco, Alex, 163
Paramilitary operations, 3
Patriot militias, 75, 85–92 (*see also* Patriot militias, contemporary)
  Colonial America, 86–89
    Bacon's Rebellion, 85–86
    Green Mountain Boys, 88
    New Jersey land rioters, 87
    Paxton Boys, 87
    South Carolina Regulators, 88
  contemporary times, 127–35 (*see also* Patriot and militia groups, contemporary)
  core goals, 85
  left-wing extremism, 92–99
    Black Liberation Army, 96–97
    Black Panthers, 95–97

    Students for a Democratic Society, 92–95
    Weather Underground, 92–95
  1930 to 1950s
    Farmer's Holiday Association, 91
    fascist groups, 91–92
      American Nazi Party, 92
      Defenders of the Christian Faith, 92
      Silver Shirts, 92

post-Revolution, 89–92
Molly Maguires, 90
Shays' Rebellion, 98
Whiskey Rebellion, 99
Patriot and militia groups, contemporary, 127–37
militias, 130–34
apocalypticism, 131
Arizona Patriots, 134
core beliefs, 131
Militia of Montana, 132
organization and activities, 131–34
patriots, 127–30
common law, 129
core beliefs, 128, 129
federal government antipathy, 128
Freeman of Montana, 129–30
leaderless resistance, 128, 129
organization and activities, 128–30
Republic of Texas, 130
Paxton Boys militia, 87
Pelley, William D., 91
People for the Ethical Treatment of Animals, 163–65
organization and activities, 183–65
social changes as result of activism, 164–65
People's war, 56
Peru, Sendero Luminoso (SL), 68
historical overview, 68
Peters, Pete, 127
Phineas Brotherhood, 117
organization and activities, 117
Pierce, William, 113
publications, 113–15
Resistance, 115, 208
Turner Diaries, 113, 114
PKK (Kurdistan Workers' Party), 25
Political activism, 9
Political extremism, 8–9
definition and characteristics, 8–9
Political extremism, case studies, 8, 173–200
commonalities, 173, 201–2
Freeman of Montana standoff, 195–96
Murrah Federal Building, Oklahoma City, OK, 191–93
Ruby Ridge, ID, 174–80
Unabomber, 197–200
Waco, TX, Branch Davidians, 180–85
World Trade Center, 186–90

Political violence and political goals, 10
Posse Comitatus, 117–18
organization and activities, 117–18
Post, Jerrold M., 16
Proactive operations, 4
Pro-Life Action Network, 157, 159
organization and activities, 157–59
Psychological profile of terrorists, 15–17
aggressive, 16
extremist thoughts, 17
group identity, 17
moral judgment disruption, 16
narcissistic, 16
psychopathic, 16
risk-takers, 17, 18
self-regard and identity, 16

Q

Qaddafi (*see* Muammar al-Qaddafi)

R

Rabin, Yitzhak, 20
Racial-religious terror groups, 108, 121–24, 135
(*see also* Ku Klux Klans; Neo-Nazis)
Ordinism, 123–24
White Aryan Resistance, 122–23
World Church of the Creator, 121–22
Radical revolutionaries, 69
Radicalism for political change, 6–7
Ransom, 20–21
Red Brigades, 18
Removal Act of 1830, 41–42
Cherokee, Creek, Chickasaw, Choctaw, Seminole, 41–42
Trail of Tears, 42
Repression, terror for power, 6
Reservations, 42
Revolutionary vs. evolutionary, 19, 30, 35–68, 74
historical continuity (*see also* Historical continuity of terrorism)
ancient times to 1800, 36–39
1800 to 1900, 39–45
1900 to 1950, 45–50
1950 to 1979, 50–60
1980 to 2000, 60–68
motivations, 35–36

Right-wing extremists, 7, 127–37 (*see also* Militias and patriot groups)
  conservative extremes for status quo, 7
  hate groups, 107–27 (*see also* Hate groups)
  militias and patriot groups, 127–37
  overview of social longevity, 136–37
Roadless Area Review Evaluation 142
Robb, Thomas (Thom), profile, 112
Rockwell, George Lincoln, 92, 113
  American Nazi Party, 92, 113
  platforms for public appeal. 92
  white power, 92
Roe v. Wade, 156, 158
Round River Rendezvous, 142
Ruby Ridge, ID and Randy Weaver: case study, 174–80
Rural radicals (*see also* Vigilantes)
  core of beliefs, 75, 85
  patriot militias, 75, 85–92
  political violence re perceived threat, 75, 85–92
  scapegoating vigilantes, 75
Russian revolutionaries
  Bakunin, Mikhail, 44
  Kropotkin, Peter, 44
  Nechaev, Sergey, 44
Rwanda
  Hutu genocide of Tutsis, 65–68
  historical overview, 65–68

S

Scapegoating vigilantes (*see also* Vigilantism)
  17th century colonial America, 75–91
  witch hunts, 76
Second Coming of Christ and Christian Identity, 118
Self-esteem, 16
Sendero Luminoso, Shining Path of Peru, 27, 68
Shays' Rebellion, 89 (*see also* Militias)
Shoulder-fired precision launchers, 25
Silent Brotherhood, 119
Silver Shirts, 92 (*see also* Militias)
Singer, Pete, 152–54 (*see also* Animal rights movement)
Skinheads (*see* Neo-Nazi Skinheads)
Slavery, 11, 36–38
  American slavery, 22, 36–38 (*see also* American slavery)

enslavement, subjugation, 19, 21–22, 36–38
  property status, 38
Smith, Benjamin N., 121
  World Church of the Creator, 121
Sobrero, Ascanio, and nitroglycerin, 26
Socialism, anarchism and Haymarket Square Riot, 43–45
  absence of power among working class, 43–45
  anarchists: Russian revolutionaries, 44
    Heinzen, Karl and bomb usage, 44–45
  capitalism's power, 43
  class structure, 44
  Communist Manifesto, 44
  democrats, emergence of, 43–44
  socialism: Marx and Engels, 44
Socialization process phases, 18
Socio-economic-political profile of terrorists, 14, 15
South Carolina Regulators, 88 (*see also* Militias)
South Korea, 9
Southern Poverty Law Center, 107
  observance of memberships
    American Front, 213–14
    Christian Identity movement groups, 117
    hate group growth, 107
    patriot militia groups, 107, 128, 136
  United Klans of America, case history, 110
Special-interest extremists, 7, 140–66
  animal rights movement, 152–55
  anti-abortion activists, 156–61
  ecological resistance movements, 140–52 (*see also* Ecological resistance movements)
  Greenpeace, 161–63
  overview, 140
  People for the Ethical Treatment of Animals, 161, 163–66
Spira, Henry, 154 (*see also* Animal rights movement)
SPLC (*see* Southern Poverty Law Center)
Stalin, Joseph, 46
State of emergency, 10
Students for a Democratic Society, 92–95
  civil disobedience, 93
  Establishment, protests against, 93–94
  Vietnam War protests, 93–94
  violence and militancy, 93

Columbia University, 93
Democratic National Convention (1968), 93
Kent State University, 93
war protests, 93
Suitcase wire-guided missiles, 25
Supreme Court decisions
  African Americans
    Brown v. Board of Education, 84
    Dred Scott (property status), 38
  Asian racial determination
    Takao Ozawa v. U.S., 81
  Indian nations' sovereignty, 40–41
    Cherokee Nation v. Georgia, 41
    Johnson v. McIntosh, 41
    Marshall Trilogy, 41
    Worcester v. Georgia, 41
Surface-to-air missiles, 25

T

Terror cycles, 12, 69
Terrorism, defining
  broad definition, 9
  categories, 5–6
    analytical re violence toward innocent victims, 5
    legal re criminal violence, 5
    simple re political change, 5
    state-sponsored re
      repression, terror for power, 6
      Western viewpoints, attack, 5–6
  definition and characteristics, 8–9
  definition complexities, 3, 5, 29–30
    criminal violence, 5
    force for political change, 5
    innocent victims, violence, 5
    power via repression, terror, 6
    Western influence retribution, 6
  from above, 8, 10–13, 29–30, 35 (*see also* Terrorism from above)
  from below, 8, 10–13, 29–30, 35 (*see also* Terrorism from below)
  government manipulation, 6, 12
  interpretation re political adversaries, 9–10
  motivations, 5–6, 10–11
  pejorative connotation, 6
  terrorism vs. terror terminology, 6, 8
Terrorism from above
  American slavery, 36–38
  Argentina's covert dirty war, 51–54
  Armenian genocide and Turkey, 46–48
  cycle of violence, 12–13
  definition and characteristics, 8, 10, 13, 69
  government repression/oppression, 12–13
  Guatemala's covert reign of terror, 54–55
  Native Americans, genocidal policies, 40–43
  overt/covert characteristics, 10, 13, 51
  tools of terror
    assassination, 19, 38–39
    banishment, 19
    enslavement, 19, 36–38
    genocide, 19
    imprisonment, 19
    kidnapping, 19, 36
Terrorism from above and below
  Afghanistan, 61–65
  Black Panthers, 95–97
  Hutu genocide of Tutsis in Rwanda, 65–68
Terrorism from below
  Algeria and FLN, 58–60
  Assassins, Order of the, 38–39
  communal values preservation, 13
  definition and characteristics, 8, 11, 69
  FLN and Algeria, 58–60
  ideology fostering, 13
  Ku Klux Klan, 48–50
  national self-determination, 13
  political system reformation, 13
  revolutionary philosophers, 55–58
    Che Guevara, 56
    Fanon, Franz, 57–58
    Mao Tse-Tung, 55–56
    Marighella, Carlos, 57
  Sendero Luminoso of Peru, 68
  socialist, anarchist influences, 43–45
  tools of terror
    arson, 19
    assassination, 19
    bombs, 19
    guns, 19
    hijacking, 19
    kidnapping, 19, 36
    mass destruction weapons, 19 (*see also* Weapons of mass destruction)
  Weatherman, 94
Terrorism, historical continuity
  ancient times to 1800, 36–39

contemporary times, domestic terror, 105–216
  randomness, 105
  vulnerability, 105
  1800 to 1900, 39–45
  1900 to 1950, 45–50
  1950 to 1979, 50–60
  1980 to 2000, 60–68
Terrorism-incident management
  preparedness, 255–58
    case study, Oklahoma City, OK, 256–58
    terrorist target evaluation criteria, 256
  strategies and tactics, 242–64
    case studies, 249–51
    critical infrastructure protection directive points, 243–45
    information infrastructure protection strategies, 245–47, 248
    partnerships for infrastructure protection, 243
    proactive criminal investigations, 247–51
    threat assessment, 251–52
    weapons of mass destruction, 242–63
  threat analysis, 252–55
    Dept. of Defense, 253
    Dept. of Energy, 253
    Dept. of Health and Human Services, 254
    EPA, 253–54
    FBI, 252
    FEMA, 252–53
  threat assessment motivational trends, 254–55
  unified response to weapons of mass destruction, 258–63
    Biological Weapons Convention, 259–63
    characteristics, biological agents used by terrorists, 261–62
    characteristics, chemical agents used by terrorists, 260
    GEDAPER, 259
    preparedness components, 258–59
Terrorists
  application of term denied to
    citizens using violence for acceptable causes, 14
    U.S. allies, 14
  application of term to
    citizen threats to conservative America, 14
    left-wing political violence, 14, 55–58
  core of legitimacy, 14

definition(s), 14–18
  left-wing political violence, 14, 55–58
  profiles
    group socialization identity, 17–18, 30
    psychological background, 15, 30
    social destruction advocates, 18, 30
    socio-economic-political background, 14, 15, 30
  value-laden application, 14, 30
Terry, Randall, 159–60
Third Position
  goals, 213
  organization and activities, 213–14
Tools of terror, 18–29 (*see also* specific forms)
  arson, 24–25
  assassination, 19–20, 38–39
  banishment, 23
  bombs 25–27
  enslavement, subjugation, 19, 21–22, 36–38
  genocide, 23–24
  guns, 25
  hijacking, 27–28
  imprisonment, 22–23
  kidnapping, 19–21, 36–38
  revolutionary and evolutionary, 19, 30, 60
  weapons of mass destruction, 28–29, 208, 210–13, 242–64
Tree spiking, 144
Trochmann, John, 133
Tupac Amaru, 21
Turkey and Armenian genocide, 46–48
  historical overview, 46–48
Turner Diaries, 113, 114

U

Unabomber: case study, 197–200
Urban guerilla warfare tactics, 96–97
U.S. terrorism (*see also* Domestic terrorism)
  Murrah Federal Building, Oklahoma City, OK bombing, 5, 27, 105, 191–93
  historical overview, 74–100
    colonial extremists, 74

V

Vail, CO, ski area fires, 146, 147, 249
Victim status, 10
  civilian, innocent, 10

political violence and political goals, 10
Vigilantism
  colonial America, 17th century, 74–91
    extremists, 74–75
  definition and characteristics, 8–9
  Ku Klux Klan, 48–50
  rural radicals, 75
Violence
  and innocent targets, 5
  forced response to circumstances, 17
  key ingredients to terrorism, 11
    continued acts of terror, 11
    political motivation, 11
    social, economic, ideological grievances,
      11

W

Waco, TX and Branch Davidians: case study,
  180–85
Warriors of the Rainbow legend, 163
Weapons of mass destruction, 28–29, 208,
  210–13, 242–64
  biological weapons, 29, 208–13, 260–63
    ————use incidents, 262–63
  chemical weapons, 28–29, 208–13
  lethal gases, 28–29
  mustard gases, 28, 29
  nerve gases, 29
  nuclear weapons, 208, 212
Weatherman, 92, 94–95
  Days of Rage, 94
  Students for a Democratic Society offshot,
    94–95
  use of violence as a means, 94
  Weather Underground, 94–95
Western political influence retribution, 6
Whiskey Rebellion, 90
White Aryan Resistance, 122–23
  hate targets, 122
  organization and activities, 122–23
  publications, 123
White Citizen Councils, 84

White supremacist groups, 108–21, 135
  Christian identity movement, 116–21
  KKK splinter groups, 108–12
  neo-Nazi Skinheads, 113–16
  neo-Nazis, 112–13
Winrod, Gerald B., 91
Wise Use
  agenda, 150–51
  core beliefs, 148
  organization and activities, 147–52
  Sagebrush Rebellion influence, 148
  state vs. federal control of land usage, 148
  statement of purpose, 147
  violence, and terror incidents by, 151–52
Witch hunts, 11, 76–77
  characteristics of accused, 76
  historical overview, 76
  Salem, MA, 76–77
  socio-economic-political environment, 77
Women, terrorist profile, 16
Women's Frontier of the World Church of the
  Creator, 16
Word derivation, 11
World Church of the Creator, 121–23
  core beliefs, 122
  hate targets, 121, 122
  organization and activities, 121–23
  publications 121
World Trade Center
  bombing, 105, 186–90
  case study, 186–90
World Wide Web
  cyberterrorism and internet, 208
    high-energy radio frequency guns, 208
    logic bombs, 208
    viruses, 208
  digital infrastructure, 208
  internet profile, 209

Z

ZOG (Zionist Occupied Government), 114, 118,
  119, 136

ABOUT THE AUTHORS

MIKI VOHRYZEK-BOLDEN, Ph.D.

Miki Vohryzek-Bolden received her Ph.D. and M.S. in Criminology from Florida State University. During her career, Dr. Vohryzek-Bolden has conducted research at the Rand Corporation, California Assembly Office of Research, and California Department of Consumer Affairs. She served as a member for eight years on the California Judicial Council Advisory Committee on Trial Court Coordination and has written numerous articles on teaching and learning, ethics, and correctional issues. Dr. Vohryzek-Bolden has also conducted training on the legislative process, investigative interview skills, and expert witness testimony. In addition, she is currently serving as a research consultant to the California Commission on Correctional Peace Officer Standards and Training. For twenty years, she has taught in the Criminal Justice Division at California State University (CSU) Sacramento, including courses on policy analysis, planning, and violence and terrorism. In addition to her instructional responsibilities, Dr. Vohryzek-Bolden is Director, Graduate Academic Programs at CSU Sacramento and maintains an active research agenda.

GAYLE OLSON-RAYMER, Ph.D.

Gayle-Olson Raymer received her Ph.D. in American History—with a specialization in the History of the Criminal Justice System—and her M.A. in Public Historical Studies at the University of California, Santa Barbara. She worked for several years with the U.S. Department of Justice and the California Office of Criminal Justice Planning, where she conducted research on a wide array of criminal and juvenile justice topics. For over fifteen years, Dr. Olson-Raymer has been teaching various courses on international and domestic terrorism—first in the Criminal Justice Division at CSU Sacramento; then in the History Department at the University of California, Santa Barbara; and currently, in both the Political Science and History Departments at Humboldt State University and at Texas Woman's University's Law

Enforcement Management Institute. In addition to her teaching responsibilities, Dr. Olson-Raymer is a consultant to the U.S. Office of Juvenile Justice and Delinquency Prevention and Assistant Editor of the *Criminal Justice Abstracts*. Her first book, *Terrorism: A Historical and Contemporary Perspective,* was published by American Heritage Custom Publishing in 1995.

JEFFREY O. WHAMOND, MS, HMS

Mr. Whamond earned a M.S. in Criminal Justice from CSU Sacramento. He is a California State Certified Hazardous Materials Specialist (HMS) and nationally certified as a Hazardous Materials Technician. As an Investigator with the California Highway Patrol, he has twenty-four years of law enforcement experience specializing in white-collar environmental crimes, criminal intelligence, and domestic terrorism. Mr. Whamond holds a lifetime California Community College Teaching Credential and has instructed at the University of California, Riverside Extension, for the past ten years on a variety of law enforcement related topics. He has also instructed Hazardous Materials Incident Response and Incident Command courses at the California Highway Patrol Academy and for private industry. He helped to develop the basic and wrote the Advanced Environmental Crimes Courses for the California Specialized Training Institute where he instructed for six years as an adjunct instructor. He has been a guest instructor for the U.S. Environmental Protection Agency in their Environmental Crimes Investigations Course held at the Federal Law Enforcement Training Center in Glenco, Georgia. His most recent assignment has been as a member to the Federal Bureau of Investigations, Sacramento, Joint Terrorism Task Force (JTTF).

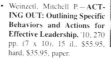

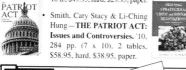

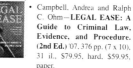
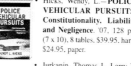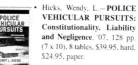